Resilient Russian Women in the 1920s & 1930s

Marcelline Hutton

Zea Books
Lincoln, Nebraska
2015

Copyright © 2015 Marcelline Hutton.
All rights reserved.

ISBN 978-1-60962-068-4   paperback
ISBN 978-1-60962-069-1   ebook

Set in Palatino Linotype types.
Design and composition by Paul Royster.

Zea Books are published by
the University of Nebraska–Lincoln Libraries

Electronic (pdf) ebook edition available online at
http://digitalcommons.unl.edu/zeabook/

Print edition can be ordered from Lulu.com, at
http://www.lulu.com/spotlight/unllib

Contents

Introduction	9
Gratitude	17
Russian Names and Places	19
Glossary	21

Part I: Russian Women in the 1920s

Chapter One. Political Life	25
A. Russian Women in the 1917 Revolutions	25
1. February 1917 Revolution	25
2. October 1917 Revolution	28
B. Women in the Communist Party	35
C. Political Activists	46
D. Disenchantment with Communist Politics	50
1. Educated Women	51
2. Gentry-Class Women	52
3. Nelly Ptashkina	52
4. Kyra Karadja	54
5. Other Disenchanted Educated Women	55
a. Maria Shkapskaya	55
b. Marina Tsvetaeva	56
c. Alexandra Tolstoy	57
6. Social Revolutionaries	59
7. Marguerite Harrison	60
8. Maria Spiridonova	65
9. Socialist Opposition	67
10. Aida Basevich	67
E. Conclusion	70
Chapter Two. Women and Religion	71
A. Nuns and Priestly Families in the 1920s	73
B. Other Religious Experiences	76
1. Mme X	76
2. Maria Shkapskaya	77
3. Marguerite Harrison	79
4. Alexandra Tolstoy	82
C. Failure of Belief	84
1. Raisa Orlova	84

      2. Valentina Petrova   85
  D. Religion in the Countryside   85
      1. Vera Panova   86
  E. Religion and the Intelligentsia   88
      1. Alexandra Berg   89
      2. Tatiana Tchernavin   90
  F. Antireligious Songs   91

Chapter Three. Marriage and Motherhood   94
  A. The Countryside   94
  B. Urban Marriage and Motherhood   105
      1. Working-Class Women   106
      2. Bourgeois and Educated Women's Weddings   108
          a. Marguerite Harrison   108
          b. Elena Skrjabina   110
          c. Nelly Ptashkina   111
          d. Maria Shkapskaya   114
          e. Anna Akhmatova   117
          f. Alexandra Kollontai   119
          g. Nadezhda Mandelstam   120
  C. Marriage and Everyday Life   122
      1. Maria Shkapskaya   122
      2. Marina Tsvetaeva and Olga Forsh   124
      3. Tatiana Tchernavin   126
  D. Conclusion   129

Chapter Four. Education   130
  A. Irina Tidmarsh   131
  B. Vera Broido   132
  C. Nelly Ptashkina   133
  D. Elena Gortskina Skrjabina   134
  E. Larisa Reisner   137
  F. Alexandra Tolstoy   138
  G. Conclusion   140

Chapter Five. Women's Employment   143
  A. Agriculture   144
      1. Alexandra Tolstoy   145
      2. Elena Ponomarenko   147
      3. Praskovya Pichugina   148

B. Manufacturing	151
1. Marietta Shaginian	151
2. Marguerite Harrison	153
3. Ekaterina Strogova	154
4. Anna Balashova	156
C. Service Personnel	157
1. Domestic Servants	157
a. Nelly Ptashkina	159
b. Elena Skrjabina	160
c. Alexandra Tolstoy	162
2. Mid-Level Service Personnel	163
a. Elena Skrjabina	163
b. Helen Dmitriew	168
3. High-Level Service Personnel	169
a. Teachers	169
b. Teachers in Art Academies	171
(1) Nadezhda Udaltsova	171
(2) Anna Ostroumova Lebedeva	172
(3) Aleksandra Exter	172
c. Teachers in Public Schools	173
(1) Tatiana Tchernavin	174
(2) Lidiia Seifullina	177
(3) Alexandra Tolstoy	178
d. University Professors	179
(1) Olga Freidenberg	180
(2) Anna Bek	182
e. Writers	185
(1) Maria Shkapskaya	185
(2) Marietta Shaginian	187
(3) Anna Akhmatova	189
(4) Vera Inber	192
(5) Nina Berberova	193
(6) Marina Tsvetaeva	194
(7) Émigré Writers	195
f. Artists	196
(1) Liubov Popova	197
(2) Varvara Stepanova	203
(3) Zinaida Serebriakova	206
(4) Anna O. Lebedeva	206
Conclusion	209

CONTENTS

Part II: Russian Women in the 1930s

Chapter Six. Peasants ... 217
- A. Young Stakhanovite and Udarnik Workers ... 218
  1. Rural Udarnik Workers ... 219
  2. Stakhanovite Tractor Driver Pasha Angelina ... 219
  3. Other Udarniks ... 222
- B. Songs and Celebration of Rural Women ... 227
- C. Generational Differences ... 229
- D. Disgust among Peasants ... 230
  1. Louise Huebert ... 230
  2. Hilda Schulz Mielke ... 239
  3. Collectivization ... 245
  4. Dekulakization ... 247
  5. Memoirs of Peasants' Dekulakization ... 248
     a. Tatiana Izyumova ... 249
     b. Maria Andrievskaya ... 249
     c. Maria and Olga Orlova ... 251
     d. Regehr Family Letters ... 252
  6. Factors in Peasant Resistance ... 255
  7. Untouchables ... 257
  8. Famine ... 259
  9. Low Productivity of Kolkhoz ... 259

Chapter Seven. Working Women ... 263
- A. Problems of Older Workers ... 264
- B. Idealistic Udarnik and Stakhanovite Workers ... 266
- C. Hard Lives during Industrialization ... 269

Chapter Eight. Education ... 271
- A. Harsh University Conditions ... 276
- B. Problems of Social Origins ... 278
- C. Education and Upward Mobility ... 279
- D. Women Teachers and Professors ... 285
- E. Technical Intelligentsia ... 290

Chapter Nine. Surviving the Purges ... 293
- A. Purges and Social Origins ... 295
- B. Purges and the Intelligentsia ... 297
  1. Tatiana Tchernavin ... 297
  2. Olga Sliozberg ... 303

3. Markoosha Fischer	306
4. Lydia Chukovskaya	308
5. Olga Freidenberg	311
6. Lydia Ginzburg	315
7. Lydia Seifullina	318
8. Anna Akhmatova	318
9. Anna Barkova	322
10. Natalia Sats and Larisa Lappo-Danilevskaia	323
C. Purges of Social Revolutionaries	326
D. Purges of Communist Party Members	328
1. Yelena Sidorkina	328
2. Olga Berggolts	330
E. The Purges: Knowing and Not Knowing	332
1. Elena Skrjabina	333
2. Markoosha Fischer	335
3. Anna Larina	336
4. Galina Shtange	336
5. Liubov Shaporina	337
6. Lydia Chukovskaya	339
7. Valentina Kamyshina	340
8. Nina Kosterina	341
9. Valeria Gerlin	345
10. Anna Larina and Nikolai Bukharin	346
F. Righteous Russians during the Purges	348
Chapter Ten. Religion in the 1930s	349
A. In the Countryside	350
1. Lifting of Some Restrictions, 1936	354
B. In the Cities	355
1. Helen Dmitriew	355
2. Elena Skrjabina	357
3. Alexandra Berg	357
C. In the Camps	361
1. Maria Joffe	361
2. Evgenia Ginzburg	362
3. Marie Avinov	362
4. A Dispossessed Peasant	363
Chapter Eleven. Marriage	365
A. Peasants	366
B. Educated Women	371
1. Galina Shtange	372

2. Anna Larina	372
3. Maria Astafeva	373
4. Helen Dmitriew	374
5. Margaret Wettlin	376
6. Sofia Pavlova	378
7. Nadezhda Mandelstam	378
C. Marriage and Family Difficulties	380
1. Galina Shtange's Demanding Children	381
2. Markoosha Fischer	384
3. Wives of Prisoners	385
a. Surrogate Families in Prison	385
b. Plight of Nonimprisoned Wives	387
D. Unequal Marriages	387
1. Happy Unequal Marriages	388
2. Unhappy Unequal Marriages	389
E. Marriage and Maids	390
Chapter Twelve. Osoaviakhim	394
A. Housewives and Osoaviakhim	394
B. Youth and Osoaviakhim	396
Conclusion	402
Afterword	403
Notes	404

Introduction

Some friends and readers have enjoyed my recent book *Remarkable Russian Women in Pictures, Prose and Poetry*, so I have continued these women's stories in *Resilient Russian Women in the 1920s & 1930s*. Some of the writers, artists, families, and issues are the same. However, the cataclysmic events of World War I, the Russian revolutions of 1917, and the Civil War made the 1920s a difficult time, as did the purges, industrialization, and collectivization in the 1930s. For these reasons, I have applied the term resilient in discussing women's lives in those decades.

Marriage, family, and work remained important to women during the 1920s and 1930s. Religion comforted many older women, especially peasants, while education and adventure became significant for young women. Just as Nadezhda Durova fought in the tsar's army in the Napoleonic War and Maria Botchkareva served in the Russian army in World War I, so too several thousand women joined the Red Army during the Civil War, 1918–1921. Starry-eyed, energetic young women also responded to the challenges of the Five-Year Plans in the 1930s.

A significant change occurred in women's political life. In the nineteenth century, only a few thousand mainly gentry-class women participated in revolutionary parties. After the Bolshevik revolution in October 1917, thousands of women—including working-class women—became politically active in the Russian Communist Party, especially in the Komsomol, the young people's section of the party. Another striking difference is that the numbers of women imprisoned increased dramatically during the 1920s and 30s. While a few hundred were arrested and imprisoned in the Tsarist period, many were sentenced to exile in Siberia or allowed to go into exile in western Europe. Under the new Soviet regime, some Russian women—like gentry-class, pacifist Alexandra Tolstoy—were repeatedly detained in the early 1920s but then released after a short time. Anarchists and Social Revolutionaries were also confined. In the early 1930s, this same pattern of short imprisonment continued, but by the middle and late 1930s detention became more draconian, and sentences lasted from five to twenty years. Moreover, women prisoners were often exiled

INTRODUCTION

to more severe detention and punishment in work camps in Siberia—the infamous Gulag. By the mid 1930s, they were not allowed to go into exile in the West, nor were they allowed to accompany their husbands or have their children with them.

For all these reasons, it is not as easy to "fall in love" with turbulent Soviet history as it is with romantic Russian history. The defunct economy and widespread famine, disease, and misery of the 1920s and the policies of collectivization and terror of the 1930s make them dark periods. Extreme poverty following World War I and the Civil War adversely affected all classes, especially the urban educated classes and their subsequent writings. Joseph Stalin's "revolution from above"—which included education, collectivization, industrialization, and the purges—make the 1930s a difficult period to interpret because of the different impact these policies had on various groups and generations of women.

Between 1917 and 1927, 10 million peasant women were able to create new households as the result of Bolshevik land redistribution. It meant a lot to these women to have their own household instead of the subservience of living with dominating in-laws. While low grain prices and famine along the Volga River adversely affected peasant families in the early 1920s, during the middle of the decade, most farmers flourished, and their life expectancy increased dramatically. Yet their gains disappeared during collectivization in the early 1930s, when non-cooperating farmers lost their land, houses, and even their lives. Some were exiled; some became "untouchables," wandering around, begging to survive; some died of starvation. The human destruction of collectivization and the purges coupled with the high cost of construction during industrialization cut short millions of lives during the 1930s.

Soviet history, generally, lacks the sparkle, grandeur, and enchantment of the nineteenth century. Gone are the charm, romance, and glitter of the aristocracy and gentry class. While young women in the Soviet Union still fell in love and got married, their lives were not as carefree as those depicted in Tolstoy's novel *War and Peace*. Instead, many upper-class women had to sell their jewels and furs to buy bread after the Bolshevik revolution. Still, Russian women in the Soviet period proved as idealistic and dedicated to serving their families and society as their nineteenth-century counterparts. Just as the

INTRODUCTION

mid-nineteenth-century Russian literary critic Nikolai Dobroliubov found women heroines whom he called "Rays of Light in the Kingdom of Darkness" so too one finds these "rays of light" in all classes in Soviet society in the early twentieth century. Their writings attest to the triumphs and tragedies in their lives.

Of course, there is a lot to admire about Russian women in the early twentieth century. This book traces the effects of war and revolution upon women, as well as women's activity in and response to those events. Despite all the messiness in ordinary life, women muddled through, supporting their families as well as they could while faithfully serving their country despite their low-paid work. As a result, I have titled this book *Resilient Russian Women* because it shows how women struggled, survived, and even flourished during very difficult and dangerous times. While some of the characters remain the same as in the nineteenth century, for writers such as Anna Akhamatova, Marina Tsvetaeva, Alexandra Kollontai, Alexandra Tolstoy, and Elena Skrjabina, their milieu is harsher. Moreover, political discontent, destitution, and starvation pushed some gentry-class and bourgeois Russians to leave the country after the Bolshevik revolution. Writers Zinaida Gippius, Marina Tsvetaeva, and Nina Berberova and artists Zinaida Serebriakova and Alexandra Exter emigrated to the West.

During World War I, manufacturing in Russia slowed to a trickle. With the introduction of the Bolshevik policy of War Communism in 1918—a policy of worker takeover of the factories and attacks on bourgeois factory owners, which lasted till the end of the Civil War— the economy almost ground to a halt. So in 1921, Vladimir Lenin and other Communist Party leaders made some concessions to capitalism to get the economy going again. They adopted a New Economic Policy (1921–28), called NEP for short. It retained government control of the commanding heights of the economy such as the banks, railroads, and communications systems, while allowing entrepreneurs once again to run small enterprises like publishing houses, restaurants, agricultural cooperatives, town markets, and so forth. This produced a more vibrant economy, and life for most women and their families improved in the mid-1920s, as many of the memoirs in this work attest.

INTRODUCTION

The shortage of manufactured goods during and after World War I and the Civil War made Russian peasants reluctant to market their grain because they couldn't buy any goods with the currency the government paid for their crops. The new regime paid very low prices for agricultural products during this period, and the peasants remained stubborn about selling their wheat for money that couldn't buy much. The result was famine and depopulation in the cities. Tatiana Tchernavin's poignant writings *We Soviet Women* and *Escape from the Soviets* show how difficult it was for her to feed her baby during the Civil War in Petrograd. Likewise, Alexandra Tolstoy's autobiography *I Worked for the Soviet* indicates how scarce food was in Moscow and how she had to scrounge the countryside to secure provisions while she edited her father's works.

Both Alexandra Tolstoy's autobiography and Elena Skrjabina's memoirs *Coming of Age in the Russian Revolution*, reveal how important the American Relief Agency (ARA) was in alleviating starvation along the Volga and in the cities during the Civil War. Their writings also attest to how fortunate they were in having relatives and friends in foreign countries who sent them foodstuffs and clothing. Tolstoy recalls that one of her family members gained needed employment with the ARA. After the revolution, many former gentry-class people and clergy, called "byvshie liudi," or former people, were excluded from jobs and the food rationing system. They were punished for their social origins and the sins of their fathers.

Of course, the new Soviet system had redeeming qualities. Idealistic revolutionaries devoted themselves to making the new regime work, and thousands of young women soldiers were as brave as their nineteenth-century counterparts. Bolshevik feminists and revolutionaries like Inessa Armand and Alexandra Kollontai worked tirelessly to improve the situation of women. Moreover, the Communist Party established a special bureau called Zhenotdel (Women's Department) to promote women's social, economic, and political equality. These activists labored indefatigably to improve the status of Russian working women. Indeed, Armand and several other female party leaders died early because of malnutrition and overwork, which weakened their resistance to contagious diseases like cholera and typhoid. Artists Liubov Popova and Olga Rozanova also died from disease shortly after the revolution. Only the strongest survived.

In 1918, Commissar of Social Welfare Alexandra Kollontai drafted legislation to make marriage and divorce cheaper and easier. Fewer complaints about arranged marriage, which bedeviled women in the nineteenth century appear in twentieth-century writings. Marriage reform and access to education and employment remain stars in the crown of the government's service to women.

The real problem during and after the revolution was that the social, sexual, economic, and political transformation that women needed to gain true equality was not possible because of the poverty of the new state and the political agendas of political leaders like Lenin, Leon Trotsky, and Stalin. These men focused on winning the Civil War, and that took scarce government resources. In the 1930s, the party's Five-Year Plan for large-scale industrialization sapped the country's wealth. While the Soviet government and Communist Party gave lip service to women's equality and opened higher education and employment to them, it did little to eliminate Russian patriarchal culture, which continued to undermine women's social, sexual, economic and political situations.

Still, *Resilient Russian Women* features writers, painters, peasants, prisoners, workers, wives, and mothers who expressed in their own words their experiences and feelings. This volume uses memoirs, novels, poetry, songs, diaries, autobiographies, biographies, interviews, and other printed sources translated into English to reveal women's inner lives. While some of the gifted women writers and artists of the late Tsarist period emigrated to the West, many doctors like Maria Pokrovskaia, poets like Anna Akhmatova, and artists like Anna Ostroumova Lebedeva as well as educated but less well known women like Elena Skrjabina and Tatiana Tchernavin continued their work and family life throughout the Bolshevik and Stalinist periods. Equally admirable but less well known are the workers and peasants who also steadfastly labored for their families to survive. Stories and voices of peasant women echo in the lives of Masha Scott and Pasha Angelina, who are highlighted in this volume.

Not all of the intelligentsia were able to or wanted to leave their native land. Anna Akhmatova refused to ever leave Russia, although

INTRODUCTION

many colleagues encouraged her to do so. Some like Elena Skrjabina and her mother were caught up in the turbulence of the twenties and were unable to leave during the Civil War. Elena had one brother in the Red Army and one in the White Army, so she and her mother had divided loyalties. In the early 1920s, they traded the family jewels for food. Despite her early gentry-class upbringing, as an adult Elena never enjoyed the pampered life her mother had lived. Instead, Elena adjusted to the rough life of the 1920s and 1930s, working at poorly paid jobs to help her family survive.

While the Bolshevik revolution and later policies such as collectivization and industrialization captured the enthusiasm of many Soviet young people, they took a tremendous toll on ordinary farmers and workers. The closing of churches by the League of the Militant Godless as well as the purges during the 1930s made this a harsh period for many Russians. Still, young Communist Party and Komsomol members saw some of their dreams come true in the building of socialism during the Five-Year Plans. Moreover, broader access to elementary education in the countryside and to higher education in major cities allowed increasing numbers of women to follow their dreams of becoming teachers, doctors, engineers, and even pilots.

Gradually, life in the cities became more Sovietized, while life for women in the country remained traditional with marriage, work, religion, and village culture prevailing. Current observers have found that rural women had subtle forms of social capital that did not diminish during the Soviet period. Village women's social status often resulted from their storytelling ability, healing powers, gossip, magic, and position as head of the household. In the 1930s some village women like those in Masha Scott's family achieved not only elementary education but higher education as well. Still, others like Pasha Angelina became tractor drivers and even members of the government.

Women in both urban and rural areas were able to adapt to the new Soviet government. One remarkable peasant folksinger, Agrafema Glinkina (1898–1972) knew more than three hundred songs, and she was able to adjust old songs to new situations. She praised both Lenin and Stalin in her songs, and she became a member of the Soviet Union of Writers in the 1930s; her memoirs were published posthumously in 2007.

INTRODUCTION

Most Russian women worked ceaselessly for their families to survive and thrive. Many demonstrated remarkable resilience during these difficult decades. Some of their lives were like that of Elena Skrjabina, who worked unpleasant, marginal jobs in factories in the 1920s and then attended university in the 1930s in an effort to support her children, in case her husband was arrested. Fortunately, he was not purged, but her anxiety persisted. Indeed, the purges in the middle and late 1930s spread fear throughout the population, especially among the "old" intelligentsia, many of whom felt "doomed."

In addition to printed sources, pictures of famous Russian women in the 1920s and 1930s have become available free on Wikimedia Commons. The St. Petersburg Film and Photo Archive also provided many reasonably priced images. Women's art of the avant-garde flourished in the early 1920s, tending toward the abstract and concentrating on material objects such as the design of clothing, household items such as dishes, costumes for ballet, and theater sets. Artists who could not conform to changing Soviet doctrine or preferred not to paint Bolshevik commissars—such as Zinaida Serebriakova and Alexandra Exter—emigrated to Paris in the mid-1920s. Some, like Liubov Popova and Olga Rozanova, died early from contagious disease. In the 1930s the government and party adopted the doctrine of Socialist Realism, and abstract art lost official support along with innovative, absurdist, existential, and overtly religious art or writing. Still, this left traditional artists like Anna Ostroumova Lebedeva and others to continue on in acceptable genres like landscape and portraiture.

As in the Tsarist period, Soviet censorship limited what women could write and publish. Those who wrote diaries, autobiographies, and memoirs were usually educated, unusual women. Some were able to focus on their own lives and selves, while others wrote more about their milieu, or even wrote biographies of others. Some peasant women wrote not diaries but song notebooks. Most faced special constraints in how they depicted events. Communist Party members like Alexandra Kollontai wrote many political tracts and some fiction but very short biographies or autobiographies like her *Autobiography of Sexually Emancipated Communist Woman*. Likewise, the Russian physician Anna Bek wrote her memoirs in 1948, a few years before Stalin died. She did not elaborate in great detail on the events of the 1920s

INTRODUCTION

and 1930s for fear of endangering her family. So, let the reader beware that women's writings were sometimes filtered by political considerations. All these constraints as well as the availability of sources in English translation and my own personal choices and understandings of Russian and Soviet history have shaped the depictions of Russian women in this book.

The Communist Party also chose particular peasant and working-class women to eulogize during these decades. They were not necessarily representative of those in their class. Russian and Soviet ethnographers provided glimpses into peasant and working-class life by collecting their songs and life stories. Their work showed a remarkable amount of continuity in peasant life from the 1890s to the 1930s. Rural women, influenced by village culture, continued many of the marital and religious traditions of the Tsarist period well into the Stalinist period and beyond.

Educated Russian women continued describing their lives in their poetry and memoirs. Some who left the Soviet Union, like Alexandra Tolstoy and Tatiana Tchernavin, had lived through the 1920s and part of the 1930s before leaving. Many had to hide their writings from government censors as well as the secret police, and some like Evgenia Ginzburg and Nadezhda Mandelstam wrote their stories only after the death of Stalin. Their memoirs could only be published illegally at home or abroad in the 1960s and 1970s. Some kept their writings secret until after the ascendance of Mikhail Gorbachev and during the 1990s when civic human rights groups like Memorial tried to preserve the memory of life during the Stalinist period. Then, Western scholars briefly gained access to Soviet KGB files. Veronica Shapovalov has made many Soviet women's prison writings available in her work *Remembering the Darkness,* and likewise Semen Vilensky presents prison memoirs in his book *Till My Tale Is Told: Women's Memoirs of the Gulag*. Recent publications of the lives of Russian holy men, such as Father Arseny and Father Sebastian, contain captivating memoirs of their "spiritual children," or followers, in the 1920s and 1930s. Stories of Russians and Germans who escaped during and after World War II have yielded insights into life during the interwar period.

INTRODUCTION

Literary critics, translators, folklorists, and historians have provided many texts of Russian women's voices in English translation. They include the following: Barbara Clements, Toby Clyman, Jane Costlow, Heather De Haan, Barbara Engel, Diana Green, Sheila Fitzpatrick, Jehanne M. Gheith, Anne Gorsuch, Helena Goscilo, Page Herrlinger, Laura Olson, Temira Pachmus, Cathy Porter, Bernice Rosenthal, Veronica Shapovalov, Isabel Tirado, Christine Tomei, Semen Vilensky, Christine Worobec, Glennys Young, and Mary Zirin.

Gratitude

I want to express special thanks to archivists Liubov Pyzhova and Elena Liubomirova at the St. Petersburg Film and Photo Archive for their assistance in obtaining fascinating pictures of Russian women. Thanks also to Irina Ivanova, curator of the Anna Akhmatova Museum on the Fontanka, for her gracious provision of pictures of Akhmatova. Thanks also to archivist Janet Weaver at the Iowa Women's Archives, University of Iowa, for pictures from Elena Skrjabina's archive. Mrs. Skrjabina had been one of my Russian language professors at the university in the early 1960s, so it was with great interest that I looked at her family photos and reread her memoir *Coming of Age in the Russian Revolution* for this manuscript.

I am also grateful to the Russian and East European and Central Asian Center and Slavic Library at the University of Illinois for the opportunity to work there in the summers during the 1980s and 90s as well as 2009 and 2010. The staff and resources are outstanding. Moreover, the summer laboratory provides opportunities to meet old friends and make new ones when discussing Russian and Soviet history and culture. I also benefited from the use of resources at Love Library, University of Nebraska Lincoln. Its impressive collection of Slavic women's holdings has been very helpful in my research.

I am extremely grateful to my editors, Paul Royster and Linnea Fredrickson, at the University of Nebraska–Lincoln, and to my proofreader Miriam Gelfand, who was also my Russian language teacher at the University of Iowa in the early 1960s. Their encouragement, help, and expertise are deeply appreciated.

Special thanks to friends and colleagues who have provided intellectual insight, emotional support, and computer help, including Connie Backus-Yoder, Linda Carlson, Gwen Colgrove, Cathy Dickinson, Dick and Debra Dorzweiler, Sarah Fairchild, Chuck and Margaret Felling, Thomas Gillan, Elaine Kruse, Joyce Gleason, Elle Hart, Loren Horton, Kathryn Hutton, Birgitta Ingemanson, Michael Johnson, Faye Kartrude, Ann Kleimola, Katharine Morrison, Kent Nelson, Mary Roseberry-Brown, Martin Stack, Richard Sullivan, Terri Swanson, Tom Tiegs, Jack Wheat, Julie Yardley, and Janet Yoder.

Russian Names and Places

Russian names sometimes confuse American readers. The same sound or syllable may be transliterated differently by American, English, or French spelling systems. For example, in French, the sound ch and the names Tchernavin or Tchaikovsky are rendered with a "Tch." In contrast, the American Library of Congress system writes them Chernavin and Chaikovskii. Since most Americans would recognize only Tchaikovsky with a T, and since the author Tatiana Tchernavin chose to write her name with a T, this spelling convention is retained.

Because of the variety of transliteration systems, the name Maria may be written two ways: Maria and Mariia. I usually employ the more common form of Maria, but when an author or translator uses the form Mariia in a quote or a title, it is necessary to keep that spelling. Likewise, the name of the poet Maria Shkapskaya may be written thusly or as Mariia Shkapskaia. The sound yah can be written "ya," "ia," even "ja," depending on the translator. In the nineteenth century, "ya" was the more common form, but in the twentieth century American historians tend to use the "ia" spelling. Yet, Elena Skrjabina chose to write her name with "ja," not "ya" or "ia." Because the 1920s was a time of transition in Russian history, I use all these forms, trusting the reader to recognize that the names Maria Shkapskaya and Mariia Shkapskaia are the same name and person. Fortunately, many of the women writers possess simple names—like Bek, Tolstoy, Orlova, and Larina—which are not as difficult to understand.

Another idiosyncrasy is that Russian women's names usually end with an "a," as in Orlova and Larina, but some writers do not use this ending—for example, Alexandra Tolstoy and Tatiana Tchernavin. Thus, I have omitted the feminine endings where writers or publishers do. I generally omit the patronymic (father's name) as well. Although its inclusion is a form of politeness in Russian culture, it is not required in American writings. Moreover, it lengthens names considerably and seems to confuse American readers; an example is the name Galina Vladimirovna Shtange. So, patronymics are omitted unless needed in footnotes or quotations.

Russian and Soviet place names also pose some problems. For example, St. Petersburg was renamed Petrograd during World War I, and then changed to Leningrad in 1924 after the death of Lenin. After the fall of the Soviet empire in the 1990s, it resumed its historical name St. Petersburg. This city simply had different names at various times.

Glossary

byvshie liudy: "Former people," including aristocrats, bourgeois, merchants, Tsarist officers, priests, and others

Cheka: Secret police, 1917–1922 (followed by GPU and NKVD)

Civil War: Struggle between Bolshevik Reds and Tsarist supporters called Whites, 1918–1921

CPSU: Communist Party Soviet Union, 1917–present

delegatki: Women delegates, representatives elected from factory workers, a quasi-political organization

FYP: Five-Year Plan, beginning in late 1928, to collectivize agriculture and industrialize the Soviet Union

GPU: Secret police, 1923–1934

Komsomol: Youth section of the CPSU

Komsomolka: Female Komsomol member

muzhik: A peasant, farmer

NEP: New Economic Policy, 1921–1928

NKVD: Secret police, 1934–1954

OGPU: See GPU

Proletcult: Organization for purely proletarian unconventional art, 1917–1932

pud (or pood): Measure of weight, about 36 pounds

purge: In the early 1920s called chistka, or a cleansing of undesirable elements in the CPSU, not connected to imprisonment or death. In the late 1920s and 1930s, purge meant the elimination of those who threatened Stalin's control, such as Trotskyites. The NKVD used purged prisoners for labor in the construction of dams and railroads, mines, and forestry. Extreme purges, 1936–1938.

rabfak: Rabochie Facultety, or worker's faculty, which was remedial education for workers and peasants during the 1920s and 1930s, usually high school

raikom: District Party committee

raion: District geographical area

ruble: Russian currency worth about fifty cents during the nineteenth century. The ruble was divided into 100 copecks, or kopecks.

SD: Social Democratic Party, in 1903 divided into Mensheviks and Bolsheviks

GLOSSARY

Socialist Realism: A doctrine promulgated by the party and government in 1932 that urged artists and writers to praise the Five-Year Plans and party officials as positive heroes; to present optimistic themes, characters, and happy endings; and to make music, art, and literature easily understood by the masses

SR: Socialist Revolutionary Party, late nineteenth and early twentieth centuries. Illegal political party in the Tsarist and Soviet periods.

Stakhanovite: A worker who far exceeds production norms, named after coal miner Alexei Stakhanov, who achieved amazing results in 1935

udarnik: A worker who exceeds work quotas; part of an effort of socialist competition to get workers to produce more for the same wages in the late 1920s and early 1930s

vydvizhentsy: Upwardly mobile workers, socially promoted cadres

War Communism: An economic policy with worker control of factories, 1917–1921

Zhenotdel: Women's section of the CPSU, 1918–1930

Part I

Russian Women in the 1920s

Women Demonstrators with the Banner 'Long Live the Soviet of Workers and Soldiers Deputies,' *Spring 1917 (St. Petersburg Photo Archive)*

Chapter One

Political Life

A. Russian Women in the 1917 Revolutions

> War abroad could lead to revolution at home.
>
> Admiral Shestakov, 1885

Admiral Shestakov's prophecy proved true in Russia in 1905 and 1917. World War I doomed the Russian empire. The February 1917 revolution occurred in the midst of World War I, and its influence was profound. The provisional government that replaced the monarchy was weak and unable to extricate Russia from the war or to equitably and quickly distribute land among the peasants. Within a few months, Russia experienced the October revolution, bringing a socialist government to power. How did these events affect Russian women, and how did Russian women influence these events? While Russians in all classes welcomed the February revolution, the October revolution was not as widely acclaimed. Let's look at Russian women's voices and pictures of their activity to see how they responded to war, revolution, and the new Soviet state.

1. February 1917 Revolution

> The REVOLUTION! My parents had lived for it; all their friends had lived for it; they had all been ready to die for it. I imagined it as something unspeakably glorious and wonderful. And now it had come!
>
> Vera Broido

Since the incomplete 1905 revolution, hopes and prayers for fundamental change had been in the air throughout Russia. Economic and political crises during World War I intensified peoples' longing for change. Yet many Russians were surprised when workers, students, and government employees brought down the monarchy in the

February revolution of 1917. Most surprised were professional revolutionaries like Lenin, Trotsky, and Kollontai, who were living in exile away from Russia.

When revolution came in February 1917, it provoked different responses from various groups in Russian society. For women workers it offered hope of food, fuel, and dignity in the workplace. For all workers it promised better factory organization and more involvement in how work was performed and paid. It also meant the formation of greater trade union and worker political organization. For many male soldiers, who deserted in 1917, it meant the end of a losing war. For a few thousand exceptionally patriotic women, it meant a chance to continue fighting on the Eastern Front against the Germans and an opportunity to shame deserting male soldiers. For many artists it meant an apocalyptic and spiritual time, a restructuring of society along more egalitarian lines.

For feminists, both socialist and bourgeois, the revolution promised freedom from patriarchy and some social, sexual, and legal equality. For believers it meant more religious freedom, especially for religious dissidents like the Old Believers, Baptists, and others. For reformist Russian Orthodox priests, called Renovationists, it meant the possibility of a revitalized church. These clergy supported the revolution, had some sympathy for socialist ideals, and wanted to democratize the church and modernize the liturgy. The democratic February revolution led to the release of religious and political prisoners from Siberia and the return from European exile of many intellectuals and revolutionaries.

For Utopian Bolsheviks like Maxim Gorky and Anatole Lunacharsky, it meant the creation of a new, more humane and scientific society. For Bolsheviks in exile like Lenin, Trotsky, and Kollontai, it came as a great surprise. They wondered how the revolution had occurred without them! For political prisoners in Siberia like Catherine Breshkovsky, Maria Spiridonova, and Stalin, it meant freedom from imprisonment and time to work for the yet to be achieved socialist revolution. For various nationalities like the Poles, Lithuanians, Latvians, Estonians, Ukrainians, and Georgians, it represented a chance to form new nation-states and governments for themselves. Some oppressed members of Russian society, like Jews and other minorities, saw new opportunities for self-expression and more social and economic advancement. Certainly the February revolution meant the end of the moribund Tsarist society.

Vera Broido was only ten years old when the February revolution occurred, but in her memoirs she remembered it as an exhilarating experience even in far-off Siberia, where her Menshevik mother and she were living in exile. Vera, many years later, described her reaction to the release of political prisoners, including the famous social revolutionary Katherine Breshkovsky, in the following words:

> It was still winter when the news of the (February) Revolution reached us. I had grown up with that word, from my earliest days I had been taught to expect that universal festival, that fulfillment of all hopes.
>
> Even in Minusinsk, so remote from the hub of events, life changed overnight. The local policemen disappeared and the exiles amused themselves by looking for their personal folders in the files of the police station. It emerged that each one had been given a nickname: Mother was described as Surovaya (the stern one). Everybody longed to get back to Russia to take part in these exciting events; everybody wanted to leave as soon as possible, or almost everybody ... The general desire to leave Minusinsk at once met with two obstacles. The ice on the Yenisey was expected to start cracking any day, and then the frozen road would become unsafe. Also the townspeople objected to the sudden departure of all the professionals. At a hastily convened general meeting at the town hall, the mayor was in tears: "Siberia has been a mother to you, yet you are leaving us without a thought for the hospital, the pharmacy, the school, the bank. They will have no staff and will have to close ... What will become of us?" So it was decided that departures should be staggered so as to permit at least partial replacement of key personnel. And by general agreement Yekaterina Breshko-Breshkovskaya was to be the first to leave. There was a festive send-off for the old lady. Speeches were made and the word Revolution came into all of them. I liked to listen and to see everybody so happy and jolly, quite unlike their former selves. But I felt very puzzled. No doubt, I thought, I will get to know what it is all about when we ourselves return to Petrograd.[1]

While large segments of Russian society celebrated the revolution, Countess Alexandra Tolstoy, youngest daughter of the writer Leo Tolstoy, expressed a more muted response in her memoir *I Worked for the Soviet*. She had been working as a nurse administrator at the front during World War I, and although she had longed for an end to the Tsarist regime, she was dismayed at the messiness of the revolution. She didn't like the new equality and familiarity of soldiers at the front, and she hated the desertions and disorder that the revolution provoked on the frontline. She wrote in her memoir:

> Nothing had changed with the revolution. The soldiers stayed on in the trenches, lazily exchanging bullets now and then with the Germans. In the rear, life went on as usual. The men cut wood, heated their mud huts, and stood duty. Only, instead of calling the officers "Your Honor" and "Your Excellency," they began using the absurd and not less bourgeois "Mr. Colonel," and "Mr. General." In some regiments the officers themselves took off their epaulettes; in others, the soldiers tore them off. As before the hospital detachments, having little to do, were bored and listless; and the officers continued to flirt with the nurses.
>
> Yet, officers, doctors, nurses, the zemstvo workers—everybody— pretended that with the change in government we had a group of intelligent people at the head of our country instead of Nicholas II, and that everything was utterly changed. Officers and men forsook the Tsar. There were no monarchists left in the army. The officers were suddenly very polite to the soldiers, calling them "you" instead of "thou," and adding "please" to their orders.
>
> And I who had awaited a more liberal government for many years, one without militarism, and with religious and political freedom, and with land for the peasants, watched these changes with mixed feelings. Like other Russian liberals, I had considered an overthrow of the monarchy essential, but felt that it should not come until after the war. With the grand Duke Michael's refusal of the throne, and the war going on, anything might happen.[2]

Alexandra's words show her displeasure that the revolution occurred in the midst of the war. What she and many others discovered was that while revolution was liberating, it was also inconvenient and messy.

2. *October 1917 Revolution*

> So we welcomed Lenin by walking around the village with these icons, with prayers. Free at last, free at last. We went round the entire village, and then we put the icons back in the church.
>
> Irina I. Kniazeva, Siberian peasant girl

The October 1917 revolution likewise met with different responses from Russian society. Many liberal, bourgeois elements who had welcomed the February revolution distrusted the Bolshevik October revolution, while the aristocracy and gentry class absolutely feared the Socialist takeover. However, many artists and workers saw it as a dream come true.

Poet Alexander Blok celebrated it in his poem "The Twelve." He depicted Christ as head of a column of Red soldiers. This poem had an enormous impact on Russian society. Writer Marietta Shaginian was distraught when Blok later distanced himself from his famous poem. She wrote to him complaining:

> The deepest thing that I have experienced in the last five years is connected with your "The Twelve." ... Why are you now renouncing Truth with a capital letter ... in favor of truth with a small letter? ... For me "The Twelve" is a symbol of ... innermost religious experience, which was experienced by only a few of us, the "intellectuals," and by almost all the "common" souls in the October Revolution.[3]

She laments that although the revolution had become distorted, still his poem had allowed people to experience the miracle of it. She thought that Blok had repudiated the best part of his spirit in renouncing his poem before his death. In some of her writings in the 1920s, Shaginian confessed that she was a believing Christian, that it was the essence of her personality, and that her religious and political beliefs did not allow her to join the Communist Party.[4]

Religion and politics remained interwoven in many Russian women's lives after the revolution. For many, religion and politics were not mutually exclusive in the 1920s. One young Siberian peasant girl remembered her family and village celebrating the revolution the following way:

> Well, when freedom was declared, everyone went to the church, the people gathered in the church, and we dragged out all the icons. Our village was good. The streets were straight and even; the houses were good. So we marched around the village with these icons and the Gospels. My grandfather welcomed the revolution with the Gospels, too, but he was the first to be branded a kulak and dispossessed.[5]

Another Siberian girl, Elena Ponomarenko, also remembered the revolution ushered in with prayers:

> My mama, Mama prayed for Lenin. She even, you know, requested that Lenin's name be put in the pominalnik: "Be sure to write down

Vladimir, be sure to." And she prayed for him. Because, see, we always, our whole life were very poor, but when the revolution came, there was this new order, and somehow we started to find work and started to live much better. Death was no longer at our door. It used to be that we lived from hand to mouth, but now, you see, we were really living—well, it was also very hard, but it was completely different. Mama, for example, she welcomed the revolution, and the kids also welcomed it.[6]

The Bolsheviks did not really control the countryside during much of the 1920s because the party was weak in rural areas. For the peasants this meant freedom from landlord control and a certain amount of religious freedom. Peasant calendars in the 1920s still listed all the High Holy Days, and women could become members of church councils after 1918. Many peasant women were active in rallying others to prevent church closures, organized petitions to local and national authorities, and physically guarded the holy places and objects of their villages from hooligan destruction. They helped provide a spiritual and cultural link to the past. But the divisions between traditional Russian Orthodox priests and reforming Renovationist priests often confused country people. The Renovationists wanted to reform the liturgy and work in peace with the Bolsheviks. Many peasants didn't want any change in the liturgy or church life. So the church in the countryside became divided.[7]

Obviously the October revolution meant different things in the cities and in the countryside. Still, for many young girls, it was an exciting time, as Sofia N. Pavlova remembered it in Siberia. Because her uncles had both been underground members of the Bolshevik Party during the Tsarist period, she had fond memories of the revolution. Describing it eighty years later, she said:

> How could I forget! I remember we all ran to the train station because political prisoners were traveling back from Siberian exile. It was a major railroad junction. Special trains always stopped there, meetings and mass demonstrations in favor of the revolution were organized there, and we, all us girls, always took part in these meetings and mass demonstrations. I remember Breshko-Breshkovskaia, who spoke here in Taiga. First of all, her speech was very emotional. That's the way I would characterize it now, very emotional. Of course I can no longer remember very well what it was about, but at any rate, it made a good impression on us, in the sense that the revolution, see,

had liberated the political prisoners and they were going to Moscow, to the capital. And undoubtedly they would accomplish something good. And in general we too were full of enthusiasm.[8]

Sofia was a teenager when the revolution occurred, but because of her uncles' political involvement, she became active in the Komsomol, the young people's Communist organization. Interviewed many years later, she remembered:

> And it was my Uncle Shura who kept urging me, Join, join the party. And I would say, but I'm not ready. I can't. Just how old was I then? In 1917 I was almost fourteen years old. And he would say, Join, join. They were accepting young people. But we quickly organized a Komsomol organization with their help, and I worked, I immediately began working in this Komsomol organization. I was in charge of mobilizing the ranks of young people for a certain length of time. Then I was an instructor for work among girls, and I rode around the district on horseback. Then I was the editor of the district Komsomol newspaper, where I wrote my own poetry, or rather published my own poetry. Yes. So I immediately took an active part, and it was thanks to Uncle Shura's influence. At first it was imperceptible; he didn't propagandize. As I said, I loved Uncle Shura very much, and he too loved us very much—especially me, he loved and spoiled me.[9]

In 1920, Sofia worked as part of the Extraordinary Units on Special Assignment. These were military units composed of Communist Party and Komsomol (young party) members organized to fight in the Civil War. Among the thousands of women soldiers during the Civil War, she fought bands of the White General Kolchak who were marauding in Siberia. A sense of adventure, escape from ordinary life, and devotion to a cause excited Sofia, just as these had stirred some women soldiers during World War I. Later, she was encouraged to join the party, and she worked on the district committee of the Komsomol while serving as secretary of the party. She remembered this period, especially the chistka, or party cleansing, which involved self-denunciation, as follows:

> Only at that time and only in Taiga could that have happened. The organization included all party members: those who belonged to the party's regional committee, to the Komsomol's regional committee, to the police, and to the court. Party members of all these bodies formed a single cell. That's what they called it. I was secretary of this cell. Then

in 1921, actually at the beginning of 1922, we had a chistka or party cleansing. Here in Moscow it occurred earlier, in 1921, but ours took place at the beginning of 1922. And at the time of the purge, the party members met and decided that I should be promoted to full membership in the party. And they accepted me.[10]

On the weekends, she and her friend Roma Kvopinskaia walked seven kilometers out of Taiga to teach adults to read and write. They were part of the liquidation of illiteracy program that the party sponsored. She received milk and bread for her services. She also worked as an agitator for the Komsomol, urging young girls to join, but they resisted. Many peasants saw the Komsomol as a godless organization and refused to let their children join it. Since the revolution had disrupted Sophia's education, the party and Komsomol decided to send her and her friend Roma to a rabfak, or special worker's school, in 1922.[11] The painting by Alexander Deineka could be depicting girls like her.

A. *Alexander Deineka*, Defense of Petrograd, *1928*

Roughly fifty thousand to seventy thousand women—about ten times the number that fought in World War I—served in the Red Army during the Civil War. Even some Socialist Revolutionaries (SRs) participated. A case in point was Irina Kakhovskaya (1888–1960), member of the SRs' Fighting Detachment. She organized assassination attempts on German Field Marshal Hermann von Eichhorn, the Kaiser's viceroy in occupied Ukraine, and she fought against the White generals Denikin and Kolchak.[12]

Still, it was usually difficult for village girls to participate in political life until the late 1920s when some were elected to the village soviets, or councils. The struggle against patriarchal culture in the village and in one's family continued long after the revolution, and few married women took part in the Komsomol or in the drama clubs. Because peasant women usually married in their late teens, this meant that few participated in political life.[13]

While some girls and women welcomed the revolution with prayer, and some well-to-do women feared the Bolsheviks, others came to the revolution as impoverished, exploited, and exhausted workers. These women's hard lives during World War I and the long queues for bread during that period made their participation in the revolution understandable. A good description of women's patient queuing and a factory worker's death in February 1917 is recounted by the English governess and journalist Rhoda Power, who was living in Rostov on Don at that time. She observed:

> Peasants stood shivering hour after hour outside the bakery, their tickets clutched between blue fingers, waiting for a loaf of bread. If there were not enough to go round they went away empty handed. Some of them lined up at midnight and waited till the shops opened in the morning. They had families to feed and could not be turned away. I used to watch their patient, tired faces, and the pale little children, sitting in the snow on overturned baskets, and wonder how long it would be before they would rebel. A little white-faced factory-girl haunted my dreams. It was Anna Ivanovna, an orphan with two small brothers. She used to stand at the bakery door, her head wrapped in an old brown shawl, her thin body shivering with cold as the snow beat relentlessly against her. She always carried a large basket and waited ... in the long queue outside the shop.... Day after day Anna stood at this door, sometimes in the middle of the line of women, sometimes at the end. Her position depended upon the time it took her to walk from the factory where she worked, and though she tried to move quickly

she had often to stop and rest because her limbs, weary with standing, refused to support her.... As the little procession passed the bakery where Anna had spent so many weary hours, the women crossed themselves, and one whispered to another: "Yesterday Michael Grigorovitch, today Anna Ivanovna.... It is the price of war."[14]

While the opening photo is of women in Petrograd, not Rostov, it seems to represent those whom Rhoda Power was describing. The price of World War I proved high throughout Russia, and it led to the revolution. In Rostov, Power witnessed the revolution and described one procession involving working-class and bourgeois women as follows:

> At eight o'clock we went to the windows and saw, coming towards us, hundreds of men, women, and children, wearing the scarlet revolutionary caps, and marching under banners printed with the words: "Hail to Democracy," "Long life to the Russian Republic," "We have won Liberty, now we want Peace," "Land for the People," etc. When they passed our house they burst triumphantly into song, throwing back their heads as they sang, some with tears in their eyes, others with a smile on their lips. One by one the procession came, the voices swelling in volume.... First a troop of women passed, red-clad, walking under an arch of banners, greeting a democracy that had recognized the justice of their claim to citizenship; after them, a vast horde of peasants and work-people demanding an eight-hour day; then the students, future doctors, lawyers, teachers, all types; the starved workers who had paid for their books by going without meals; the dreamers with eyes full of vision.... After the students walked the schoolgirls in brown dresses and neat black aprons, singing in sweet, clear voices.... Then, again, hundreds of factory-girls, some pathetically young and delicate, whose white faces contrasted horribly with their scarlet caps of liberty. They, too, carried banners demanding an eight-hour day. At intervals soldiers marched under flags printed with the one word "Land," and crying at the tops of their voices, "Peace without Annexation and Contribution." ... After the soldiers came quantities of Jews; old, bearded men, young, eager boys with dark eyes ..., full-bosomed women, and children, ... singing in unison and carrying flags with Hebraic inscriptions. And still they swept on in crowds.[15]

In Rostov, servants and workers seemed to interpret the revolution as a source of dignity and license as well as egalitarianism. They met and resolved that employers should no longer use the familiar form of "you" with them. Nor would they work more than eight hours a day. This meant that a servant who began work at seven in the morning refused to work past three in the afternoon, even if they had not done much all day. Any complaint brought the reply: "Now it is liberty." Chauffeurs and drivers were unavailable for night duty when a family wanted to drive to the theater. A dismissed chauffeur hinted that very soon the bourgeoisie would not require drivers, as they would have no car, and shortly afterward, all motor cars were commandeered by the Union of Soldiers' and Workers'.[16] Power observed:

> Home life, and in many cases labour, became completely disorganized. In households where a sense of humour lurked, the phrase, "Now it is liberty," became a standing joke, and the members of the family just shrugged their shoulders and did the work themselves. Servants, who wished to go to the cinema, sauntered out of the house when they pleased; workmen, bored with what they were doing, temporarily downed tools and strolled off to meet with friends or organized meetings during working hours to discuss any grievance that was rife. The streets were disorderly. There was no bloodshed, but meetings were held everywhere, so that it was impossible to walk ...[17]

B. Women in the Communist Party

> You all remember when a washerwoman was a washerwoman and nothing more. She could never be anything else. Now she can be anything she pleases. The working women of Russia have come into their kingdom.
>
> Inessa Armand, 1920

Despite the privations of the Civil War, which lasted from 1918 until 1921, the 1920s were a mixed time for Russian women. Some women gained educational and economic opportunities as well as more political, social, and legal equality. Still, in a patriarchal society like Russia, it was impossible to legislate women's equality. Yet, several hundred thousand women, out of a total female population of 60 million, became more active and visible in politics as the decade wore on. The Bolshevik Party promoted women's emancipation in its rhetoric, representatives such as "delegatki" (women delegates in factories and villages), and Zhenotdel (the party's separate organization for women). The organizations were meant to draw peasant and working-class women into the party and Komsomol. One of the leaders of Zhenotdel, Alexandra Kollontai, declared: "Here in Moscow there are weekly meetings of women delegates from the large factories once a week. But women are encouraged to go to all political meetings and to work in conjunction with and on an equal footing with men."

In areas remote from the capital, political life was complicated, and it was more difficult to draw women into party life. Yet, stalwarts like Inessa Armand, Alexandra Kollontai, Konkordia Samoilova, Vera Golubeva, Sofiia Smidovich, and others exhausted themselves agitating among and organizing nonparty women to support the new Soviet state during the Civil War. Indeed, Samoilova and Armand died from overwork during one of the epidemics that swept through Russia in 1920. Kollontai suffered a heart attack during this same period. While Samoilova's work before the revolution had drawn women into supporting International Women's Day from 1913 to 1917, during and after the revolution she, Armand, and others organized conferences of nonparty women to gain their support and participation on the Bolshevik side.

Still, women's work was not highly valued by the party, and Zhenotdel suffered from a high turnover in personnel at all levels. Female as well as male party leaders criticized it, as the following quote by Anna Rodionova indicates:

> Our work at the local level has suffered. Hence we must now eliminate all these *Babkomy* (*baba* committees); we must merge our work with the general party work, so that our district committees will acknowledge our circulars and (not) laugh at us. When everything will come from our sections through the provincial committees, then the district committees and neighborhood committees and trade union fractions will take our work seriously. I think we should eliminate the provincial *Babkomy* right here at the congress.[18]

Inessa Armand was the first leader of Zhenotdel. Armand had worked for the party in Moscow during 1917, and she was one of the few women elected in the Moscow Duma (city) elections of May 1917. She also served on the Bolshevik Executive Commission in Moscow. Like Kollontai and Krupskaia in Petrograd, she edited a journal for working women in Moscow. While the Petrograd paper was entitled *Rabotnitsa* (Working Woman), the Moscow equivalent was entitled *Zhizn' rabotnits* (Life of a Working Woman).[19] However, her

Inessa Armand, 1916 (Wikimedia)

untimely and early death in 1920 cut short her work in the women's department.

Kollontai briefly directed Zhenotdel, but her opposition to the party's New Economic Policy in 1921 led to her dismissal in March 1922. Sofiia Smidovich took over for two years. Finally Alexandra Artiukhina chaired it from 1925 until its closure in 1930.[20]

Lenin and other party leaders feared that women might resist and sabotage the Bolshevik revolution. They realized that its success depended on women's acceptance, and it was female Bolsheviks who worked to secure women's participation in the new Soviet society. During the Civil War, about twenty thousand women trained as Red Nurses to tend the Red Army men or to give help in supplying the Red Army and the workers; another thirty thousand served in administrative work, while others served in supply detachments to gather quotas of grain and other products. While sixty thousand or so women fought in the Red Army, less than two thousand were made prisoners of war or died in combat. Women workers were sent to look after the children — to organize nurseries, children's homes, hot meals in the schools, sewing shops, and so forth. In the words of L. Katasheva, the young generation that was building socialism during the second Five-Year Plan owed their lives and strength to the active women of the first women's congress.[21]

Eleven hundred women participated in the first nonparty women's conference, but their influence extended to hundreds and thousands of workers who had sent them as factory and trade union delegates. Samoilova dealt with the organizational questions of the conference and had numerous talks with the delegates. She explained to them how the women workers and peasants must take part in constructive work. Out of this conference grew Zhenotdel. Indeed, Samoilova and Armand worked so unstintingly for and among women—agitating, organizing, and writing for the new women's journals *Rabotnitsa* (Woman Worker) and *Kommunistka* (Woman Communist)—that they burned themselves out and died young. Still, Samoilova saw success in her work. She thought the Volga nonparty women's conference of 1920 not only helped secure much-needed grain but also, because of the publicity of their work among Saratov women workers, that it would serve as a model in other towns.[22]

Agitating among working women in the fisheries on the small islands of the Volga River near Astrakhan in 1918, Samoilova discussed the importance of education, saying:

> For the men and women workers to be able to organize national economy on new socialist lines, they must not only be literate but they must have professional technical education, for which purpose the soviet government is organizing technical course and schools. We must uproot illiteracy—this cursed heritage from the old order.... Only by knowledge can we conquer all our enemies and put national economy on its feet.[23]

In her last article before her untimely death in 1920, Samoilova summed up the difficulties of the women workers in the following words:

> The many fisheries of Astrakhan form a veritable desert in the sense of cultural and educational work. Scattered about the Volga delta, separated from the city educational sections, they receive no help either from the educational sections or from the political education departments. But the thirst for education can be felt at every step among the working population. Schools to teach adults reading and writing are springing up all over the fisheries, on the initiative of the workers themselves. Local clubs are being formed. But they are dragging

out a miserable existence because they have no books; the clubs have no newspapers and the workers of the fisheries do not know what is happening in the world. It is true that the shortage of school books is explained by the general economic ruin through which we are passing, but this is not the whole explanation. The Political Education Department possesses a certain number of school books and school supplies.... The most serious attention of the party, trade union and educational organizations must be devoted to the education of this mass of toilers.[24]

Adding to Samoilova's problems was the death of her protégé Shpakova, who had been sent to Astrakhan by the Moscow Zhenotdel. Shpakova had tried to educate and mobilize women workers, only to be undone by "hostile elements" in the fisheries—poverty and cholera. She died shortly before her mentor, Samoilova.[25] By 1926 the Soviet government was finally able to exert its will in the fisheries in Astrakhan.

After the revolution, the Bolshevik Party especially appealed to women on International Women's Day, which is celebrated on March 8 every year. Nevertheless, married factory women remained overworked, had to stand in line for food at cooperatives up to four hours per day, and had little time for political work. Mainly young women unencumbered by family duties had time or energy for political activity. Male Bolsheviks wanted women workers to support the new Soviet regime and to undermine the Menshevik influence in the trade unions. Yet, political activists in the delegatki and Zhenotdel groups often felt used and without proper direction. Some complained that Bolshevik propaganda in the papers was ineffective and unhelpful. One argues:

> The stranichka in *Pravda* is awful. I am a worker myself and we hope to receive something for directing our work. But there's nothing in the women's pages for us. There are only agitational little articles which would have been useful three years ago for the factories . . .[26]

Indeed, much of the propaganda and agitation work did not impress them. One remarked:

> "These little articles in which some comrade writes why she joined the party in 1902 and why she became a Communist. Any one of us could write that, but such a stranichka gives us nothing for our work."[27]

Yet another complained:

Neither the leaflets nor *Kommunistka* (Woman Communist journal) stand up to criticism. When you read them, you are struck by the poverty of the propaganda. Is it really possible that among women workers there are no manifestations of creativity?[28]

Women were brought together in congresses of various kinds: some for factory workers, some for peasants, some for party members. The following picture shows women peasant delegates engaged in political discussions in 1925.

While the male Communist Party elite remained sympathetic to women's political emancipation, in fact they spent their time on "more important economic and political matters," relegating young women to low-level positions in the party and government and keeping old female party members, with few exceptions, in obscure positions. Speaking to the First All Russian Congress of Women Workers in 1918, Lenin observed that there could be no socialist revolution unless a vast section of the toiling women took an important part in it. He praised Bolshevik law, which promoted women's social, political, educational, and legal equality. However, he saw women's housework as domestic slavery that "crushes, strangles, stultifies and degrades her, chains her to the kitchen and to the nursery, and wastes

A Congress of Poor Peasants in a Hostel, 1925, Leningrad
(St. Petersburg Photo Archive)

her labor on barbarously unproductive, petty, nerve-racking, stultifying and crushing drudgery." He and other socialists did not believe in paying women for their domestic work but thought that this work could be socialized and done through canteens and model dining rooms as well as crèches and child care centers. He correctly forecast that the emancipation of workers and women had to be brought about by themselves since others would never do so.[29]

For a variety of reasons, including poverty, the new socialist society was never able to properly transform women's drudgery, freeing them exclusively for "productive labor." Instead, working women continued the double burden of paid work and unpaid housework that they, like their European sisters, experienced under capitalism. It proved much harder to go beyond providing legal equality for women and to secure true social and political equality. Of course, the Bolsheviks tried harder than European bourgeois democracies to emancipate working women, but this daunting task still awaits a solution in the twenty-first century.

The following picture shows the "Old Bolshevik" Elena Stasova (1873–1966) in 1920. In 1919, she had been appointed party secretary, and she tried to make the party's central administration more efficient.

Elena Stasova with Fellow Workers, 1920, Petrograd
(St. Petersburg Photo Archive)

But in 1920 Lenin appointed three men to replace her. She was sidelined into a less significant job, becoming the party's historian. Like many other old Bolsheviks, she shunned work in Zhenotdel, but she did work on party history and the Political Red Cross.

Food and fuel deprivation during World War I pushed thousands of women workers and housewives into political demonstrations during the February revolution. Unhappiness with these lingering problems as well as the new provisional government drew thousands of working women to the streets again in protest in April and May 1917, as the following picture shows.

Prior to the February revolution, no women could vote and few belonged to political parties. However, working-class women slowly joined the Bolshevik Party, their numbers increasing from ten thousand in 1917 to twenty thousand in 1922 to fifty-eight thousand by 1927. About 430,000 young women belonged to the Komsomol in 1929. About 16 percent of Komsolmolki lived in rural areas, but not all were peasants. Nearly half were from families of the intelligentsia, such as daughters of teachers in village schools. In 1926, 43 percent of women voted in city council elections, and 28 percent of village women voted in rural soviet elections. Yet by the end of the decade 29,000 were elected to positions in the city Soviets, and 273,000 were elected to village Soviets. While these are not huge numbers, especially out of the total 60 million female population, they were thousands more than in Tsarist times.[30] Generally it remained easier for women to participate in the soviets or government councils than to obtain party membership. Igal Halin's study of student Communist autobiographies in the 1920s shows that not all men and women who applied for membership were allowed to join. Even if women were exemplary workers, their "class consciousness" might be inadequate.[31] If workers and peasant women were rejected for membership, this may have deterred others from even trying to become party members.

Recruiting young women to join the Komsomol proved equally daunting in the 1920s. In her study *Youth in Revolutionary Russia*, Anne Gorsuch found that many young women felt politically illiterate and unwanted in the Komsomol. Others expected political and social equality, only to be jeered at during Komsomol meetings or to be assigned cleaning, not political, work. Still others liked the dancing, drama, and singing groups that the Komsomol fostered but found the

Women Demonstrators, April 1917, Petrograd (St. Petersburg Photo Archive)

political lectures dull and boring. Little attention was devoted to family issues. As in the Communist Party, the Komsomol was a bastion of male fraternity. One married woman, Nadia Borisova, complained:

> I want to work and be a productive Komsomol member; I don't want to be left behind in the Komsomol work ... but escaping from the oppression of the kitchen is beyond my strength. My husband works during the day and in the evening he goes to classes or participates either in some kind of social work or political work. Alone I have to deal with the everyday cleaning, prepare the dinner, run to the cooperatives, clean the swaddling clothes, feed the baby.... What does the Komsomol do? Absolutely nothing. We married Komsomol women with children are without hope, in the dark; I am thinking of the future when the baby will grow a bit older so that I can work again. But the Komsomol sleeps, leaving its members behind; if a girl gets married there is no place for her in the Komsomol.[32]

In both the countryside and city, women made inroads into low-level party and government positions. The party organization that best succeeded in the countryside was the Pioneers, which recruited children. They attracted large numbers of peasant girls. Adolescent women often shunned the Komsomol in the countryside because of its rude, crude treatment of them. Male Komsomol members were often patronizing, scornful, and nasty to women, even raping them. Needless to say, peasant fathers wanted to protect their daughters from debauchery and usually kept them from joining the Komsomol. Parents also feared that joining the Komsomol would make a young girl unmarriageable—the worst disaster in peasant culture. Young women often courted shame in their villages if they joined the Komsomol.[33]

In her memoir *I Worked for the Soviet*, Countess Tolstoy provides negative glimpses of several young Communist women who worked at the family estate Yasnaya Polyana. She describes an idealistic one (Comrade Malvina) who becomes disillusioned, one who enjoyed life (Comrade Alexandrova), and one who was ruined by a male Komsomol who had been rejected as her lover (Comrade Marina). Tolstoy initially feared Communist supervision and the introduction of "political grammar" into her school in 1925 because it would lead to militarism and antireligious doctrine. Yet none of the women proved a threat, as her writings show:

> In school special hours were set for classes in political grammar. The new Communist teacher was supposed to give a report of her work in teacher's meeting. But when, as chairman of the meeting I called on her, she said that her report was not ready. It was not ready at the second meeting either, and I had to reprove her. When this happened a third time, Comrade Malvina simply covered her face with her hands and sobbed:
> "Please leave me alone, won't you?"
> The poor girl did not know anything about teaching or writing reports.... But Malvina got too tame. We corrupted her with our ideas. Once, as I was coming out of the museum, I met her on the porch.
> "I want to speak to you," she said, and burst into tears.
> "Well, what's the matter? Has something happened?" I asked.
> Sobbing like a child, she told me that she could no longer belong to the party.
> "Why?" I asked. It flashed through my mind that if Malvina should leave the party, I would lose my "tame Communist," and another one would be sent to us. "Why, Malvina? Don't you want to be a member of the party?"
> "I can't, Alexandra Lvovna! If only you knew how mean they are! They make us denounce you and say all kinds of bad things about you, and spy.... No, No, I can't stay with them any more. Oh, tell me what to do!"

Her grief was so real that I forgot my own worries, and forgot to make fun of her as I always had.

"Malvina," I asked her, "tell me the truth. Do you believe in the work of the Communist Party as you did before?"

"Well ... no," she said. "I don't. Maybe I still believe in socialism, but not in the Bolshevik Party".... Poor Malvina! As soon as she lost her membership, she lost almost everything else. She went from one job to another until at last she became an under clerk in an office, and even this work she did badly.[34]

The next Communist supervisor sent to Yasnaya Polyana was "too stupid to be harmful," according to Tolstoy. She describes her as follows:

> Our next Communist was a member of the Komsomol. She was sent from Moscow in 1927 as the leader of the Young Pioneers. Comrade Alexandrova lived at Teliatinki and taught the second grade of the primary school. Luckily this girl was also too stupid to be harmful. She was a plump, rosy-cheeked, lazy, sleepy creature. The only subject that aroused her was sex. Everyone in the school made fun of her.
>
> "Which do you like better: the instructor of the workshops or the bookkeeper?" the teachers would ask her.
>
> Alexandrova opened her red lips, her small gray eyes shone. "Ivan Stepanovich is a real man, and I love men like that. He is so big and strong, and well built ... the bookkeeper is too gentle, too refined . . ."
>
> Everyone laughed, and I was happy that we had another harmless member of the party. But soon rumors were heard that the "Komsomolka" had received several men during one night. And the tutors insisted upon her leaving Teliatinki when they learned that she had made love to some of the older boys in the orphan home.
>
> For several months, I could not get rid of the girl. Not until the director of the Department of Experimental Schools, who sent her to us, was discharged, did I succeed in dismissing her.[35]

At first, there was no Komsomol cell at Yasnaya Polyana, but eventually one was established because if the high school students wanted to attend the university, they had to join the Komsomol. Trouble erupted when a young Komsomol organizer named Vorobiev came to the estate. He was from Tula, and soon a student named Katia became pregnant. Tolstoy learned that the father of the child was Vorobiev. Further trouble arose when Tolstoy learned that another Komsomolka named Marina had been expelled from the Komsomol because of problems with Vorobiev. Tolstoy asked her what happened, and Marina explained:

> "What's the matter, Marina?"
> "I'm lost, Alexandra Lvovna!"
> "Why?"
> "I've been expelled from the Komsomol."
> "What for?"
> "Comrade Vorobiev has reported that my father was an employee of the old police..."
> "But they knew it before, didn't they?"
> "Yes, but they paid no attention to it. My father was a clerk in the police office. He was not a policeman. But now Vorobiev is angry..."
> "Why?"
> The girl blushed and lowered her eyes: "He made love to me, and I sent him off ... I hate him..."
> The next day I spoke to Vorobiev. The boy was impudent. I went to the secretary of the Tula cell and begged him to help Marina. The secretary refused. Marina was expelled from the Komsomol. She was graduated from our school, but she could not go to the university, and as the daughter of a police employee, and disfranchised, could not become a member of the trade-union and get a job.
> For a year I lost sight of Marina. Then one day as I was walking through the main street of Tula someone called to me,
> "Alexandra Lvovna!"
> "Marina!"
> She was as good looking as ever, but her face and lips were painted.
> "How do you do, Alexandra Lvovna."
> "I am glad to see you, Marina. Where are you living now? Are you working?" Marina did not answer. She turned away her handsome head and wept."[36]

The implication is that Marina had been ruined by the Komsomol boy Vorobiev, and she had become a prostitute since she couldn't get a job.

C. Political Activists

> The business of emancipating women workers and peasants is far more complicated, far more difficult, and demands much more time than it had seemed to us at first.
>
> Inessa Armand, *Kommunistka*, 1920

Not all revolutionaries were disenchanted with the Bolshevik takeover. Many Old Bolsheviks—those who had joined the party before World War I—saw the revolution as a way to morally rejuvenate the country. As they considered themselves moral and spiritual reformers of society before the revolution, so many Bolshevichki (female Bolsheviks) perceived working-class women as moral beacons after the revolution. They thought the job of working-class women was to become literate and then enlighten others, providing needed social services such as crèches, canteens, and other communal services so that women would be liberated from housework and childcare, free to participate in socially and economically useful work in the public sphere. The revolution was supposed to change women from objects of social transformation into agents of social and moral change—improving their lives, raising their self-esteem, and renewing Soviet society. Socialism became the new religion for many, and the party the new liberating community offered women political, spiritual, and moral rebirth.[37] Just as many European and American women viewed themselves as morally superior to men in the late nineteenth and early twentieth centuries, so many Russian women saw themselves and were seen as moral elements elevating and improving their society.

One of the most famous and hardworking Bolshevichki was the socialist and feminist Alexandra Kollontai. She was a party agitator, publicist, and organizer—equally concerned about women's emancipation and the socialist revolution. She thought the right time to redefine women's position was when the new socialist state was being formed. She served as Commissar of Social Welfare from 1918 to 1921. In that position, she introduced legislation for civil marriage and divorce and equality of spouses in marriage and abolished distinctions between legitimate and illegitimate children.

Kollontai, along with others in "The Workers Opposition," fell afoul of the new party line in 1921 when they criticized Lenin for introducing the New Economic Policy (NEP). She thought NEP was harmful to workers and a capitulation to capitalism. As a result, Kollontai lost her post as head of Zhenotdel in 1922. However, her lover and comrade Shliapnikov, as well as others in the opposition, were later expelled from the party and purged, while Kollontai was effectively silenced by exiling her as ambassador to various Scandinavian

Alexandra Kollontai, 1930s, Moscow (St. Petersburg Photo Archive)

countries in the 1920s and 1930s. Still, she did not go quietly and voiced her opposition to NEP in feminist short stories and novellas she wrote until 1925.

As a feminist and socialist, Kollontai criticized NEP for its pernicious influence on women. She thought NEP represented a return to capitalism, with bosses, not workers, in charge of the factories, and greedy NEPmen and managers in charge of the economy. During this period, women's unemployment skyrocketed and prostitution and abortion increased, as did abandonment of children. Her works, along with those of several male writers like playwright Valentin Kataev and novelist Fedor Gladkov, reflect women's personal and political struggles. She wrote, "Life creates the new woman, but literature reflects them," and Kollontai used her literary writings to reveal women's situation.[38]

Her novella *Vasilisa Malygina* shows the young starry-eyed revolutionary Vasia married to a fellow who had become a corrupt NEPman. She found it hard to leave him because the ties that bound her to him were "artfully tied." Only after he took a mistress was she able to break with him. When she discovered she was pregnant, she decided to keep the baby and raise it in true communist fashion in a communal crèche that she hoped to establish at the factory where she worked.[39]

In her short story "Sisters," Kollontai criticized another nasty aspect of NEP—the return of wide-scale prostitution. Prostitution had initially declined under the Bolsheviks, but high unemployment among women, even white-collar workers, had distressing effects in the mid-1920s. One socialist observed: "Men with money and women without" lead to prostitution. "Sisters" depicts a woman whose husband has betrayed her by bringing a prostitute to their apartment. Slowly the wife realizes that she too could fall into prostitution if she lost her job or her husband. After a conversation with the prostitute, the wife feels compassion, not jealousy for the "other woman."[40]

A third casualty of the new regime is a change in ethical values. Kollontai deals with this subject in "Love of Three Generations." This work focuses on Zhenia, a young, sexually emancipated Communist woman, darting hither and thither during the Civil War, heeding the party's call. Her lifestyle during the early days of the revolution allows her no time to develop relationships because just as she gets to know someone, she has to move to a new place at the front. At one point, Zhenia says:

> I've read enough novels to know just how much time and energy it takes to fall in love, and I just don't have the time. At the moment we've got an enormous load of work on our hands in the district.... I never want to fall in love like mother did! How would you ever find the time to work?

Sometimes she has so much work to do that she forgets about her lover. She thinks the main thing is to enjoy the time she has and not become too committed to any one man. When she stops liking a fellow, that means it is over. As a result of her many assignments and noncommitment, Zhenia ends up having a sexual affair with her mother's partner. Her mother is so extremely busy working, Zhenia doesn't think she would mind their rendezvous! But she does.[41]

In many ways, Zhenia symbolizes the "new woman" who behaves like a man. The implied criticism is that women revolutionaries display better, more ethical behavior. Kollontai does not fault the mother for having a lover. She supports women's sexual liberation and portrays the mother as a responsible, sexually emancipated woman. Only the daughter is considered too cavalier.

50   CHAPTER ONE: POLITICAL LIFE

The earlier picture of Kollontai is from the 1930s, and her mouth and eyes reflect some of the sorrow that she experienced in the 1920s: her "unacceptable" involvement in the Workers' Opposition; her unhappy divorce from her second husband, Dubynko; her exile as an ambassador in Scandinavia; and no further discussion of "Winged Eros" and women's sexual emancipation.

Despite her personal problems, Kollontai apparently remained personally charming and helpful to others. In the early 1920s, Countess Alexandra Tolstoy was given an appointment to meet Kollontai, a pass out of prison to talk with her, and describes her encounter with Kollontai as follows:

> I did not expect to find Comrade Kollontay so pleasant. She was ladylike, cultured in manner, and apparently clever. I do not know what impression I made on her, but in about ten days ... the members of the Central Party Committee ... voted for (my) freedom.[42]

D. Disenchantment with Communist Politics

> No, we do not stone our neighbors,
>   Our bullets rip their hearts in two.
>   Anna Barkova, poet, *Woman*, 1922

While only a few female "Old Bolsheviks" were openly critical of the Communist Party in the early 1920s, some found membership precarious later in the decade when Trotskyites were attacked. Devout party member and historian Anna Pankratova had to be careful working with bourgeois professors in the History Institute in Leningrad in the mid-1920s. Later, she had to sever all ties with her husband, who was also a party member and graduate of the Academy of Red Professors (where they had studied together). Accused of Trotskyite sympathies, her husband had been arrested and imprisoned. Presumably fearing "guilt by association," she broke completely with him. Party members like Maria Joffe, who was an avowed Trotskyite, suffered in the late 1920s. While allowed contact with her son in the late 1920s when she was in prison, her situation became almost unbearable in the 1930s when she refused to recant her Trotskyite position so was imprisoned in the Gulag and denied contact with her son.[43]

1. Educated Women

The social and political situation of some nonparty intelligentsia also became bleak during the 1920s. Poets like Anna Akhmatova, Vera Merkova, Sofia Parnok, Anna Radlova, Maria Shkapskaya, and others who chose to remain in Russia did not reckon on the new government forbidding the publication of their work in the mid-1920s. Nor did they guess they could barely eke out a living doing translations or working as journalists. Trotsky's denunciations of poets Akhmatova, Tsvetaeva, and Shkapskaya in 1925 in his book *Literature and Revolution*; the fall of Minister of Culture Lunacharsky from grace; and the Central Committee's strict guidelines for "fellow travelers" in 1925 all made life more difficult for nonparty women writers. Likewise, Nadezhda Mandelstam, wife of the poet Osip Mandelstam, did not imagine how miserable her life would become. She began the decade as an artist, painting slogans on buildings to celebrate the revolution, but slowly felt the long arm of the state, which refused to publish her husband's work or provide rations for poets whose writings did not please the new government.

Disenchantment with Bolshevism can be seen among some who initially favored it. Anna Barkova's first book of poetry, *Woman*, was published in 1922 under the patronage of Anatoly Lunacharsky, minister of Culture. In the mid-1920s, she also wrote poems that were published in several major literary journals and the newspaper *Pravda*. Still, by 1925 she had a sad, sardonic tale to sing, as the following poem shows:

> Scarlet blood and yellow bile
> Feed our life, and all we do;
> Malignant fate has given us
> Hearts insatiable as wolves,
> Teeth and claws we use to maul
> And tear our mothers and our fathers;
> . . .
> Oh! Better not to think like this?
> Very well, then—as you wish.
> Then hand me universal joy,
> Like bread and salt, upon a dish.[44]

2. Gentry-Class Women

In addition to disenchanted party members, several hundred thousand devout, priestly, and gentry-class families found the new Bolshevik order unbearable. Most gentry-class families were chased from their homes by peasants desiring their land and goods. In her memoir, Alexandra Tolstoy tells about the confiscation of her estate Novaia Poliana and that of her brother-in-law, who also lived near her mother at Yasnaya Polyana. The peasants at Yasnaya Polyana protected Countess Sofia Tolstoy because Leo Tolstoy had treated them well. Mobs broke into bourgeois or priestly residences to kill and pillage. Some well-to-do people fled to the south and some to western Europe. Nina Berberova gives us poignant stories of Russian women dying from typhus and broken hearts during the Civil War. Her stories "The Ladies from St. Petersburg" and "Zoya Andreyevna" show the difficulties women in marginal positions and young orphaned girls faced during the Civil War.[45] Most sympathetic accounts of bourgeois women's lives were not printed during the Soviet period. Some writings like Berberova's were published only in Paris in the 1920s.

3. Nelly Ptashkina

> Yes, it is very terrible. When reading the papers, all that is happening creeps quite close to us; the trivial incidents of every day, which formerly stood between us and these horrors, seem to vanish and there comes in their stead something huge, which crushes us with its weight.
>
> Nelly Ptashkina, 1918

Poignant accounts of the lives of a bourgeois family after the Bolshevik revolution are recorded in the diary of a young nationalistic Russian girl named Nelly Ptashkina. In Moscow in the winter 1918, the fourteen-year-old feared for Russia as the Germans advanced into Ukraine and toward Petrograd. Fearing German rule, she reluctantly agreed that the separate peace the Bolsheviks had brokered with the Germans was necessary. In February, 1918, she wrote:

> It seems to me that it is superfluous to dwell on the ignominy, the baseness of what is going on. After all that Russia has done with regard to the Allies, what does a separate peace matter? Have we taken

DISENCHANTMENT WITH COMMUNIST POLITICS 53

any part in the war since the advent of the Bolshevists? The answer is clear—"No!" According to my opinion, the separate peace will not come as a surprise to any one. And such a remarkable event must pass unnoticed, as in olden times did the fall of the Eastern Roman Empire.... Yes; a separate peace is a disgrace, but it seems to me more infamous still to live under the German yoke.... At such moments we surrender hope; terror and sorrow grip our soul and we want to forget everything—forget, above all, the world which has become such a nightmare.... What is still ahead? What is going to happen? When will all this end ... or is it without an end?[46]

Although Nelly was a convinced Socialist, she was not a Bolshevik. In her November 1918 diary written in Kiev, where her family had fled, she explains her political views:

My decision was made long ago. For a long time past my feelings and my thoughts have inclined towards Socialism. I do not know when this happened, or how it came about. My convictions have been formed for some time past, not with regard to everything, but on certain questions.... I consider myself a Socialist, and hope that when I grow up, I shall really become one. In the meantime ... of what does my Socialism consist? In my views on the form of government, on the situation of the working classes, on the question of political equality. Yes, of course, the Socialists are in the right. There is no doubt in my mind as regards this.[47]

In Moscow, she fears that her father will be arrested, but it's after they have fled south to Kiev that Cheka agents (secret police) come to arrest him. Her mother tells her:

"They have come for Father, they want to arrest him," she explained.
As usual when terrible things are happening, I feel as if my heart was bursting. But there is no time to think, one must act.
Mummie stuffs the belt with the diamonds into my hands; I put it on. I hide the money and the papers, the rest Mummie gives to the servant, and her cupboard is ready for the search.
In the meantime, Uncle gives our cook Father's note-case to hide; Lena has been with us for ten years, but she crosses herself and refuses; "That I should be drowned with it, no thank you" ... But Uncle's nurse, who has brought up his children, takes it at once.[48]

As the Cheka agents are being shown in, they enquire from Nelly's uncle:

"Ptashkin lives in your house?"
"He does, but he has just gone."
"How is that?"
"He is a business man, he comes and goes."
"We want to see his room...."
"This way, please."[49]

Then the Cheka summoned the House Committee representative and a militia man, who came and searched their apartment. One was kind hearted and performed his work quietly. The other was more eager and searched with a sense of his importance. While her father escaped this time, they were afraid for his safety and made plans to leave Russia for Paris, which they thought would be more peaceful.

4. *Kyra Karadja*

After the Bolshevik takeover, some gentry-class people realized they had been greedy and unwise before the revolution.[50] Many, like Nelly's family, fled south. Young gentry-class Kyra Karadja and her family escaped to the Caucasus. She remembered the frightening triumph of the Bolsheviks in Tiflis in the following words:

> At night the red glow of burning villages could be seen beyond the mountains. Regiments of soldiers marched through town. Wounded, clay-smeared men were brought back from the trenches just outside the summer resorts on the road to Tiflis. Tales were told and repeated of what took place after the occupation of a town by the Reds.... The searches and arrests took place mostly at night. So did the executions. The children would wake up with a terrified start, instantly sweaty, their hearts thumping, when around midnight came the rumble of heavy wheels over cobblestones in the distance and long, moaning wailing.... The truck advanced heavily, jerkily, swinging round the tramcar rail, blotting out the lantern light for a second. The dark mass of prisoners swayed with every jerk. The soldiers' bayonets glistened. The truck went by. It disappeared from view, headed for a field outside of the town. Only the horrible howling remained hanging in the air.... Crouching on her bed, her nails digging into her neck, Kyra prayed frenziedly, "God, all-powerful God, don't let it happen. Save them, save them. Do a miracle.... God, let them escape this very moment, right at this instant before it's too late." ... She listened unmoving, trying to still her trembling.... She sobbed till she fell asleep from utter exhaustion.[51]

5. Other Disenchanted Educated Women

a. Maria Shkapskaya

In her 1918 poem "No Dream," Shkapskaya laments the hanging of an officer during the Civil War. It isn't clear whether he's a Red (Communist) or White (Tsarist) officer, but to Shkapskaya it shows the dreadful, senseless cruelty of war:

> "You hear? Tomorrow, they say?"
> "I thought it was today."
> "There'll be crowds out to see it."
> "In public, what is the world coming to?"
> "But it'll be interesting, admit it."
> "They say the Swiss do it in public, you know."
>
> All round town they put posters up.
> They fixed up a gallows in pride of place.
> Next to a wall by the cathedral porch.
> To give them plenty of space.
> A swing like a cross with two ends.
> . . .
> It was the feast of St. Peter and Paul.
> And he hung there for three days and nights,
> And God's own people walked by,
> On errands, or to stare at the sight.
> They came past and past.
> As they went to morning and to evening mass,
> And the bell tolled on and on.
>   And he swung in the wind, and listened.
> "Starting to stink now, with the heat."
> "Eh! Have a look at them filthy crows!"
> "I've five mouths to feed, you know!
> I've got nothing against the revolution,
> I'm all for the constitution."
> . . .
> "We'll be quits, you can be sure,
> Not in the next world, before."
> "What about God?"
> "Nothing to do with us, is it?
> The powers-that-be will answer for it."[52]

b. Marina Tsvetaeva

Tsvetaeva wrote a similar indictment of the Civil War when her husband was away fighting for the White Army. Her poem "Swans' Encampment" laments both the Red and White soldiers dying in misery. Her poem captured the devastation but did not please the Soviets:

> Swans' Encampment, 1917–1921
> . . .
> On either side, mouths lie
> Open and bleeding, and from
> Each wound rises a cry:
> —Mother
>
> They all lie in a row,
> No line between them,
> I recognize that each one was a soldier.
> But which is mine? Which one is another's?
>
> This man was White   now he's become Red.
> Blood has reddened him.
> This one was Red   now he's become White.
> Death has whitened him.[53]

During the 1920s, some educated Russian women became more devout and more anti-Bolsevik. One such woman, Iuliia Nikolaevna Danzas (1879–1942), was a librarian and history teacher who became a Catholic and a nun. She had been a fervent monarchist and hated the dismemberment of the Russian empire. Initially, she thought the Bolshevik takeover was just one more "changing of the guard." Along with many Catholic priests, she was arrested and imprisoned in the early 1920s. After her release from prison in 1932, the writer Maxim Gorky and his wife intervened on her behalf, and she was allowed to emigrate to the West.[54]

Artist Vera F. Shtein (1887–?) and teacher Olga V. Sinakevich (1875–1959) belonged to the religious circle Voskresenie (Resurrection). Both were arrested in 1929 for participating in that organization. Shtein had philosophically opposed the Bolsheviks from the beginning. In letters to her brother, which she wrote in 1921 but never sent, she complained that she was "living in a prison from which there is no escape." What depressed her most of all was the "prison monotony and hopelessness of everyday life." She saw the Cheka (secret police) as criminals and scoundrels. In another letter, she complained about the execution of sixteen seemingly innocent women in a "supposed conspiracy." The authorities needed to "sacrifice some lives" in order to intimidate others and show that they were not bluffing. In 1929 Shtein was arrested in conjunction with a case against Voskresenie. Sentenced to three years in penal camps, she was released and exiled to Vologda in 1931. She later worked as an art teacher in Novosibirsk.[55]

c. Alexandra Tolstoy

Like many others, Countess Alexandra Tolstoy thought the Bolsheviks would not last, and early on she was disillusioned with Soviet rule. Nothing worked in Moscow, where she was trying to publish a complete edition of her father's writings for the centennial of his birth. She found neither the phones, heating systems, trolleys, trains, nor food distribution worked for several years after the October revolution. Bartering goods and clothes from her family's estate was the only way to obtain food from the impoverished peasants.[56]

Her gentry-class status and critical attitude made her suspect to the Bolsheviks, and the Cheka arrested and briefly imprisoned her four times. Like many others, she was accused of having counterrevolutionary ideas when she was really nonsupportive. Luckily, she was able to trade on her family name and usually received reasonably lenient treatment in prison. A communist even secured Tolstoy a meeting with Kollontai, who helped arrange for her freedom.

Describing one imprisonment, she explains how ineffective Bolshevik safeguards were. A group from the Workers and Peasants' Inspection, set up to investigate abuses of government and party officials, came to visit the prison where Tolstoy was, and she describes how unresponsive the prisoners were to inquiries about their treatment. As Tolstoy records it,

> "And now, comrades, please tell me how you are living here. How are you fed? Are you given clothes? Do you get enough wood for your stoves?
> The prisoners were silent.
> "Comrades, I am asking you are there any complaints about the food? How does the commandant behave toward you?"
> "What is the use of asking all those questions?" I asked irritably.

"Don't you understand that if we are silent, it is not because we have nothing to complain of? Every one of us knows that if we tell you the truth we will be punished as soon as you leave the camp: thrown into the cellar or worked to the bone?"

"Comrades?" the little inspector exclaimed, "Comrade Tolstoy is not right. I will answer for your safety!" and she planted her head on her chest. "Please tell me everything. Don't be afraid!"

And again the prisoners were silent.

"Well!"

"Let me ask you a question," I said. "How can we say anything when we do not know what is due us? We only know that they are feeding us frozen potato peelings, that we haven't got enough bread, that we are given old dirty clothes that are good for nothing ... but we don't know what we ought to have!"

"Is all this true?" the inspector asked.

"Of course it's true," one of the prisoners said. "We never get the food that is due us, the commandant punishes us for no reason at all .. we don't get our share of sugar ..."[57]

Tolstoy went on to say that the inspector returned several times and the commandant was dismissed, but conditions remained the same. She shares some humorous stories about one imprisonment where the commandant let her out to go to the dentist, and another let her out to visit Kollontai, who arranged for her release from prison. The most ironic was a commandant who let a thief out every day to rob and then took one half of her earnings.[58]

Olga Sinakevich's writing, "Epiphany in the Taiga," shows an unexpected leniency in Soviet penal behavior in the late 1920s and early 1930s. Arrested for participating in the religious-philosophical circle Voskresenie, she was sentenced to three years in corrective labor camps. She spent her time in the Solovetsky camps and exile in Vologda. On Epiphany in 1931, she and a friend were granted a day pass, and they walked to a neighboring village to buy some supplies for themselves and their friends. She remembered this twenty-five years later when she wrote her story. In the village, they tried to buy some fish, but no one wanted Soviet currency; they wanted only to barter for other goods. Still, it was refreshing seeing the "everyday life of free Russian people, who lived at home, surrounded by their family." Describing their situation, Sinakevich wrote:

> Everywhere, we waited on the threshold, gazing at the clean floors meticulously covered with clean, handmade carpets and the warmly

lit icon lamps; and in every foyer were freshly cut branches of fir trees reminding us of the happy Epiphany celebrations of our childhood, within our family circle. Everywhere was the appetizing aroma of food and fresh bread. Obviously, at every house, the families were ready to sit down for a holiday supper and were waiting with irritation and impatience to close the door behind us.... One way or the other, it was useless to continue walking from door to door. Besides it was late and it was high time for us to start back. It was sad to return with empty hands to our dirty, hungry, noisy barracks.[59]

Finally, the local storekeeper stopped them and sold them some sugar, candies, and gingerbread. They walked back to their camp in the magical moonlight, remembering past Christmases. Sinakevich recalled the time before her arrest, musing:

> None of us had any inkling of my impending arrest, which a week later would separate me from everybody I loved, from my native city and everything I had known up till then.[60]

6. Social Revolutionaries

Following the Bolshevik takeover of the Constituent Assembly in January 1918, the Communists became the only legal party in Russia. After the attempted assassination of Lenin by Social Revolutionary (SR) Fanny Kaplan in 1918, many SRs were arrested and persecuted. Some famous ones, like Katerina Breshko-Breshkovskaya, emigrated abroad. Leading figures in the bourgeois women's rights organizations were disfranchised as class enemies, and many of them also left Russia. By 1921 some SRs, Anarchists, and Mensheviks had been imprisoned, but as "political prisoners" they received special treatment. In the early 1920s, relatives and friends were allowed to send food parcels to prisoners. Prison fare itself was poor, often herring soup and black bread. Anarchists and SRs were often sentenced to the more lenient Butyrki rather than the Lubyanka prison in Moscow. The SRs made demands on prison administrators, and their demands were usually met. The Socialists had a special bloc at Butyrki, where husbands and wives could share the same cell.[61] SR Bertha Babina Nevskaya, who was arrested in 1922 along with many other Left and Right SRs, recorded their stay in prison in the following words:

A crowd of men and women rushed to greet us, and I was passed from one embrace to another. Blinded and deafened, I did not recognize any of them. Later I found out that many old comrades were there from the Petersburg underground, from my student years, and from many different towns and cities where we had lived during our wandering. We were in the "socialist block." Members of various left-wing parties were held there, and some had already been imprisoned by then (followers of either Slyapnikov or Safronov, I don't remember which). The "socialist block" was locked from the outside, but inside everything was run by the prisoners themselves.

After the uproarious welcome, they took us to the "club." The table was laid with vast copper kettles of boiling water and small teapots containing a strong brew. Every conceivable kind of food that our comrades possessed in those Spartan years, from their rations or parcels, was laid out. Around a table in one of the corridors, the Council of Elders was seated in grand session. Most of its members were leading Right SRs ... ; others came from the Menshevik Central Committee. Later we would jokingly refer to the council as the "shadow cabinet." They were busy allocating cells to the new arrivals: husband and wife were given their own cell, while the single shared with others.[62]

Some of the SRs did not initially take their imprisonment seriously. According to Berta Babina-Nevskaya,

> We were convinced that, in the end, the differences between us and "them" (the Bolsheviks) would not hinder the building of a new world. Although we would always have to argue, and argue stubbornly, they would release us from prison and we would build the new world together! We did not take what was happening to us seriously: it seemed more of a fairground staging of the French Revolution—without the guillotine, of course. Wasn't it Marx who said that history repeats itself, first as tragedy and then as farce? No one, including the various shades of Marxists, suspected what an enormous guillotine awaited us all in the not so distant future.[63]

7. Marguerite Harrison

According to Marguerite Harrison, an American reporter who had entered the Soviet Union illegally, and who was imprisoned there for eight months in 1921, prison life was wearing. As she described it:

> There was a universal groan of dismay, as tea was used for laundry and bathing purposes, there being no other way to get hot water. The

cups were filled under the stern eye of the Ganymede, who, however, allowed himself to be prevailed on by various blandishments to consent to the filling of two empty bottles. Then we all proceeded to munch black bread and drink the apple paring tea. In the midst of breakfast a soldier appeared at the door.

". . . to the washroom," he said solemnly.

There was nothing for it but to leave our tea to get cold, and we all filed out to the washroom, preceded by the dezhyurnyi, carrying the parashka, the tin refuse can, which stood in the corner of the room; those who had them with towels flung over one shoulder, soap and tooth-bushes in their hands. In the washroom we took turns two at a time washing in a big tin trough with ice cold water.[64]

In the washroom, women often found notes left by male SR members. Some left notes written on cigarette paper and stuffed into tiny cracks in the wall or behind the sink. In the early 1920s such communication was tolerated. Despite her ill health and despair, Harrison found prison life curiously liberating and extremely egalitarian. After she had been released, and after writing about her experiences from afar, she realized that all the conventions that had bound her in the past had been swept away by her time in gaol. She felt free from all the prejudices of race and class, or caste and tradition. Describing her prison stay, she wrote:

> I had seen human nature at its best and at its worst, for prison life has a way of stripping even the most skilful moral camouflage.
>
> I had found what the dreamers, idealists, fanatics and opportunists in the Kremlin had been looking for in vain — the true International. For internationalism cannot be expressed in terms of a political dogma or a social creed. The way to its realization lies in grasping the fact that not only the Colonel's lady and Judy O'Grady are sisters the world over, but that the Colonel and Judy's husband are brother-in-law as well.
>
> . . . Whatever the morrow held in store for me it could hold nothing richer than the friendships and the memories I would take with me from my Russian prisons.[65]

While Harrison ended her prison story on an upbeat tone, others wrote in a more doleful voice. Dismal stories of prison life in the 1920s were reported in *Letters from Russian Prisons*, a book published by the International Committee for Political Prisoners in 1925. Famous revolutionary Vera Figner headed the Russian Political Red Cross, and it published many letters and reports. One was from eighteen-year-old anarchist Olga Romanova; another from Maria Spiridonova, the head of the Left SRs; as well as others. In her report, Romanova complained that she and eight Russian Orthodox priests were banished to Narym (a swamp). They had to go by rowboat, and only a small cabin was there. They had no books, newspapers, paper, or people to talk to. There were no paths or roads in the taiga, only insects and mosquitoes. She was a-religious and left the cabin in the evenings when the priests had their three-hour worship services. She didn't like their services or singing and preferred the cold outdoors to their company. She baked bread for them all, and the priests made fires outside to heat water for their daily "tea," which was sometimes only hot water. Her greatest tortures were loneliness, lack of food, and an untended dislocated shoulder. After four months, she was released from this detention and sent with a taiga guide to the small settlement of Parabel. When she arrived there, she was suffering from frostbitten feet since she was transported in the winter in her summer clothing.[66]

Female political prisoners could have quite different experiences. One Menshevik, Nadezhda Peremeschko, was initially sentenced to three years exile in Turukhansky Krai, but her sentence was changed to exile abroad without privilege of returning to Russia. When questioning this change, she was told by the GPU magistrate: "Because three years in Turukhansky Krai are equal to a lifetime abroad."[67]

Another letter told of political prisoner Sonya Bogoyavlenskaya, who fled her place of banishment, was rearrested in Orenburg, and again escaped. Punishments varied. Tatyana Rayevskaya and Helen Yegelskaya were taken prisoner in Petrograd in connection with an underground printing office of the Left SRs, and were sent to Suzdal for three years. Others imprisoned in this same affair were sent to Solovetsky Monastery, which had been turned into part of the penal system. The latter prisoners were not allowed any visits from relatives, correspondence, or food parcels. Another political, Lydia Surkova, had no work, starved, and suffered from tuberculosis. Of the sixteen exiles there, only two had jobs. One of them committed suicide.[68] Among students arrested, some were sent to concentration camps for two or three years, others to exile for two to three years.[69] At Solovetsky, some political prisoners were shot in a massacre in December 1923.

One of the greatest degradations that political prisoners faced was being imprisoned with criminals instead of other politicals. The criminals both in the 1920s and 1930s often became the cell masters, and political prisoners detested the rule of these cruel, unsavory elements. Other deprivations they endured at Solovetsky were lack of heating, bathing, and laundry. These indignities led 233 political prisoners to sign a declaration about the massacre and their lack of rights. Of this number, 27 were women.[70]

Judging from letters dated in 1924, many of the illegal actions protested by the Political Red Cross in 1921 continued unabated. Vera Figner, an old populist, terrorist, and former prisoner, was president of the Council of the Political Red Cross in 1921 and noted that abuses by the government and party leaders condemned in 1918 still continued. Some of these misdeeds included taking prisoners away from their cells in the dead of night and not informing anyone where they had been taken; wholesale deportations; transfer of prisoners without adequate food and clothing; secrecy in the removal of Butyrky prisoners with neither relatives nor the Red Cross having the opportunity of rendering assistance; relatives having to stand in queues to send a parcel, and then not having their parcel accepted; prohibition of innocent games like chess; overcrowded and unventilated cells; inactivity; lack of beds, pillows, underclothing, and soap; lavatory use only twice per day; coarse behavior of lower officials, especially swearing; ambushing of prisoners at the time of their arrest; detention without examination; and accusations of spying for simple interactions with foreigners. All these things the Political Red Cross denounced to the Presidium, hoping for improvement. This was the "Protest by the Non-Partisan Political Red Cross" in 1921.[71]

An account of someone identified only as "N." shows that conditions for politicals did not improve as the decade progressed. She describes her time in various prisons as follows:

> We had spent much time in different "G.P.U." prisons, in damp cells, never breathing the open air, forbidden to see our relatives, deprived of the right of correspondence, the windows of our cells always closed under orders.... We had been through the filthy and crowded association with common criminals on the route, suffering from bugs, lice, the absence of bunks, traveling in packed prison cars, frequently stopping at provincial prisons, and having endless encounters with squads of G.P.U. guards ... clicking the musket triggers just for the sake of terrorization.

All of that wore the nerves of the healthy prisoners out and knocked off their feet the weak ones. We had cases of tuberculosis and heart disease among us. Towards the end only three to five comrades from among the party of 25 were capable of carrying their own luggage . . .[72]

After having settled in at Kalpashova, Siberia, they found living quarters, organized a common kitchen, and began studying. Then the authorities began to hound them: "You live here as if you were on a vacation!" Some of them were then sent to swampy regions that were not on the map, or to places infested with malaria or areas populated by indigenous peoples.[73] An unusual feature of Soviet life in the 1920s was that banished SRs were allowed to work in exile, just as they had been under the Tsarist regime. N. describes their work situation as follows:

> The exiles receive none of their allowances. During the entire period of six months several comrades received from 1–2 roubles, including cash, flour and millet. We began to look for work. It was not difficult to find it, as in the whole region there is an enormous demand for educational resources. We occupied a number of positions in the government service, in the educational field, but the Soviet and local party committee, composed of total ignoramuses, under the leadership of the semiliterate chairman of the Soviet, commenced a campaign against us.[74]

Suddenly six in their group were to be exiled. Two even had children. The cold was 35 degrees below zero, so the SRs refused to let their comrades leave. After their protest, they were again ordered to leave in December. While a physician and two clericals were allowed to stay, the rest were being exiled to tributaries of the Ob River north of Kolpashova. They lacked money and adequate clothing but set out on foot, carrying their luggage, which was restricted to one pud (36 pounds). Included in their party were old party members who had been imprisoned during the Tsarist regime, as well as two young factory workers, Fanja Lissina and Anna Yefimova, who had to carry her little girl.[75]

Rape was probably fairly common but rarely reported since the perpetrators would not be punished. However, the anarchist G. M. Yudevitch gives an interesting account of how prisoners' solidarity saved her and three other women at the temporary detention prison in Vologda:

Before leaving, the wardress warned us to be on our guard; the inspector, or even the chief might come late at night for a certain purpose. Such is the "custom." Almost all the women who pass through this prison are abused that way. In addition, almost all the officials are diseased and infect the women. "Any woman who is here for a certain period of time leaves it diseased."

The warning was not superfluous. During the night a man with a lamp came into our cell.

"Who is there?"

"Never mind ... I have come for the control," was the reply.

We jumped up together. There were four of us; myself, the woman doctor, a Lettish woman and one other woman, a would-be socialist-revolutionist (it was afterwards found out that she was planted as an *agent-provacateur*). The visitor saw, no doubt, that this time his call was futile. He examined us, stamped his feet and left.

When morning came he appeared again and—doubtless as revenge—ordered: "Clean the lavatories."

We refused. He threatened "to take measure." We still refused to go.... The following night another individual appeared in our cell. He came in without a light.

"What is the matter?" we asked, and again jumped up together. The man lit a candle, examined us and mumbled between the teeth: "I have come for the control."

We protested energetically and shouted:

"After the evening inspection you have no right to come into our cell ... Get out."

The man left. We did not know who he was. We learned the next day that it was the Assistant Chief of the Vologda Prison.[76]

It is hard to know the exact number of political prisoners in the 1920s. Some estimated one thousand to fifteen hundred. Many were sent into exile in desolate places. Political prisoners were defined as spies, counterrevolutionaries, or members of other political parties.

8. *Maria Spiridonova*

One of the most poignant political prisoners in the 1920s was the leader of the Left Social Revolutionaries, Maria Spiridonova. While she initially supported the Bolsheviks during 1917–18, she eventually split with them over their treatment of the peasants and the grain requisitioning that began in 1918. Imprisoned by the Tsarist regime from 1906 until 1917, when she was freed by the February revolution, she was a heroine until her arrest by the Bolsheviks in 1919. Since she had been beaten and raped by her guards in the Tsarist regime, she had a nervous disposition, and her imprisonment by the Cheka almost drove her insane. She disliked being watched, and her Chekist guards watched her unceasingly, fearing she would escape. In prison, she suffered from lack of sleep, food, visitors, fresh air, heat, soap, and bathing facilities. Kept in a damp section of the Kremlin, her tuberculosis worsened, and she engaged in hunger strikes to protest her treatment. She thought the Cheka invented plots about SR revolts, and she was convinced they were invented on purpose and were part of a systematic fabrication. In these ways, prisons became the harbingers of the NKVD system of the next decade under Stalin. She hated the Cheka and the planting of spies in her cell. As she wrote to a friend in 1919:

> I cannot wash, I cannot read, write, eat, think calmly, when *uninterruptedly* I am the object of the curiosity of these sleuths.... You know well enough what it is to serve long sentences of penal servitude, but in *this manner* we were not treated even by the servants of the Czar.... When I applied for open-air exercise, I was refused. When I asked for newspapers, I was refused. With great difficulty I secured soap. Why are no visits permitted?
>
> The sentinel convoys me to the toilet, which harmonizes fully with the general style of my cell.... The guards are changed every two hours. Every half hour here is some kind of an additional inspection. They are watching. At night there is the banging of the doors, loud conversation, rattling, and every two hours, every hour, every half hour, somebody looks through the door to see that I am lying here under my coat.
>
> This was never done to me even when I was a penal convict.[77]

Spiridonova notes that she had not tried to escape, so all the watchfulness was unnecessary. Her only way to secure better treatment was the weapon that many politicals used, a hunger strike. A friend's description of her hunger strike is incredibly poignant. Still Spiridonova did eventually escape, only to be imprisoned again from 1921 until 1941, when she was shot. These gloomy accounts of prison were only part of women's difficulties in the early days of the Bolshevik regime.

As we can see, women became disenchanted with Bolshevik institutions for a variety of reasons. Galina Shtange, wife of a high-ranking transport engineer, wanted to get involved in community work after the revolution, and she was elected to the Village Council in Udelnava. However, she didn't last long because there was a campaign to rid the Council of an "aristocrat," which was how they viewed her at the time. She found it very insulting and turned in her resignation.[78] Shtange's diary reveals the hostility to "byvshie liudi," or former people, which smoldered in Soviet society during the Civil War and later.

9. *Socialist Opposition*

Socialist intellectuals like Angelica Balabanova, Emma Goldman, and Rosa Luxemburg initially welcomed the revolution but soon became disgusted with it. After visiting Russia, Goldman wrote two books about it: *My Disillusionment with Russia* and *My Further Disillusionment with Russia*. Angelica Balabanova returned after the revolution and in her memoirs accused Lenin of using Zinoviev to do the "dirty work" he would not do himself. She wrote of this in her books *Impressions of Lenin* and *My Life As a Rebel*. Rosa Luxemburg also found fault with Lenin's "bureaucratic" Communism. This was not the form of socialism that Luxemburg had worked and hoped for, and she too felt betrayed.[79]

10. *Aida Basevich*

Some Anarchist young women like Aida Basevich initially wanted to join the Komsomol, but when she witnessed the violence of the anti-religious agitation, she changed her mind. The robbery of St. Vladimir Church in Petrograd in 1923 angered her.[80] Other Anarchists and Social Revolutionaries became similarly disenchanted, were arrested and imprisoned for their political views in the 1920s. SR Anna Skripnikova (1896–1974) was arrested when one of her friends offended the Soviets. She was imprisoned in 1918, and again in 1925, and 1927. When she tried to protest some of the brutal behavior of the guards, a gaoler told her:

> Forget these Russian intellectual habits of protesting in prison, they are old fashioned and worth nothing today! Take care only of yourself, otherwise you will fare badly under Soviet power![81]

The Soviets used provocateurs to trap people and arrest them in the 1920s, and some women were duped into becoming spies. Still, deals with Soviet guards could be made. In some ways the Bolshevik prison system was more "humane" than during the purges of the 1930s. When the anarchist Peter Kropotkin died in 1921, imprisoned anarchists were let out of jail to attend his funeral. Indeed, the memoirs of anarchist Aida Basevich (1905–1995) show a lax political police. She noted that during mass arrests when student anarchists were being arrested, some simply ran away and evaded the police. She observed:

> At that time everything was different, the screws were not turned so tightly, and the regime in the prison was different. We managed to learn the day and the time when they would be transported.... There were thirty-eight people in this case. Maybe they had arrested more, but by the time of the trial there were thirty-eight of us. The GPU let all the rest go, because many had connections and then it was still possible, the GPU was a different organization back then.... Political prisoners enjoyed special treatment, different from that given common criminals. First of all, by the rules, we could not be housed together with common criminals, although they had already started doing this.... Usually my parents brought me very good parcels, and I shared them with all my cell mates.... Political prisoners still received better food and had special rights with regard to the lights—we were allowed to keep the lights on longer. We were taken on "normal" walks—all cell mates together.... Cell-to-cell visits also had been allowed.... We announced hunger strikes to have visitation rights; for example, to have a visitation before a prisoner's transport. Our hunger strike was very short. We fought for everything; we did not give an inch. From the outside I received so many letters expressing moral support! I was simply flooded by these letters. Financially I was well off. Lida Chukovskaia did so much for me: She kept sending letters and parcels.
>
> When I was in Shpalernaia, my parents came to visit me. Generally, I was given better treatment than other prisoners because a number of scholars had issued petitions on behalf of our group.... On Jewish holidays the Jewish community of the city always brought parcels to Jewish prisoners, both political and common criminals. The same was true in Samara.[82]

Roza Vetukhnovskaia (1904–1993) belonged to the Socialist Revolutionary Party in the 1920s, and she too was arrested in 1924. She spent three years in camps and two years in exile. Indeed, she spent much of the 1930s in exile and was rearrested during World War II, as many others were.[83]

Not all women arrested for "political crimes" in the 1920s fared as well as anarchist Basevich. A more somber note appears in the autobiography of Evgeniia Iaroslavskaia Markon (1902–1931). She had led the life of a pampered and protected daughter of the intelligentsia before the revolution. A convinced revolutionary before the Bolsheviks took over, Markon soon became disillusioned. In 1922 she graduated from Petrograd University but was tired of studying. She wanted to fall in love and marry and did so after meeting the poet Aleksandr Iaroslavsky. While they lectured against religion in Russia in the early 1920s, they soon found the regime oppressive. Living abroad in Berlin and Paris in the mid-1920s, they wrote some articles critical of the Soviet regime. Yet they decided to return even though they thought they would be killed upon their return.

After her husband was arrested in 1928, Markon sold newspapers in Leningrad and Moscow to support herself. With a university diploma, she could have taken a job in a Soviet office, but she despised the "clean, self-assured, and inaccessible" Soviet office. She "could not even think of going to work in such a nest of scribes and pharisees!" Moreover, taking parcels to and visiting her husband in prison was time consuming and not congruent with a regular job. Markon had a strong antisocial streak, and she preferred selling newspapers and petty thievery to office work. Once, she sold out of papers easily when the news was of a bomb thrown at an OGPU office. She described this event in her memoirs, which she wrote in prison, and which were kept in a police file for decades after she was executed in 1931:

> So I stood on Nevsky Prospect, and when someone passed by, I would say distinctly and loudly, looking aside, "A bomb in Moscow OGPU! *Vecherniaia krasnaia gazeta*! A bomb in Moscow OGPU!" A passerby would stop as if he had been whacked on the head. With trembling hands, he would take out his wallet and open the newspaper. It was like a birthday present to everybody—who in Soviet Russia did not hate the GPU?[84]

Like many other Russian women, Markon moved from Moscow to Leningrad to be near her husband while he was being investigated. After he was sentenced to serve in the north, in Solovetsky, she also visited him there. Since she hated the Soviet regime, she resorted to petty thievery to survive, and she was arrested several times before being sentenced to three years in exile. In prison, Markon struck a guard, and she was sentenced to execution by firing squad. She wrote her autobiography while imprisoned, and it was kept in her file until the fall of the former Soviet Union. One report in her file mentioned her agitating among the prisoners, calling for a work stoppage and an uprising against Soviet power. The report also mentioned that Markon believed that Soviet power discredited the idea of revolution, covering itself up with the name of the Soviets. She thought the country was governed by a clique of the intelligentsia headed by the Central Committee of the CPSU. Another guard wrote of her defiance and how she even spat in the face of her executioner.[85]

E. Conclusion

While some women participated in the revolution and profited from it, others resigned themselves to the situation with stoical acceptance. Some intellectuals like Anna Akhmatova never accepted the legitimacy of the Soviet regime and became "inner exiles." Others, like poets Gippius and Tsvetaeva, left the Soviet Union. Some were imprisoned. The Bolsheviks did not have to arrest everyone to ensure compliance. Seizing some aristocrats, priests, bourgeois, or political dissidents served as a warning to others. Statistics are not available to show how many people left, but some Mennonite farmers did, and other peasants in the central region did not quietly accept Bolshevik rule. Going to Kiev in 1924, Nadezhda Mandelstam noticed that all the carriages on their train were guarded by three machine gunners because "peasant resistance had still not been completely stamped out in the central regions."[86]

Chapter Two

Women and Religion

While the February revolution resulted in the release of religious prisoners and represented new freedom, not everyone rejoiced at the separation of church and state introduced by the Bolsheviks in 1918. Moreover, the Bolsheviks soon closed some churches and monasteries and took some antagonistic priests prisoner. So, religion in the post-revolutionary period provoked a problematic response, as the following sections reveal.

> Go where? Where to? God only knows!
> Perhaps to a hermitage somewhere,
> Repent my sins in tears and prayer—
> Where is Zosima, faith's defender,
> Or is the world without end ended?[1]
>
> Sofia Parnok, *Through a Window-Light*, 1928

While the Bolsheviks separated church and state in 1918, the new regime became embroiled in a three-year Civil War and spent little

Sofia Parnok

energy combating religious influence. Many intellectuals and some workers had become disenchanted with organized religion prior to the revolution, but the bulk of the population remained Russian Orthodox. Sofia Parnok's poem shows the legacy of Russian Orthodoxy in mentioning Zosima, a hermit in Dostoevsky's novel *The Brothers Karamazov*. It illustrates the skepticism of the intellectual in asking whether her religious world had ended. After the Civil War in an effort to invigorate the economy and increase production, the government made some capitulations to businessmen and peasants, giving them considerable financial freedom during the New Economic Policy. Under these conditions, religion did not disappear, and religious life flourished in the countryside but more surreptitiously in the city, where priests often ministered secretly in homes rather than in churches.

While the Bolsheviks separated the church from the state, and confiscated church property, it did not make worship illegal and allowed active church communities to lease buildings for worship. Some monasteries and convents were tolerated and allowed to function until the middle and late 1920s. However, the church had been declining in influence since the revolution of 1905 and the incident of Bloody Sunday, when the Tsar forbade the burial of the dead demonstrators in sacred ground. The Russian Orthodox Church agreed not to bury the dead workers, since it had been subordinated to the state for two hundred years and was used to following orders. After the 1917 revolution, it proved unable to redefine itself. Some reformers known as Renovationists, or the Living Church, wanted to modernize the Orthodox Church by changing the language of the liturgy from Church Slavonic to Russian, adopting a modern calendar, enlarging women's role as deaconesses, and eliminating corruption and stagnation. Although the Russian Orthodox Church had opened a theological academy for women in 1916, and approved of women in modern vocations of teaching and medicine, after the revolution it was unable to implement changes to allow women to serve as deaconesses.[2] Moreover, most peasants resisted change in church liturgy, and the Bolsheviks were able to use dissension between the two church factions to weaken and discredit the church's authority. However, women, generally, still believed in God, and like many other features of Soviet society, religion remained a rather mixed affair in the 1920s.

Mikhail Nestorov, The Song, 1923

A. Nuns and Priestly Families in the 1920s

After the revolution, the number of nuns declined from more than one hundred thousand in 1914 to less than two thousand listed in the 1926 census.[3] While the Bolsheviks took over the lands of the convents and monasteries in 1918, some nuns and monks were allowed to maintain their religious way of life until the middle and late 1920s. Initially, the Bolsheviks pursued a moderately repressive policy toward religion. In 1920 novices and workers were still harvesting hay at the Borodino Monastery outside Moscow. Moreover, the policy of closing churches, monasteries, and convents varied by locale. In Dmitrov, a town outside Moscow, the "wonder-working Life Giving Cross" and some icons of the Dormition Cathedral were removed by the state in 1924, but the Boris and Gleb Monastery was not closed until 1926, and the Dormition Cathedral until 1932.[4] More draconian treatment of the church occurred in the 1930s.

Mother Rachel, eldress at the Borodino Monastery, met and counseled innumerable pilgrims until her death in 1928. In addition to lifting the hearts and souls of troubled peasants, Rachel also offered spiritual advice to workers, clergy, monastics, doctors, Communist Party members, teachers, students, lawyers, merchants, craftsmen, along with the elderly, poor, destitute, and beggars.[5] While troubled souls came to Mother Rachel for spiritual counsel or physical healing, they left with tears in their eyes, relieved, renewed, and reborn. One pilgrim in her collected writings put it this way:

> What a great eldress Mother Rachel is! It was so difficult for us to go to see her. How much grief and suffering we carried within us, and now how light, how easy it is, as if she gave us wings. Now how serene and joyful are our souls.[6]

Mother Rachel spoke with these pilgrims in small groups or individually. It was her full-time work at the monastery. She often missed confession and communion at church to make herself available for visitors. She refused to see only those who had come because they thought it "fashionable." Mother Rachel was perceptive and distinguished between true and false pilgrims.[7]

Like most Russian Orthodox believers, Mother Rachel was especially attached to the Mother of God in her prayer life, and one of her prayers went like this:

> Mother of God, thou thyself dost see the warm tears of these good people; direct their life unto good. Strengthen in them faith in thy Son, our Lord Jesus Christ. Warm them with love towards one another and towards their neighbors. O, Mother of God, I entrust them to thee, thyself. Be to them a helper in all their affairs and set them on the right path. O Mother of God, do thou, thyself bless them with thy all powerful right hand, and not with mortal hand, as thou thyself didst promise me . . .[8]

Mother Rachel healed many, urged her flock to pray for everyone, and to gently treat atheists, enemies, and Communists. She confounded Communists who came to discredit her healings, miracles, and spiritual counseling. She recounted one experience in her writings as follows:

> Three men from the Communist Party called on me once: they were men who reject the life of God. They came with the intention of refuting our Orthodox Christian hope. I blessed them with the sign of the Cross. They spoke for a long time, but my answers dampened their ardor, and at the end of the conversation, I saw an iridescent light on the

head of one of them, as is represented in icons of holy god-pleasers. Do you understand what I am telling you? Even those people are good.[9]

In her counseling, Mother Rachel encouraged people to read the scriptures, go to confession, receive Communion, pray for their enemies, and love their family members and neighbors. It was only after her death in 1928 that the Communist Party completely closed both Borodino and Optina Monasteries, dispersing the monks and sisters.[10]

While some nuns were arrested and imprisoned in the 1920s, many merged back into society by living with their families or working in low-level jobs as domestic servants, cooks, nannies, or hospital orderlies. Bolshevik policy toward priestly families was mean spirited. Priestly families were defined as nontoilers and were deprived of their ration cards during War Communism (1918–1921). Jobs and access to higher education were also forbidden to the children of priests. As Vera Fleisher, the daughter of a priestly family, remembered:

> But I have to say that already at that time, even in the first years of Soviet power, priests and their families were really suspect. I already sensed that people didn't treat us the way they treated other children. And the older I got, the more strongly I sensed this.[11]

Yet Vera was luckier than most because she had a brother who had served in the Red Army. He was able to attend a pedagogical institute in Perm in the 1920s and invited her to study there too. She recalled:

> And so in December 1924, I left Akhansk for Perm, and there I enrolled in school, and graduated in 1925. I did well, but it was the same thing: Because of my social origin—as the daughter of a priest—I was not given preference for admittance into an institute of higher education. I could only get into a teacher-training school. I graduated from this teacher-training school in Perm in 1927. I was eighteen at the time. I graduated from the preschool division of the Perm Teachers' College, as it was then called. In addition to the program of study for the preschool division, I also passed all the exams that were required for the elementary school division and received a diploma with the right to work in preschool and in elementary school. Well, in the beginning I worked in a preschool, but the way things turned out, I didn't work there long. And then I started to work in a school, I worked in an elementary school.[12]

B. Other Religious Experiences

1. Mme X

Surprising sources give us glimpses into women's religious life in the Soviet period. Just as Nadezhda Durova and Maria Botchkareva's military memoirs reveal a bit about their religious lives, so does the diary of Mme X, who was drafted into the Red Army in 1918. While Durova and Botchkareva entered military service to escape unhappy marriages, Mme X was drafted into the Red Army. An aristocrat, she had a choice of serving in the army for six months or in a forced labor unit for two years. She chose army service. It was a shorter period, and she thought her odds of surviving greater. (In 1918 the Bolsheviks had decreed compulsory labor mobilization of "bourgeois" elements, which included those from gentry and priestly families. This lasted on and off until the end of the Civil War.)

A dedicated monarchist, she and some other princesses had received military training to safeguard the Tsar after the February revolution in 1917. Since she had some familiarity with military matters, she was appointed head of a Girls' Proletarian Battalion. Her upbringing made it difficult for her to relate to the women under her command. They didn't really want her since she was a "lady" and they were working girls. Mme X lived in danger of attacks upon her person and property from her female subordinates, and in terror of her senior male officers. Several officers tried to seduce her, and one finally raped her. She analyzed this experience in her diary, initially wanting to die, yet ultimately felt comforted by God's presence:

> Never shall I speak to a living soul about these four days and four nights ... which have branded me for my life ... soul and mind ... and body alike ... And it is the soul that aches most ...
>
> The worst of this is that one has to take up life again in spite of all. That one is given no oblivion, no share in the Great Nothingness....
>
> And is it not the summit of all cruelty—these days are holy, have been holy to me up to now ...
>
> I am twenty in years, I am at least forty at heart....
>
> Dear, kind God, grant me, if not death, then madness, take away this strength which makes me capable of living on....[13]

In a passage written about a week later, she comments:

One catches a glimpse of one's God, one's real living God, amidst all these hardships, hardships of body, hardships of soul, hardships of spirit, hardships of mind—surely these are eased by the everliving realizations of God's presence in all of them....
Christianity is coming home so vividly.
Russia's sufferings will be her greatest glory in the future.
To me, and to all those innumerable others in Russia, Christ ought to be doubly, trebly dear.
Why, we, all of us, have gone through our Gethsemane watches, our bitter hours on the Mount of Calvary, left alone by all, sometimes we deemed ourselves even forsaken by God, and yet always stretching the weary helpless hands of our souls towards HIM, THE CRUCIFIED.
And never without response.
In this horrible afterwards, the inevitable outcome of those nights and days of hell, I would have tottered down physically and morally from the weight of this burden. It holds more than I can speak of.... It has branded with the seal of unspeakable horror my very soul, and I doubt not that this seal will remain.
And yet . . .
My beautiful white queenly girlhood—now crucified—has it not found an echo in the love of The Crucified? I wish I could send out this message of strength to all other girls.... Wish I could tell them that all sorrow is worth bearing if borne with God's help and in His love.[14]

Although Mme X is later slightly wounded during skirmishes and becomes deathly ill, she doesn't discuss her faith when writing about those events. Her major crisis was being raped, coming to grips with it, and finding some redeeming value in her suffering. Her writing shows that many kept their faith and found solace in it under Bolshevik rule.

2. Maria Shkapskaya

Russian women's religious experience varied considerably. After the revolution, poet Maria Shkapskaya (1891–1952) wrote some poems with religious overtones. In one, she describes the merciless hanging of an army officer during the Civil War, the miraculous trooping of saints from the local church to venerate the hanged man, and the toppling of church crosses in response to the savage event. In her poem "No Dream," she writes:

> And when the third day was ended,
> And a dark summer night had fallen,
> The doors of the church were opened,
> The royal doors burst apart,
> And through them came, marching in procession,
> The whole company of saints,
> All the holy men of Orthodox Russia:
> John the Baptist, the Preacher,
> Panteleimon the Healer...
> And all the Mothers of God Most Holy,
> Of Smolensk, Vladimir, and Kazan
> ...
> And others without special names.
> Going sadly as new made monks,
> To the carnival tree they went,
> Stared up at his blue bruised face,
> Bowed low at his twisted feet,
> Sprawled in the dust of the road,
> As the most terrible vow dictates.
> They lay there until first light.
> In the morning when God's people came there,
> The hanged man still swung in the air.
> His shoulders still stooped and humble—
> But the crosses on the church had tumbled.[15]

Poets like Shkapskaya even depicted miracles in their early Soviet writings. Whether the events just described happened in fact or only in Shkapskaya's imagination is not so important. It's significant that she wrote about them. In a later poem, "Mater Dolorosa" (1921), Shkapskaya reflects a more critical attitude toward God and prayer and does not accept suffering as readily as many Russian Orthodox did. Her long poem includes the following stanza, full of reminders and demands:

> Lord, did I not stand up when You called to me? Truly I'm only a small loop in Your heavy lace....
> But give us time and term to ripen under warm rays, so that flowers may rise in bunches in the field, so that the ear might ripen.
> Don't stretch out your thin fingers to us before it's time, don't tear off the green berries, don't touch the empty ear, don't remove the heavy weave unfinished from the frame in the night.
> Let the children given me by You grow up.[16]

Boris Kustodiev, The Consecration of Water on the Theophany, 1921

3. Marguerite Harrison

Living in Russia in 1921, the American journalist Marguerite Harrison was surprised to find Moscow churches packed. She visited various sanctuaries at vespers and high mass on Sunday and always found enormous congregations. As a reporter, she interviewed the Russian Orthodox Patriarch Tikhon and discovered him living under house arrest in Moscow. As a Constitutional Monarchist, he thought the Soviets had done well to separate church and state. People were no longer required to support the clergy, and they did so voluntarily and adequately. The Soviet government initially allowed as many churches and priests as parishioners were willing to support. While they left some icons, robes, and sacred vessels to local churches, they took over all church lands.[17]

The Patriarch thought that initially 322 priests and bishops had been executed. Yet, he believed that the influence of the church on the lives of the people was stronger than it had ever been in all its history. Still, he was dubious about the future if the Communists remained in power too long. Like many others, the Patriarch thought the Bolsheviks would be a "flash in the pan" and would not rule very long. Still, he found it impossible for the church to hold convocations of the clergy or to ordain new priests. Seminaries were closed, so no new priests could be trained. Without their schools, the Russian Orthodox Church found it difficult to educate the youth, while the Soviets conducted antireligious propaganda in state schools.[18] Despite this situation, Patriarch Tikhon complained little about the authorities, until he was arrested in 1922. After his imprisonment, the Patriarch was forced to recant his opposition to the regime in order to gain his freedom. He died in 1925.

In many places, the peoples' tithes proved adequate for priests to survive. Churches remained crowded, and famous opera singers sang in the choirs of many Moscow churches. Journalist Harrison was "astonished at the piles of 500 and 1,000 ruble notes heaped on the plate during the offertory." Despite the lack of food and fuel in Moscow, she saw "hundreds of votive candles, and at all hours of the day there were always scores of devout worshippers with votive offerings before the shrine of the Virgin of Iberia at the entrance to the Red Square...."[19]

When the Soviets tried to disparage religion by opening the relics of the saints, credulous people told Harrison what a miracle it was that the holy saints disappeared to heaven and substituted rags and straw when their tombs were desecrated by nonbelievers. Harrison thought Soviet propaganda remained lost on naive, illiterate peasants.[20]

In Moscow, Harrison discovered that the Novo Devechi Convent remained open, and nuns continued living there. About twenty nuns and twenty lay sisters lived there with the Mother Superior, whom she described as a sweet-faced, gentle-voiced woman, utterly resigned to her fate, utterly uncomprehending of the great movement that had swept away her world, and she lived on a bit bewildered by all the changes, clinging instinctively to the shelter of the familiar walls, her long black robe and medieval headdress. She told me that the nuns were given their quarters free by the Soviet Government, that they were quite unmolested and had excellent relations with the working people who occupied the rest of the convent buildings, but that they received no rations for food, fuel, or clothing, and were debarred from work in all government offices or institutions. She ... regretted being cut off from work among the children whom she loved. The nuns supported themselves, she said, by going out for the day as domestic servants or seamstresses, and doing fine needlework, making underclothes and summer dresses for the wives of the rich commissars. Their former pupils brought them donations of money and food and thus they managed to get along, living from hand to mouth.²¹

Studying the Orthodox Church, Harrison found some Communist sympathizers and some Theosophists among the bishops. She also discovered that the Catholic and Baptist churches were also strong, despite the arrest of some of their clergy. Old Believers still flourished among the Don Cossacks. The Bolsheviks generally considered evangelical churches counterrevolutionary. In 1921 she met several members of the Salvation Army in prison.²²

She, and others, thought the most popular new "religion" among Russian youth was Communism. It appealed to both the young and mature idealists.

> "There are many people who take a fierce delight in the renunciation of their individual freedom for the collective good, and there are many features of the Communistic doctrine which, when studied from this angle, have a tremendous appeal."²³

While she thought the religion of Marxism was doomed for political and economic reasons, she observed its success among Communist youth, especially boys and girls of the working classes. They did not see the practical failure of Communism, and were at the age which hopes and believes all things. She wondered what effect the spiritual and intellectual side of Communism would produce in the next generation.²⁴

4. Alexandra Tolstoy

While Countess Alexandra was a Tolstoyan, and as such had yearned for the end of the Tsarist regime and the control of the Russian Orthodox Church, she was still dismayed to see old religious sites destroyed in the 1920s. Her account of a visit to Yaroslavl Monastery in 1929 and her life in Moscow shows how much religious life had changed since the beginning of the decade. She writes in her book *I Worked for the Soviet*:

> In July, 1929, I was in Yaroslavl, one of the most ancient cities of northwest Russia. I wanted to visit a monastery that was built in the thirteenth century.
> "You won't see much of it," a woman whom I asked about it told me. "They've turned it into a factory for felt boots."
> I could hardly recognize the monastery. The walls lay in ruins, and there was a pile of stones in the middle of the yard. One of the chapels was being demolished.
> "What do you want here?" a man asked me.
> "I wanted to see the monastery."
> "Well, you won't see it. They started a factory, but it didn't work. Now they want to use the stone for something"....
> "I'm on my way home from Moscow," the old clergyman said. "What do you think of their destroying the Iberian Chapel?"
> "I was in Moscow the day they tore it down," I answered. "I saw it one evening; the next morning when a friend and I were passing through Voskresenskaya Square on a street car, it was gone!"
> "And the people?"
> "They did not dare say anything. I opened my mouth, but I said nothing. We were afraid to speak, we only looked at each other."[25] (Alexandra had already been arrested four times, so she was not too outspoken by the late 1920s.)

Alexandra Tolstoy was the head of the Tolstoy museum, and also the head of a school there. She was dismayed at the Bolshevik attempts to introduce militarism and atheism into the schools. As a pacifist, she had hoped to prevent this happening at the school at Yasnaya Polyana, but she was fighting a losing battle, as her memoir shows. Toward the end of the decade, she complains of the hypocrisy of having two lives, a private life for one's own thoughts, and a public one of which the Bolsheviks approved. She thought that it was not only she, but the teachers, museum workers, peasants, and even children had to dissemble. In one chapter, she writes of being invited to discuss religion in one of the classes. The teacher was presumably too cowed to broach the subject. She writes:

> "Oh, I'm so glad you've come!" the teacher said. "Please tell us what you think about God!"
> "God?"
> "Yes, yes!" one of the children shouted. "We want to know whether God exists or not."
> "Of course He does, children," I said, avoiding the alarmed glance of the teacher.
> "I told you so!" a boy shouted. "I knew He did."
> One of the Pioneers with a red necktie jumped up: "No, no, no! It's only the bourgeois who believe in God. And the priests who darken the poor people's minds and then rob them."
> "My parents believe in God. They haven't thrown their ikons away ... !"
> "Ikons, pieces of wood!" the Young Pioneer shouted.
> "Who created the world, if there is no God?"
> I stayed for almost an hour. The children wanted to know a great deal: Was it true that all priests were greedy? What did my father believe? Did I believe in a future life? I told them frankly what I thought.
> "Please come and talk to us again—please!" one of the boys called as I left the room. The teacher followed me. "Well, what will happen now?" she asked.
> I did not care. It was such a joy to be oneself. The excited childish voices were still ringing in my ears.
> What is the use of trying to keep antireligious propaganda out of the school, I thought, and giving them nothing in its stead?
> The Komsomols proposed to organize a society of "militant godless" at Yasnaya Polyana, and established "godless corners."
> On Christmas Eve and the Saturday before Easter, the Komsomol, with the help of the local Communist cells, presented antireligious plays and movies and lectures. The older peasants were indignant; the girls and boys welcomed any kind of a show. Sometimes after the performance the Komsomols would go to the church where services were being held, and shout down the priest and sing ribald songs.
> Some of the children had never heard the name of Christ. Others got their ideas of him from the antireligious posters....
> The children were ignorant in religious and moral matters, and the teachers were afraid to instruct them. If a child happened to have an interest in such subjects, the teacher would either not answer his questions or would try to avoid giving a clear answer. Sometimes I

thought of my father. I knew that he would have said: "It is better to let all those children be illiterate than to darken their minds as you are doing!"

And I was troubled.[26]

C. Failure of Belief

1. Raisa Orlova

In her *Memoirs*, Raisa Orlova describes the transition from belief in God to the new Soviet ideology. As a young child, she believed in her nanny's God. She went to church and kissed the holy icons until the mid-1920s. As she remembered:

> I imitated everything my nanny did. Nanny's God was kind. It was easy to talk to him. He readily forgave you and absolved you of your sins.

On holidays after visiting her relatives, nanny and Raisa would stop at a church on Briusovsky Lane. She quotes her nanny saying:

> "Oh, Lord, I, your servant, have made you angry, I am leading a sinful life," Nanny would begin noisily. And I too would imitate her and repent before God the Almighty. I didn't know why I was being repentant, but God loomed over all of my childhood actions, games, and fantasies.
>
> In fact, there was not one but two gods in my childhood. Grandmother—my mother's mother—lived with us; she was very old. She slept in the middle room, and I can only recall her lying in bed. It was stuffy in there and smelled bad and was somehow frightening. Grandmother told me stories about her God, about the Bible. Grandmother's God (in contrast to Nanny's) was malicious, hurled stones, and was forever doing battle. For a long time stones remained for me the sole image of the Bible. Perhaps it was also because Nanny and Grandmother were ever at odds, and I was always on Nanny's side.[27]

Raisa remembered that her educated and reasonably well-to-do parents were not devoutly religious. By the time she joined the Pioneers in 1928, when she was about ten years old, she no longer believed in God. Raisa didn't remember any one event undermining her belief in God, but one day she realized that she no longer believed. For a while she continued going to church with her nanny, but soon even that ended when she became active in the Pioneers. Gradually, her belief in Communism and building up Russia became her new religion.[28] This probably happened to many Soviet youth for whom traditional religion was no longer enforced, whereas Communism was. Raisa noted that as a student she was well paid to read the journal *Ateist* (The Atheist) in the workers' dorms. She didn't recall any questions or arguments. The workers listened, or pretended to listen, and her atheism was subjected to no tests.[29]

2. Valentina Petrova

A worker named Valentina Petrova wrote about her problems adjusting her religious beliefs in her memoir. She joined the Communist Party in 1917 and described her religious confusion after the revolution. She remarked: "I understood about priests and monks and that there was no God, but still I wasn't convinced." It was hard for her to surrender the beliefs of her childhood and youth. According to historian Page Herrlinger, Russian female culture defined a good woman as religious. As a widowed mother, needing help from the female community in raising her daughter, it was impossible for Petrova to give up her faith. It would have alienated her from her mother and her peers. Being an Orthodox woman was the model that her mother had inculcated in her. Pious behavior was the essence of the good woman. This was one reason even working-class women continued to baptize their babies after the revolution.[30] However, the situation was different in rural areas.

D. Religion in the Countryside

The Orthodox Church survived in rural areas, and its religious rites, rituals, traditions, superstitions, incantations, and taboos hung on there. On the eve of church holidays and Sundays, no one in the villages worked. According to Soviet ethnographers, religious celebrations began two weeks before Christmas and one week before Easter. Holidays continued playing an important part in farmers' lives. People usually took a steam bath before holidays, cleaned their homes, changed the bedding and curtains, whitewashed the walls, and prepared special food. While more trained midwives helped in births than in the late nineteenth century, some superstitions continued. Women still strove to protect themselves and their newborn from the "gaze of strangers" and the "evil eye."[31]

As in the nineteenth century, the line between religion and magic was blurred. Women still learned many of the incantations that their mothers had practiced. Incantations were not part of Orthodox prayers, but of folk Orthodoxy. Mothers especially used crosses and candles and invoked the names of the saints to heal their sick children. As late as 1950, one Russian woman in Arkhangelsk oblast describes the following incantation to help frightened children:

> Jesus Christ himself was flying in the clouds. He brought three bows, three wooden arrows, and thirty-three metal arrows. Come to us, Jesus Christ, to your divine slave X (insert name of patient). Jesus Christ, shoot all evil eyes, evil glances, and fears. Amen, Amen, Amen.[32]

Although the Bolshevik government closed monasteries, convents, and some churches, especially during the famine of 1921 so that they could sell religious artifacts to raise money for famine relief, millions of Russians continued going to church, celebrating holidays, weddings, baptisms, and burials as well as praying at home in their icon corners. The antireligious policy of the government shrank the number of bishops, monks, and nuns in the new Soviet state, but the number of churches remained almost the same as in the prewar period. There were 54,000 Russian Orthodox churches in 1914 and 50,000 in 1929.

A survey of rural women showed that they spent 199 hours per year in religious ceremonies, but only 10 hours in education. Age was a factor. Seventy-one percent of peasant women aged 25–39 participated in religious rituals while 100 percent of those age 40–59 did so. Many rural men were also religiously active, and some village soviets had icons as well as pictures of Lenin and President Kalinin on their walls.

1. *Vera Panova*

In a short story titled "Evdokia" about small-town family life, author Vera Panova (1905–1973) depicts an adulterous woman praying in her house after an argument with her husband:

"Choose," he said. "That means that I'll choose what I want, choose who's to stay here and who's to go."
And comforted by that thought, feeling that a weight had fallen off her shoulders, she washed her face, said her prayers, smiling happily and guiltily as she prayed for Evdokim's health and that of the children and her own, then went to bed.[33]

Most peasant women did not give up their faith. One peasant woman remarked to some visiting Americans in 1917 that the revolution had been a miracle. Almost echoing Shaginian's belief in Blok's poem "The Twelve," she exclaimed:

> When I remember those days and nights when the revolution started — the light that was in the peasants' eyes — then I know that God is in all of us. In the fields I often believe that He is in the cattle, too, and in the very grain itself when it waves in the wind. And if we can learn better ways to cultivate not only the grain but men and women and children, too, then the wonderful God that is in them all will rise up toward the sun.... When it comes to all the children on earth, that will be the Great Revolution. And that is what the women will care about.[34]

As the decade wore on, government antireligious policy intimidated city people more than country folk because the party and regime were stronger in urban than rural areas. While believers were not barred from party membership during Lenin's lifetime, after 1924 it became an impediment. Of course some peasants and some villages were anti-clerical and resented having to pay the priest for performing the rites of baptism, marriage, and funerals. In other villages peasants were grateful to their priests and provided them food and fuel.

During both the Tsarist and Bolshevik periods, rural priests were often impoverished, surviving mainly by the fees they collected from providing the sacraments. So, many did not suddenly become poor when the Soviets took over. Indeed, during NEP some rural priests survived by obtaining jobs at village cooperatives as managers and accountants. Since priestly families were educated, family members could also find positions in the co-ops, especially in the northern provinces of Moscow, Leningrad, Vladimir, Ivanovo-Voznesensk, and Saratov. In her fascinating article "Trading Icons: Clergy, Laity, and Rural Co-operatives, 1921–28," Glennys Young tells how priests provided peasants with icons, candles, and oil for the icon lamps in many co-ops. Naturally priest managers closed the village co-ops on

Sundays and religious holidays. Young indicated that religion flourished in some places, and seven new churches were built in Vladimir Province in 1928.³⁵

E. Religion and the Intelligentsia

> Many of the intelligentsia looking down their noses at the "popular piety" of the masses and at "backwards" monks and clergy, could only accept an abstract and idealistic Orthodoxy of their own devising, one that would suit their high opinion of themselves.
>
> Father Paul Florensky, 1908

Judging from Father Florensky's quote and other sources, some of the intelligentsia were alienated from the church both before and after the revolution. Still, a remnant of educated people remained believers and secret practitioners. For urban, educated women, religion remained problematic. Elena Skrjabina's memoirs and those in secret religious circles under the direction of various priests, indicate that religious life in the cities in the 1920s had to be conducted clandestinely. In her memoir *Coming of Age in the Russian Revolution*, she recalled that her wedding by a priest had to be done in secret, and she had to hide her family's Christmas tree for fear of being reported to the secret police.³⁶

As early as 1916, groups of ecumenical students were meeting to discuss the scriptures in Moscow in private. From 1920 till 1941 small groups of cultured, educated people, often former gentry class in origin, joined special Christian Study circles under the direction of various Moscow priests. They pursued their religious education and experience quietly. Usually priests like Father Arseny were able to offer confession, communion, and direction to their spiritual children in these groups. But it had to be done secretly—outside of church buildings in people's apartments. In the 1920s, there were many such circles, but beginning in 1928 the Bolsheviks launched a new policy closing more and more churches and arresting more and more priests. While the Communist Party's League of the Militant Godless was not well funded, it discouraged church attendance and destroyed some church buildings.

1. Alexandra Berg

> I answered all their questions, and prayed to the Mother of God in between.
>
> Alexandra Berg

One friend and disciple of Father Arseny was Alexandra Berg. A "blinding beauty" in her youth, she also became a spiritual beauty in the 1920s. Although she had apparently been charmed by her own good looks in her youth, she developed more spiritual depth after a priest refused to grant her absolution when he felt her confession was insincere. He also told her that her beauty was destroying her. She records her third attempt at confession after some deep soul searching in the following words: "A week later, on Sunday, I went back to confession with Father Theodosy, and after Communion, I was overwhelmed for the first time in my life by a feeling of true joy, not an earthly joy, but a spiritual one."[37]

Berg also relates miraculous prayers that saved her when she was taking food to Father Arseny in exile near Vologda, in the late 1920s. She had made the trip alone, and was almost raped and robbed before she arrived at his hut. After alighting from the train in Vologda, she hired a cart to take her to Father Arseny's village. However the driver suddenly stopped as night came on and made her get out. She was eight miles from the priest's village and had heavy food and luggage to carry. The driver mentioned a nearby barge where she could rest and left her. She remembered:

> I said to him, But it is nighttime and my luggage is heavy, I will never be able to make it!
> But he whipped up his horse and left. It was –20 degrees and there was a piercing wind. I suddenly saw a barge standing on the shore, so I started walking towards it, pulling my bags with me one at a time.... I climbed onto the barge.... I entered and smelled the strong odor of cheap tobacco. I heard someone say, Hey, guys, look a woman has come here to hide from the wind!
> I froze. I realized from the voices that there were three men in the cold booth. I was scared: who were they? Only God could save me, so I started praying, asking for help from the Mother of God, from the saints, but my prayer kept getting interrupted since the men asked me one question after the other and I had to answer.... I decided to tell only the truth. If I survived till the morning, they would be able to see

anyway where I was going and whom I wanted to see. I answered all their questions, and prayed to the Mother of God in between.[38]

At sunrise they all left the barge, and two of the men helped her with her luggage. They realized they had scared her the night before and told her:

> "I will tell you, girl, around here you should not be walking by yourself. People could steal from you, or they could rape you. There are many camps around here and there are criminals on the roads; in the forests, they attack and rob. You were lucky you met us."

When Alexandra arrived at Father Arseny's, she found that he had also been praying for her safety all night. Then she resolved to never go alone to visit her spiritual advisor again.[39]

In the late 1920s many priests were arrested and exiled or sent to concentration camps, so many spiritual groups remained without a leader. In the case of Father Florensky, the Soviet government cultivated him because of his scientific genius and was loathe to arrest him for refusing to renounce his priesthood while serving as an engineer, inventor, and lecturer at a technical college. However, Florensky rejected the Bolshevik appointment of Metropolitan Sergius Starogorodsky, and this proved unacceptable. Many priests objected to the new metropolitan, who in 1927 accepted Soviet control of the church and issued a declaration stating that the "joys and sorrows of the Soviet regime" were those of the Russian Church. Florensky found this an absolute falsehood.[40] In contrast to Florensky's public denunciation, some nuns, monks, and priests just quietly retired to the countryside and survived unmolested. However, those who strenuously opposed the new metropolitan were arrested and imprisoned.

2. Tatiana Tchernavin

Writing about the situation of the church in the 1920s, high school teacher Tatiana Tchernavin thought much of the intelligentsia was unchurched prior to and after the revolution. In the prerevolutionary period, she thought students seldom went to chapel, and families sent their children to church to keep up appearances. In her memoirs, Tchernavin seemed more a-religious than antireligious, had a certain reverence for the clergy, and disliked the idea of liquidating them as a class.[41]

Before the war, Tchernavin observed that peasants still wanted a priest to bless their apples and honey, but she thought it more a pious tradition than religious faith. Spending time in a Siberian village before the revolution, Tchernavin had known the local priest Father Alexei. On a visit there some years later to secure paintings from an estate for the Hermitage Museum, she learned about the closing of some of the churches. One peasant told her:

> It's the only one left in our neighbourhood; all the others are closed. We manage to keep up this one. People are afraid to die without a priest. About marriage, now, they no longer mind—they just go to a registry office. Girls, of course, prefer a church marriage, it is more secure somehow, but the young men are chary of it. They can't get a job if they go to church; it's downright persecution, I call it.[42]

Father Alexei told Tatiana that people's spirits sink if they don't hear God's word and have Holy Days. Still without rations, it was hard for priestly families to survive. Father Alexei's daughter Vera would have graduated at the top of her class, but she couldn't have that honor because of her social origins. After graduation, Vera could not get employment as a teacher or even as a worker because of her priestly origins. She did needlework, washed clothes, laid out the dead, anything to earn food. Her father hid in the cemetery waiting for funerals to bless, and people would sometimes pay him a few kopeks. At the end of the decade, Vera committed suicide, abandoning her old father.[43]

F. Antireligious Songs

Before and after the revolution some antireligious and anticlerical peasant chastushki (songs) ridiculed church-going and the clergy. Chastushki could be used to shock, and the following verses do:

> Only the old, old men
> Frequent the temple of God.
> The young people think
> That the saints are trash.

Sunday has come,
I will not go to pray.
For me this time has passed,
I will go to study.[44]

There is no one in the world more vile and wicked
Than the potbellied priests.
They steal without compunction
From the country peasants.

But the new priest
Really has some conscience:
From everyone he takes
Two rubles for their sins.[45]

I am now a Komsomolka
I no longer wear a cross,
Without any shame,
To a meeting I will go.[46]

Of course, the percentage of women in the Komsomol in rural areas in the 1920s was very small. So the views expressed in this song were not widespread. Still, the Bolsheviks made sneering at religion respectable, and disdain became widespread in the cities and among some rural youth and Red Army soldiers. In the late 1920s, the Bolsheviks organized the League of the Militant Godless to fight religion among the Muslims in Central Asia, to close churches in the cities, and to combat religious observance among the peasants. This movement was only marginally successful; most peasant girls still wanted and had church weddings. Many feared that their parents would withhold their blessing and dowry if they didn't have a church wedding.[47]

In many villages, peasants and clergy united to retain religious traditions and church holidays. Some priests were innovative in organizing Bible studies, choirs for youngsters, and opportunities for gathering for food, drink, and listening to the gramophone. These events were tolerated during NEP but ended with an attack on the kulaks and clergy in 1929 during collectivization. Members of small religious sects like the Skoptsy, Khlysty, and Fyodorists often rejected the Soviet state and military service. These were persecuted by the government; trials were held in 1929, and some were arrested and some executed. The followers of the Fyodorists were exiled after their leaders were executed. By 1930, there were only a few hundred Skoptsy scattered in various settlements. Still, there were about five hundred in Moscow in the 1930s. Persecution of Roman Catholic and Russian Orthodox priests also became more intense then.[48]

Chapter Three

Marriage and Motherhood

A. The Countryside

"I don't want to marry anyone else, and nobody else'll want me anyway—I am getting so old now, and I love Anton, I love him, father, and I want him. Save me, dearest, save me, and I'll always love you!" That's what she said.
Peasant girl, in Maurice Hindus, Broken Earth

During the 1920s, new Soviet, secular culture coexisted with the old traditional one in the countryside. Church weddings predominated in the countryside—about 75 percent married in the church—and the number of rural churches did not decline much. Traditional wedding laments of the nineteenth century continued without much change. These were songs that the bride sang to express her grief at leaving her home, before going to live with her in-laws.

However, a deficit in the male population occurred during World War I, and the Civil War, which left many girls of marriageable age without husbands. One result was that some men demanded large dowries, and not all fathers could afford them. If a father provided for his eldest daughter, the younger ones sometimes had to wait until he could accrue dowries for them. According to Maurice Hindus, even in the 1920s neighbors would shun an unmarried woman, and "no unhappier lot can befall any woman in a peasant village than to remain unmarried." At a fair, one man was trying to sell his dog to get money for a dowry for his daughter, and Hindus quoted another man, father of a twenty-two-year-old daughter, saying:

> "Do you know how much of a dowry he wants? A horse and wagon and one hundred poods of rye! Think of that, brothers! I have talked to him, and so has my wife, but it's done no good. He is stubborn as an ox. He said if I won't give it to him, some other man will. And where can I get one hundred poods of rye? That's more than I'll harvest this year, and I have taxes to pay and bread to provide for the family for a whole year and seed for the fall's sowing. And what'll I

do if I give away the only horse I have? What's a muzhik nowadays without a horse? ...

"Father, dear," she cried, "get me the dowry for Anton. Please do. He won't marry me if you don't.... He wants to drop me, father, my dearest; he said he does, and if he should, then, father, what'll I do?"[1]

Throughout the 1920s, village girls continued traditional courting and marriage customs. Young couples could flirt. A fellow could even kiss a girl on her cheek or neck, but not on her lips unless they were engaged. Many peasant girls remained as strict about courting as their mothers and grandmothers had been. To be seduced and abandoned remained a terrible disaster in village culture. Still, illegitimacy rates among peasants and workers had climbed before the First World War and prebridal pregnancy also increased.[2] Old patterns persisted. The banns announcing a couple's intention to wed were read at church, the bride had a party the night before her marriage, she had a ritual bath before the wedding, and her hair was plaited into two braids instead of one. Village culture remained strong, and appropriate clothing for different occasions was very important. Maria Iakovlevna, born in 1912 in north-central Russia but married in the 1920s, asks her mother in the following bridal chastushki, or ditty, to check her outfit to make sure it is correct:

> My mistress, my good mother,
> Look at me, please!
> Have I dressed myself skillfully?
> Can I be considered worthy?
> Does the colorful dress look well on me,
> And the sky blue flowers on my head?[3]

Gift giving remained important, and the bride learned as a teenager to spin and weave so she could present a beautiful shirt to the groom and her father-in-law before the wedding. She would prepare special embroidered towels for the groom's family. She also wove a special towel to cover the icons in their hut so they were shielded when they made love. In their youth, girls learned lullabies and wedding laments as well as folk stories to amuse younger siblings, whom they helped raise. They also learned to cook and do domestic and field chores growing up. Thus, their education was an informal one of established behavior—rites, rituals, and songs—rather than the formal one of school, which may or may not have existed at the village level in the 1920s.

Wedding laments resembled those from earlier times. Some honored a girl's family and friends and alluded to the loss of freedom that marriage brought. Some showed the pampered existence of young girls living at home who were allowed to sleep in, whereas mothers-in-law demanded they rise early to work, as the following song illustrates:

> How that bold mother-in-law
> Gets up quietly in the morning
> Gets up very early,
> She moves about and bangs about
> As she speaks, she roars:
> "Get up now, my oversleeping daughter-in-law,
> Get up now, oversleepy one!"
> Out in the clear field
>   . . .
> And I, a little orphan,
> I got up, yes got up early,
> I washed up, and brightened my face,
> And as I walked out on the clear field,
> I, an orphan, looked . . .[4]

Historian Isabel Tirado sheds light on village culture and has translated chastushki from the 1920s. They resemble those in the late nineteenth century, as the following ones show:

> Come to me, my sweet friends,
> And all my dear aunties,
> My closest neighbors.
> You should have visited me long ago,
> In my sadness.
> In my great travail,
> Come and listen to my bitter songs.
>
> I sing them loudly.
> My girlish days I will recall.
> Gone are the good times and my freedom,
> Gone are my walks with my girlfriends
> Down the wide street,
> Gone are the late night games with them.
>
> I won't enjoy myself at night at my mother's
> And sleep till the red sun rises.

> I am off to live with strangers,
> Not the same as living with my dear mother.
> Where I'll have to ask for leave,
> Wherever I will go.[5]

The chastushki—or short ditties of two, four, or six lines—were composed and sung on various occasions. They showed only a few changes in word and rhyme from the Tsarist period. Some girls were remarkably honest, almost shocking, as the following version reveals:

> Our river is so shallow
> I can cross in my galoshes.
> I'm a feisty girl—I'll marry
> Any man who'll have me.[6]

While relatively few peasant girls and women joined the Komsomol or party, many patronized traditional courses in sewing, cooking, child care, church choirs, or village gatherings (called posidelki). Still, some songs showed the resolve of young peasant women:

> Scold me or not
> It won't be as you say
> I'm off to a meeting
> You can't bar my way.[7]

Despite parental opposition, some girls set their caps for a young Komsomol man in the village, as the following verses show:

> Save your yelling mama
> No need to give me dark looks
> I'm going to sign up for Komsomol
> And I'm going to read some books
> I don't have use for rings now
> And bracelets not at all
> Because together with my girlfriend
> I've got my eyes set on a guy
> From the Komsomol.[8]

A feisty peasant woman is the heroine of Lidiia Seifullina's novel and play *Virineia*. She does not romanticize peasant life and says at one point:

> They talk about love and so forth. But it is not like that for our village lads. They seldom speak to their sweethearts and never to their

Russian Women Peasants, 1918 (Library of Congress)

women. To the cow or horse a man sometimes says "dear," but no tender word does he find for his old lady. She is in the house for work and children, not for his affection. And at work, he pities his cattle, not his wife.⁹

When Virineia goes to work for a widower named Pavel, he says he cannot promise not to pester her at night. But he would promise not to do anything against her wishes. She decides to accept his job offer and boldly replies:

> Well, let's try to live and sleep together.¹⁰

Virineia could well look like the proud peasant girl illustrated above.

Other songs reveal humor, like the following one, speaking of exchanging boyfriends:

> Girlfriend of mine,
> Let's make an exchange.
> You take mine and I take yours,
> Let's organize a gathering.¹¹

This song refers to the "posidelki," gatherings that occurred most evenings between the fall harvest and the beginning of Lent. The meetings took place in a hut, a bathhouse, even a barn. It was a time of merriment when the unmarried youth gathered to sing, play games, dance, and court.

Some of the peasant girls' songs spoke of marriage matters like these:

> I'll go home
> And stamp my foot.
> Mother, sell the cow.
> And marry me off.
>
> Oh, mother, my dear mother,
> Pamper me, let me sleep late.
> When I'm married off.
> No one will pamper me.
>
> My mother is too zealous
> She plucked the blossom in July
> She ruined my youth
> And gave me away in marriage too soon.[12]
>
> Mama woke me up
> She was crying at the bed.
> "Wake up, daughter dear,
> I gave you away in marriage."
>
> They betrothed me; didn't tell me
> I pour my tears into my kerchief.[13]

Some chastushki were like those of the earlier nineteenth century and told of the misery of marriage: the beatings, unhappiness, reluctance to marry a man of one's parents' choosing. While some sociologists thought that Soviet society had no need for arranged marriages, they were probably speaking of city culture, and not the more traditional life in the countryside, where marriage was designed to suit the needs of the family and community, not necessarily those of the bride. The following lines show that some girls were still being married against their will:

> I approach my house
> Smoke rises high from the Chimney.
> Mama gave me away in marriage,
> To a man I do not know.
>
> Oh, my mother
> Would have given me to Ivan.

CHAPTER THREE: MARRIAGE AND MOTHERHOOD

> Cut my head off,
> I won't marry him.[14]
>
> Vanechka, oh, Vanechka
> You and I don't make a pair.
> Your beard is turning gray
> And I am still a young girl.[15]
>
> A husband taught his wife,
> His sad wife.
> How the wife implored her husband,
> She implored her father-in-law,
> Her father-in-law, her mother-in-law:
> "Father-in-law take me away
> From my cruel husband,
> My cruel husband, who's so angry
> The father-in-law ordered to beat her more,
> Until the blood flows, he ordered,
> Until the blood flows to beat her.[16]

For a variety of reasons, some peasant couples decided to have secular weddings, and the following songs describe these events:

> My dear friend
> I will share some news:
> My sweetheart proposed
> That we marry at the volost (district court).
>
> I'm betrothed to a Komsomol fellow,
> I want to marry him . . .
> He is not asking for a dowry,
> We won't have to pay the priest.[17]

In her research, Isabel Tirado found the writing of a young Komsomolka who did not lament her wedding day but praised her new married life and work in the Komsomol journal *Zhurnal krest'ianskoi molodezhi* (Journal of Peasant Youth, 1925):

> I'm not bitter on my wedding day. I don't cry, but feel happy with all my soul, as I start a new life. My first duty: to be a conscious citizen, to participate in the construction of the new life. I will strive to strengthen and bring to life everything that the October Revolution has given us peasants. On my shoulders I carry the burden of the household and family: I have the responsibility for raising children, the new generation, the builders of the new life.[18]

Interviewing a woman teacher named Manka, who lived in a village in 1925, the journalist Maurice Hindus found that the revolution had not produced enough women like the one just quoted. It had not changed the hard lot of most peasant women. Rejecting his pity, Manka informed him that all the villagers thought her frightfully old to be unmarried at twenty-two, and they were constantly trying to arrange a marriage for her. Having lived in the village for a few years she saw what life was like for brides. As a young teacher, she was satisfied with her life but described most peasant women's lives in the following words:

> However, take the peasant girl. She marries young. She has never been outside of the village, unless to visit another village in the neighborhood. She knows nothing of the world. She never reads anything. She knows nothing of love. She talks of it with a kind of light-hearted earnestness, but she has no conception of its meaning, its purpose, the power of exalting the individual. Unlettered, unread, inexperienced, she mistakes a fleeting physical passion for love, and how fleeting it is she finds out soon enough. After marriage her life becomes a deadly routine, an endless round of toil and worry and dullness. She ceases to go to the parties of the young people; she is not wanted there after she is married. That is the custom of our peasants. Occasionally she will join the older people in a spree on Sundays and holidays, and they, the older people, like nothing so much as getting drunk. For the rest, she drudges day and night. Evenings in winter her husband goes off to a gathering to talk, argue, sing, and listen to stories. On Sundays he hitches up the horse and drives to town. He sees new fields, new faces, hears new voices, new words. But she has to choke in her filthy hovel, always washing, scrubbing, spinning, weaving, sewing, and—caring for the babies! And she has so many of them.... They never wake him, the husband. He sleeps in peace, and if he does wake it is only to curse the wife for not having quiet in the house.... And have you observed the way the muzhik woman tends her baby, binding it in rough linen so the poor thing can hardly breathe, and feeding it the disgusting chewings of bread or potato? ... No wonder so many peasant babies die before they reach their first birthday.... Oh, these interminable rounds of epidemics that sweep our villages—the waste of it, the pity, the agony that follows in their wake ... you have no idea how ghastly were the ravages of the recent typhoid epidemic ... and it is all so needless. If only the muzhiks would learn to keep clean, to leave their deadly home-brew alone, and to eat and drink as men should!
>
> Heavens! Look at our women when they are thirty—beauty gone, gaiety gone—misshapen, shriveled, flat-chested creatures, irritable,

morbid, given to swearing and cursing their husbands, their neighbors, their children, and beating them, too, without mercy, with fists and feet and clubs, and often crippling them for life ... women, mothers! God how terrible! ... nu [well], tell me please what sort of a life is that? No rest, no pleasure, no diversion, no inspiration, no love, no sympathy—nothing but toil and quarrels and beatings ... of course our men beat their wives with fists and whips ... beastly creatures! ... that many of our peasant women are mere hags, drained of the beauty, sweetness, glory, with which they glowed when they were girls, and turned into coarse, callous, sharp-tongued creatures ... yes such is the lot of our peasant women.[19]

However, Manka sees her mission to awaken the peasant women so that they can "regard themselves as somebody, not a mere drudge, but a human being, a woman with a life all her own and entitled to her share of joy and inspiration. Oh it is a colossal task, I tell you, to redeem our unfortunate muzhik woman." Maurice Hindus realizes that she has found her life's work in the village, and she agrees. She has found her lifework among the peasant women, and she is quite happy. She not only teaches school in the village but reads and has organized a chorus and a theater group. She also wants to work with the older women whose lives are so desolate.[20]

While most peasant women wanted church weddings that offered security, men often preferred secular marriages because then party officials wouldn't bother them, and they needn't fear the possible loss of their job. Marrying at the government offices, called ZAGS, was also cheaper—no priest to pay. Finally, fellows thought a secular marriage less binding than a church one. Recognizing this attitude, some girls insisted on the traditional church wedding.

The new Soviet marriage law of 1918, amended in 1926, made divorce easy in the ZAGS registration office. A married person could even send a post card notifying a spouse that he or she had been divorced, and this became known as post-card divorce. Of the five hundred thousand divorces listed in the 1926 census, about half were obtained by peasants, showing they had some knowledge of the new laws. One peasant woman explained:

"When the revolution came and I learned that the new government made it easy to get a divorce, I put in my claim at the court. It was hard enough to be living here, without having a drunken husband, too. I had my child to think of."[21]

Another remarked in 1927:

> Yet I think it is a little better. Men are ashamed to beat their wives so often. Formerly after holidays one could not get up from the beating....
> I think also they are afraid. A woman in the next village got a divorce.[22]

According to Soviet sociologist A. S. Marchenko, divorce still carried a stigma and represented the disgrace of the deserted wife. It was more common for husbands to leave their wives than for wives to divorce their husbands, because few wives could support themselves and their children as single mothers.[23] Soviet law was weak in the 1920s, and customary law held sway. According to Beatrice Farnsworth, divorce was more common among younger than older peasant women. The Land Code of 1922 was silent about whether a departing divorced woman was entitled to a share of the land. As a result, most divorced women were landless. They could work as farm laborers in the summer, earning 60–75 rubles for the season, but they had no income in the winter. Some then worked for the local priest or teacher in the village as domestics. To get a share of the household land, a divorced woman often had to go to court. Many were illiterate and unable to navigate the new Soviet legal system. Moreover, those women married in the church and not registered in the Soviet ZAGS were not considered legally married, and hence not entitled to land. Divorced women also complained in the peasant women's journal *Krest'ianka* (Woman Peasant) that they received no alimony for their children and no property settlement. The advice to young women became "get to know your husband before marriage, because divorce is hard." With the collectivization of land in 1929, women's right to land became a moot point. Legal battles about divorce and land show peasant society slowly adapting and women pursuing their self-interest. Party sources show a significant proportion of delegatki, or politically active rural women, were divorced.[24]

Many of the chastushki refer to divorce, as the following indicate:

> Don't threaten me, I'm not afraid
> Tomorrow I'll register with someone else.

> Before it wasn't
> As it is now:
> The commissars allow folks
> To marry forty times.

I didn't want to dance,
I feared my husband.
Just think, just guess,
Tomorrow I'll divorce him.[25]

Slightly different marriages are described by Yelena Shershenyova, who lived in the New Jerusalem Tolstoyan agricultural colony outside of Moscow in the 1920s. Daughter of Leo Tolstoy's associate Feodor Strakhov, Yelena grew up in a gentry-class family, thinking of a life of chastity and service to others. So, she refused her first marriage proposal from Vasia Shershenyov at the colony. Eventually she decided marriage was acceptable, and she and the other members of the colony had an idyllic, dedicated life. When they first formed the colony, life was simple. Although Yelena was born into the educated Russian intelligentsia, she became a farmer—acting out her Tolstoyan convictions. She joined the New Jerusalem Tolstoyan Commune in the early 1920s, noting:

> We had no equipment, no seeds, no money, and nowhere to get any. We had no clothing and no shoes. We had only our unity of convictions, our confidence in one another, our love of work and devotion to our common cause, and our youth with its endurance and optimism. It mattered not at all that we had only one pair of boots for five men and had to decide every evening who would need them the most the next morning, and who would most need our most presentable jacket....
>
> There were disappointments, mistakes, and blunders; but in general the farm developed vigorously, and soon it attracted the attention of the district land department.[26]

Hard work turned the colony into a showplace, but the members had fun in the evenings singing, playing instruments, acting out plays, and joking. While marriage did not separate Yelena from the duties and rapport of the colony, motherhood did. She was passionate about motherhood, and caring for her son left little time for work and attending the general meetings or evening entertainments. She admits that she probably romanticized motherhood, but her baby was sickly and required a great deal of care. She remarks:

> To a certain extent motherhood cut me off from the joys of ... work within our communal family. I did not have enough strength to combine the two. I would often sit up all night with Fedya who was sick and then get up at four in the morning to do the milking.[27]

It wasn't the tradition of the colony to spend so much time on a baby, but she couldn't help herself. Some of the other women criticized her, but not all. Some other mothers also wanted to raise their own children, so gradually everything got straightened out, and everyone calmed down.[28]

The colony did well until collectivization, when it was forced to merge with the Red October state farm outside of Moscow. Although the Tolstoyan commune members were popular with the local population, who sought their advice on farming, their ideology was alien to the authorities, and eventually members of the New Jerusalem Colony left to farm in Siberia. It seems ironic that Tolstoyanism was anathema both to the Russian Orthodox Church in the late nineteenth century and to the Soviet government in the early twentieth.[29]

B. Urban Marriage and Motherhood

> I wondered whether I have the right to marry; whether I must not sacrifice my personal happiness and devote myself entirely to the service of others? But I have not solved this problem.
>
> Nelly Ptashkina, Muscovite girl, 1918

Although she was only fifteen years old at the time of the revolution, Nelly felt conflicted over marriage and careers. Indeed, the Soviet economy was so weak during and after World War I that almost all married as well as unmarried women had to work, thus creating dilemmas of putting their energy into their family or career. Perhaps easy divorce, which the Soviets introduced in 1918, is one reason that one doesn't encounter as many bitter accounts of marriage among women writers in the 1920s as in the Tsarist period. In Moscow in 1927, there were ten thousand divorces compared to thirteen thousand marriages. Moreover, the difficulties of building the new Soviet state required many men and women, especially true believers and party members, to sublimate and subordinate their sexual energy into building the new Soviet society rather than putting a great deal of time and energy into marriage and family life.

While many Russian women kept traditional views of marriage— thinking it women's whole life—other patterns also existed, especially among party members and the intelligentsia. Some women took a rather cavalier attitude. In the 1920s, party leader Alexandra Kollontai indicated in her *Autobiography of a Sexually Emancipated Communist Woman* that when her lover no longer esteemed her as a person, and saw her only as a sex object, she would end the relationship.[30]

Writing about this topic years later, Nadezhda Mandelstam, a member of the intelligentsia, observed: "We otherwise attached no importance whatsoever to the registration of our marriage, since it was a totally meaningless formality." Like others of her generation she despised the hypocrisy of conventional family life by having a free union based on love not marriage. She also noticed that people had a "free and easy attitude to divorce," and it was "easier to separate than to stay together." Mandelstam also decided that the post-revolutionary period and the 1930s were not good times to have children. Although she was basically a housewife, tending to her poet husband's needs and not directing her energy into her career, she wrote: "I realized in time that one must not have children. Writing her memoirs in the 1970s, she had some second thoughts about marriage and the family, noting: "I sometimes think that my generation was wrong to undermine marriage, but I still feel I would rather live by myself than in the false atmosphere of the traditional family.... People should not live together if the inner link between them is broken." Needless to say, Nadezhda and many intellectuals completely rejected the idea of the trophy wife, which arose with the advent of NEP in 1921. She saw herself as a girlfriend and partner, not a doll or manikin all made up, as some of the NEPmen's wives and mistresses presented themselves.[31]

1. Working-Class Women

In a short story, Vera Panova depicts a woman who has an affair as a teenager, and her father condones it. Eventually she marries a worker with a steady job, but when her lover reappears, she goes to him. When her husband discovers the deception, he doesn't beat her but tells her to choose whether to stay with him and their adopted children or to leave and live with her unreliable lover. She chooses her husband, family life, and being a mother, but she misses the kisses and caresses of her lover. Although her husband loves her, he is unable to express his love, is rather taciturn, and their relationship lacks romance. Evdokia muses:

It was very quiet in the house. Evdokia thought that Evdokim wasn't a bad man, of course, but it was dull with him. He kept silent all the time. When he caressed her he wouldn't say a word, and what kind of love was it without words?[32]

An account of working-class marriage and divorce is found in Anna Balashova's writing "A Worker's Life." A devoted worker at the Trekhgorka Textile Factory, she married in 1925, but unhappily. Her husband found her not submissive enough. He discouraged her from joining the party or engaging in volunteer work. He wanted her to "stay home with him." Balashova describes the deterioration of her marriage in her autobiography with the following words:

> Basically he was not happy with the amount of volunteer work I was doing. At first he just knew he had an obedient wife who would spend all her free time at home waiting for him. On Sundays I used to beg him to stay home with me and cry over his neglect, saying I could not even tell whether I was married or single, but then, after I got involved in volunteer work, I no longer cared what my husband did. He had his life; I had mine. My eyes had been opened to a different kind of life, different social interests.
>
> I stopped worrying about what my husband thought of me; I worried about whether this or that government campaign was going to succeed at our factory. At first I was often nervous, afraid I would not be able to do the work I had been assigned. I tried very hard and wanted to do the best I could.
>
> Soon after I became a candidate party member, I was elected to the supervisory board of Osoaviakhim [Civil Defense organization] and then a delegate to the provincial trade union congress, and then a member of the board of the factory club.
>
> When my child was born, and while I was still in the hospital my husband left me for good, taking quite a few of my personal things with him. He did not even leave me a note. I sued him twice, to get my things back. He had even taken the table. The court made him return my things and pay alimony.
>
> So I started living on my own, but my spirits were high. Aleksei came over a couple of times; he obviously was having doubts. He would have stayed if I had asked him, but I didn't.[33]

According to Soviet law, Balashova received alimony for her child, but none for herself. She doesn't mention factory crèches or how she raised her son, but presumably she had help. She seemed happy to make her own way, devoting herself to her work and the party.

She obviously had a strong ego and sense of accomplishment. Not all working-class women possessed such personalities. Many were abused and put upon.

According to Glebov's play "Inga," some working-class housewives felt trapped in abusive situations, especially when they had several children. In his play, the character Nastia tells a comrade:

> I encouraged you for nothing. I thought something would come of it. ... You can see for yourselves ... I can't cope with him—the shark! He bends me like a straw! He's squeezed everything out of me as it is. It's worse than a sentence of hard labor to live with him! But where shall I go? Alone, with the kids? You young ones are free.... But I ... it seems I'll die under the iron.[34]

Nastia's words show how different a housewife's reality was from a young factory worker's like Balashova's, who was educated, having been sponsored by her trade union to study at the rabfak. She was also strengthened by her political work and comrades. She wasn't dependent on her husband for her identity or her finances. There were often generational differences among working women. While older working-class housewives schemed to provide food and clothing for their children, young, unmarried workers were freer to spend money on clothes, cosmetics, the cinema, and dancing. Some Puritanical party members condemned free love, jazz, flapper culture, and the romantic escapism of films, but their warnings usually fell on deaf ears among the youth.[35]

Fascinating accounts of wedding culture are provided by the American reporter Marguerite Harrison, who was living in Moscow from 1920 to 1921. She observed that some working-class women remained engaged for long periods because of the shortage of housing. Other workers couldn't marry because they had dependents to care for. The Soviet government recognized only civil marriages as legal, and they were simple and cheap. A couple needed only two witnesses to declare there were no hindrances to their marrying. Many Russian women kept their own names as a sign of independence.[36]

2. Bourgeois and Educated Women's Weddings

a. Marguerite Harrison

> In the Russian churches there are no organs, but the unaccompanied Gregorian chant is often very beautiful, and it was superb on this occa-

sion, for this particular church had one of the finest choirs in Moscow.

Marguerite Harrison, *Marooned in Moscow*

Harrison meticulously recorded the events of a fashionable wedding to which she was invited in the summer of 1921. The aunt of the bride owned a flourishing tailoring enterprise, which provided gowns to the wives of well-to-do, high-ranking Bolsheviks and wealthy NEPmen. The wedding took place one afternoon in a huge Moscow church. Harrison described the experience as follows:

> I went to their home and walked to the church, which was only a short distance away, with an elderly friend of the family. The bridal party was driven in carriages. My escort was very correct in a frock coat of somewhat antiquated pattern, it is true, and the cousin of the bride was smart in an English morning coat and striped trousers, with a white boutonniere in his buttonhole. The same costume was worn by the groom, a prosperous young engineer, and his best man.
>
> On entering the church, the bride, with her attendants, ten pretty bridesmaids in white frocks, carrying large bouquets of phlox, accompanied by the members of her family and intimate friends, turned to the left of the door and waited.... He [the priest] advanced to where the groom was standing with his best man, took him by the hand and led him across to the bride, placing his hand in hers. Then turning, he led the way to the sanctuary, followed by the bridal couple, the attendants and family, among whom I was included, while a wedding march was chanted by the choir.
>
> The ceremony was long and exceedingly complicated. During the entire time the best man and maid of honor held huge gilt crowns over the heads of the bride and groom, there were many prayers and a short homily on the married state by the priest. Then, followed by the bridal couple and their two attendants, still holding the crowns over their heads, he marched three times around the huge Bible.... During the entire ceremony the guests and spectators remained standing, for there are no pews or chairs in Orthodox churches. There were many places in the service where they all bowed and crossed themselves several times. After the final blessing everybody present kissed the priest's hand, and the Bible, filing in line before the lectern, then the priest and all the guests kissed the bride and we all went home to a beautiful wedding supper.[37]

At this bourgeois wedding, no expense was spared on the dinner of cold meat, salad, hot meat croquettes with fried potatoes, white rolls, cakes, bonbons, fruit, and coffee. Kvass was served, instead of champagne, and it cost 35,000 rubles per bottle. Many speeches were made, toasts drunk, and then dancing lasted until after midnight. The cost of the wedding was exorbitant: the white satin material for the wedding gown cost 80,000 rubles, her white silk stockings 18,000 rubles, white kid slippers 40,000, bridesmaids' dresses 30,000 each, bouquets 5,000 rubles each, the priest's fee 10,000, the choir 10,000, a fee for using the church, and about 500,000 rubles for the supper. All together it was a million-ruble wedding! The raiment of the guests was not quite so spectacular because many of them had had to sell their prettiest frocks to get money for food, and consequently they covered up old dresses with family furs. The married couple had no honeymoon because they could not obtain travel permits during the Civil War. Luckily for them, the bride's aunt, Mme B., gave them two rooms in her extravagant seven-room apartment for their abode.[38]

Soviet observer, Margaret Wettlin, who lived in the Soviet Union from 1932 to 1982, noted that her husband's first marriage had also taken place in a church in the 1920s. So, church weddings remained not unusual among some segments of the middle class and intelligentsia.[39] Some educated women continued to have modest church weddings but did so clandestinely.

b. Elena Skrjabina

> We were married in the evening two weeks later, in the semi-dark Tikhvin Church, behind closed doors.
>
> Elena Skrjabina, *Coming of Age in the Russian Revolution*

In her memoir, gentry-born Elena Skrjabina describes her wedding as follows:

> Already in the spring, Sergei Skrjabin had proposed to me; and in October we registered for marriage, to the great joy of my mother, who found him completely acceptable as my husband. She was impressed both by his age — he was seven years older than I — and by his solidness. My numerous romances had disturbed her and she always found something to say against each of my dates.
>
> We registered in that very house of Kuntsevich on Oshara where we had once lived and which, as I have already mentioned was now ZAGS. Most amusing of all, the registration took place in my former nursery.

Elena and Sergei Scrjabin (Iowa Women's Archives)

> We were married in the evening two weeks later, in the semi-dark Tikhvin Church, behind closed doors. Among those invited were the four attendants and only the closest relatives.[40]

The photograph of Elena and her husband was found in her archives. Although it was not marked wedding picture, judging from their expression, youth, and clothes, it may have been.

c. *Nelly Ptashkina*

> I do not know what love is . . .
>
> Nelly Ptashkina, diary

Just the opposite of the church weddings were the reveries of a young Russian girl from a bourgeois family who recorded her ideas about romance, marriage, free love, and feminism in her diary in 1918. Nelly Ptashkina mused:

I do not know what love is, I cannot analyse it, but it is a wonderful exquisite feeling.... The most beautiful on earth....
    When I see a pair of lovers who at any rate seem pure, I am seized with emotion and want to go on looking at them. It does me good....
    How beautiful is love! ...
    Of course, it is ridiculous for me, a fifteen-year-old girl, to try and unravel these questions, but once they come into my head I shall speak about them.
    What is occupying me considerably is the question whether I can, or rather whether I have the moral right to *marry*.... Naturally, this doubt only acquires significance if my plans mature and if I really show myself fitted for a public career.
    The family, and children in particular, whose education is so incalculably important to the human race, represent a certain responsibility which takes up much time and of that I shall have but little....
    ... And supposing that not I alone but hundreds of women devote themselves to public work, neglecting their families in consequence. What will happen then? Will this arrest the growth of the human race?[41]

In a different philosophical tone, she records her feminist ideas:

And, even if I should fall in love and meet with no response, my life will not suffer from this. I shall arrange it, so as not to depend on love, let alone wait for it as so many girls do. I shall live. If love comes I shall take it; and if not, I shall regret it, wildly regret it, but I shall *live* all the same....
    Is it necessary to add that I believe with all my heart and mind that women have absolutely equal rights with men, because I consider them in no wise their intellectual inferior?
    This year I have added to the books on social subjects, some that are concerned with the feminist question, and I shall read them with great enjoyment.[42]

She views married life critically:

In any case, love must and can only be an appendix to life, it certainly must not form its substance. Pitiful are those for whom that is the case. Thank God that is not so with me.
    Does eternal love exist? I don't know. There are many examples in history, but I do not know that there are any *en masse*. At least, in conjugal life, love turns into a habit.
    ... In many cases I have seen enmity and hatred spring up often between husband and wife. It is what is called "family happiness!"

... And, on the other hand, the ties created by the children, or something else, habit, are too strong and they go on dragging the shackles of their grey, melancholy existence....

Therefore from marriage there remains only the outward form without any substance. It does not prevent illegitimate love, but only increases the evil and the immorality. But if it is only a husk, let it be removed from life.

I am unquestionably *against* marriage.

The ideal is to live in separate houses; the children with the mother.

It seems to me that in such conditions love must be more beautiful and more attractive: it always leaves something unexplored and, through this, entices.

And for this reason also I should like to experience love in order to know whether I shall act as I believe I should now.[43]

Musing in the summer of 1919, Nelly continues:

Probably I am at the age when one begins to think about love. I do not know how it is with others, but this thought sometimes haunts me....

"Mummie, what is love, without which people say life cannot be complete? What is it? Is it really such a radiant thing?" I asked Mummie a few days ago in an excess of frankness and expansion. "Yes," she replied and talked a little on this subject.

But, all the same, I still do not know the meaning of love. I try to, but simply cannot understand this feeling....

I have been thinking about L.A. It always seems to me that we shall meet in life, that we shall be near to each other....

And Mummie also thinks of him for me; she does not mention this, but I know.

Is this not a coincidence? It is a pity that we know each other so little. Especially that he knows so little of me.[44] [L.A. was a friend and tutor of Nelly's in Moscow.]

Meditating on the themes of love, sexuality, and free love, Nelly writes in January 1919:

I see life without sexual love. I do not know whether this can be, but I should incline to think that it is possible....

The feeling exists. And at present it expresses itself in uncouth and misshapen forms. New ones must take their place. That is what I think.

Love is a feeling, and like every feeling it cannot be made quite subservient to the mind. It has its rights, which people refuse to admit. One speaks of eternal love, love burdened with chains. Probably eternal love exists, yet it is possible that this is not the case. It may be a passing thing, yet passionate and sincere.[45]

d. Maria Shkapskaya

A harsh, yet passionate and erotic view of love, marriage, infidelity, and mothers' lives is found in Maria Shkapskaya's poetry written in the early 1920s. She wrote about taboo topics such as menstruation, abortion, stillborn babies, absent husbands and fathers, and the painful lives of mothers' in the new Soviet state. In her prose poem "Mater Dolorosa," written in 1921, Shkapskaya cries:

> My still born child,
> We didn't lay you in the cradle to rest,
> Nor caress you with the sign of the cross,
> Your lips didn't know my breast.
>> People go to the graveyard—
>> A task that's dear to the heart—
>> They weep with tears that are living
>> And bring flowers for those who depart.
> I could search all over the world—
> For your dear little grave there's no place,
> But, flesh of my flesh, vein of my veins,
> In my heart there's your quiet trace.
>> . . .
>
> Behind her children's coffin,
>> Shoulders hunched, she walked,
> Her hands more weak than a child's,
>> The look on her face distraught.
>
> O God, on the other shore,
>> Will there be, must there be a meeting—
> But I cannot comprehend,
> How she managed to walk without falling.
>> . . .
>
> And I feel so sick and sorry,
>> Resentful, my heart grown numb.
> That my unborn boy
>> Does not see such a sun.
>> . . .

> I should like to be a good wife to you, the mother of
> your children. But the Lord decreed me a different fate,
> and these dreams are smoke.[46]

"Mater Dolorosa" suggests that men are necessary for conception, but few remain to become solid husbands or fathers. Indeed, she depicts women as peaceful, long-suffering, compassionate, and loyal while men are rapacious. She says:

> My body was impenetrable and scorched with black smoke. Bent over it rapaciously was the black enemy of the human race.
> And forgetting my pride, I gave him my blood to the end in return for a single hope for a son with a dear-featured face....
> Oh, the seduction of the blessed burden, the overpowering temptation to be called "mother" and to feel every evening in your body the new beating of new life.
> To walk down the street like a queen, proud of your double fate. And to know, that your blind womb has been summoned, to be sovereign to it and slave, and to be confident that the Lord's sword of wrath will not rise over you in the night.
> And to be like an animal, like a wild she-wolf, in her unappeasable forest anguish, when the time comes to be disembodied and become individual and separate again....
> You knew? Oh, you doubtless knew, that I have been waiting for you all these years.
> That I am all yours and all afire, filled with you, as a cup with mead. You came, you tasted and . . ., and here is the child—mine and ours.
> My arms are full now, my evening is quiet and the night peaceful. Lord, measure me to the core,—I am worthy to be called mother.[47]

As the poem winds down, its frenzy increases:

> Quickly life flows, not in meeting, but parting.
> Now how can I help you live, poor ones.
> And what sun on a somber evening
> Can I place in your empty hands?
>
> May God in our blood-filled days,
> Often both now and forever,
> Remember the Sorrowful Son
> And shelter every mother
> Let her not see his ghastly face
> On a rope between two posts,

> The one who turned his stumbling step
> By custom to her the first.
>
> Let her not see another's blood,
> On him whom she bore in her own.
> If, dear God, it must be so,
> Before time call her home.[48]

In an even sadder poem titled "Blood Ore," alluding to ancient pagan charms, Shkapskaya reveals a mother and wife's grief in 1922, saying,

> Oh, a woman's Golgotha!—again give all your robust strength to the child, carry it inside yourself, nourish it with yourself—no rest for you, nor breath.
> Until, dried up, you collapse in the road—those who wish to come devour you from within. Earth's rules are simple and stern; give birth, then die.
>   . . .
> I bloom a woman in the fields of earth—unacknowledged, unvoiced and unseen, and my lot is simple and unenviable (for us, perhaps, there is no other lot): to bloom in the morning, give succulent fruit at midday and droop towards evening—as the dew falls—from the fading and paling heights.
>   . . .
> It is hard for me to cook the dinner,
> Cook the dinner, wash the dishes,
> Put the children to their bed,
> Talk like a human being.
>   I would like to howl at the moon!
>   To embrace a pine in the wood!
>   . . .
> Ah calamity, calamity,
> The blood-ore has boiled in me.
>   . . .
> Ah, my blood—I have nothing to soothe it,
> Ah my strength—I have no way to use it.[49]

In her poem "Lonely Like a Crane" (1923), Shkapskaya laments the loss of a husband during NEP, moaning:

> But in the past at least a place was found for her, and if You chase me out today, I don't even know where I'll go.

. . .

    A woman gets all from her man: if he desires, she will remain forever young like a pine tree sustained by fresh water.
    Ponds shield themselves from the sun with yellow water lilies, but if water leaves the pond, water lilies fall on the bottom, into the sleazy slime.
    The husband is like water, the wife is like a water lily. How can I go on living, if my husband has abandoned me?[50]

e. Anna Akhmatova

Despite the popularity of marriage and the ease of divorce in the early 1920s, poet Anna Akhmatova found marriage as unreliable as Shkapskaya did and described it as jail:

> Obey you? Dearest, you cannot be sane.
> No, nothing but God's will I will obey.
> I hate all trepidation and all pain.
> A husband is a gaoler; home, a gaol.
>
>   (*Anno Domini*, August 1921)

Akhmatova's poem shows that some Russian intellectuals were still critical of marriage in the new Soviet period, and her critique sounds similar to those from the nineteenth century. Writing in 1921, she curses a former lover:

> Ah, you thought I too was the kind
> That's easy to forget,
> And that I would fling myself, pleading and sobbing,
> Under the bay horse's hooves.
>
> Or I would start asking witches
> For a root in charmed water?
> And I would send you a frightful gift—
> My intimate, perfumed kerchief.
>
> Damn you then. With no moan, with no glance
> Will I touch the cursed soul.
> But I swear to you by the angels' garden,
> I swear by the wonder-working icon
> And the fumes of our fiery nights—
> I will never go back to you.[51]

Natan Altman, Anna Akhmatova, *1914*

In contrast to many married, educated women, Anna Akhmatova had a self and began many of her poems with "I." Moreover, she didn't believe men were monogamous more than seven years. She gave as an example Boris Pasternak, who left his first wife though she thought herself irreplaceable.[52] Anna Akhmatova had three husbands—Lev Gumilev, whom she married and divorced prior to the revolution; Vladimir Shileiko, 1918–1924, and Nikolai Punin, with whom she lived during the 1920s and 1930s until he was purged. It was an odd arrangement because Punin's wife and daughter also lived with them in their apartment on the Fontanka embankment. This ménage à trois resulted partly from the shortage in housing and food. Most byvshie liudi, or former gentry-class people like Akhmatova, were impoverished and lacked decent housing. This, as well as love, Punin provided for Anna.[53]

f. Alexandra Kollontai

Fewer arranged marriages in the 1920s did not end criticism of marriage as an institution. In a short story, written in exile in Scandinavia during the mid-1920s, Alexandra Kollontai presented the dilemma of an ambitious, educated woman whose love of a worker threatened her career. Titled "Thirty-Two Pages," the saga reveals how difficult it was to balance the head and heart. Kollontai's character realized that if she continued her love affair with a worker and moved in with him, she would never progress beyond the current thirty-two pages of her research. Yet, her heart wouldn't let her give him up. An unstated part of her dilemma lay in the class difference between them. While the woman was an educated person, the man was "nekulturny," an uncultured worker. He wanted her to be his housewife and homemaker, to cook and clean for him. He couldn't understand that this interfered with her intellectual work, that if she moved in with him, she would not have access to her mentor, lab, and research. At one point he told her that he would be holding her by the bridle, the way a woman should be kept. She was unable to accept the lonely life of a researcher without a lover and passionate sex. It was safer to be silent about her work that he didn't understand. He thought her pretentious; she thought him boorish. Some of the dialogue showed the struggle and distance between them:

> I can no longer stand the fact that you love me not as your friend or comrade, but as your woman ... and you don't grasp the fact that I need to work, to work ... no, I can't go on with you like this.

He asks:

> You can't go on with me like this? Why can't you? ...

She explains:

> Please try to understand; it's been five months since I've touched my work, with only thirty-two pages written.... Why can't you understand that if I don't finish my work, I won't get my degree, and if I don't get it, I might as well say goodbye to all my dreams and to continuing my research?

He counters:

Oh, come now! You say you love me. What kind of love is this? When people love each other they strive to be close together. That's how "unlearned" folk understand the word love. I don't understand your problem.

He doesn't understand her work/love dilemma and ridicules her:

> Yes, of course, why should an "educated person" be bogged down with the cooking.[54]

Still, Kollontai wrote no more essays like the one in 1923 titled "Make Way for Winged Eros: A Letter to Working Youth," describing the joys of tender romantic love, castigating vulgar sex. After her participation in the "Leftist Opposition" of 1921 and her exile as an ambassador to Scandinavia, Kollontai's sexual ideas were limited to her short stories and novellas, and no other party members championed women's sexual liberation or freedom from patriarchal control as she had in the early 1920s.

g. Nadezhda Mandelstam

> In Moscow, before I had time to look around me, he lassoed and bridled me...
>
> Nadezhda Mandelstam, *Hope Abandoned*

Another educated woman Nadezhda Mandelstam described some of the difficulties she encountered in her marriage to poet Osip Mandelstam in the 1920s. The title of her book *Hope Abandoned* is a bit misleading because it's really about finding her "self" and her aim in life after her husband's death in the Gulag in 1938. Initially, she was her husband's shadow, pampering him, pumping him up to write, believing in him when he found it hard to believe in himself. She suffered through his marital infidelities. At times, she tried to set aside time to pursue her painting, but he didn't want her doing that. He demanded her undivided attention and devotion. Nadezhda remembered their married life in Moscow as follows:

> In Moscow, before I had time to look around me, he lassoed and bridled me, and at first I tried to kick over the traces. I was eager to meet people and join in what was left of the carnivals.... Nor would he let me go anywhere by myself, so I never got to know the Moscow salons

Nadezhda Mandelstam, center, Anna Akhmatova, far right, and Osip, between them, 1933, Moscow (St. Petersburg Photo Archive)

in those early days of the new imperial epoch then beginning. People came to invite me out to a basement nightclub ... but M. would not hear of it. "But you used to go to the Dog," I protested, to which he replied: "I'm very sorry," or "Times are different now."[55]

Only in old age could she become a "self", an "I," a writer. So her marriage was not so avant-garde since he wanted her to devote herself entirely to him, quite like many husbands of the nineteenth century. Still, she slowly came to believe that "love is not merely a source of joy or a game, but part of the ceaseless tragedy of life, both its eternal curse and the overwhelming force that gives it meaning."[56]

Women often had different marital expectations and experiences in the 1920s. Nadezhda Mandelstam tells the experience of the cavalier poet Khodasevich and his long-suffering wife:

> Khodasevich was in a cheerful, talkative mood, and very pleased at the prospect of getting away. He told us he was leaving together with Berberova and begged us not to pass this on to anybody, in case it should get back to his wife .... I was amazed he was going away with-

out telling the woman he had lived with during all his years of hardship and called his wife. M. was also a little put out by this, but it was not his habit to think badly of a poet—there must be a good reason, he decided, telling me that Khodasevich was a sick man whom Anna Ivanovna had looked after like a child. Life had been very difficult for them, and according to M., Khodasevich would not have survived without his wife: she went out to hunt for food, chopped the firewood, lit the stove, did the washing and cooking, and bathed her sick husband, never allowing him to do any heavy work.... Though upset that he had left without a word, she showed everybody his new verse sent to her from abroad, never saying anything bad about him and insisting that she loved only him.[57]

Women like Skrjabina and Tchernavin seemed content with traditional devout marriage. Yet, Skrjabina also reported an episode in her uncle's family that showed how common infidelity was. Her uncle—like the poets Gumilev, Mandelstam, and Khodasevich—felt entitled to affairs while married. She noted in her memoirs:

> My uncle ... had apparently hoped that she [Skrjabina's mother] could establish equilibrium in his family relationship. Having recovered from the famine of the last years, he had begun to work at the Aleksandrinsky Theater, looked ten years younger, was courting actresses, and had all sorts of romances. My aunt, terribly jealous, was also counting on Momma's support to tame my light-headed uncle. Perhaps their hopes were realized. During the nine months of our stay in their apartment on Khersonskaya Street there were no special dramas, except for minor flare-ups caused by her constant jealousy."[58]

C. Marriage and Everyday Life

"How can I live, if my husband has abandoned me?"
Maria Shkapskaya, "Lonely like the Crane," 1923

1. Maria Shkapskaya

Indictments of everyday life drip from the pens of poets Maria Shkapskaya (1891–1952), Marina Tsvetaeva (1892–1941), and teacher Tatiana Tchernavin during the Civil War and early 1920s. While some welcomed the new Soviet easy divorce of 1918, Shkapskaya's bitter criticisms of men abandoning women shows the greater emotional investment women made to marriage compared to men. This comes through in her poem "Lonely like the Crane," published in 1923. Although ostensibly writing about the plight of Chinese wives, she could be describing the situation of Soviet women during the Civil War when she mourned:

> From ancient times there survives the custom of driving out a wife, if she grows old and ugly.
> Formerly they at least found a place for her somewhere, but today you drive me away, and I don't know where I'll go.
> I don't know where my family is, because I made a new family with you.
> I'll return to the place where stood my home, and will weep at the gates of strangers.
> . . .
> At fifteen springs I had already decided to marry you. But our hair did not mingle on one pillow for long.
> You went away on a journey, and I stayed home alone.
> All other families are happy, because husband and wife are together.
> But I was always alone, and when I was sad—there was no one to comfort me.
> In my own room, as in a remote forest, I was always sorrowful and lonely, like the crane.
> Sorrow ages a woman, her face loses colour, her eyes their shine.
> But I thought that you too would be sorrowful in parting and waited for your return.
> The covers on my bed were wet with tears. My voice became hoarse from long silence. I didn't paint my cheeks, didn't oil my hair, and my face became as if covered with dust.
> And my thoughts flew over the seas and rivers to the land where you were.
> But the happy years melted like frost: you returned and I was already old.
> You loved me while I was beautiful—old, I bored you.
> I stop my tears, sorrowful as autumn grass I leave my room.
> I was happy in it for a short while, but in it my eyes wept much.
> I take little with me out of your house: only one gown and a flute.
> A little life is left me, but I don't even know where to spend it.
> How could I stay beautiful? For even yellow flowers fall in autumn into the dark pond. For the wind shakes the poplars and divests them of their withered leaves.

A woman depends on her husband: if he wishes, she will stay young forever, like a pine-tree, nourished by fresh water.

Ponds are concealed from the sun by yellow water-lilies, but the water will go from the pond, and the water-lilies sink to the bottom, into the slippery slime.

A husband is like the water, a wife like the water-lily. How can I live, if my husband has abandoned me?[59]

2. Marina Tsvetaeva and Olga Forsh

Like many other women, Marina Tsvetaeva had a hard time providing for her children during the Civil War. When her family was starving, she thought her younger daughter would be better off in an orphanage where she would be fed, but her daughter died there. Bitter, Tsvetaeva left the Soviet Union and went to Paris to live. There she could work and feed her children.

Widow and writer Olga Forsh also captured the pain of the period in writing about the problems of everyday life and mothers of victims in the Red and White armies in her short story "The Suitcase." She tells about a woman's search for her suitcase containing her family's winter clothes, and also portrays the grim lives of ordinary women who happened to have sons fighting on opposite sides during the Civil War. She recounts the story of a village woman who had one son in the White Army and another in the Red Army. She had to check the battle scenes daily for traces of one of her sons as the armies moved back and forth near her town. She laments:

> "They were twins, you know," Marinchika said very quietly. "It came out so wrong! Old folks say God gives twins the same soul, but brother went after brother. When the White Army takes our town, I look for mine among the Red Army dead; when the Reds take us, I search among the Whites. I still haven't gone after the last; they're lying five versts off. You catch a whiff, then there's a wind. They say there's a lot of ones unclaimed, though it's a week it's been quiet. My legs swell like logs, that's my affliction. 'It's your heart,' the doctor says; says I shouldn't walk so many versts. Tomorrow, I'm going. I'll take my shovel and be off, even if I end up burying a stranger. It still helps...." They sat for awhile, silent.[60]

Compared to Marinchika's misery, Maria Ivanovna's lost suitcase seemed insignificant. Yet her problem overwhelmed her. With little firewood to heat apartments during the Civil War, warm clothes were essential. Her winter things were in a suitcase, which she had checked with the railroad when taking the train south. Upon arrival it turned out that someone had stolen her receipt for the suitcase, and she had a terrible time dealing with rude Soviet bureaucrats, who refused to surrender her suitcase without a receipt. She discovered that under the Bolsheviks nothing made sense. There was no logic.

Rejecting her request for her bag without the receipt, the clerk in her story "The Suitcase" contemptuously commented:

> "Ah, you're the one without a receipt? Nothing'll happen without it. They've jammed so many suitcases into the shed there, that a person with a receipt could go goggle-eyed and still not find his own; without a receipt, it's hopeless."[61]

Later the baggage master lets her look in the shed for her suitcase, and she spies it. But before she can take it, he becomes officious, saying:

> "The baggage department storeroom is an official establishment and unauthorized persons are strictly prohibited."[62]

He pushed Maria away, telling her she had to have a receipt or a special stamp. Not knowing what to do, she prayed and vowed to stay in the village until she got her suitcase. Everything she owned was in the suitcase, and she was lost without it. She gasped:

> It was midnight; where could you get a stamp? The train was on its way—miss it, and there's another day in this station, or else a week, or even a month, the way things were . . .
> "And just where's it to be found this time of night?" cried Maria Ivanovana. "Here's two hundred, three hundred for the one who'll buy it tomorrow and stick it on for me. Let me leave on this train."[63]

But the baggage master ignored her and stomped off, scorning the Kerensky notes she offered and muttering that an official stamp was required. About midnight, Maria came upon a businessman who was willing to sell her a stamp to use for the release of her bag. Finally, she was able to sign on the stamp for the release of her luggage and to catch a train to return to the nearby town where relatives awaited her.[64]

Many widows lived in poverty during the Civil War. In 1918–19, artist Zinaida Serebriakova's estate was plundered, her paintings destroyed, her husband arrested, and she was widowed when he died of typhus in prison. In her *Autobiographical Notes* written in the 1970s, Anna Ostroumova Lebedeva noted that Zinaida unwillingly left the countryside for Petrograd, where she and her four children and mother lived in extreme poverty. Anna maintained that Serebriakova's "works were taken by unscrupulous dealers in exchange for food and second-hand clothes."[65] So, everyday life for many women in the intelligentsia was painful and perilous.

3. Tatiana Tchernavin

Writing about the poverty of intellectuals after the October revolution, Tatiana Tchernavin described how disorganized and distressing life became in her memoir *Escape from the Soviets*. Initially she didn't find the Bolshevik government frightening. She had been brought up in a liberal household and believed the end of the Tsarist regime would lead to real political freedom. She thought that because she and her husband were educated, hard-working people, they would be able to earn a living. However, after the birth of their son in 1918, she discovered that they had little money, and she and the baby were always hungry. She writes of this period:

> We had practically no money left: we could just manage to pay the doctor. I was to have been paid for some literary work, but the publisher had to wind up his business suddenly and I never received my fee.
>
> My husband took another job in addition to his work at the University, I returned to my teaching, but prices of food-stuffs were soaring, and our joint monthly salaries were not enough to keep us for a fortnight.... I did not dare confess even to myself how I suffered from hunger, especially after nursing the baby. My head reeled, my back ached, I felt so weak that I could have given anything for some really nourishing food. But in those days we could get nothing except the daily ration of half a pound of black bread ... and potatoes. Meat and fish were an inaccessible luxury. I had never imagined in the old days that food could be such a problem! ...
>
> In those days we often avoided each other. Meals were particularly trying: we were both hungry, and neither could make the other eat....

And the baby screamed and could never wait in patience for his next feed. He was rosy and his eyes were azure-blue, but his stomach was drawn in like that of a borzoi pup, and he cried so much that we had to call in a doctor.[66]

Not knowing their situation, the doctor told them their baby was well but needed more food. He suggested they apply to a government Infant Welfare Center for bottled milk, but said that the milk was bad because there was too much oatmeal water added to it.

> Left alone, we could not look each other in the eyes. What had we done! We had brought a child into the world and now could not feed it. We both worked from morning till night, and yet our child was crying with hunger.
> "I will try to get one more job," my husband said. "They say that at the Agronomical Institute they give the professors a bottle of milk a day.... You see, the Imperial dairy farm at Tsarskoe Selo is theirs now."[67]

Tatiana's husband was able to get this third job, and it improved their food situation, but at the cost of his health. She observed that around the town there were villages with cows and milk to sell, but special police at the railway stations took the milk away from the peasant women who brought it to town to sell because the government wanted to buy the milk for worthless paper money, and the peasants wanted to barter it for goods like clothes, pillows, watches, even pianos. Tatiana had nothing to offer because they had just started their household, so she was unable to get milk from the peasants. A letter from her mother informed her that her mother and sister were badly off too. Tatiana's sister worked from 9 a.m. until 11 p.m., but they still lacked food. She told Tatiana that another professor lectured in five or six university schools, but it wasn't enough to feed their family. Famine increased as did undernourishment. Together they produced weakness and indifference in the population.[68]

Tatiana lost her teaching job and began to work in a museum and do translations, but these earned so little that for translating a long novel of Balzac, she received paper money to buy two pounds of black bread. Moreover, her museum work was unappreciated. Writing a children's story earned her three lumps of sugar. Publishing a book of Italian fairy tales earned Tatiana 56,000 rubles, and she felt wealthy enough to buy extra food.[69]

Tchernavin thought the hard times of the Civil War led Lenin and the party to adopt the New Economic Policy since "War Communism" was not producing enough goods to obtain grain from the peasants and feed people in the cities. While many Communists hated NEP, it worked to encourage the peasants to market their fruits, vegetables, and grain for the urban population. According to Tatiana, "in the course of one year the country recovered to such an extent that bread, vegetables, butter, eggs, meat appeared on the market and ration cards somehow disappeared of themselves. There was enough food to go around." Food remained available until collectivization in 1928, and then it became scarce once more and ration cards were reintroduced. Although wages for intellectual work were low, and Communist supervision detested, life improved during NEP. Still, Tatiana had to put up with dishonest, rude, and suspicious Communist bosses in the museums where she worked. She slowly began to realize that her class was doomed by the disorganization that the Five-Year Plans produced in industry and agriculture because the government was blaming the "experts" like her husband for the failure of the plans.[70]

While these writings show the hard side of women's lives in the 1920s, there was a lighter side. Some young women just wanted to have fun—go dancing, wear pretty clothes, and enjoy life after the hard years of World War I, the revolutions of 1917, and the Civil War. Apparently the tango and the fox-trot were the rage, and some American jazz bands toured the Soviet Union during NEP. Some young women wanted sensuality, not marriage. Some flaunted the bourgeois idea of respectability and touted women's sexual liberation. Some working-class girls and peasants wanted to imitate chic urban dress and shoes. In a chapter on flappers and fox-trotters, Anne Gorsuch includes the following chastuchki, which shows that this culture had also permeated the countryside:

> Don't refuse me money, Papa
> Twenty-five rubles,
> To buy a parasol and leather boots,
> Just like cultured people have.[71]

One of the dark sides of youth culture was prostitution. Some young, unemployed girls, especially orphans, became prostitutes to survive. Gorsuch indicates that since the brothels had been closed by the Bolsheviks, prostitutes, especially young ones, plied their trade on the streets. Apparently they were aggressive on paydays when young male workers had money, and they had none.[72]

D. Conclusion

Mandelstam's account of her marriage recalls Tolstoy's nineteenth-century novel *Anna Karenina* when Anna's brother Stepan invites her to Moscow to smooth things over between him and his wife, after he has had an affair with a servant. Thus it appears some aspects of marriage did not change so much for Soviet women.

Most peasant women continued having traditional weddings and marriages, although they could threaten to leave and divorce their husbands if they abused them too much. Some peasant women may have gained more power in the marriage relationship. Of course many continued as drudges and were abused by their husbands, but at least some found the new Soviet law on their side. Moreover, free divorce allowed women to exit unhappy marriages. Some young textile-factory working women were pretty independent at work, and possibly at home as well.

Sources indicate that there was a great deal of alcoholism among workers as well as abuse of wives and children in the 1920s. Lack of food during the Civil War and lack of employment during NEP meant that many women's everyday lives remained difficult in the 1920s. This ongoing misery shows how marginal the improvement in women's lives was.

In an article "Motherhood in a Cold Climate," Barbara Heldt notes that the new Soviet state simultaneously empowered and devastated women. It was a state not organized by or for women. She observes that Shkapskaya's poetry dealt with the anguish of motherhood, but this became a taboo topic by the end of the decade. Shkapskaya's poem "Mater Dolorosa" lamented women's and mothers' harsh situations on the job and at home. Her poetry defined men as the problem, not the solution. Her criticism of patriarchy was no longer appreciated in the late 1920s. Although initially welcomed by Gorky as a strong poet early in the decade, she was lumped with lyric poets Tsvetaeva, Akhmatova, and Radlova by Trotsky in an unflattering essay in 1925. Along with Radlova's and Akhmatova's, Shkapskaya's poetic voice was effectively silenced.[73]

Chapter Four

Education

> I was at a private school, which after the Revolution was taken over by the state and made co-educational. Oh we loved it. We managed the school ourselves, and we had the boys there. It was such an interesting time.
>
> Irina Tidmarsh

Despite Irina Tidmarsh's enthusiasm for coeducation, the 1917 revolutions and the subsequent Civil War interrupted most children's and young people's schooling. Indeed, fewer youth attended school in 1923 than in 1914. Following the revolutions, life was difficult for people in all classes but especially so for working-class and peasant families, many members of which had to quit school to earn food for their families to survive. Working-class girls typically had only four years of education. Many were kept at home to help raise their siblings. Sometimes even gentry- and middle-class girls had to quit school to work during the hard times of the Civil War.

Certainly their education changed. A decade after the revolution, women had made strides and were constituting about a third of all university students, almost half of worker high-school students, and about 10 percent of technical institute students. Moreover, class dynamics changed, and more women from working and peasant groups were engaged in higher education. Also, more married women—even women with children—were attending institutions of higher education, especially medical school.[1]

While higher education had traditionally been linked to upward mobility, in the 1920s it sometimes proved mentally destabilizing for some.[2] Since the Bolsheviks distrusted gentry-class and bourgeois youth as counterrevolutionary, they attempted to curb such students' access to higher education in the 1920s. The low educational attainment of children from other classes meant that the universities still teemed with middle-class students, and Communists remained a small minority among university students and professors.

A. Irina Tidmarsh

The voices in this education section are primarily those of gentry- and middle-class girls and young women. They had the leisure time to keep diaries and write memoirs. Describing her educational situation in an interview decades later, gentry-class Irina S. Tidmarsh remembered the revolutionary period when she was a teenager as an adventurous time. She described the changes in her education during the period of the Provisional Government, February to October 1917, as exciting:

> We in the upper forms organized the whole curriculum; the school life was in our hands. The teachers only taught. This happened after the first Revolution; the idea was to put everything into the hands of the pupils so that they should organize their own school life. We used to invite all the artists from the theatres in Moscow to give us talks and perform in the school. We organized all kinds of clubs, dancing circles and singing circles. We produced lots of plays. All the private exhibitions opened, and in the same street as our school, which is now called Kropotkin Street, there was the famous Impressionist collection of two Russian merchants. We used to go there for hours from school to look at those masterpieces.[3]

Although they had a good time, Tidmarsh explains that they also had to assume responsibility for getting food to the school, and this took a lot of their time as she remembers:

> We also had to manage to feed the school. We organized different meeting points in different parts of the town where you had to go and fetch the food, and bring it back to all the schools. We used to go with enormous churns to all those communal kitchens to bring back soup. Awful soup it was with herring bones and herring heads. We had our little ration of bread; it was just a tiny bit. So we were very busy. Instead of working at our studies we spent a lot of time doing all that. But it was fun; you know in youth everything is fun. We had big sledges and we used to fetch all the provisions. We really enjoyed ourselves. We went to every imaginable theatre and cinema because we had free tickets to go anywhere. Everything was free—all the private exhibitions. They were wonderful those summer months before the October Revolution. My main recollections of Moscow were that everywhere there were meetings, on every corner someone was talking ... about how we must be faithful to our allies, and that we must continue with the war and wait for the constitu-

tional assembly. We would have a democratic government, but first of all we must finish the war because we've got our allies and we've promised them this and that.[4]

B. Vera Broido

Vera Broido, daughter of Menshevik parents, found the new life, especially school, less exciting than did Irina Tidmarsh. Living with her mother in exile in Siberia, Vera was unused to formal education and preferred reading books on her own. However, as she recalled:

> Meanwhile mother had decided that I could remain ignorant and untutored no longer; I must go to school. This met with passionate opposition from me. I was not ignorant; since we moved into the flat in the Furshtatskaya, I had discovered the shelves full of books in one of the rooms. There was nobody to direct my reading, so I devoured indiscriminately Russian classics and foreign classics in Russian translation.... I was in fact a widely read eleven-year-old. And poets! When I was not writing poetry myself (a fact I did not mention to mother), I was reading it. Lermontov was my hero, and of the moderns, Alexander Blok and Nikolay Gumilev. I could think of nothing more wonderful than to have my nose in a book, even when ... I had to wrap myself in a blanket. Besides, I had always been alone and school scared me out of my wits—but that, too, I did not tell Mother.
> And Mother was adamant. There was, she said, quite near our house, on the famous old street, the Ligovka, a school founded before the revolution by a family of well-known liberal educationalists: that would do nicely. It was a boys' school, but this did not worry Mother; a government decree issued some months earlier had made all schools co-educational. True, people seemed slow to send their daughters to boys' schools, and the one on the Ligovka numbered as yet no girls among its pupils. But this did not worry Mother either; there must always be a first to seize any opportunity offered, so I was taken to the headmaster, inscribed into the junior school and told to report next day. This was the beginning of six months of martyrdom. The boys were outraged at the intrusion of a mere girl and determined to get rid of the intruder by making life hell for her. In class, my thick plaits of hair were nailed to the desk behind me, ink was spilled over my clothes and books, I was pinched and cuffed whenever the teacher's back was turned. Worst of all was the cold dislike and contempt shown me by the boys, from the youngest to the oldest. All of them believed that if they succeeded in driving me out, no more girls would come.[5]

Vera refused to be bullied, and eventually the authorities helped her out by moving half of the boys to a girls' school and putting half of the girls into the boys' school. She recalled that overnight she was no longer a "repulsive toad," a "carrot-headed monster," but suddenly everybody's darling, an old timer. A year later, in 1919, teachers, paper, and books were in such short supply that the school barely functioned, and it stopped completely in the winter. Vera and her friends went to school only to warm up a bit at the stove that the janitor warmed for them and to have a bowl of gruel before dispersing.[6]

C. Nelly Ptashkina

Gentry-class Nelly Ptashkina found life less of an adventure than Irina Tidmarsh did, but she did record her dreams for her future in her diary in 1918. At fifteen, she imagined being a social worker. While she had initially thought she would study the arts, she decided that law was a more appropriate study for a social worker and believed that the path to being a woman lawyer in Russia was open:

> It is my intention—and I think I shall be able to carry it out—to take a share in social and political work. The visions of my future life all centre round it. It seems to me that to bring enlightenment to the masses is very important, and that I shall direct some of my energies in this direction. But only a part.
>   So many things are of interest to me that I want to crowd all I can into my life. I do not know as yet what I shall do. Perhaps, and how wonderful that would be,—I shall write. There is one thing that I can see quite clearly in the time ahead of me, and that is a life full of activity and occupations. [January, 1918]

Several months later she added:

> It seems to me that for social work, in which I have definitely decided to take a part, the most fitting education is the law. Apart from this all the roads are open to the woman-lawyer; in this profession I can be the defender of the feeble and the oppressed, and in the very end perhaps I, too, shall become a barrister....
>   As a voluntary student I can attend lectures in the Faculty of Arts; books on all subjects are at my disposal. At twenty-two or twenty-three I shall finish the University, and then I want to travel.... And af-

ter that, made wise by life, with a reserve of energy, experience and knowledge, I shall return to my mother country, and devote myself to the work of serving others.[7]

In addition to thinking about social work as a career, Nelly also longed to become a writer. Shortly after the Bolshevik revolution and during the end of World War I in January 1918, she wrote about this. While she says little about religion in her diary, she describes writing as sacred and consoling:

> I considered my diary as something sacred, which I wanted to keep safe from prying eyes.
> ... When the day does not bring vivid impressions I sit down to my diary without any wish to do so, or, to be more exact, with the wish which is merely the result of habit.
> It is easier, on the whole, for people to record in writing the thoughts that preoccupy them than to talk about them; a diary does much to relieve a full heart. Mine, I must say, is generally more full of sorrow than of joy ...[8]

Unfortunately, Nelly died in France two years later, and she was never able to fulfill her dreams. However, her parents thought her diary worth publishing. Certainly her diary provides a fascinating entrée into a young girl's life and thoughts in the post-revolutionary period.

D. Elena Gortskina Skrjabina

Another gentry-class girl, Elena Gortskina (later Skrjabina), kept a diary about her life and dreams, but since her brother was arrested early during the Civil War, her mother burned Elena's diary because it contained incriminating items. Her father and one brother were fighting for the White Army, and her reference to that might have caused the arrest of her mother and herself. So we don't have a complete record of Elena's thoughts and dreams about her educational future. At one point in her later memoir *Coming of Age in the Russian Revolution*, she mentions that her mother was preparing her to take exams so she could enter a girl's gymnasia in St. Petersburg. However, the revolutions changed her education. In November and December 1917, when she was in the town of Lukoyanov, where the gentry-class families of her area came together after being forced out of their family estates, she, like Irina Tidmarsh, found some fun in her new life. She describes it thus:

> All the landowners, not only of Lukoyanov but also of the surrounding districts, for some reason chose to gather in this town. Every day we found out that others had arrived, and the population continued to grow. Marina and I liked this, because it was interesting to make new acquaintances. Many had children of our age with whom we quickly became friends. We began to put on children's shows; we even organized dance lessons. Classes were begun on various subjects: mathematics, geography, history, botany, and foreign languages. Uncle taught the more serious subjects, and Mother began to give us French and Russian language lessons. She especially tormented us with grammar, toward which neither of us felt any attraction. Thus all of November and half of December passed without incident.[9]

After the Christmas holidays, Elena enrolled in the local school, but her best friend was not allowed to attend because it involved doing janitorial chores to which her conservative parents objected. Elena recalled that it was not so bad:

> Right after vacation Marina and I were accepted by a school located in the large red building on the main square, opposite the cathedral. But Marina's extremely reactionary parents took her out of school almost immediately. They found that the instruction was not being conducted in the same manner to which they had become accustomed in pre-revolutionary Russia; however, what irritated them most was that the children had to do the janitorial work. Every Saturday we either loaded wood (essential not only for our school but for all municipal organizations) or, if we remained in town, washed all the huge windows and scrubbed the floors of the classrooms and the corridors....
> Despite the fact that I had engaged in a lot of sports, loved to work in the orchard and garden, and rode horseback, the carrying of the very heavy wood and scrubbing the concrete floors often was too much for me. In my class there was a strong, healthy girl Marfushka, from one of the neighboring villages, who was accustomed to all types of household work. Marfushka felt a great sympathy for me and offered the following exchange: she would wash the windows and floors and I would help her with the French that gave her trouble no matter how hard she tried. My salvation was found. Soon Marfushka began to receive good marks instead of her usual D's; I, however, would write various exercises and short compositions on Saturdays that she would pick up the same day, rewrite, and give to our teacher....

Toward spring the preparation of wood and the scrubbing of floors ceased. It was no longer necessary to heat the quarters, and the pupils had done such a poor job of scrubbing and cleaning that the administration decided to hire two healthy scrubwomen entrusted with keeping order in the school building.

... However, for old times sake I continued to help Marfushka with her difficult French so she too did not suffer from the changes that occurred. I had entered into my new role of teacher and would not have wished to turn her down, which later apparently influenced the career I chose.[10]

Changes were taking place in Lukoyanov. Her brother George, a Latin teacher, was arrested but let out of prison because of typhus. Later, he joined the Red Army. Their father and brother Paul left to fight for the White Army. Then, Elena and her mother moved to a new flat. Because of the shortage of fuel, all the lower school classes were closed. Elena remembered:

The girls' school and the boys' high school were joined. I was in the fourth class, so for me there arose the important question of how I would continue my education. Having discussed this with Mother, I said that during the vacation—from the 1st to the 15th of January— I would try to cover the entire year's program and enter into the fifth class.[11]

Elena's mother sacrificed a beautiful turquoise and diamond bracelet to barter for food and to pay three teachers to prepare her daughter for the fifth class. Elena recalled:

I shall probably never forget those lessons. There was no kerosene and all the lamps were out of service; the only thing that served for illumination was little "koptilka," as they were called. They were made by pouring kerosene into a saucer and inserting a wick. This apparatus would be placed right under the nose, and then one could read only with difficulty. January is a dark month, and it was necessary to study from morning until late at night. Nonetheless, we succeeded in overcoming all difficulties; and in the middle of January, to my unbelievable joy, I was accepted into the fifth class. Among the students of the fifth class were many former friends and acquaintances. But mainly I was proud that I had overcome a difficult obstacle and had become one year older.[12]

However, Elena did not get to rejoice for long because her brother George returned from his military service and wanted his mother and sister to come to live in Simbirsk with him. This was right before the end of the semester, and Elena was hoping to go to Nizhny-Novgorod to see the city with her classmates and to visit the theaters and other attractions. Going to Simbirsk meant an end to her schoolgirl dreams. In Simbirsk, Elena began high school, but her studies were interrupted by serious bouts of typhus and measles.

In 1921, the American Relief Administration (ARA) began distributing food to the schools. Food was in such short supply, they had only herring and dried cod, but the ARA provided powdered milk, all kinds of canned goods, and white bread. Her mother had also received a special package from relatives in Holland which the ARA delivered. So now Elena could eat at home and at school. Before her second year in high school, it was announced that her school would be organized into a teacher training institute with evening rather than day classes. This delighted Elena because then she could work in the day and study in the evening. Once again her brother George arrived, asking them to move. In Simbirsk, Elena worked at a variety of jobs, and she doesn't mention finishing her teaching degree. It may have become too difficult for a "former gentry-class person" to attend teacher training classes. Or, her mother may have needed Elena's contribution to the household for them to survive. She never mentions wanting to attend the university.[13]

E. Larisa Reisner

> They lead hard lives in the crowded dormitories . . .
>
> Larisa Reisner, *The Front*

While Elena was able to obtain a modicum of education under difficult circumstances, many working-class students encountered harsher conditions. Writer and Bolshevik Larisa Reisner in her piece "The Front" described Soviet education rather gloomily:

> There are large, grimy, gloomy buildings in Moscow in which thousands of workers', peasants' and soldiers' offspring receive their schooling. They lead hard lives in the crowded dormitories, and the air in the lecture halls is foul and damp, not at all like the air which the old-regime students breathed as they walked down the vast, sunny corridors of St. Petersburg University. These new people, "marching Left," must in the space of several fleeting years absorb the old bourgeois culture

and not only digest it, but smelt its best qualities and elements into the new ideological forms; these are the new people of the Workers' Faculties, tomorrow's judges, the heirs and successors of this decade.

The revolution takes a great toll of the physical energies of its professional cadres.... But a few years from now there will hardly be anyone left from those who stormed the Winter Palace and make up the vanguard that proclaimed the social revolution in October of the great year.... And so the new proletarian culture ... will not be brought about by the soldiers and commanders of the revolution, nor by its defenders and heroes, but by ... very young people who are now sitting in those stuffy, dirty lecture halls, digesting science, selling their last shirt in order to eat, and absorbing Marx and Lenin through every pore in their bodies ...

These tumultuous, uncompromising young people are materialists. They have calmly and courageously tossed out of their lives and outlook all the laws and platitudes, all the sweet dreams and mystical consolations of bourgeois science, aesthetics, art and mysticism. If you say "beauty" to them they will boo as if they were insulted. "Creativity" and "emotions" cause a stampede. And this is only right.

However, while booing and ridiculing bourgeois sentimentality, you young people, you proletarian children, must not ... ever forget the immortal recent years which had just departed in the delirium of typhoid and starvation.[14]

Reisner urged Soviet youth not to forget the sacrifices of the revolution and its true values. Certainly the promise of more widespread education was one of the better kept promises of the revolution.

F. Alexandra Tolstoy

> Salaries were so low and conditions so hard that we had trouble finding teachers for our schools.
>
> Alexandra Tolstoy, *I Worked for the Soviet*

In her memoir, Countess Alexandra Tolstoy, daughter of the writer Leo Tolstoy, wrote quite a bit about how destabilizing government educational policies were. She established a school at the family estate Yasnaya Polyana, near Tula, and encountered many difficulties. For several years after the revolution, wages for teachers were unbelievably low—seven rubles a month. She recalled:

Salaries were so low and conditions so hard that we had trouble finding teachers for our schools. We had no lodgings. A great number of our teachers had to live in peasant huts in the village. For more than a year, we could not find a teacher of physics and chemistry. At last we got a woman from Siberia. Although she had been told that life at Yasnaya Polyana was rough, she never expected to find it so bad. Living too close to the calves, cattle, and sheep, she was miserable, wept during most of the winter, and in the spring returned to Siberia.

The courses of study in the high schools worked out quite spontaneously. The nine year school emphasized agricultural subjects, the seven year school industrial ones.

... Farming was at a low level in our district.... The peasants could not make a living by farming, and had to work in town as cab drivers. Our nine year school set out to teach agriculture to the students and help the peasants in their work....

The industrial school trained locksmiths and carpenters so that they could mend machinery and make furniture in the winter months when outside work was impossible. Yasnaya Polyana is surrounded by forests and much of the timber is excellent for carpentering. We had ambitious plans, but their realization was difficult. The industrial school was closed several times because the government would not give money for keeping it up; and again and again it was transferred from one department to another. We did not want to abandon the school because we felt that it was needed. It was always full of pupils. The parents realized that here they could learn a trade which would enable them to earn a living; and the boys liked the work. In the daytime they studied; in the evening they returned to the workshops and made furniture—tables, chairs, chests, and trunks for their families.

The cow barn that we had made over into workshops was too small. We were flooded with applications for entrance to the industrial school, and there were hundreds of boys that we could not admit. I could not bear the sight of little chaps coming on foot for miles, and begging to be admitted. They would stand watching the boys who had been admitted, and sometimes cry bitterly if we refused to let them in.

The houses in the village were full of students. They came from distant villages, went home each weekend and brought their food back with them. Sometimes they paid a ruble or two a month for this lodging.[15]

To make matters worse, the Commissariat of Education kept changing official teaching methods.[16] Tolstoy remembered:

The sabotage on the part of the intelligentsia that characterized the first years of the Revolution was over. The intellectuals came back to work;

many experienced teachers assisted the Commissariat of Education in trying to bring some system and order into the schools. Many of us believed that we could not only save the old treasures of Russian culture, but could build up new ones, and these hopes filled our lives.[17]

She generally found the government's new educational policy called the "complex method" confusing for teachers and students. She noted:

> A country school teacher with meager education had to abandon the routine he had followed all his life. Instead of teaching reading, writing, and arithmetic to eight-year-olds, he was ordered to discuss with them the aims and purposes of the October Revolution, and the changes that followed. To this discussion, he had to link arithmetic, spelling, and drawing. It was no wonder that he often did not understand what was expected of him. In vain the inspectors drove from one school to another and called conferences and meetings.[18]

One of the school's established teachers complained:

> "I've been teaching children twenty-six years, and they've never made any mistakes in their spelling after the four years of the primary school, and now, with these new methods and tests of theirs, the students who've been through the nine-year school make seventy mistakes on one page!"[19]

By end of the decade, Countess Tolstoy felt beleaguered by changing educational programs and interfering Tula Communists who harassed her school and teachers. Eventually, she found life unbearable and left the Soviet Union in 1929.

G. Conclusion

Soviet higher education was not without cost. Peasant and working-class youth who attended technical schools and universities often found life difficult. Food and clothing were scarce, housing crowded. These physical problems, however, paled in comparison to the mental anguish some students encountered. While education and upward mobility were praiseworthy, they sometimes caused nervous breakdowns among students from working-class and peasant backgrounds. Moreover, the lack of jobs during the high unemployment of NEP meant that education was not necessarily a passport to a good career.

Sergei Luchishkin, A Book Festival, *1927*

Soviet social scientists busily measured youth during the 1920s, studying student diseases such as epilepsy, schizophrenia, mental breakdowns, syphilis of the brain, manic-depressive psychosis, psychological traumas, and intellectual fatigue. They found that many workers and peasants who became students had difficulty exchanging manual for intellectual work. Psychologist E. Troschenko found that the move to the university could easily undermine young proletarians' "fragile psyche." In some cases "nervous fit follows nervous fit, escalating all the while, rapidly developing into a wild form of insanity." Troschenko noted that peasant students were more prone to suicide. They had to acculturate to the city as well as to university life.

This transition could be relentless and cruel.[20] She observed:

> Strain induced by the imperative to cope with a high level of engagement in mental labor, an activity for which they have not been previously trained, creates psychological instability and anxiety and destroys the peasant psyche.... The individualistic nature of mental labor, the solitude of the struggle with the book, the one-on-one encounter with one's memory, can bring a peasant to the brink of despair.[21]

A study of student Communist autobiographies by Igal Halfin shows that education was not necessarily a path to party membership. Peasant A. Dubrovskaia's autobiography indicates that while the party was willing to send her to a worker school, or rabfak, for training in the 1920s, it didn't grant her membership. Although her sister and brother were Komsomol members and her husband a member of the Communist Party, her application was not accepted, despite her antireligious propaganda work among the peasants.[22]

A decade later, tractor driver Pasha Angelina refers to her unsuccessful period of study at an agrarian technical institute in her autobiography. She felt very badly that she could not do well in higher education, whereas she was a first-rate tractor driver.

A decade after the 1917 revolution, Soviet educational statistics indicated that the social origin of students had changed significantly from the late nineteenth century. A questionnaire from students in the medical faculty at the Second Moscow University in 1927–28 showed that students from working-class families made up 25 percent of the total, peasants 35 percent, and employees 40 percent. In terms of nationality, Russians predominated at 73 percent followed by Ukrainians at 3 percent, Belorussians at 2 percent, Jews at 14 percent, and others totaling 8 percent. Continuing the trend during World War I, women outnumbered men 58 percent to 42 percent. The average age of a student was twenty-seven years. Peasant students were the oldest, employees the youngest. About 29 percent were married, 65 percent single, 2 percent widowed, and 4 percent divorced. Of the married students, 45 percent had children: 36 percent had one child, 6 percent two children, and 3 percent three children. Most students with children came from the peasantry. About 67 percent of these medical students were nonparty, 11 percent were party members, and 22 percent belonged to the Komsomol. Interestingly, 85 percent belonged to trade unions.[23]

Chapter Five

Women's Employment

> Beginning in 1929, no one had to worry about jobs any more. The Unemployment Exchange, one of the busiest offices in Moscow during the NEP, closed its doors. On the other hand everybody began to worry about food.
>
> Markoosha Fischer, Russian/American observer

Employment ebbed and flowed in the 1920s. During World War I, female agricultural, factory, and office employment rates remained high because men were away fighting. In 1918 the Bolsheviks introduced an economic policy called War Communism. It functioned well enough for the army to wage war on several fronts. But by commandeering all private businesses and requisitioning grain, industrial and agricultural production plummeted further than they already had under the Provisional Government of 1917. Then during most of the 1920s, unemployment remained high, especially among women.

Peasants hated giving up their grain in return for low prices and few manufactured products during War Communism, so in 1921 the Soviet government abandoned that policy and adopted a New Economic Policy, or NEP. Under this scheme, the government retained control of the banks, railroads, and heavy industry. Grain requisitioning stopped, and peasants began producing and marketing more grain since more consumer goods were available to them in exchange for their grain. Small-scale businesses like textile mills, printers, publishers, bakers, shoemakers, tailors, dressmakers, small shopkeepers, movie theaters, and nightclubs reopened.

Along with NEP came corruption, degradation, drugs, alcoholism, and high unemployment among women and youth. The petty capitalism of the 1920s led to men with money and women without, which increased prostitution, abortion, and abandonment of children—all problems that female party leaders lamented. The Left Opposition, which included Alexandra Kollontai, thought Lenin's NEP policy represented a step backward from socialism. She and others felt betrayed by Lenin and the party majority. Many youth also felt disillusioned by NEP. According to Anne Gorsuch in *Youth in Revolutionary Russia*, the Russian economy did not return to its pre-war level until 1926. By then, unemployment had taken its toll, and many youth had fallen into homelessness, drunkenness, hooliganism, and debauchery. High female unemployment intensified the struggle of widows and single mothers with children.[1]

A. Agriculture

> The last three years I spent there showed me the enormous difficulties in overcoming peasants' ignorance and superstition, and most importantly, their deeply rooted mistrust for the intelligentsia.
>
> Lidiia Seifullina, writer

Much of what we know about Russian peasants comes from the pens of intellectuals like Lidiia Seifullina. With the exception of songs and laments, it's hard to find peasant women's writings about their own lives because most were illiterate. While some industrialization and urbanization took place in the late nineteenth century, Russia remained an agricultural country with 82 percent of the population still on farms in 1926. This meant high employment rates among married rural women, while many young peasant women migrated to the cities to become workers, nannies, or cleaning women. According to the 1926 census, 32 million women and girls over fifteen worked in agriculture—19 million were wives and several million were teenage daughters; 800,000 women farmed alone; 200,000 were employers; 330,000 worked as employees for wages; and 4,000 were unemployed. Fewer than half a million women had joined communes or collective farms according to the census. Most continued in family farming, and the number of individual farms increased by 10 million: from 17 million in 1917 to 27 million in 1927. This meant that women could now be mistresses of their own household and not have to work to please their mother-in-law, sisters-in-law, brothers-in-law, or father-in-law.

While 35 percent of farmers remained poor, this represented a decline from 65 percent in the nineteenth century. By the mid 1920s, about 60 percent of peasant families were middle peasants, up from 20 percent in the nineteenth century. And the number of rich peasants, or kulaks, who hired workers fell from 15 percent in the 1890s

Russian Peasant Women Working, 1918 (Library of Congress)

to 5 percent.² Some peasant poverty resulted from the decline in large extended families and the division of land holdings into smaller ones. Still, most couples preferred nuclear family life to living with parents or in-laws, but the result of this was the division of land into smaller and smaller parcels and much rural poverty.

1. Alexandra Tolstoy

Rural immiseration increased when men were away fighting in World War I and during the Civil War. Famine occurred in many parts of the Soviet Union, especially along the Volga. Some agricultural experiments were tried, but not all were successful. In her memoir of the 1920s, Countess Alexandra Tolstoy observed that the Tolstoyans she invited to come to Yasnaya Polyana to farm turned out to be incompetent and lazy. They were not at all like those earlier described in the New Jerusalem Tolstoy Commune by Yelena Shershenyova. Instead, Tolstoy observed:

The inhabitants of Yasnaya Polyana disliked the Tolstoyans, and hated one Grushkin, especially. He was a dirty, illiterate young fellow with uncombed hair, filthy clothes and great self-assurance. All day long he would strut about the yard, giving advice or orders to his companions, or he would harness my favorite stallion, Osman, and drive off, bringing the handsome horse back in a lather.

"The idea of bringing all those loafers to Yasnaya Polyana!" grumbled the cook, one-eyed Nikolayevna, when I went into the kitchen. "What did we need them for, the do-nothings, the God-forgive-me trash!"[3]

Later Alexandra commented:

The Tolstoyans did not know how to work. They had no discipline or system, they did everything carelessly. When they went to get water, they overturned the barrel. When they hauled manure to the fields, their carts stuck somewhere in the mud or snow. The peasants watched them and shook their heads.[4]

In 1922, the Tolstoyans were replaced with a rural cooperative made up of the workers at the Tolstoy estate and museum. They worked hard and were successful, but in 1924 they willingly gave up their agricultural work to return to classroom teaching, which was now better funded at Yasnaya Polyana. Describing their first successful season, Alexandra wrote:

We were glad to be working, but also, like all the members of the cooperative, we knew that farming was our only salvation from hunger, and we worked with triple energy. Everything went well during the summer of 1922, and one task followed another. From the vegetable garden, we moved into the fields and planted potatoes and beets. We had plenty of milk, the cows were well cared for, and the dairy in good order....

I was so tired after the first morning's work in the rye fields that I could hardly get home. After lunch it was easier, but the next day all my body ached. I could hardly move. On the third day, I worked like the others....

When autumn came and we divided our crops, we found that we had so much that we could even sell some of the vegetables. There was plenty of bread and cereal, too. Everybody was happy.[5]

2. Elena Ponomarenko

Yet, the fact that life expectancy grew in the 1920s indicates that peasants may have been keeping and consuming more of the grain they produced and is testimony to their hard work. One journalist, Elena Ponomarenko, remembered her impoverished childhood when she couldn't go to school because she had no shoes and had nothing to wear. She reminisced:

> When I was seven, after father died, in the summer I started to earn my own bread. I tended other people's cows. All in all, it was awfully hard, but I loved school, I would have walked even further. I wanted so much to learn! Oh! You cannot imagine how much! Well, I finished the fourth grade here (in Siberia), and then we went back to Bogorodichnoe, the village in Ukraine where I was born ... but I didn't like the way people treated me. "Siberian contingent," katsapka that's what they began to call me at school.... This made me terribly indignant. Well, I wanted to get out of there at any price, and I did.[6]

She returned to live and work in Siberia when she was fourteen, and she didn't return to school for many years because one sister and brother-in-law died of typhus and she had to raise her sister's three daughters. Yet, Elena Ponomarenko was luckier than her siblings, who remained illiterate. Commenting on her family's life in the late 1920s, she remarked:

> We really had a hard time, a very hard time. Mama was illiterate, my older brothers set up separate households, they already had large families with nine, eight, seven children apiece, and all of them were illiterate. I was the only one to receive any sort of higher education, out of all seventeen of us.[7]

During the 1920s, the Bolsheviks recruited women, even some rural ones into the party, Komsomol, and the delegatki. Some women were critical of the hooliganism of the male Komsomol members, and some criticized unemployment during NEP and rural poverty. In 1926, one delegatka wrote:

> Here you hang a poster showing a muzhik harnessing himself to pull a capitalist and a priest in a cart and the Godmother is shown to put on a yoke. Shameless people you are! Obscene people you are! You have lost all shame. It is not the Godmother who puts on a yoke, but you,

the Communists, who have put a yoke on us peasants and are strangling us. Why do we need freedom and equality if there is no bread and there is nothing to eat? Yes, indeed, you have already equalized everybody—men and women are all hungry and barefoot. Yes, indeed, you can say there will be good life. But now there are no jobs. Your plants are idle. There are no jobs for our men. They are sitting at home and what results from that is only a bunch of kids. There is nothing to eat. This is what you've led us to.[8]

3. *Praskovya Pichugina*

A biography of Praskovya Pichugina, who was born in a village in Ryazan Gubernia (province) and married during the Civil War, shows how patriarchal and cruel village life continued to be. Her life reveals how awful a father-in-law's tyranny was. After her husband went to fight for the Red Army, Praskovya returned to live in the village with her children and her father-in-law. He was a very mean alcoholic. The women in the house had no shoes, and he forced them to walk barefoot in the winter, refusing to even let them wear his son's felt boots. He also vented his anger on Praskovya and her two children. When the youngsters were sick, he forbade them even to cough. Despite his abuse, Praskovya was beloved by the village for helping the peasant women. In return, they elected her to the village Soviet. Only in 1929 did her husband, who was working in a city and building a house for them, send for her and their children to come live there and escape their rural poverty.[9]

Indeed, superstition, ignorance, low levels of education, and patriarchal family life bedeviled peasant women throughout the 1920s. Sociologists who studied the peasants of the village of Viriatino found that many families forbade their daughters to attend school. Some villagers opposed the antireligious education of the Bolsheviks and prevented their children from going to school. Moreover, education during the period of War Communism (1918–1921) was difficult because schools lacked teachers, books, paper, pens, and heat for the classrooms.[10]

However, many observers saw an improvement in the lives of peasants in the 1920s. Visiting his home village in 1929, the naturalized American citizen and journalist Maurice Hindus reported that children no longer wore the homemade bast sandals called lapti but had factory-made shoes, and on Sundays and holidays young girls wore factory-made clothes instead of the former homespun.[11]

Other improvements also occurred. Peasant women's life expectancy rose from thirty-three years in 1897 to forty-seven in 1926. Infant mortality declined from 133 per one thousand babies to 79. Despite these improvements, farm life remained arduous. Most peasant women worked fifteen hours per day in the summer: eight hours in agricultural labor cutting grass, raking and staking hay, tending the family vegetable plot, and caring for cows, pigs, chickens, and other animals. They worked seven hours in the household, cooking, cleaning, minding the children, and making bread. While the term "household chores" may imply easy work, making bread took incredible strength. One batch of bread took sixteen kilos (or thirty-five pounds) of flour. Kneading this huge dough took considerable strength. Usually, the matriarch, or Bolshukha, controlled the bread making. In the winter, women worked four hours per day at farm labor and nine hours at home. They did weaving, sewing, embroidering, and knitting as well as other household chores. Women also participated in handicraft production to earn money for their family. In the summer, they helped in crop production and tended the vegetable garden. In addition, they produced and sold meat, poultry, eggs, vegetables, and berries at local markets. Sometimes, they rented out their dwellings to city folk to use during the summer, while they slept in the barn or even outside.[12]

The millions of widowed and the thousands of divorced rural women had an especially difficult time surviving unless they had family members to help them with the heavy plowing—they usually helped harvest crops but seldom plowed the land to plant them. The 1926 census shows some 4 million peasant women as heads of household, out of a total of 32 million, presumably without a husband. This was a significant number. Some of these women may have welcomed collectivization because they could then participate in agricultural life when the fields were plowed by collective teams.

Families who worked hard and flourished began to be dispossessed in 1928 in the dekulakization campaign. One observer saw this occur and noted:

> Once in a torrential rain, I stopped at a hut where the local peasant committee was dispossessing the owner, a kulak, and his family. The

Anti-kulak poster, 1920s

committee members were poor peasants of the neighborhood whose only complaint against the Soviet government was that they had not been permitted to lay hands on the kulak earlier. They searched every corner of the attic and cellar, and emptied the closets and trunks. They packed everything into bundles: bedding, clothing, saucepans, and toys. They disregarded the wailing of the women and children and the threats of the men. All the kulak's agricultural implements were loaded on carts. But the worst came when the farm animals had to be caught. The desperate sobbing and hysterical screaming of the family, the shouting of the committee men, the howling, barking, cackling, squealing of animals, all this under a terrific downpour, turned the place into utter confusion.[13]

Of course the enmity between the poor and wealthy peasants had existed for a long time. Kulaks had often mercilessly squeezed the poorer peasants. They were hated and called "bloodsucker" and "cutthroat" in Russian literature and folklore. As Markoosha Fischer saw it:

> In releasing popular feeling against the kulak, the Soviet government set free a long-repressed popular desire for cruel vengeance.

The authorities felt that the power of the kulak had to be eliminated in order to pave the way for village collectivization. But there must have been other ways of destroying the economic power of the kulak, whom the government permitted to become powerful during the years of NEP, without bringing misery and dire poverty to countless women and children.[14]

B. Manufacturing

> I liked my work right away. Factory life brings people together, and soon I became friends with the weavers who had helped me when I first started.
>
> Anna Balashova, textile worker

The urban population grew from 12 percent in 1897 to 18 percent in 1926 but produced only a slight increase in the number of women in manufacturing. Whereas domestic service employed roughly 1 million nonagriculatural women in the late nineteenth century, it was factories that utilized more than a million workers in the 1920s. Of course, the 1926 census may have undercounted domestic workers, so the difference between the two occupations may have been more nominal than real.

1. Marietta Shaginian

The lives and work of factory women workers did not change so much in the 1920s. They suffered from wage discrimination, earning only 67 percent of men's wages. Because their job roles clustered in unskilled categories, it was legal to pay them less than men. Writer Marietta Shaginian's investigations of workers in the 1920s revealed low wages of working women and discrepancies between the harsh lives of married women and better standard of living among single women.

She reported that workers with families lived in crowded conditions—as the "Family of Workers at Tea" photograph indicates—had no newspaper, no cinema, no cigarettes, and no amusements. They often lived on tea, bread, meatless soup, and porridge. She observed working women supporting other family members—mothers, children, and others. One lived so shabbily that she shared a room with ten other people, having one blanket for four people. The house was damp and dirty. Moreover, the toxic conditions in some factories led to the declining health of workers and increased incidences of miscarriages.

Yet, she found that a single woman earned forty-three rubles per month, had enough to eat, could afford to go to the bath-house once a fortnight, to the theater once a month, to the cinema to lose herself in fantasy five times a month, and ate soup and macaroni for dinner, and bread and tea for lunch. After researching the situation of workers, Shaginian was so overwhelmed by the findings that she was unable to write it up. Instead, as a privileged Soviet writer, she fled south to the Caucasus to recuperate.[15]

Although women working in tobacco and rubber factories often suffered from toxic poisons, the new government did lower their workday to seven hours and tried to improve ventilation and sanitation in the workplace. Because more than a third of female factory workers were married, most also had domestic responsibilities,

S. Magaziner, Family of Workers at Tea, 1924, Leningrad
(St. Petersburg Photo Archive)

including shopping, cooking, doing the family laundry by hand, child care, and coping with family life in extremely crowded housing—usually one room. Often apartments had more than eight people per room, only 35 percent had running water, and just 11 percent central heating.[16] Working women who raised their families in such conditions were commendable. However, they had little time for trade union participation or Communist Party work.

2. Marguerite Harrison

The difficulties working women faced are reflected in the memoir of Marguerite Harrison, an American reporter living in Moscow in 1921. She found, for example, that acquiring a saucepan could take an entire week. First, she had to obtain an order entitling her to purchase a saucepan. This order was countersigned by three officials in the Food Administration, the process taking an entire day. The second day, she exchanged the order for one permitting her to survey various kinds of saucepans on display in a government store. Then she had to get another coupon entitling her to purchase it at the government cooperative in the district where she lived. Then she had to find out which day saucepans were sold. The morning of that day, she was obliged to stand in line until the shop opened in order to make sure they would not be sold out before her turn. The entire process occupied a large part of a week, but the saucepan was good and cheap—3 rubles at the co-op compared to 2,500 rubles in the market.[17] The trade-off for working-class women was time versus money. This bureaucratic process was one reason some workers engaged domestics—to shop and stand in line for them.

Despite life's hardships, working-class women's literacy and participation rates in political organizations increased during the 1920s. Women workers in textiles, clothing construction, and other fields joined trade unions. It cost half a day's pay to join, and 2 percent of a worker's pay for membership dues. Because housing, childcare, and holiday accommodations were distributed through the trade unions, women were probably glad to join, even if they did not have much time to participate. Women accounted for the majority of textile workers, but by 1929 they accounted for only 6 percent of top textile union officials, 7 percent of union delegates, and

12 percent of paid union organizers.[18] Their participation rate in the Communist Party remained low but was higher among female representatives elected to the city Soviets. Of course, European and American women workers also had low participation rates in politics and unions at this time.

3. Ekaterina Strogova

Some remarkable vignettes about women textile workers are recorded in the writings of Ekaterina Strogova, who may have been a party worker in the 1920s. In a story called "The Baroness and Her Maid," she shows the vindictiveness of a villager who had become a factory worker after the revolution. A maid named Klavdiya had worked for a cruel mistress in St. Petersburg prior to the revolution. The Baroness had herself been a kitchen maid, but after marrying a baron she had experienced upward social mobility. After the revolution, he left Russia, and she became penniless, reluctantly returning home to her village. She then took a job at a factory, where her former maid Klavdiya tried to prevent her from being hired. The factory committee allowed the baroness to work, but when she tried to enroll in the party in 1924, Klavdia tore up her application saying:

> "Comrades, what is going on here? We are defiling Ilich! [Lenin's patronymic] Our enemy is sneaking into the party.... So a Baroness from the enemy class is trying to sully our vanguard?" And grabbing the Baroness's application from the table, Klashka tore it to bits.[19]

Strogova's story "A Day in Trimmings" reveals both negative and positive features of women workers—some are gossips, complainers, and whiners. Yet, they engaged in good-natured teasing of pregnant coworkers and were generous in sharing food with destitute new employees. Some even offered housing to a new worker. Strogova concluded, "Our womenfolk begrudge their comrades nothing, they share everything one and all."[20]

In her sketch "The Foreman and the Forewoman," Strogova described young factory girls' love of finery and ways they decked themselves out for a party. This story also shows how workers made the lives of their supervisors miserable. The altruistic Dusia Boikova—who had established a reading hut in the village, brought in books,

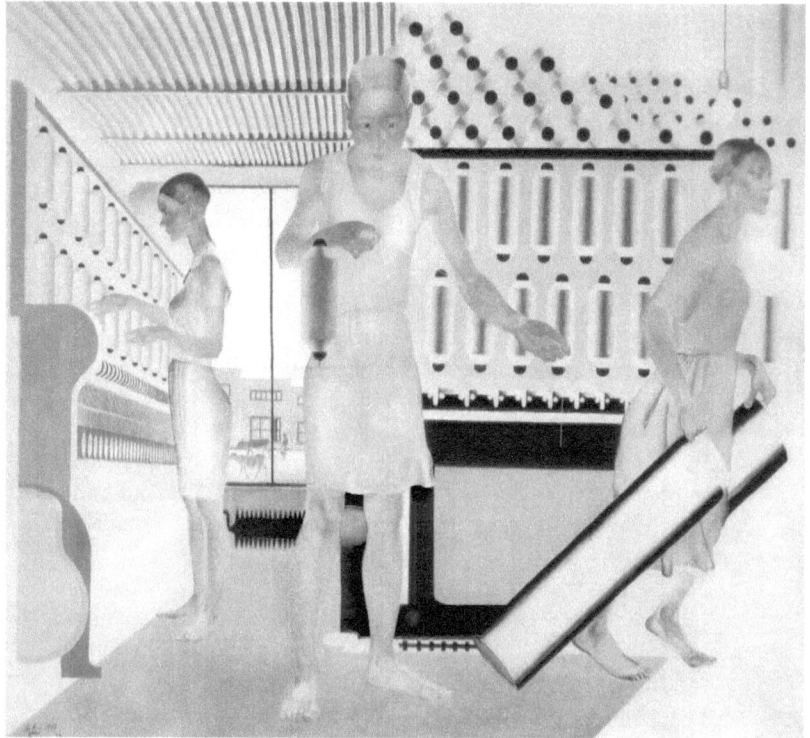

A. Alexander Deineka, Textile Worker, 1927

and started clubs—was undone by the very women workers who initially loved her. Dusia fell out of favor with the winders, who did everything possible to make trouble: they disobeyed her instructions, purposely didn't turn off the electricity after the evening shift, "forgot" to turn off the motor, and played other nasty tricks.[21]

Strogova praised workers who engaged in political affairs. She lauded woman factory committee chair Olga Kozlova and all those serving as shop delegates or members of party and Komsomol organizations. In the factory, women often made up half of the political positions, while the men dragged their feet in doing volunteer work. Strogova described one organizer with the following words:

> Olga is so good at wounding women's soft hearts with her words that at her discussions and reports the womenfolk weep copiously, they are prepared to follow Olga to the ends of the earth.[22]

4. Anna Balashova

Anna Balashova's biography reveals a woman much like Strogova's heroine. Balashova's story was chosen for publication by a Commission of the Institute of Party History at the Communist Academy (1932) partly because she was a dedicated and devoted worker at the Trekhgorka Textile Factory. She liked working and organizing the other weavers into more efficient groups. She did not perceive increased work as exploitation, and she led other workers to participate in competitive "shock work" in the late 1920s. While not all workers were happy to increase the work tempo, Balashova won many prizes for her industrial feats. At one point she says:

> At first I only had one machine, of course, but within three months I already had two, as a relief weaver. I worked very well, and after one year (very quickly for those days) I was assigned two machines of my own....
>
> I never missed work and always tried hard, so the foreman's assistants and even the foreman himself treated me well. Soon I was asked to become the collector of union fees. I enjoyed it and did it willingly and carefully.
>
> I felt that I was more developed and better educated than most of the weavers so I considered it my duty to share my knowledge with them and to explain to them the actions of the Soviet government. Soon I became known as the "Communist."
>
> Shortly afterward I was elected a shop union representative, and then in 1926, a union activist. I was sent to the factory's night school of the trade union movement. At first I was placed in the beginning group because I was unfamiliar with union work, but later I was transferred to the advanced group. I liked the school. I came to understand the structure not only of the union organizations but of the party organizations as well.... I felt I was growing politically....
>
> While I was still nursing (my baby), my volunteer work had to be limited to the shop. It was at that time that socialist competitions and shock work came along.... We shop Communists were the first to challenge one another to a socialist competition. The nonparty weavers followed suit. At first the workers did not take it seriously. But when results began to be posted regularly and prizes awarded to the best workers, they began competing in earnest, everyone trying to achieve the best results possible.[23]

Anna ends by saying that she received prizes, and the unit where she worked was always the best. Of course, stories of working women who resisted the speed-up in production were not published, or they were criticized as laggards. According to Soviet questionnaires, some working-class girls, like their European counterparts, did not want to work in factories. They preferred the cleaner work of shop assistants and clerical personnel. While they wanted upward mobility, not so many joined the Komsomol. Like their European counterparts, they preferred romantic escapist films to the politically didactic, and they loved dancing the fox-trot. Their love of "flapper culture" created anxiety among their parents, just as youth in Europe and the United States did.[24]

C. Service Personnel

The 1897 and 1926 censuses used different terms for employment. Many jobs in 1926 were categorized as low-, middle-, and high-level service. Low-level personnel included about 1 million domestic servants, laundresses, office cleaners, bath attendants, janitors, guards, messengers, couriers, and hospital orderlies. Mid-level workers totaled slightly less than a million and included women typists, stenographers, shop assistants, bank clerks, conductors, tram drivers, police women, a few hundred in the military, and those in general commerce, service, and transport. There were 400,000 high-ranking personnel composed of teachers (190,000), doctors (20,000), lawyers (450), engineers (1,400), paid political workers (4,000), dentists (5,000), pharmacists (12,800), midwives (27,000), and others.[25]

1. Domestic Servants

> Their situation is very hard, one of the hardest, of which their personal dependence is an extremely unpleasant feature. There is much in this that should be altered. First it should not be despotism on one side and bondage on the other, but a free contract made by both, with the mutual respect for each other's rights and liberties.
>
> Nelly Ptashkina, Muscovite teenager, 1918

Domestics made up the largest category of low-level service workers. It seems strange to us that servants even existed after the proletarian revolution of 1917. However, standing in line to shop took

158 CHAPTER FIVE: WOMEN'S EMPLOYMENT

Avram Arkhpov, Laundresses, *1920s*

an enormous amount of time, and factory workers as well as career women hired maids to do this job for them. Living conditions were harsh and food was in short supply for several years after the revolution. Queuing for long hours to provide food for their family was part of most workers' existence.

Russian Women at the Market, 1918 (Library of Congress)

a. Nelly Ptashkina

A thoughtful analysis of the situation of servants appears in the diary of a Moscow teenager after the Bolshevik revolution. A confirmed socialist, she believes that maids should be treated better. Writing in the summer of 1918, Nelly Ptashkina notes:

> I should like to discuss the social status of servants.
>
> People of a lower rank should be treated with still greater consideration than one's equals: the latter, without danger to their material independence, can answer back, whereas the inferiors must remain silent. This is one of the rules of my life, by which I direct myself even now.
>
> ... For the moment we must strive for the nearest possible approach to this ideal, that is try to improve the conditions of the servants, both physically and morally.
>
> When I think about their work, I feel appalled at the idea of its hardness. How many thousands of people are waiting for betterment. Isn't it the highest duty of man to help them?
>
> I shall devote all my efforts to this. There is so much to do that it becomes a daily and necessary task.[26]

None of the other women's accounts of servants during this period is as compassionate and empathetic as Nelly's. The economy almost ground to a halt in the last days of the Provisional Government in the summer of 1917, and it slid further into chaos during War Communism when workers were put in charge of factories, businesses were taken over by the government, and grain was requisitioned from the peasants. During this time, rationing meant families often had only bread. For other commodities, one had to stand in long, time-consuming lines at cooperatives, or trade at local markets where farmers brought goods to barter or sell at more expensive prices than the government stores.

Often, people had to make trips to the countryside to obtain food directly from farmers. Since few manufactured goods were available, the peasants often refused to take paper money because they could buy nothing with it. People bartered whatever personal goods they had for food. All of this was time consuming, and those who could hired servants to do it for them. Of course, not all house workers were a blessing. Some gentry-class families found supporting disgruntled domestics a burden.[27] The new Soviet government also stipulated that employers pay into an insurance fund for their servants, so the 450,000 house workers listed in the census may have been undercounted for this reason too.

Grain requisitioning and the devastation from two wars—World War I and the Civil War—undermined agricultural production. Famine was rampant along the Volga in 1921. After World War I, Herbert Hoover and the American Relief Administration (ARA) sent aid not only to Poland and Eastern Europe but also to the Soviet Union, especially along the Volga River. At one point the ARA was feeding more than 10 million people in the Soviet Union, including 5 million school children.

b. Elena Skrjabina

Living in Simbirsk at this time, Elena Skrjabina fondly remembered the ARA mission and cherished her relatives in Holland for sending packages via this relief organization. Recalling this event years later, she wrote:

> The Americans had organized help for the starving in the Volga area ... those who had relatives abroad began to receive packages through the American mission, both of foodstuffs and of other items. We received packages from Holland. One of my mother's sisters had been married to the czarist Russian ambassador to Holland and had lived

in the Hague. My uncle had long since died, but the Dutch authorities allowed the family to live in that very house where the ambassador's office had formerly been. Our relatives had also searched out Mother through the Swiss Red Cross and, having received our address, had paid some money in Holland so that we could receive a quantity of food. Having received a summons to the ARA, Mother sent me there alone, supposing that there would be one small package I could easily bring home. The American distributing the food and products questioned me through an interpreter and inquired about our material circumstances. He then supplied me with such a quantity of things that I could not have carried even half of them with me. I requested permission to leave all the things there for the time being and ran to the center of town, where there were always some beggars. I hired two beggars, promising them part of what I received.

An array of good things was in the packages prepared by the wonderful Americans: sugar, fat, coffee, flour, condensed milk, and what especially delighted me, two lengths of material for coats (for my mother and me), and material for dresses. I returned home in triumph, having generously rewarded my two companions with products they had not seen in a long time.

Simultaneously with the help to the needy population of Simbirsk, the Americans began to supply the schools. Now, instead of our dinners of herring and dried cod, there appeared powdered milk in cans, all conceivable types of canned goods, and white bread.[28]

Russian Women at the Feet of American Relief Worker, 1920s (Library of Congress)

c. Alexandra Tolstoy

Countess Tolstoy also had good things to say about the ARA. It gave a useful job to her brother Ilia. It also provided medical supplies and a set of instruments to the dispensary recently established at Yasnaya Polyana, which was near Tula.[29] As the 1920s photograph shows, Russian women were so grateful for the food they received that they bowed to the ground at the feet of the ARA official.

The miserable situation in urban areas led to depopulation of the cities and yet also an in-migration of young women from farms to the cities. These youthful migrants made up most of the servants in the 1920s. This pattern resembled that of the late nineteenth century when most domestics also traveled long distances to work in urban households.

Unfortunately, many other negative aspects of this work also continued. Many families lived in just one room, so maids still lacked beds and slept on the floor in the communal kitchen because that was the only available space. Wages remained low, sometimes as low as twenty-five rubles per month.[30] This meant that a widowed charwoman with three children lived very poorly. And yet young peasant girls continued this employment as a way of adjusting to city life. Positive changes occurred, as there were more literacy classes available in the cities than the countryside, and many young girls learned to read and write. Half of domestic servants were literate in 1926. This represented a change from their illiterate cohorts of the nineteenth century. Since there was a high demand for these workers, there was also a high turnover, and girls could leave an abusive master or mistress to look for better working conditions. Some even became factory workers and earned higher wages, had two days off a week, and enjoyed higher social status.

While some domestic servants enjoyed upward mobility, some like their nineteenth-century counterparts experienced downward mobility into prostitution. Soviet sociologist Wolfson found that 43 percent of prostitutes in Moscow in the 1920s had peasant backgrounds and worked as servants.[31] While prostitution declined, almost disappearing during the Civil War, the New Economic Policy created men with means and women without, thereby producing high levels of prostitution and contributing to alcoholism and drug abuse. To deal with this problem, the Commissariat of Health established

Prophylactoria, or halfway houses and treatment centers, for prostitutes. Moscow had eight prophylactoria in 1927, and each one housed about two hundred residents who stayed from six to eighteen months for medical treatment, job training, and rehabilitation. Venereologist V. M. Bronner estimated that these centers provided care for half the known prostitutes. So aid was available, but there was not enough.[32] With the beginning of the Five-Year Plans for industrialization in 1929, prostitution declined. As Russian-American Markoosha Fischer innocently observed:

> The Women's Prophylactic Institute, whose task it was to return prostitutes to normal lives by teaching them trades, now discontinued its work for lack of new inmates. There were plenty of jobs, and no woman had to recur to prostitution for a living....[33]

The only problem was that jobs were not always available in the cities where the prostitutes lived, and unemployment remained but without pay for jobless women.

2. Mid-Level Service Personnel

Among young mid-level service personnel, unemployment increased during NEP. Moreover, a wide discrepancy existed between married and single women. Married women had to use their wages to provide food and clothing for their families, whereas young female clerks earned enough to smoke, buy nice things, and go dancing. Indeed, puritanical Bolsheviks deplored young women's penchant for "free love," cosmetics, silk stockings, jazz, the fox-trot, romantic movies, and "flapper culture." They also lamented women's penchant to starve themselves in order to spend their wages on frivolities.[34]

a. Elena Skrjabina

A good account of a married, mid-level worker is found in Elena Skrjabina's memoir *Coming of Age in the Russian Revolution*. Born shortly after the turn of the century into a high-ranking, gentry-class family, she seems an unlikely source of information for this work. A pampered yet well-educated and strong girl when the revolutions of 1917 occurred, she was able to deal with the changes in life that the new order brought, whereas her mother was more set in her ways. At times, her mother referred to Elena as "Sovietized."[35] Having one brother in the Red Army and another brother and her father in the pro-Tsarist White Army, she must have felt some ambivalence. Yet she was able to come to terms with life, live in the present, and make the best of it.

Because she and her mother were homeless after their estate was taken over by peasants in November 1917, they initially survived through the help of friends and the sale of her mother's jewels. Eventually, her mother obtained a job as a typist and later as a seamstress. Elena attended school during the difficult days following the revolution, and she took a daytime job in Simbirsk when her school switched to evening classes. At the Simbirsk Practical Institute in 1923, Elena studied fifteen subjects: linguistics; Soviet government; political economy; pedagogy; educational psychology; Western European culture; history of culture; Greek, Roman, and Russian history; Russian literature; Latin language; chemistry; and physics. Her certificate from the People's Commissariat of Enlightenment shows grades of satisfactory and highly satisfactory, but not outstanding as her record book showed in the late 1930s when she studied French at the Pedagogical University in Leningrad.[36]

In one of her first clerical jobs, Elena worked as a low-paid file clerk in the district finance office. One day the head of the finance office noticed her and inquired the name of her father. When she told him, she was worried that as a gentry-class "former person" she might lose her job. Instead, she received a promotion because her father many years previously had befriended this man by giving him a cow as part of a dowry so he could marry. Thus began a series of intercessions on her behalf. After her promotion, she was earning good money, had boyfriends, and even acted in the local theater. She remembered, "Life seemed happy to me, and the Soviet regime no bother at all."[37]

A fire in their apartment entailed a move to Nizhni-Novgorod, where her brother George was living. There Elena met Comrade Burov, who came to her aid several times. He helped her and her mother find housing and furniture and provided her with a typewriter so she could learn to type—thereby getting a better job. High unemployment in the 1920s meant that when Elena got a job as a typist, she was often the first one fired as layoffs occurred. Unemployment pay was too little to live on, and she had to repeatedly seek Burov's help in getting new positions.

Elena Skrjabina as a young woman (Iowa Women's Archives)

In 1924, Elena married a friend of one of her brothers, and in 1925 she was attending shorthand classes. Her neighbor in the class was the wife of Lazar Kaganovich, who at that time was the director of the Nizhnygorod Trade Commission. Elena and Mrs. Kaganovich became good friends and helped each other. Elena was invited to participate in a bazaar and entrusted with one of the kiosks. Flattered at being invited, Elena feared that her kiosk would earn less than the others. Therefore she invited all her friends to attend. As she remembered it:

> My sister-in-law, my husband's sister, made a charming outfit for me with white silk with gold oranges woven in it. When I took my place in the prettily decorated kiosk, I began to look over all the other saleswomen; and my heart sank, for I felt that I was out of my element and that the wives of such highly placed people undoubtedly would have much greater success than I.

Then she remembered the old Russian proverb, "Don't have a hundred rubles but a hundred friends." That night she found it absolutely true when her friends supported her in her kiosk:

CHAPTER FIVE: WOMEN'S EMPLOYMENT

Nizhni Novgorod, 1902 *(Library of Congress)*

All those young men I used to date before my marriage, colleagues from work, fellow students, and finally Burov himself, kept filling my kiosk without stop, choosing one thing or another. Soon I forgot completely about the existence of the other kiosks and lost interest in where and how the trade was going. I saw that my cash intake was growing and was happy that my friends were supportive and were not allowing me to disgrace myself.[38]

Shortly after the kiosk episode, Elena became pregnant, but she continued working. In January, she had gotten a job at the Fish

Kombinat, but she also continued her courses in stenography in the evenings. It all fatigued and irritated Elena. Her mother and her husband, who worked as an accountant, begged her to quit her job. But Elena knew that her income was essential for the family to function. In the 1920s, both husband and wife usually had to work in order for a family to survive.

Before her marriage, Elena had worked at the Nighzni Novgorod fair because she needed money for her dowry, and she made good money there. A year after her wedding, they moved to Leningrad at the request of her uncle. His two children had moved out of their rooms in his apartment, and he preferred having family members to new people in the rooms.

In Leningrad, she and her husband had two rooms but shared a common kitchen and bath with fourteen others. This shows how crowded housing was—not only for workers but for mid-level people too. Since Elena was pregnant, she received compensation from her relatively high-paying job at the Nizhni fair, and they were able to live on this for four months. Her husband was advised to take courses as a bookkeeper, which he did. While training, he met a former colleague from Nizhni who offered him a job as an accountant at the textile factory where he was the director. Despite his position, the family needed income from Elena's work, so she studied shorthand and eventually got a job at a company on the outskirts of the city.

It wasn't the sort of place that Elena wanted, but she knew if she refused it, she might not get another job. So for the next four years she worked at this factory as a secretary. She had to rise at 5:00 a.m. to take a bus and trolley to get to work by 8:00 a.m. She had no alarm clock, could not buy one, and found it hard to get up in the dark in the winter when the sun didn't rise until 10:00 a.m. Fearful of being late to work and losing her job, she slept fitfully. Her job also imposed burdens on her mother, who had to come each day to care for her grandson and do the shopping and cooking. Although Elena had grown up with servants, she was unable to afford one during the 1920s. The stress of work and household life made this an unhappy period, and she found these some of the hardest years of her life.[39]

Nor was work easy. The head of the factory, Polyakov, was a bully and sexual predator. He shouted at the employees all day, even slapped some of them around, and conducted orgies with many of the young women. Elena lived in fear of him. Then one day she received a summons from the NKVD (Soviet secret police) to appear at one of their offices in Leningrad. She knew this was not how they arrested people, but still she was terrified by the time an NKVD officer interrogated her. It turned out they wanted her testimony about Polyakov's behavior before removing him. She hadn't initially realized that others had already denounced him, and she was only one witness among many. This unnerving experience illustrates one way politics intruded into ordinary people's lives.[40]

b. Helen Dmitriew

While life was difficult for most working women in the middle levels, the daughters of some village officials had a good life. Helen Dmitriew recalled in her diary that her family lived very well during the 1920s because her father worked for a cooperative and was able to keep his family well supplied. She noted: "The majority of the population, however, experienced great shortages during these years. World War I, the Revolution, the Civil War, and the Bolsheviks' rise to power all contributed to the ruin of our country's economy and doomed our people to terrible poverty."[41]

A woman librarian in Taganrog complained of extreme poverty even among the educated. She was so destitute she could hardly keep from prostituting herself to earn money for food. In her letter of lament to a party official, she cries:

> I have been in the party since 1919. Now I am exhausted. I have no strength any more; it is all gone after five years of hardship. I have no place to live. Is selling your body the only way to survive? At every corner you are confronted by your own colleague, a man, who asked you to come by in the evening. If you go, you are finished. Some of them say: "You are poor and hungry—why don't you find a man who would provide for you?" In response you would just start crying and go away, and he would say: "Who do you think would worry about you for nothing?" I don't know what to do. There is no food and there is no hot water for two months already. Should I beg? Should I go to the mines? Barefoot? And I am not the only one in such a situation. Please help women workers. Please save us from prostitution. Save us from selling our bodies for a piece of bread.
> With Communist Greetings.[42]

3. High-Level Service Personnel

> At the beginning of the 1917–1918 academic year I entered Petersburg University. The university still looked as it had in the old days. The lectures of its famous old professors were now open to the public. I remember the lecture halls and the professors in their black frock coats reading from the rostrum. A new freedom was born in the Revolution. People from cultivated circles came to listen to anyone they chose.[43]
>
> Olga Freidenberg, scholar

In the 1920s, high-level service personnel often earned lower wages than factory workers and had the highest rate of unemployment among service workers. With the advent of NEP, local Soviets could no longer pay teachers' and doctors' salaries, and a hundred thousand high-ranking employees were unemployed in 1926. Teachers earned 678 rubles per year, medical personnel 200 to 400 rubles, but factory workers 843. Provincial doctors worked under trying circumstances, having inadequate drugs, consultation rooms, and transportation. Although doctors could engage in private practice, taxes were heavy and fees difficult to collect, so most worked in state clinics. Married women teachers and doctors often had a servant to shop and tend their children while they worked.

a. Teachers

> I liked teaching at the Rabfak. In my second year I had six groups of thirty pupils. I was engaged every evening till half-past eleven; sometimes I felt utterly exhausted, but I could not forsake them—they were just as overworked as I was. It was delightful to watch their progress and see how clumsy lads who could scarcely put two words together ... learned to use their brains, to express their thoughts clearly and understand complex historical situations.
>
> Tatiana Tchernavin, history teacher

According to Soviet statistics analyzed by Jiri Zuzanek in *Work and Leisure in the Soviet Union, A Time Budget Analysis*, women teachers spent about 25 hours per week teaching, 9 to 13 hours in preparation, 5 to 7 hours in administrative work, and several hours in unpaid required social-political work. Men spent the same time teaching and preparing but more time in administrative work and at second jobs. Women teachers spent 10 more hours per week than men in unpaid household work and additional time in childcare. Men spent more time in sociopolitical work than women teachers did, but they both spent similar amounts of time in professional training, meetings, travel, and reading. Still, Soviet married career women did not encounter as many difficulties as their European cohorts. Fifty-five percent of female Soviet educational and cultural personnel were married, widowed, or divorced, contrasted with only 42 percent of French career women, 15 percent of English, and 5 percent of German in the 1920s. Russian women doctors and teachers belonged to unions but constituted only 1.5 percent of paid union positions.

Unemployed women totaled eight thousand in medicine, thirteen thousand in education, and two thousand in cultural positions. In Leningrad alone, the 1926 census reported forty-two thousand unemployed women: fourteen thousand in factory work and twenty-eight thousand in various service occupations. Young women in the city were particularly hard hit with 16 percent of those 15–19 years of age unemployed; 17 percent of those 20–24; 13 percent for those 25–29; and 12 percent for those 30–39. This happened partly because during NEP the central government withdrew its support from many schools and clinics, and local Soviets refused or were unable to tax themselves to pay qualified personnel. Unemployment may also have resulted from the reluctance of Soviet institutions to hire gentry and middle-class women who had been educated during the old regime. It also resulted in part from the unwillingness of career women to leave the major cities to live in provincial places where jobs may have existed but where wretched housing, working conditions, and wages prevailed. Unemployment and the increase in divorce, which provided alimony for children but not wives, may also have contributed to the high proportion of gentry-class and bourgeois prostitutes reported by Soviet and American sociologists and doctors in the 1920s.[44]

Teachers encountered a variety of problems during the 1920s. At most levels, they were poorly paid and lacked supplies—books, paper, pens, and technical equipment. Schools suffered from inadequate dormitories for rural residential high school students who traveled from villages without high schools to nearby towns and cities to study. Depopulation of the cities in the post-war period led to pressures in the provinces and countryside. Lack of food, fuel, and electricity from

1918 to 1921 meant teaching at any level in Petrograd or Moscow was extremely difficult.

b. Teachers in Art Academies

> Our groups opposed contemporary bourgeois society. The Futurist poets thundered out against the bourgeoisie in their poetry while we painters demolished it in our paintings.
>
> Nadezhda Udaltsova

(1) Nadezhda Udaltsova

Some artists, like Nadezhda Udaltsova, embraced the revolution and worked for it. She had resented the bourgeois press calling women in the avant-garde "hooligans" and "boors." In her 1915 essay "How the Critics and Public Relate to Contemporary Russian Art," Udaltsova asked:

> One feels like crying out: How long is this going to last for? How much longer is artistic innovation going to encounter only ridicule, mistrust, insults? In science the law of evolution is acknowledged, so why should art be doomed to stand still and go on with the same old truths?[45]

After the revolution, Udaltsova enthusiastically supported the new regime. In her memoirs, she writes:

> My colleagues and I gladly accepted the October Revolution and, from the very beginning, we went to work for the Soviets and then for the People's Commissariat for Enlightenment. I played a vital role in the reorganization of the art institutes and, beginning in 1918, worked in various departments and studios.[46]

In 1920 Udaltsova became a professor and senior lecturer in the Higher Artistic and Technical Studios organized as Vkhutemas. She remained on the staff until 1934. She also taught painting courses at the Textile Institute and then the Institute of Printing in Moscow. A longtime friend and colleague of Lyubov Popova, Udaltsova did not abandon easel painting as Popova and others did in the 1920s. From 1926 to 1934, she and her husband traveled in the Urals. Her painting became more like that of the impressionists—more from nature and less abstract.[47]

(2) Anna Ostroumova Lebedeva

After the revolution, artist Anna Ostroumova Lebedeva also taught at a Soviet art academy but had to do so in her winter coat because of the cold. Without heat, the oil paint froze, and instruction was very difficult. She taught only a few years because her philosophy of teaching remained rather traditional. She was not a part of the avant-garde as Popova and Udaltsova were. Materials for sculptors, filmmakers, and oil painters were in short supply. Sculptors had to make their art from plaster or low-grade cement; hence few works from this period survived. The best-paid artists in the early 1920s were the poster artists. Their art was easily understood and provided useful propaganda for the state. Relatively few professors or students in the art institutes in Petrograd belonged to the party or Komsomol.[48]

Many teachers encountered political and ideological conflicts. Most teachers had been trained in the Tsarist period and were considered "byvshie liudi," or "former people" — the "old" intelligentsia. They were suspected of not really supporting the new Soviet state and its policies but were necessary for educational institutions to function. One noble girl, Kyra Karadja, a high school student, remembered the denunciation of librarians and teachers by Komsomol members in her school in the 1920s:

> Grigori Alibekoff banged his fist against the table on which he was perched. "Comrades, I see we're unanimously agreed. We shall not allow ourselves to be poisoned by rotten reactionary ideas, whoever the scribblers of those books might be. Down with the accursed bourgeois notion of culture — we fight for the rights of the proletariat." . . .
>
> Alibekoff's despotism was growing rapidly, especially since he had formed a Comsomol cell in school whose power seemed to be unlimited. He terrorized both his fellow pupils and the teachers by the mere threat of reporting them as "undesirable counter-revolutionary elements." . . .
>
> Their mother had recently been threatened with dismissal from teaching on the grounds of undesirable social origin. Others already had been purged.[49]

(3) Aleksandra Exter

By 1921 the Bolsheviks had established new policies in higher education. In art institutes, easel painting was replaced with industrial art.

SERVICE PERSONNEL   173

Some professors like Nadezhda Udaltsova resigned their positions in protest against such changes. Aleksandra Exter participated in agitational art to spread the word of the revolution in 1918, and in the Moscow Art Academy from 1921 to 1924. She was an abstract artist and colleague of Popova, moving from easel painting to design, particularly theater design. She teamed with Alexander Tairov's Chamber Theater to create innovative costumes and sets in the early 1920s. However, she emigrated to Paris after Lenin's death, when changes in Soviet art and social policy occurred. Minister of Culture Anatoly Lunacharsky's tolerant cultural policy ended, as Osip Brik's 1924 speech indicates:

> Only those artists who once and for all have broken with easel craft, who have recognized productional work in practice, not only as an equal form of artistic labor, but also as the only one possible—only such artists can grapple successfully and productively with the solution to the problems of contemporary artistic culture.[50]

In Paris, Exter became a professor at the Academie der Moderne, and then from 1926 to 1930 she taught at Fernand Leger's Academie d'Art Contemporain. Soviet art also became more prudish in the 1920s. While Zinaida Serebriakova depicted nude bathing women and some erotic peasant women prior to World War I, her works *Ballet Dressing Room* in 1922 and *Ballet Dancers* in 1923–24 were partly clothed. Not many nudes appeared in Soviet art after Lenin's death in 1924. Male artists also depicted many more nudes in their pre-war paintings than they did in the 1920s.[51]

c. Teachers in Public Schools

Another issue for schools, teachers, and students was the introduction of new teaching philosophies and systems without adequate preparation. Nadezhda Krupskaia, Lenin's wife, was the Commissar of Education in the 1920s, and she was a devotee of the American educators Horace Mann and John Dewey. She tried to introduce some of their innovative, experiential educational ideas. However, as Alexandra Tolstoy's memoirs about teaching at Yasnaya Polyana indicated, the "old" intelligentsia was not always "in tune" with the new ideas and methods. Moreover, the government lacked money to retrain elementary and secondary teachers in the new ways.

With the abolition of grades and student participation in teacher councils, students sometimes showed a lack of respect toward their instructors. Empowered by revolutionary rhetoric, students sometimes decided on the curriculum and then required teachers to teach it. Students often failed to take "group work" seriously, making their teachers' lives more difficult. Some students studied episodically because they lacked food, clothes, or shoes, and they had to work in order for their families to survive.

Educators found this a trying period. A teacher in both the Tsarist and Soviet periods, Tatiana Tchernavin observed many changes in the new educational system. She had no sympathy for the Soviet system in which history was haphazardly taught and teachers' wages were lower than those of unskilled workers. It proved impossible to live on a teacher's salary. So, in 1918 she left her high-school teaching job to work in the Hermitage Museum.

(1) Tatiana Tchernavin

In 1923, Tchernavin agreed to teach at a rabfak, or school for workers, where she taught in the evenings after her museum work. These students were older and generally more serious. She felt that she would be educating uncultured peasants and workers who were going to become the leaders of the new society, and she found this worthwhile. Moreover, the government treated the rabfak schools better than others—spending more money on them and selecting the best teachers, since they were especially intended for working people. However, only some of the students obtained government grants. Others had to work an eight-hour day in a factory and then study for four hours in the evening. Many found it too tiring, and about half of the students dropped out.[52] Commenting on this teaching, Tchernavin remarked:

> One also had to teach them to behave more or less decently, and above all not to pick quarrels with one another and be rough with the girls.
> The girls were our misfortune. They were not many, only one or two in every group; they were usually more backward than the men and, what was worse, introduced disorder by their very presence, even if they were plain and not inclined to flirt. The young men were not used to any restraint; the Soviet Government zealously fostered in them contempt for "bourgeois morality," they had not as yet acquired any moral standards of their own, and every day there was some "painful incident," especially with the first-year students.

They "grabbed" at the girls and made crude jokes more reminiscent of the farmyard than suggestive of any conscious depravity. The girls squealed with excitement and were quite ready in their turn to pinch, or lean against a man in a "comradely" way.[53]

Tchernavin remarks on some of the sexual difficulties among the youth. The boys were rough on the girls, badgering them until they yielded sexually. Then the trouble of having abortions arose. Trouble erupted when a really beautiful girl came to class. This happened when a student named Dunia arrived. She was unlike the others who wore short hair and skirts. Instead, she wore a plait and simple frocks, threadbare, but clean and ironed; the boys found her a distraction. She knew how to write and helped the others.[54] Commenting on her other students, Tchernavin noted:

> Besides, all had to work extra hard for the half-yearly examinations. An order had been suddenly issued that these were to be in writing instead of oral as usual—and writing was the weak spot of Rabfak students. Many of them had a fair command of language, since most of them were used to speaking at meetings, but practically all found writing difficult. It was the case even with the most aristocratic of our

Housing Collective Members Studying in the Red Corner, 1927–28, Leningrad (St. Petersburg Photo Archive)

176   CHAPTER FIVE: WOMEN'S EMPLOYMENT

Students Studying, Leningrad (St. Petersburg Photo Archive)

pupils—the judge, a former political instructor in the Red Army, a Red director of a tramcar station and a co-operative store manager, though they were all quick and business-like men.

"I am used to my secretary writing for me," the judge said with a sigh.

"Writing is sheer waste of time," the political instructor grumbled, "the chief thing is to be politically sound and to have ideas— and I have plenty."[55]

The above picture of the members of the Leningrad housing collective may have resembled Tchernavin's rabfak students, except there are more women in the picture than there were in her classes. To her dismay, she discovered that only twenty of the thirty students in her history class finished, and then only five places in the university were available. She also found that the few female students who participated in the rabfak courses tended to disrupt the male students' concentration.

An interview with a former rabfak student confirms Tchernavin's observations. Sofia Pavlova, a political activist, remembered her rabfak training sponsored by the regional Tomsk Komsomol as follows:

At the end of 1922 the Komsomol raikom sent me and my friend Roma Kvopinskaia to Tomsk to study at the *rabochii fakultet*, the rabfak. We set off for Tomsk and enrolled. I don't remember whether we took an entrance exam or not. Most likely there weren't any exams; they simply accepted us. They made sure we could read and write, but of course we were literate because the elementary school provided a very good education.

At the rabfak there were very few girls, in general. Mainly there were returnees from the civil war, young men who were already quite grown up, and for some reason there were Germans. The guys really courted us. They really went after me, for example.... The student body was largely composed of returnees from the civil war. From the Red Army. Because everyone had either a Mauser or a revolver.[56]

The picture *Students Studying* shows students both studying and participating in recreational activities at their housing collectives. One of the wall slogans in the photograph reads, "One who doesn't rest, can't work."

(2) Lidiia Seifullina

While city students frustrated Tchernavin, other teachers were disappointed with rural pupils. Writer Lidiia Seifullina began her career as a teacher and librarian in Omsk in 1906. During the years 1912 to 1917, she taught in Siberian and Mordvinian villages. She taught peasant children and adults, and she organized reading rooms and wrote letters for illiterate villagers during World War I. Working in rural areas, she joined the Socialist Revolutionary Party and was a member from 1917 to 1919.[57] However, she found her work among peasants disenchanting, describing it as follows:

> I began my work among peasants as a schoolteacher in the most remote regions of the Orenburg province ... These three years opened my eyes to my own ignorance and demonstrated to me the poverty of ideas which I brought to the countryside.... I left the village with deep dissatisfaction and a depressing understanding of how microscopic my contribution was, especially when compared with the energy and hopes I had invested in it. But, besides this bitter feeling, I left the village with a significant plus: better knowledge about peasant folk and my experience in their environment.[58]

Forsaking teaching, Seifullina became a writer and dramatist in the early 1920s, graphically describing the lives of peasant women and orphans. Her popular novel and play "Virineia" was based on a woman custodian at her school. It portrayed a simple, ordinary, yet vibrant woman who became an active supporter of the Bolshevik cause. Virineia possessed great energy and was able to defend herself against unwelcome lovers. She was stubborn and self-willed yet feminine. In the words of one Soviet critic, Virineia was a drunk and good for nothing but sober-minded and prudent when it was necessary. She was a mother, lover, sister, friend, comrade, worker. Most importantly, she did not have a trace of peasant passivity.[59] Seifullina's intimate knowledge of village life and her authentic use of folk language contributed to the novel's success. After it was published as a novel, it was made into a play and was even performed in Prague and Paris in the late 1920s. Seifullina remained a popular writer throughout the 1920s but was unable to glorify collectivization or the Five-Year Plans during the 1930s.[60]

(3) Alexandra Tolstoy

Alexandra Tolstoy not only headed the museum at Yasnaya Polyana but all the other institutions there as well. She opened a school and appealed to the Commissariat for Enlightenment for money for buildings, textbooks, and school equipment. She recorded one interview with the minister as follows:

> Once an official in the Commissariat of Education asked me what my position in the Yasnaia Poliana schools was.
> "Why, I don't know," I answered. "I am curator of Yasnaia Poliana."
> "Yes, you are under the Museum Department as curator of the museum; but you are organizing schools, and you have to deal with the Department of Education in your school work."
> It was true, although I had never thought about it.
> "Do you get wages?"
> "No."
> "How do you live?"
> "I sell honey."
> The official laughed. He might not have laughed if he had known how hard it was to carry those heavy linden casks on my shoulders every time I went to Moscow. Selling honey was my only income. The Bolsheviks had nationalized all the Tolstoy property except the bees.
> "All right. We will appoint you the director of the Yasnaia Poliana school and give you wages." So it was arranged that I was to be paid

forty-two rubles and fifty kopeks a month. In the autumn of 1923, the Jewish American organization, "Agrojoint," through their representative Mr. Rosen, gave us ten thousand rubles, and with this we put up a building that was used for the first four classes of the high school.[61]

d. *University Professors*

My enemies are already teaching the younger generation to hate my book. They roam the university and speak infamies ... The cards have been reshuffled in such a way that I have envious opponents among those who share my ideas, and sincere well wishers among scholars of the traditional school. How painful and difficult it all is! Much more difficult than the defense, which went easily for me ...

Olga Freidenberg, scholar, 1920s

While elementary and secondary school teachers faced many problems in their work, university professors were also not immune to stress. After the revolution, the Bolsheviks organized a special university in Moscow for party members called the Institute of Red Professors (IKP). It was staffed with reliable "Red" or Marxist professors. Young people like Anna Pankratova trained at the IKP in the field of labor history. Pankratova was of working-class origins and a devoted revolutionary, so it was easy for her to change her undergraduate worldview that was influenced by "bourgeois" professors and ideas to a Marxist interpretation in line with new Soviet ideology. As a committed revolutionary, she was happy to study labor history, but it was difficult for her when she was sent to Leningrad to "shape up" famous "bourgeois" historians at the Institute of History. This was a ticklish business for a young woman. Criticizing respected historians was not an easy job, especially for a recent university graduate.

In 1927 Pankratova's life became even more complicated when she became a single mother. Her husband, Gregorii Iakovin, a fellow historian from the Institute of Red Professors, was denounced as a Trotskyite, and he was exiled and imprisoned in Tashkent. Although she loved him, she broke with him to keep her job and support their child. This was not an isolated case since the Institute of Red Professors suffered first a purge of Leftists (supporters of Trotsky) in the mid-1920s and then later a purge of Rightists (supporters of Rykov and Bukharin) during 1927–28.[62]

Some young people like Natalia Sats were so devoted to the new regime that they eschewed higher education to develop new programs. Sats organized a children's theater in Moscow and spent the rest of her life, except for the time she spent in prison in the mid-1930s, working for it. Only in prison did she have time to read and educate herself in the manner she might have had she gone to university. In detention, she organized shows among the prisoners and used her talents well. Evgenia Ginzburg, like others, first studied social sciences at Kazan State University but switched her studies to pedagogy. Ginzburg also taught at a rabfak. In the 1930s, she became a specialist in party history, but her party loyalty did not save her from the purges of the intelligentsia in the mid-1930s. (Being purged in the 1920s sometimes meant exile, but during the 1930s it usually included imprisonment, life in the Gulag, or death.)

(1) Olga Freidenberg

> By graduation, I ceased to be a student and lost my "social status," without which people were not allowed to exist under Socialism. In order to legalize my unemployment, I had to be registered at the labor exchange.
>
> Olga Freidenberg, 1920s

After being registered a year and a half at the labor exchange, Olga finally received pay for her work as an academic assistant. Her pay was twenty-four rubles per month, about half that of a woman factory worker. Olga's situation shows that the intellectual life of a philologist, considered esoteric by the Bolsheviks, remained precarious in the first decade of Soviet rule. However, some integrity was possible until the very end of the decade when even the Academy of Science came under party control. Olga's autobiography, diary, and letters to her cousin—the famous writer Boris Pasternak—reveal the struggles a strong woman had in remaining true to her own values and creativity.[63]

Olga had been unable to study at the private Bestuzhev Courses for Women prior to the revolution because she was a Jew, so she was delighted to be able to study at St. Petersburg University after the revolution. In 1919 she began studying in the Classics Department with Professor Zhebelev. Her euphoria did not last long because of the food shortages in St. Petersburg. Soon she became ill because her family, along with most other urban dwellers, lacked adequate food and fuel. Some professors died of starvation. Some were arrested. Slowly, the university ceased functioning during the Civil War. By 1921 the beautiful city of St. Petersburg had become deserted, with empty streets, grass and wildflowers springing up in the cracks of the sidewalks. Yet in the midst of such destitution, the university offered Olga a research grant of one thousand rubles to travel to Moscow to study the Latin manuscripts of St. Thecla, a disciple of St. Paul. However, she was too ill to go to Moscow to take advantage of the grant. Her research suggested that the stories of the saints in the apocrypha, like Thecla, were based on the form of the Greek erotic novel, each with their persecutions, holiness, feats, martyrdoms, heroic deeds, journeys, and so forth.[64]

After graduating with distinction from the Philology Department, Olga was too proud to ask for help in getting a position. She refused her cousin Boris Pasternak's advice to go to Moscow and seek an audience with Anatoly Lunacharsky, the Minister of Culture, or to get a letter of recommendation from her mentor Professor Marr. She wanted Boris to arrange it all, but he couldn't do it unless she came first to Moscow, which she refused to do. She told Boris that in the first place, she would never regard her professors as a source of influence, would never bring pressure to bear on a scholar's kindly attitude toward her so as to turn it into cold cash.... She also told him that she had enemies at the university: "My tragedy also lies in my being as timid as a lamb despite the revolutionary trend of my scholarly thinking."[65]

Lacking an academic position, Olga decided to study for another dissertation and learned Sanskrit and Hebrew. In a return letter, Boris told Olga that she was morbidly proud. She would get nowhere if a mere trip to Moscow was such an insuperable barrier. Dejected, Olga wrote to Boris that she didn't even want to have her work published. "Who needs it? What for? ... My book is premature. No one will understand it." Initially, her works were read by various critics and reviewers, and submitted to the Academy of Red Professors for publication. But the Marxists decided her work was anathema, and refused to publish it.[66]

Reading the Communist scholar Deborin, Olga realized that her book *Procris* was an example of dialectical materialism in application.

Eventually, the Communist Academy reversed itself and decided to publish Olga's work, but its press was closed in 1930 before it could do so. In the process of trying to get her work published, Olga encountered academic politics at Leningrad University as well as in the party. She was threatened with being discharged for launching *Procris* at the Japhetic Institute of Philology instead of at Leningrad University.

Olga's scathing indictment of uneducated party members, who headed the Communist Academy and wielded power over trained intellectuals like herself, is quite astute:

> I made Aptekar's acquaintance in Moscow. He was a portly, outgoing, rather familiar fellow, in a leather coat of the sort only "those at the top" wear. He advanced with a rolling gait as if in defiance of all obstacles. Gaily and self-confidently he acknowledged his lack of education. Uncouth young men like Aptekar come to the city from the country or from small towns, master party slogans, newspaper jargon, the bare bones of Marxism, and assume the role of bosses and dictators. With untroubled consciences they teach scholars what to think and are sincerely convinced that knowledge itself is not essential to the formulation of a proper scheme of knowledge [methodology].[67]

Despite her disdain, Aptekar became her patron and shepherded her work through the academy. In 1929 Olga was able to publish two articles: "Three Plots" and "The Plot Semantics of the Odyssey." A few years later, she was offered her first teaching appointment. Heretofore, she had been only a researcher. A university administrator named Gorlovsky asked Olga to organize the new Leningrad Institute of Philosophy, Language, Literature, and History. The very next year he was arrested on trumped-up charges.[68]

(2) Anna Bek

Because physician Anna Zhukova Bek was a Marxist, her academic life initially went more smoothly than Freidenberg's, but she too faced problems as a professor in the 1920s. Bek was not a party member, and ignorant party hacks challenged her teaching. Although a medical doctor, Anna Bek had worked two decades teaching adults and children. Having read psychologists like William James, Ivan Pavlov, and Vladimir Bekhterev as well as educational theorists like Maria Montessori, she worked out her own educational psychology, which she called "pedology." She employed an experimental approach using quantitative data from tests and experiments to explain child development and behavior. She sought an interdisciplinary approach that analyzed physical and psychological changes to discuss development in children during puberty.[69] Despite her qualifications, she met hostility when she began teaching at Irkutsk University in 1923. She explains in her memoirs:

> At Irkutsk University I initially experienced hostility from the students. The staff was being purged of ideologically unsuitable teachers at that time, and because of the purge the head of the Department of Psychology, Professor Rubinshtein, had just been fired. He was renowned as an outstanding lecturer and enjoyed great authority among the students, especially among one group of women students who were called ironically the "myrrh-bearing women." . . .
> After Rubinshtein left I was assigned the upper-class course on defectology [deviations from the norm], directly connected with psychology. I, a woman of modest appearance, arriving from the district, was to replace a famous Moscow professor. This led to the students' hostility toward me. Some of the students, especially the male, reactionary ones, were obstructive: they gave me trick questions, found fault with particular words, and kept me from carrying on with the lecture. Coming from my work with the Chita teachers and having thought deeply about Marxist and psychological literature, I felt the ground firm beneath my feet. After having given a number of introductory lectures and having acquainted the students with the methodology of objective observation, I proposed that each student take one child under observation from the Bekhterev Home, where children who deviated from the norm were housed. Checking and organizing the material they collected, I built a theoretical course on it.... Students gradually became interested in the experimental method as the course proceeded.[70]

Having won over her students, she then faced changes in the party line. As she recalls in *The Life of a Russian Woman Doctor*:

> The students responded to my lectures with interest, but the Marxism department and the dean of the *pedfak* sounded the alarm. At that time Academician Pavlov was in conflict with Soviet power, he was debarred from teaching, and his teachings were not recognized. I was warned, but I was deeply convinced of the tremendous significance of reflexology to the materialistic worldview and continued to inform students of the facts of reflexology.

The psychology department challenged me to a debate. The day and hour of the debate were widely posted throughout the university. The student body was interested, and probably the audience would have been enormous, but for some reason the designated time for the debate was changed, and then, without much notice, assigned to a small auditorium in the Medical Institute. When I came to the debate, the auditorium was overflowing, people were even standing in the corridor in front of the doors. The presidium was made up exclusively of opponents of reflexology. I was worried, although I had prepared myself a great deal for the debate. I had collected many excerpts from Marx, Engels, and Lenin, guessing in advance what the possible charges would be. During the debate I answered every accusation with citations from the classics.

... At the conclusion of the debate the chairman of the presidium, Professor Odintsov, expressed the view that reflexology is a young science but that the future belongs to it. I took this as my victory. In my lectures I included information on reflexology as before. Later, I became convinced that my superiors' distrust of the direction of my work had not fully disappeared. Nevertheless, in 1925 I received notification from Moscow that I was promoted to senior lecturer in psychology and was sent for scientific research to Moscow and Leningrad.[71]

Unlike Olga Freidenberg, Anna Bek was able to publish most of her research in the 1920s and early 1930s, although she suffered some harassment. She tried to defend her husband's research, but some charlatans made her work in the medical field difficult. While her work became popular in Irkutsk and Novosibirsk, where she had been invited to give lectures, the clouds again gathered against her. She was accused of deviating from Marxism by linking reflexology with psychology. Her assistant Alya Krinskaya expressed deep interest in Bek's work, but ended up betraying Bek for her own careerist goals. Describing this treachery, Bek writes:

> She was in her last year when I began to teach in the *pedfak*. At that time there was a purge of students. As the daughter of a priest she was threatened with expulsion, but with her good looks she succeeded in captivating a Communist who was on the purge committee. She married him, openly saying to her friends that she was marrying without love. As a successful graduate of the *pedfak* and the wife of a Communist she got a job as assistant in the Pedology department when she graduated. Failing to investigate her past carefully, I trusted her fully and believed in her sincere enthusiasm for my direction in child development. But shrewder people later told me about her careerism

and hypocrisy. She had an interest in my departure, wanting to take my place herself.[72]

Bek was willing to leave Irkutsk for Novosibirsk because her daughter, son-in-law, and grandchildren had earlier gone there and she was happy to join her family. Bek also realized some students in the Komsomol would be glad to see her leave because of her strictness. Lazy students tried to get by in group work where the best students did all the work, but Bek insisted on grading students separately. She recalled:

> I knew that in the Komsomol cell there were those who were unhappy about my strict attitude concerning exams. In those days it was accepted for students to take exams as a group. If there were some knowledgeable individuals in the group, then even those who said nothing also received a good grade. I demanded knowledge from each member of the group. That was not popular. Someone speaking about my strictness characterized it with these words: "On the way to her exam, even members of the Komsomol cross themselves."[73]

Bek was proud of her legacy at Irkutsk and noted that her replacement in the psychology department began to introduce reflexology into his course and to make reference to her work. Leaving Irkutsk for Novosibirsk was not so difficult.

e. Writers

> One reads with dismay most of the poetic collections, especially those of the women. Here, indeed, one cannot take a step without God. The lyric circle of Akhmatova, Tsvetaeva, Radlova, and other real and near-poetesses, is very small.
>
> Leon Trotsky, *Literature and Revolution*, 1924

(1) Maria Shkapskaya

Life was not easy for women writers after the Bolshevik revolution. While the February revolution ushered in freedom from Tsarist censorship, women's poetic voices were muted after Lenin's death, as male culture in the Bolshevik regime asserted itself. Maria Shkapskaya described herself as a lyric poet in a time when "sterner notes" were needed. According to literary critic Barbara Heldt, Shkapskaya wrote female-centered monologues and authoritative mother voices critical of patriarchal society, two things unappreciated by the middle of the decade. Although initially welcomed early in the decade by Maxim Gorky as a strong poet, by the mid-1920s she was attacked along with other lyric poets Akhmatova, Tsvetaeva, and Radlova by Leon Trotsky in his book *Literature and Revolution*.[74] In one passage, he complains about the women's discussions of God:

> ... inevitably God, without any special marks. He is a very convenient and portable third person, quite domestic, a friend of the family who fulfills from time to time the duties of a doctor of female ailments. How this individual no longer young, and burdened with the personal and too often bothersome errands of Akhmatova, Tsvetaeva and others, can manage in his spare time to direct the destinies of the universe, is simply incomprehensible. For Shkapskaya, who is so organic, so biologic, so gynecologic (Shkapshaya's talent is real), God is something in the nature of a go-between and a midwife; that is, he has the attributes of an all-powerful scandal-monger. And if a subjective note may be permitted here, we willingly concede that if this feminine wide-hipped God is not very imposing, he is far more sympathetic than the incubated chick of mystic philosophy beyond the stars.[75]

Later, in the same work, Trotsky again castigates "poetesses" for being out of touch with the needs of new men:

> If Christ alone or Sabaoth himself bends over the poet's embraces (as in the case of Akhmatova, Tsvetaeva, Shkapskaya and others), then this only goes to prove how much behind the time his lyrics are and how socially and aesthetically inadequate they are for the new man.[76]

Maria Shkapskaya found that while her poetry had been praised and appreciated for speaking of woman's significance in the early 1920s, by 1925 a resolution of the Central Committee of the Communist Party was putting the screws on "Fellow Travelers," like herself. It spoke of an approach that would guarantee writers' fast transition to the side of communist ideology. What this really meant was that poetry reflecting women's social, emotional, and sexual struggles was no longer appreciated. Bolshevik male culture, which had triumphed during the Civil War, now dominated Soviet culture, and hopes for a social and sexual revolution to accompany the political revolution faded. Henceforth, Shkapskaya devoted herself to journalism, while socialist feminist Kollontai wrote little after 1925. No more discussions of "Winged Eros," or short stories about the harmfulness of NEP to women workers by Kollontai in Soviet publications. No more discussions of women combining love and work in their lives. Henceforth, the work ethic prevailed, and women's search for meaningful personal lives was considered irrelevant. Silenced by Trotsky's devastating criticism, Anna Radlova abandoned poetry for translation. Sofia Parnok's lyrical, lesbian poetry was no longer acceptable, and she too had to confine herself to translation. After Lenin's death, poet Anna Barkova lost her patron Anatoly Lunacharsky, the Minister of Culture, and she too ceased publishing in 1925 as the political landscape changed. Her fierce intelligence, caustic wit, and the vicious prickles of her verse were no longer acceptable.[77]

(2) Marietta Shaginian

Some established writers, like Marietta Shaginian and Maria Shkapskaya, made accommodations to the new Soviet regime by abandoning poetry for prose and journalism. According to Tatiana Tchernavin, a translator and university friend of Shaginian, Marietta was a minor but pretty and popular poet before the revolution. Author of "Orientalia" and other poems, she was a darling of the intelligentsia before the war. In that period, poets were the fashion and were well paid. In 1917 the revolution parted them. Tchernavin recalled the early Bolshevik period:

> It was a terrible time: everyone seemed to have hidden away, sunk through the ground, as it were; everyone was left alone with his own sorrow and hunger. Petersburg where I had moved just before the revolution was growing empty and dying out. Trams were not working, shops were shut, front doors permanently closed....
> It was at that time, early in 1921, that I met Marietta. We were glad to see each other. But it was a strange joy—there was so much sorrow in it at the thought of what we had become....
> Marietta who had once dressed smartly and elegantly was wearing a shapeless overcoat ... She had nothing but thin worn shoes on her feet and on her head a miserable little hat knitted by her own unskilled fingers....
> My get-up was little better than hers. Its chief advantage were topboots made of sealskins which my husband brought me from an expedition to the North. Warm footwear was essential in those days, and I did not take off my boots either at home or at the office.[78]

Like others in the intelligentsia, Tchernavin and Shaginian were saddened by the death of Alexander Blok and undone by the shooting of Nikolai Gumilev in 1921. Marietta said: "I cannot write poetry any more." She asked: "Has anyone the right to kill a poet?"[79]

Tchernavin noted that the years of famine and terror killed off many writers and made others change:

> To say that they "sold themselves" to the Bolsheviks would be crude and unfair. To say that they became "regenerated" and sincerely accepted bolshevism would be simply untrue. No one in Soviet Russia doubts that the Bolshevik power is a terrible tyranny, and that its strength lies in its ruthlessness and cruelty. No one is enthusiastic about it, but ... one has to live. People have been taught to adapt themselves to the Communist regime, not by Government slogans, which are sheer bombast, but by Soviet life.
>
> Reading Marietta's Diaries I see once more how people changed and why.
>
> Up to 1921 she wrote novels and sometimes poems, studied Goethe and Balzac, was keen on the theory of music and other arts.
>
> In 1923 she began to write about brandy, cotton, textile industry, fruit-drying, coal, manganese ore, geology, agriculture, chemistry, hydrotechnics and so in spite of being hopelessly ignorant with regard to all these matters. Like the Communists whom the party commandeers one day to manage a match factory, the next to be directors of the Neurological Institute, then to run the "Red Triangle" rubber works, and afterwards to superintend the Hermitage, she rushed from one thing to another, without studying any one subject properly. A true poet and gifted writer, she has become a mediocre journalist, writing dull novels to order.[80]

After conducting research on the lives of workers in the mid 1920s, some of which she incorporated into her "Diaries," Marietta found herself unable to write a novel about them and left Leningrad for her sunny Armenian homeland.[81] At one point, the party asked Marietta to write a detective story to counter the popularity of American detective stories. Her detective stories *Laurie Lane* (1925) and *Mess Mend or the Yankees in Petrograd* (1926) were spoofs of American mysteries but very popular. By the late 1920s, many thought she had "sold out" to the party. Tchernavin did not think Marietta had sold out so much as blinded herself to reality. This was easy for her to do because she was deaf and so short-sighted that she missed negative parts of reality which others noticed.

Other writers made different adjustments to Soviet society and policies. Some gave up their own voice and lived from the money they

Portrait, Marietta Shaginian, 1932, Moscow (St. Petersburg Photo Archive)

earned doing translations, especially ones of famous foreign writers like Shakespeare. Government publishing houses paid famous writers like Akhamatova and Pasternak well for translating. Others turned to children's literature or wrote screenplays instead of their own poetry or novels. Some poets like Sofia Parnok and Vera Merkureva became physically and psychologically exhausted by working as hack translators.[82]

3. *Anna Akhmatova*

Anna Akhmatova's poetry had made her famous during the prerevolutionary period. But because she had been married to Lev Gumilov from 1910 to 1918, and he was executed by the Bolsheviks as a counterrevolutionary in 1921, she had a difficult time and eventually stopped writing poetry in the mid-1920s. Her poetic voice was silent for thirteen years. Her lyrical poetry celebrated romance, not revolution, and a yearning for happiness—yet it contained a foreboding of misfortune. It was not valued by the regime as Trotsky's diatribe indicates, and government publishing houses did not publish her work.

Only private, NEP firms printed her writings. Her second marriage to Shileiko did not work out. In her "Brief Word about Myself," written in 1965, she doesn't discuss or divulge anything about her married life. Writing about the 1920s, she says:

> After the October Revolution I worked in the library of the Agriculture Institute. In 1921 my collection of verse "Plantain" was published, in 1922—the book "Anno Domini."
>
> From about the mid-1920's I began a keen and diligent study of the architecture of old St. Petersburg and of the life and work of Pushkin. The results of my Pushkin studies were three works—on "The Golden Cockerel," on Benjamin Constant's "Adolphe" and on "The Stone Guest." They were all printed....
>
> From the middle of the 1920s they almost stopped printing poems—or reprinting the old ones.[83]

Refusing her husband's invitation to talk about men and identify herself as a sex object, Akhmatova wrote about women. One critic suggests that Anna's preeminence in the 1920s was partly because of the death of some Symbolist poets, the emigration of Gippius and Tsvetaeva, and the displacement of others from the literary capitols, thus leaving her the preeminent poet.[84] Still, her poetry was enchanting and its simplicity deceptive, as the following excerpts reveal:

> "The Song of the Last Meeting"
> . . .
> "I've been wronged by a sad and gloomy,
> By a treacherous, evil fate."
> And I answered, "O my dearest, dearest,
> I was, too—I'll come die with you . . ."
>
> That's the song of our last, sad meeting.
> I looked back at the house in the dark—
> In the bedroom alone there burned candles,
> With their yellow, indifferent flame.
>
> (1911)

> "The Muse"
>
> When I await at night for her arrival
> It seems my life is hanging on a thread.
> For what are honors, what is youth, or freedom
> Before this guest with panpipes in her hand?

And now she comes. She's cast aside her veiling
She looks with full attention in my eyes
I say to her: "did you dictate to Dante
Inferno's pages? And she answers: "I"[85]

(1924)

Akhmatova's poetry was lyrical, haunting, even existential. The following poem conveys some of these qualities:

> As the shadow from the body wants to part,
> As the flesh from the soul wants to separate,
> So I want now—to be forgotten . . .[86]

Some of her last poems of the 1920s were somber as a stanza from "Now All Is Sold" indicates:

> And on these houses, this grime, these trivial ruins
> also, the marvel is wafted all around.
> It's near at hand, the desired, the long-despaired,
> which all men dreamed of and yet no man found.[87]

While Akhmatova doesn't mention translating, Nadezhda Mandelstam indicates that Anna received high remuneration for her translations, and that she distributed translations to others who were unemployed, taking half of the payment for herself. Nadezhda ruefully records:

> One day people will collect all of Akhmatova's translations too, but only about ten lines of them are actually her own unaided work, the rest having been done in collaboration with others. Whenever she was commissioned to do such things—which for the likes of us was tantamount to receiving a prize or a handout—she farmed them out to other people and shared the fees fifty-fifty. She managed it very shrewdly and saved needy people by getting them paid handsomely for their drudgery—she was entitled to the highest rates of payment for such work.[88]

Describing the plight of the intelligentsia under the Soviets, Tatiana Tchernavin noted that before World War I, culture and jobs flourished for intellectuals. However, after the revolution, rations were insufficient, and collecting payment for one's work was not easy. Waiting for payment of her translation of Balzac one day at the cashier's desk of the office of Universal Literature, Tchernavin realized that

Anna Akhmatova had come to collect a substantial payment for some of Gumilev's writings. Tchernavin records Akhmatova's encounter with a Soviet bureaucrat as follows:

> "I've been told that I was to receive a large sum of money, that my husband had it owing to him for his work."
> Cashier: "This is all that is due to him," the cashier said drily.
> I could not resist peeping into the receipt book. The young woman had her finger on the name of Gumilyov. The sum of money had been large two or three months before, but by the time all the formalities had been completed and the payment could be made Gumilyov had been shot and the value of the money due to him had dwindled down to less than the price of one pound of butter. The widow stood there not knowing what to do: signing the receipt meant giving up all further claim to what was her last resource, and perhaps there was some mistake about it which she did not understand.
> Cashier: "Don't keep me waiting," the cashier said impatiently. She sighed and in her distress forgot to take her "thousands."
> 'Take your money!' the cashier shouted angrily.
> Soviet officials like to be treated with gratitude and respect. The widow turned round in alarm, hastily thrust the money into her bag and went away. A decade later the Soviet Government no longer paid wives of enemies, and even took their goods and children's toys.[89]

(4) Vera Inber

While many women poets left Russia, and others complained about the Bolshevik regime, a few were loyal to it. Vera Inber (1890–1972) wrote a very touching elegy to Lenin upon his death. It shows the honor in which many held him:

> "Five Days and Nights" (On the Death of Lenin, 1924)
>
>> Before they closed him in the tomb
>> lost to the light of day,
>> five days and nights stretched in the room
>> of pillars still he lay.
>>
>> The people filed in an endless train
>> with flags borne low at rest
>> to see his sallowing profile again
>> and the medal red on his chest.
>>
>> . . .

> Five nights in Moscow no one slept
> because to sleep he had gone.
> Close watch the sentinel moon kept,
> Solemn and wan.[90]

(5) Nina Berberova

One of Gumilev's last protégées, Nina Berberova, also wrote lyrical poetry. A segment of one of the many poems she submitted to the House of Arts so she could study there, reads as follows:

> And avidly shall I detect
> The marks of your embraces
> In the folds of her dress
> Which you have helped her put on.[91]

Apparently, Nikolai Gumilev was smitten with the youthful, beautiful Berberova and wrote the following poem about her:

> I only laughed at myself.
> I only deceived myself.
> When I thought that there was in this world
> Anyone else but you.
>
> All white and all in white,
> Attired as a goddess of old.
> You alone hold the crystal sphere
> In your slender transparent hand.
>
> . . .
>
> Strange that there is in this world
> Anyone else but you.
> That I am not only a song.
> A sleepless song about you.
>
> The light behind your shoulders,
> It is such blinding light;
> The two long flames rise slowly,
> Like a pair of golden wings.[92]

However, Nina thought Gumilev was insensitive, ugly, and old. She later discovered that he was thirty-five while she thought him fifty. She did not accept his advances or presents. He told her he was never friends with a woman, only the "master." Such words amazed Nina, who from childhood had rejected others trying to control or protect her.

> Never, it seemed, had I been in such a difficult position: up to then, between myself and a man, there had always been an understanding about what was right and wrong, what was possible and impossible. Here there was an unhearing wall: the self-assurance of a mentor, the false grandeur and complete absence of sensitivity.... but I was also conscious that this was a great poet.[93]

After this encounter, she resolved never to see him again, and she didn't because he was arrested as a counterrevolutionary and shot by the Bolsheviks a few days later.

(6) Marina Tsvetaeva

The famous poet Marina Tsvetaeva (1892–1941) also had a hard life after the revolution. Her husband was away fighting in the White Army, and she could not support herself and their two daughters in Moscow during the Civil War. Impoverished, Tsvetaeva placed her younger daughter Irina in a Moscow orphanage, thinking there was more food there, but instead, Irina died of starvation. Tsvetaeva's lyrical and sometimes anti-Communist poetry did not gain her support or rations from the Poets' Union. So, in 1922 she emigrated. First she lived in Prague, then Berlin, and finally Paris. Some of her love poems from this period are particularly poignant, as the following suggests:

"You loved me" (1923)

You loved me. And your lies had their own probity.
    There was a truth in every falsehood.
Your love went far beyond any possible
    Boundary as no one else's could.

Your love seemed to last even longer
    Than time itself. Now you wave your hand—
And suddenly your love for me is over!
    That is the truth in five words.[94]

In Paris in the 1930s, Tsvetaeva was persona non grata because she praised the work of Soviet poet Vladimir Mayakovsky and later because her husband spied for the Soviet secret police. Tsvetaeva returned to the Soviet Union in 1939 but committed suicide two years later. Lacking a job and family, she had no reason to live. Her poetry was staccato, rhythmic, and unusual, as "The Return of the Chief" (1921) reveals:

> The horse—lame.
> The sword—rust.
> Who—is he?
> Chief of hosts.
>
> A step—an hour.
> A sigh—an age.
> Eyes—downcast.
> Those—yonder.
>
> Foe—or friend.
> Thorns—or crown.
> All—but dreams
> But he—the horse.
>
> The horse—lame.
> The sword—rust.
> The cape—old
> The stance—strong.[95]

Her ode to the poet Alexander Blok in 1916 was in a similar style:

> For a beast—an abode,
> For a pilgrim—a road,
> For a corpse—a hearse,
> And for each—his own claim.
>
> A woman—betrays
> A czar—rules his days,
> As for me—I shall praise
> Always your name.[96]

(7) Émigré Writers

Many Russian women writers fled the country after the Bolsheviks took power. Zinaida Gippius (1869–1952) and her husband fled in December 1919. They initially settled in Minsk, then Berlin, and finally

Paris. Both Tsvetaeva and Gippius found that prose paid more than poetry and so wrote more prose in emigration. Between 1918 and 1923, other gentry-class writers like Nina Berberova, Nadezhda Teffi, and Zinaida Vengerova also emigrated to the West. In her autobiography, Nina Berberova described the sense of impending doom that she felt in the early twenties—after the shooting of the poet Nikolai Gumilev and the death of Alexander Blok: "It was said that soon everything would close down—that is, private publishing houses—and that 'all' would be turned over to Gosizdat" (Government publishing house). She heard that in Moscow censorship already was more severe than in Petrograd. The pre-war intelligentsia wondered how long Lunacharsky would remain in power, and how long they would be safe and allowed to work, especially after Osip Mandelstam and Evgeny Zamiatin were forbidden to publish.[97]

f. Artists

"The Last Picture Has Been Painted"

Nikolai Tarabukin, lecture, 1921

While the Russian Revolution initially offered opportunity and acceptance of avant-garde artists, some Leftist critics like Tarabukin declared easel painting outmoded. The Bolshevik revolution divided the women avant-garde artists. Natalia Goncharova left in 1915, and Alexandra Exter and Zinaida Serebriakova left for France in 1924, hoping to find freer expression there. Nonobjective artists like Liubov Popova, Olga Rozanova, Varvara Stepanova, and Nadezhda Udaltsova embraced the revolution and supported the regime in their graphic designs and by teaching in various institutions.

Still, in art, like much of life, Bolshevik rule resulted in masculine dominance by the end of the decade. The Commissar of Culture, Anatoly Lunacharsky, tried to steer a middle course between Leftists who wanted to destroy the old art as bourgeois and the Right which wanted to preserve academic art and the museums, which Leftists wanted to close. Many Bolsheviks wanted to develop proletarian art on a sound basis and purge "vulgar, philistine, anti-revolutionary, religious bourgeois art." Lunacharsky did not want to impose revolutionary ideas on artists but to use education and encouragement to foster new art. Leftists believed that the revolution could give art its soul, and art could provide the regime its mouthpiece. Certainly revolutionary poster art succeeded well. Lenin and others thought music, choirs, theater, cinema, and art could be used for agitation and propaganda, especially at government festivals.

(1) Liubov Popova

> There was a large group, headed by Mayakovsky and under his influence, which felt the need to link their work with the demands of the people in their construction of a new society.
>
> Solomon Telingater, on artist Varvara Stepanova, 1920s

Although Telingater wrote these epigraphic words about the work of Varvara Stepanova in the early 1920s, he could have written them about Liubov Popova as well. After the revolution, abstract artists often gave up easel painting and turned to design—for the theater, books, journals, and textiles. Russian avant-garde painter Liubov Popova teamed with the radical theatrical producer Vsevelod Meyerhold, while Alexandra Exter collaborated with Alexander Tairov. They created stark, modern set designs for Moscow theaters and films as well as sensational, innovative costumes for the actors. While such innovations pleased many, others like Nadezhda and Osip Mandelstam were not always happy with the results. Meyerhold's new productions sometimes aroused their interest, other times their disgust. Nadezhda commented: "We never really took to the theater: underneath it was empty and frightening, despite all the surface glitter. The shibboleth of the day was 'biomechanics,' which sounded both grand and stylish."[98] The photographs of Popova's and Exter's set designs still seem avant-garde today.

The dilemma in the 1920s was that while the revolution offered new content, representational artists like Zinaida Serebriakova were not interested in depicting revolutionary ideas or people. Serebriakova confessed that she did not want to paint portraits of commissars. Artists who endorsed revolutionary ideas often belonged to the avant-garde, and their work was too abstract and nonobjective to convey revolutionary ideas to the masses.[99]

Some artists, like Marc Chagall and Natan Altman, returned from abroad to participate in the new artistic life. From 1918 to 1920, Chagall headed the Art Institute in his birthplace Vitebsk, Belarus. In 1919

198 CHAPTER FIVE: WOMEN'S EMPLOYMENT

Alexandra Exter, Set design, 1920s

Liubov Popova, Set design, 1920s

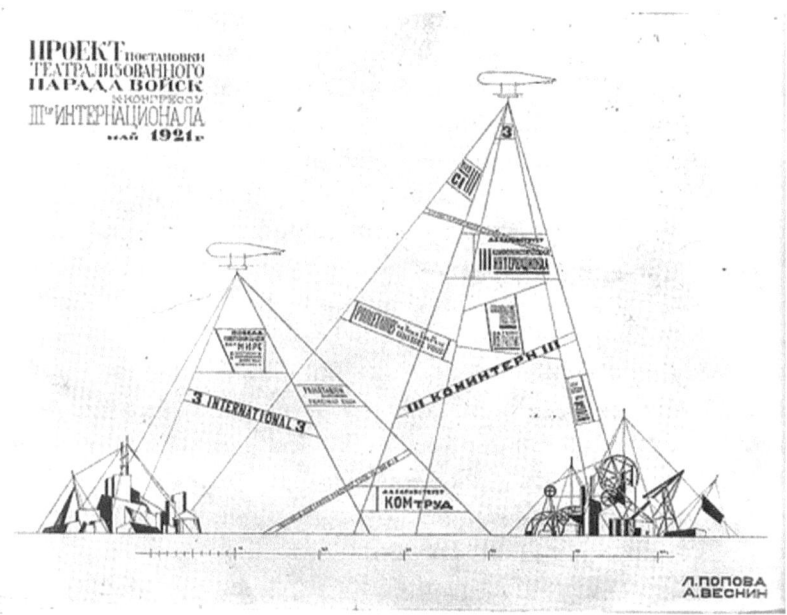

A. Vesnin & L. Popova, Design for a Mass Spectacle in Honor of the Third Comintern Congress, 1921.

artists like Aleksandra Exter and her student Nadezhda Mandelstam enjoyed decorating the streets and squares of Kiev and Odessa for revolutionary festivities. They also adorned the agit-trains (Bolshevik propaganda trains) that roamed the countryside popularizing the Soviet regime, especially in contested areas during the Civil War. Students of Chagall and Malevich in Vitebsk also painted fences, shop windows, and so forth to help celebrate revolutionary holidays. Similar mass decorations took place in Moscow and Petrograd from 1918 to 1920. However, the lack of art supplies, along with shortages of food, fuel, and electricity made serious teaching and art production difficult. Paintings, architectural designs for new buildings, monuments, and sculptures often remained on the drawing board. Some installations celebrating the revolution became too expensive for the government to fund.[100]

In 1921, Popova designed a spectacle called "The Struggle and Victory of the Soviets." It was to be produced by the avant-garde theater director Vsevolod Meyerhold. It included two monumental structures "The Fortress of Capital" and the "City of the Future" tied to the ground with cables. It became a gigantic work involving the assistance of two hundred Red Cavalry, twenty-three hundred infantry cadets, heavy artillery, armored cars, tanks, motorcycles, ambulances, teams of athletes, military orchestras and choruses, and flyovers by warplanes with searchlights. Spectators were to join in singing the "Internationale." But, Minister of Culture Lunacharsky found it too expensive to stage.[101] More modest and affordable spectacles were staged instead.

Illustrations of two dresses designed by Popova in the early 1920s are included.

Agreeing with Nikolai Tarabukin that "The Last Picture Has Been Painted," artists like Liubov Popova, Varvara Stepanova, and Stepanova's husband Alexander Rodchenko declared easel painting outmoded. Industrial construction was to take the place of traditional art. Olga Rozanova and Alexander Bogdanov along with Kazimir Malevich, Popova, Exter, and Nadezhda Udaltsova had participated in peasant craft cooperatives before World War I; but after the revolution Rozanova and Bogdanov rejected art based on folk motifs. They

Liubov Popova, Sports dress design

Liubov Popova, Dress design, 1924

joined Proletcult, which flourished from 1917 to 1932 and endorsed purely proletarian or worker art. The motto of Proletcult was "burn Raphael and trample the flowers of art in the name of our tomorrow." This ideology was replaced in the 1930s by "Socialist Realism — art that was to be realistic, have positive heroes, and be easily understood by the masses."[102]

In some ways the Russian avant-garde had gone as far as it could go with the development of Cubism, Futurism, Rayonism, and abstract art. This impasse plus Bolshevik ideology of making art for the masses lent strength to the constructivists who argued that not easel painting but industrial and applied art were the proper direction. Alexander Rodchenko wrote about photography replacing painting. Some artists were able to follow this new path. Popova and Stepanova

202   CHAPTER FIVE: WOMEN'S EMPLOYMENT

took their talent for design into textile, porcelain, clothing, and theater design. In the 1920s, this group triumphed, running art schools and theaters, organizing agitprop trains, designing posters promoting the new regime and its policies. At the Paris International Exposition of Modern Decorative and Industrial Arts in 1925, the Soviet pavilion exhibited works of the constructivists and won numerous medals.[103]

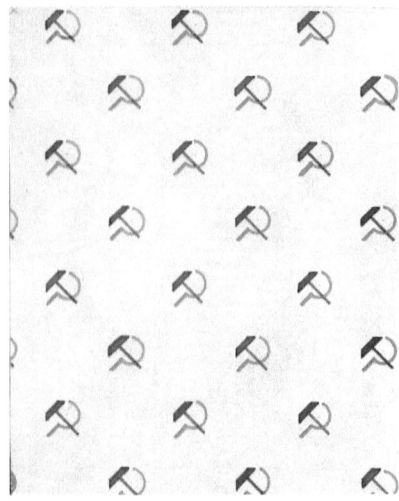

Liubov Popova, Textile design, 1920s

Liubov Popova, Graphic design for Russian Post and Telegraph Statistics 1921

Varvara Stepanova and Liubov Popova, Textile design, 1920s

Rozanova would probably have made the transition to constructivism, but she died of diphtheria in 1918. Popova likewise died young in 1924. Her husband had died of typhus in 1919, and she never returned to painting after his death. While she recovered from typhus, which she had also caught, she was unable to survive the scarlet fever that claimed her son; she died soon after him in 1924.

(2) Varvara Stepanova

> If the task of fashion in a capitalist society is to reflect the economic level, then in socialist society fashion will be the development of more and more appropriate forms of clothing.
>
> Varvara Stepanova, 1928

Varvara Stepanova was a decade younger than many of the other artists of the avant-garde. As a result, she came to artistic maturity during the period of constructivist art after the revolution. She supported the Bolshevik regime and taught at several faculties, including the Textile Faculty of Vkhutemas. Stepanova wanted to link her art with the people in the building of a new society. She eschewed easel painting; designed clothing, books, and journal covers; and illustrated books on transrational poetry by Kruchenykh and Rozanova. Writing in 1919, she remarked:

> I am linking the new movement of non-objective poetry—sounds and letters—with a painterly perception that instills a new and vital visual

204   CHAPTER FIVE: WOMEN'S EMPLOYMENT

*Varvara Stepanova, Dancing figures on a white background, 1920
(Tretyakov Museum, Moscow)*

impression into the sound of poetry. I am breaking up the dead monotony of interconnected printed letters by means of painterly graphics, and I am advancing toward a new kind of artistic creation. On the other hand, by reproducing the non-objective poetry of the two books *Ziga ar* and *Rtny khomle* by means of painterly graphics, I am introducing sounds as a new quality in graphic painting.[104]

One critic noted that these works were called "anti-books" because they utilized cheap newspaper whose printed text was blurred by Stepanova's superimposition of her diagonal text in watercolor. Reading it was incomprehensible. Stepanova further subverted the book by placing the title page at the end, so that the book in the conventional sense was entirely unreadable.[105]

By 1925, however, the Bolshevik regime took a dim view of such expressions and closed the radical journal *LEF* in which avant-garde writers and artists presented their work. Communist critics thought her art unintelligible to the masses. Earlier, Stepanova created posters and her husband, photographer Rodchenko, illustrated many of Mayakovsky's futurist poems. Stepanova presented some of her clothing designs in *LEF*, especially sports clothes, which resembled Popova's in their bright colors and geometric designs. Stepanova also designed special clothing for surgeons, firefighters, sports, leisure, and workers. She wanted clothing that was functional and fit the occasion. In contrast, her graphic designs for the cinema journal *Kino*, which she did throughout the 1920s, are quite innovative yet easily understood.[106]

Varvara Stepanova, Three Figures, 1920 (Tretyakov Museum, Moscow)

Writing about the role of art, design, and fashion, Stepanova noted:

> "Fashion" rarely comes from the pattern of the fabric—it is the shape of a garment that determines the material and patterns used. It would be a mistake to think that fashion can be abolished, or that it is haphazard or unnecessary. Fashion gives the lines and shapes to suit the particular time.... At the moment one sees an amusing phenomenon—that men's clothes are changing more noticeably than women's....
> If the task of fashion in a capitalist society is to reflect the economic level, then in socialist society fashion will be the development of more and more appropriate forms of clothing. All technological advances should influence forms of dress.... Most important of all, the artist should get to know the consumer's daily life, and find out what happens after the fabric leaves the factory.[107]

Alexandra Exter echoes some of Stepanova's ideas in her writings on fashion in 1921:

206 CHAPTER FIVE: WOMEN'S EMPLOYMENT

The pace of contemporary life demands the least expenditure of time and energy on production. To contemporary "fashion," changing according to the whims of businessmen, we must oppose clothes which are both practical and beautiful in their simplicity. The dress for general consumption must be made from the simplest geometrical forms, such as the rectangle, the square, the triangle; the rhythm of colours varies the impact of the form. They are quite utilitarian since they are constructed from a combination of parts and, in putting them on or taking them off, the wearer dramatically modifies both the form and its purpose....

By removing the wrap of an outdoor costume we have a holiday dress, and by taking off a white blouse we come to the underfrock— the working costume. A dark undershirt acts as a simple housedress which allows free movement, but add the overshirt and it becomes a holiday costume....

All the designs are simple in their outlines, material and construction so as to minimize the number of seamstresses required for their manufacture.[108]

(3) Zinaida Serebriakova

While "leftist" artists like Popova made the transition to constructivism, not all artists did so. It wasn't Zinaida Serebriakova or Anna Ostroumova Lebedeva's style. Serebriakova continued painting the female form, either as clothed peasants or naked in the bathhouse. The number of nudes painted declined in the 1920s, and Serebriakova later painted dancers who were partially clothed. Her nudes looked less directly at the viewer than Natalie Goncharova's prewar paintings did.

When the opportunity of painting murals in Paris arose in 1924, Serebriakova left, although her four children remained in the Soviet Union. Only two of them were allowed to join her in the late 1920s. Aleksandra Exter also emigrated in 1924. The death of Lenin in that year led to policy changes in the Ministry of Culture that some artists could not accept. No doubt Exter emigrated to France believing she would have more freedom to teach the way she wanted in Paris.

(4) Anna O. Lebedeva

Anna Ostroumova Lebedeva was not part of the Russian avant-garde or constructivism, but she continued painting and engraving throughout the Soviet period, living until 1955. She taught briefly for

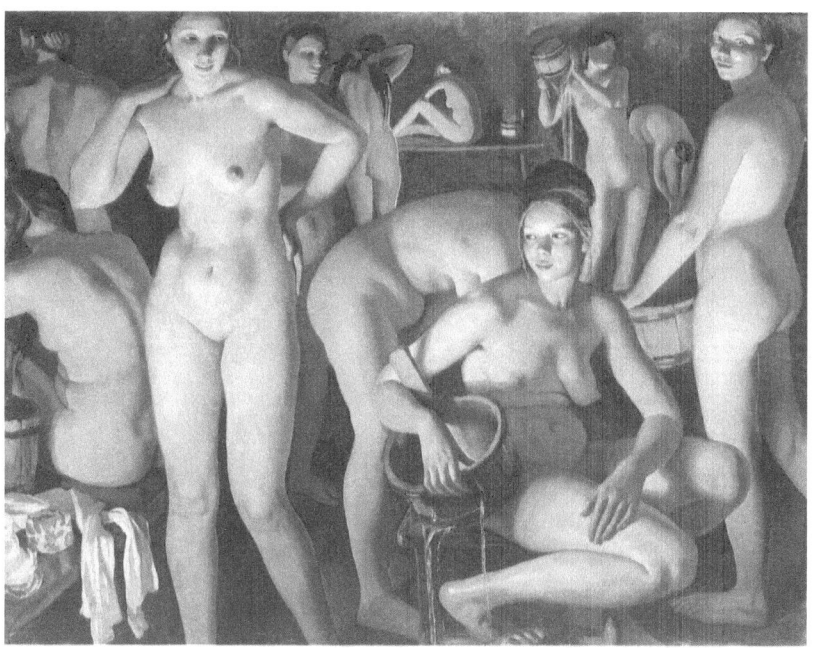

Zinaida Serebriakova, The Bathers, *1913*

Zinaida Serebriakova,
Dancers, *1920s*

N. Yanov, Anna Ostroumova Lebedeva, *1951*,
Leningrad (St. Petersburg Photo Archive)

the Soviets as a professor at the Institute of Photography and Phototecnique in Petrograd from 1918 to 1921. However, new policies and the acceptance of students without qualifications or interest in basic skills like anatomy and draftsmanship dulled her interest in teaching. Still, she remained a practicing artist and friend of the poet Anna Akhmatova. By the late 1920s, the ranks of Russian women artists had declined.

Conclusion

What sort of conclusions can we draw about women's lives in the 1920s? The new Soviet state ushered in a time of mixed messages for women. While the socialist program promised sexual and social revolution, patriarchal structures remained strong. Divorce and abortion became more widespread in urban areas, but birth control remained limited, making married women's lives difficult. For 85 percent of the female population—the peasants—not a great deal of political or religious change occurred because the Bolshevik regime remained weak in the countryside. Yet, 10 million families were able to obtain their own land and house after 1917, so the Bolsheviks produced an economic and social revolution in family relationships, where women were no longer under the control of mothers-in-law and fathers-in-law in the traditional extended family of the nineteenth century.

While many peasant men were influenced by their stint in the Red Army and participation in the Komsomol, relatively few women joined those organizations. Most continued their hard, unremitting work as usual, except more peasant girls obtained elementary education. Most continued to marry and have families. Most peasant women still prepared a dowry for marriage and continued the wedding traditions of the nineteenth century. As mentioned, 10 million married women rejoiced as they were able to separate from their in-laws and set up their own nuclear families. However, this became a Pyrrhic victory when in 1929 collectivization ended family control of land and made peasants subject to collective farm management. Still, village culture remained strong, and the Russian Orthodox Church continued serving the needs of the peasants in that decade.

For working-class women the changes may have been generational. Young women workers were more able than their elders to participate in political organizations and obtain elementary and higher education, thus becoming more upwardly mobile. Young women with one or few children were more able to take advantage of the easy divorce policy and leave abusive marriages. Most workers still wanted to marry but probably without expensive church weddings. Marriages at the local government registry office were free, as was divorce. Work in factories changed in the later 1920s when "shock work" was introduced and women were encouraged to become "udarniks," doing more work for the same pay. Again, younger workers with fewer domestic responsibilities accepted these changes more easily. Married women workers faced a lack of birth control, except for abortion. Moreover, raising children in the aftermath of World War I, during the Civil War, and during the hard economic times of NEP was hazardous.

Educated women faced a variety of changes. Those from the "former gentry, bourgeois or priestly" classes could have a hard time getting or keeping a job. Newly educated women often had to work in rural areas. During NEP, educated women suffered tremendously from unemployment and underemployment. Still, education offered upward mobility to peasant and working-class women who could take advantage of the opportunity to obtain meaningful work. Teachers and doctors earned lower wages than workers, but presumably their work was more fulfilling, and in some respects they had a lifestyle that they enjoyed. Living conditions remained crowded for women in all classes. Even educated women had to live in one or two rooms and share a communal kitchen and bath. Many were able to hire maids to help with the shopping and child care. Still, balancing work and home life was not easy. Low wages, for men as well as women, meant most educated women had to work in order for their families to survive. There was also a generational divide among educated women. Older women found it more difficult to adjust to the Bolshevik regime, whereas younger women were often "Sovietized" and accepted new policies more easily than their mothers.

Women from the upper classes who could not adjust often fled the country for France and other havens. There, however, they often discovered employment hard to find and life extremely difficult. Women in certain religious organizations and those critical of Bolshevik political policies—such as most Social Revolutionaries and Anarchists—were sometimes imprisoned. Some were later exiled and worked for the new regime in provincial places.

In general, Russian women were overwhelmingly negatively affected by the regime in the 1920s. If she could be a "fellow traveler" and go along with the regime, life was difficult but bearable. Nonparty women writers, however, suffered in many ways. After 1925, poets like Anna Akhmatova, Anna Barkova, Anna Radlova, and Maria Shkapskaya had difficulty writing and publishing their poetry. Wives of unappreciated poets, like Nadezhda Mandelstam, struggled to survive since the government gave them no rations. Without work or rations, life was precarious. A similar situation existed among the wives and daughters of male priests. These families also lacked rations and work. Except for the respite of the New Economic Policy, it proved a harsh decade for many "byvshie liudy," or former people.

Despite the poverty and famine following the October revolution, Soviet statistics show life expectancy rose from thirty-three years in 1897 to forty-seven in 1926, indicating improvement for many. Child mortality declined, and this must have eased many women's lives. While it was not an idyllic time for all women, NEP made it a time of survival for most. Although the revolution did not produce the economic or human equality it promised, and sexual liberation meant greater freedom for men than women, by the end of the decade greater equality in education and the workplace occurred. Still, Bolshevik male-dominated work culture triumphed, and women's needs and voices fell silent. Zhenotdel, which had striven to protect women and their interests, limped along after Kollontai was exiled to Scandinavia in 1921, but Stalin closed it in 1930. By the end of the decade, women's issues were no longer prominent. This is clearly seen in the triumph of the Five-Year Plan, collectivization of agriculture—which entailed once again a lack of food in the cities, the reintroduction of rationing, hardship for mothers trying to feed their families, and the general neglect of women's issues.

Part II

Russian Women in the 1930s

It was the best of times, the worst of times.
Charles Dickens, *A Tale of Two Cities*

Russian women's lives in the 1930s are difficult to assess and discuss. For millions of young, poor peasant and working-class women, it could be the best of times—of great expectations and upward mobility. Many poor peasant women obtained better housing, elementary schooling, and some higher education as well as better jobs than previously. For millions of workers it could also be a time of improved education through the rabfak (worker's school), technical institute, or university, and greater job opportunities as demand for engineers, teachers, doctors, and other professionals soared during industrialization. For many it was a time of willing self-sacrifice for building socialism during the Five-Year Plans. Thousands of young, true believers joined the Komsomol and Communist Party, feeling a sense of mission. Raisa Orlova felt she lived among those chosen to do great things. She and her university classmates felt they could work, run, draw, and play better and faster than others. Living during the Five-Year Plans, they thought they had the good life and felt that they were the first generation of happy people.

For several million others, especially intellectuals, older married workers, and well-to-do peasants, or kulaks, it was the worst of times—the bitter time of the purges, harsh industrialization, collectivization, and dekulakization, when not only "the samovar was requisitioned," as the novelist Ilia Ehrenburg wrote, but the house, land, and possibly life itself. As one woman lamented, "Hope was a rare commodity." Millions of peasants dragged their feet, barely complying with work on the collective farms. This created famine in the cities. For married working women it was a time of exhausting factory jobs with high production norms, low wages, inadequate food, and even sexual harassment on the job. During the same decade, many intellectuals and older Communist Party members were arrested, exiled, shot, or sentenced to hard labor in Siberia. Whether the numbers of party members rising and falling "equaled each other," it's hard to say. Exact figures remain hidden aspects in Russian history.

Generational differences were often pronounced. Idealistic young women were likely to profit from higher education and higher wages as they over fulfilled their quotas as exemplary "udarnik," "shock," or "Stakhanovite" workers. In agriculture, youthful Stakhanovite women, who produced above the norm, were more receptive to using new technology, such as tractors and incubators, to raise agricultural productivity. Many studied agronomy and used new techniques to increase production. Some of these energetic women became famous in films and newspaper articles or were even elected delegates to the government's Supreme Soviet. Many felt satisfaction in raising their country's industrial and agricultural productivity. They believed in "building socialism" and using technology to modernize the country. Cults developed around driving tractors and combine harvesters, piloting planes, and praising Stalin for his help in making this possible.

Yet, life for married working-class women became harsher as production rates rose while wages and consumer goods did not. In addition to generational differences, the late 1930s also witnessed increasing class distinctions. The Communist Party encouraged wives of high-ranking men to become *obshchestvennitsy*, or social volunteers. The job of these well-to-do women was to make home life easier for their husbands so they could be more productive, and to beautify and improve government institutions, such as nurseries, barracks, and reading corners.

Abandoning the New Economic Policy meant the end of a somewhat laissez-faire policy in Russian society. With the beginning of the first Five-Year Plan in 1928, the economy underwent drastic changes. To many upwardly mobile Russians in villages, towns, and cities, the 1930s represented a time of greater access to education and employment. To other segments of society, the new plans meant greater government control and suffering. Indeed, some have called collectivization, industrialization, and the purges Stalin's "revolution from above." The number of churches declined from thirty thousand in 1927 to five hundred in 1940. Increased arrests and imprisonment of priests and nuns occurred, and many pious Christians were harassed. Desecration of churches and monasteries undermined morale among believers. Some monasteries, like the Solovetsky in the North and the Boris and Gleb near Moscow, became concentration camps where NKVD officials lived and administered the miserable lives of political prisoners. Likewise, tolerant teaching policies in the 1920s changed in the 1930s when native languages, such as German among some in the

Ukraine and Crimea, were forbidden and Russian became the only language of instruction in schools.

Some intellectuals felt doomed. The arrest of specialists and their families during the late 1920s and early 1930s produced enormous fear among educated people and bewildered most women prisoners. In his book *I Speak for the Silent*, Vladimir Tchernavin, who with his wife and child escaped from the prison camps in the early 1930s, observed that the arrests of so many specialists and the use of their slave labor and that of other prisoners contributed to the infrastructure and industrial capacity of the Soviet state. It seems the use of prison labor to build the Baltic White Sea Canal and extend the fisheries north of Archangel, and the use of "kulaks" to cut timber and mine minerals in Siberia, all helped develop the country at very low cost. The GPU and NKVD acted like trusts and had their own Five-Year Plans. Low-cost prison labor increased the success of the government's Five-Year Plans.

The treatment of kulaks during collectivization and the subsequent lack of food during the famine that followed hurt all segments of society. Rationing, which had stopped during NEP, was reintroduced, and it became hard for urban mothers to feed and clothe their families. At the same time, the institutions of marriage and the family helped women survive. Moreover, religion strengthened many women during the adverse times. Finally, participation in sports and the paramilitary organization Osoaviakhim helped provide a patriotic and unifying effect in the country because they included women from all strata—peasants, workers, students, and housewives. Because the largest group in Russian society remained in the countryside, let us first look at the rural situation.

Chapter Six

Peasants

When in our village reading room
They hung up a linen screen,
Even the old, old women
Came together to see the movies.

Y. M. Sokolov, *Russian Folklore*

Perhaps the greatest struggle Soviet society faced in the early 1930s was the collectivization of agriculture. Peasants were traditional in their ways and reluctant to change. However, a shortage of grain for urban workers in 1927 and the unwillingness of many peasants to sell their grain at low government prices, since few consumer goods were available, pitted peasants against the regime. In response, the party and government adopted a Five-Year Plan (FYP) to collectivize and control agriculture and a plan to speedily develop industry. They began implementing these plans in 1929. Losses were significant. Several million peasants were exiled from their homesteads and became "untouchables." Others were arrested and sent to work on various projects, where the survival rate was low for men (survival was not as hard for women because they were not usually subject to work in the forests, factories, mines, railroads, or canals as men were). Some peasants were arrested and shot for resisting collectivization, and several million others died from starvation during the collectivization campaign. So the toll was heavy and success meager the first few years. Overthrowing "the ways" of 25 million farmers, especially 4 million kulaks, was not easy. The government moved forward and then backtracked in their dealings with peasants. Although this book is about Russian women, and Russian peasants generally suffered less than the Ukrainians did, one cannot ignore the intense famine and starvation that occurred in Ukraine at this time because it was part of the Soviet Union. Scholars generally note that resistance to collectivization and subsequent famine and starvation were greatest in three main areas: along the Volga in Russia, in Georgia, and in Ukraine and Crimea.

Kolkhozniks during Their Lunch Break, *1930s*,
Leningrad Oblast (St. Petersburg Photo Archive)

This rather "staged" picture shows some young collective farm workers taking a break over their lunch hour.

A. Young Stakhanovite and Udarnik Workers

> I decided to become a tractor driver. And that is what I became.
>
> Now it is easy to say "decided and became" but back then, in the spring of 1930, it was very hard. It cost me so much strength and so many tears!
>
> Pasha Angelina, tractor driver

While the above Kolkhozniks picture was probably posed, some peasants did experience incredible improvement in their lives as elementary education and some social services came to the countryside. It is hard to generalize about peasants and collectivization in the 1930s. While about 35 percent of peasants were bedniaks, or poor peasants—about 11 million or so—not all bedniaks profited from collectivization, yet many did. Stories like those of udarniks (overachievers) Maria Senatskaya and Natalia Romasheva, who worked at a kolkhoz on the edge of Moscow, and hardworking Stakhanovite tractor driver

Pasha Angelina, were widely celebrated in the press and "fit in" with Soviet propaganda. Many young peasant women tractor drivers rejoiced in their exhilarating work. Negative stories were not published until decades later.

1. Rural Udarnik Workers

> Before the kolkhoz was started, I was nothing. In the village, they looked down on us. I was poor and no-account. Now they say I'm one of the best in the collective farm. Now I'm an udarnik.
>
> Maria Senatskaya and Natalia Romasheva, *Moscow Daily News*

On International Women's Day, March 8, 1933, *The Moscow Daily News* carried a charming story of exemplary workers Maria Senatskaya and Natalia Romasheva. The title was "Now We Amount to Something." The article quotes the women saying:

> What did we do? We worked, that's all. We did our work.
> We like the kolkhoz.
> And so they made us udarniks. (Those who fulfill their work quota.)
> That's right. Now we have our place. We amount to something.[1]

And they proudly showed off their new coats. Peasants like them earned special prizes for fulfilling their work quotas. Some received coats, shoes, boots, bicycles, or other goods in short supply. They might also be awarded medals, access to special holidays and sanatoria in Crimea, have their photograph featured in peasant newspapers or women's journals, or be co-opted into the government.[2]

2. Stakhanovite Tractor Driver Pasha Angelina

> At first people just laughed at me, but as the district administration did not send anybody to replace him and the tractor was sitting idle, I was allowed to give it a try. My brother had taught me a few things about the tractor's engine, and after some extra preparation, I passed the test.
>
> Pasha Angelina, tractor driver

The story of Pasha Angelina and her family show the success of one poor peasant household. They worked for wealthy kulaks in the 1920s and were all members of the Komsomol or the Communist Party in the late 1920s and 1930s. All supported the Soviet regime and believed in the building of socialism. In one of her autobiographies, she writes of her Komsomol experiences as follows:

> Every evening we, the young people of Staro-Beshevo, would gather in our club around a map of five year plan projects and talk about the future of our country and our own future. They were bright and limitless, and they were inseparable.
>
> None of us was going to wait for that future with folded arms. We Komsomol members were activists playing a far from unimportant part in the tumultuous life of our village.[3]

At first Pasha wanted to go to far-off construction sites like Kuznetsk or the Dnieper Hydroelectric Station to help build socialism on the industrial front. But her brother Ivan convinced her that the Five-Year Plan, or FYP, was also developing in their village, and she could be part of it right there. As Angelina recalled:

> Suddenly Ivan—our district's first tractor driver and the secretary of our party cell—was sent off for further education. So I decided to take his place....
>
> But I was not afraid of hardship and had plenty of strength. I had just turned eighteen, but was already a "Komsomol veteran." We Komsomol members were used to hardship: there were many behind us and quite a few still ahead . . .[4]

Pasha may have been referring to an event in 1929 when she, her sister Lelia and her brother Kostia were walking to a Komsomol meeting in a neighboring village, when they were shot at with a shotgun. Her elderly mother was beaten by kulaks because she was the mother of Communists. When her family voted in favor of a collective farm, some kulaks said they simply wanted other people's property. When the vote regarding the kolkhoz was taken, seven families voted for it, but twelve kulak families voted against it, and the middle peasants abstained. After this, the poor peasants had to leave the village collective and form their own kolkhoz. It was hard work. First they "dekulakized" the wealthy peasants, taking their land and implements. Pasha participated in the dekulakization campaign. She found those difficult days filled with fierce class struggles. "It was only after defeating the kulaks and chasing them off the land that we, the poor, felt truly in charge."[5]

It was not easy to get the kolkhoz started. We worked day and night, all the while feeling the villagers' eyes upon us. We knew that the decision of the majority, those middle peasants and some poor ones who had abstained at the meeting would ultimately depend on the success of our efforts.

It was then that the party and state came to the assistance of the first kolkhoz. Our new agronomist, Nikolai Angelin (who was called a "red agronomist" to distinguish him from the old experts bent on sabotage) was told by the district party committee to start introducing new technology. The kolkhoz received a loan from the district executive committee, but, even more important, it received a tractor. That is what helped make up all the doubters' minds.

The unaffiliated farmers would come and stand for hours, watching our first tractor driver, Ivan Angelin, plow the kolkhoz field. Meanwhile at every kolkhoz board meeting more and more membership applications needed to be considered.[6]

When Pasha became a tractor driver after her brother Ivan left, she faced a lot of hostility—from men and women. Old women sometimes spit when they saw her. Other drivers from the Machine Tractor Station teased her. (The Machine Tractor Stations were set up in the countryside, and several collective farms used the tractors and machines from the same station. The government and a party deputy director retained control of the machines, however.) As she worked and broke plowing records as a "shock worker," she experienced more animosity. When she organized other women as tractor drivers, to make her work less unique, opposition mounted. One time, women blocked their way to the fields, shouting: "Get out of here! We're not going to have machines on our field! You'll ruin our crops!" They even threatened to tear out the hair of the female tractor drivers, but Pasha ran to the district party leader, Comrade Kurov, and he came and saved the day. He told her: "Nothing can be accomplished without a fight."

This proved true as the female brigade met resistance in the next kolkhoz where they were supposed to plow. Some of the drivers were threatened with beatings; others were locked up in cellars. In 1933 some kulak enemies ran over Pasha with a cart, leaving her bleeding and unconscious in a field. She recovered but worried about making good on her boast that she and the other women tractor drivers would plow 1,230 hectares each. The other women did their part, and they exceeded their pledge. After this, she promised Stalin at the Moscow All Union Conference of Best Agricultural Workers that they would exceed their previous norm and teach more cadres of tractor drivers in Russia and other republics. The support of the local party chief and meetings with Stalin strengthened Pasha's position locally and increased her fame nationally.[7]

By the end of the decade, Pasha had become a delegate to the Supreme Soviet, the highest governmental organization, and all her brothers and sisters had taken jobs as Soviet officials in agriculture, the government, and the military. Reflecting on the changes that had occurred under Stalin's leadership, Pasha wrote:

> As he talked about the affluent, cultured life of Soviet people, I thought of many recent events in our village that could illustrate his words. One collective farmer was building a brick house with a metal roof; another had gone to ... buy a motorcycle; a third was planning a trip to a resort in Sochi; and a fourth was all set on sending his daughter to a music school. The stars from the Moscow Art Theater had visited Staro-Beshevo, and new movies were being shown in the village club. All this had become so familiar ...[8]

She and her brothers all experienced considerable upward mobility. So, poor peasants with intelligence and gumption who cooperated with government policies could advance in the new Soviet system. Those who didn't fall into line fared less well, often barely eking out an existence. Those who opposed government policies sometimes starved, were exiled, or were shot. Pasha Angelina's story is one of a poor peasant who had worked for kulaks from the age of eight but became a tractor driver in 1930 during collectivization.

While Pasha eventually became a member of the Communist Party and a delegate to the Supreme Soviet in 1937, her life was not without struggle. She married and had a child but eventually divorced her husband because he pressured her to quit her beloved tractor driving and spend more time with their child.[9] Like many other achieving women, Pasha had to choose between pleasing her husband and pursuing her own work.

3. Other Udarniks

> We're going from the dark into the light.
>
> Tatiana I. Pankratova, hog farm manager, 1934

Collective farm worker Ustina also had to fight ignorance and superstition when she introduced an incubator into her farm. She realized:

> All the same, nobody really believed it would make chickens. I was chicken-woman of the commune and I could read. A little book came with the incubator and told us how to run it. When I read that, I believed it might be worth trying. But I was afraid of being laughed at so I told nobody.
>
> I put a few eggs in, just left-overs, on the chance that we might get some chickens. I kept it in my room to watch it night and day. The 21 days went by and nothing happened. I said: "You fool; the eggs are spoiled; it's lucky you told no one." But late that night I heard a pecking and a cracking. I couldn't sleep from excitement; I just kept listening.
>
> The next morning I called the women and they saw the chicks and said: "Tell us the truth, Ustina, who put those chicks there? Not that machine? No, we won't believe you!" But now we are quite accustomed to the incubator. We no longer use left-over eggs, but select eggs from Kostroma to improve our chickens.[10]

As a collective farm worker from the 1920s, Ustina had to contend with the superstition of other women, and the criticism of her sister for placing her baby in a nursery. Her sister berated her as "an unnatural mother, who lets her baby stay in the day nursery while she tends to chicks." In reply, Ustina remarked:

> I think it wrong to put my baby down in the dirt of a kulak's home while I am raising dust. In the nursery room my baby is clean and quiet and gets good care. When women bear children in the commune, we have four months freedom from work, just as they do in factories; but in old days, a woman gave birth in the fields or over a stove.
>
> Already we begin to have the new life that we fought for in the Revolution.[11]

While the following photo also may seem "staged," some peasants and workers were enthusiastic about the party's plans to develop the economy. During the second FYP, grain production increased, and peasant families received more grain and wages for their labor. Whereas households had received 36 puds (one pud equaled 36 pounds) of grain and 108 rubles in cash for work in 1932, by 1937 kolkhoz households earned 106 puds of grain and 376 rubles in money. Their wages were somewhat illusory since the kolkhozniks had to pay taxes, thereby reducing any money they might accumulate. As

Kolkhozniks from the Kolkhoz 'Avantgard' Voting for Socialist Competition in an Agitation Train Car, *April 1933, Leningrad Oblast (St. Petersburg Photo Archive)*

the decade progressed, the production of tractors and mechanization of agricultural work increased productivity, although wooden implements remained common until World War II.

By the mid 1930s, most peasant girls were obtaining elementary education, and some achieved technical and university education, becoming teachers, doctors, dentists, agronomists, engineers, administrators, and even politicians. Pictures show women tractor drivers rolling over the *staryi byt* (old ways) and forging new paths. By 1934 several thousand women headed collective farms, managed dairy farms, and drove tractors. By 1937 thousands of women earned high wages as tractor drivers (forty thousand), combine operators (thirteen thousand), or machine operators (thirty thousand). Still, the vast majority—about 20 million—remained ordinary kolkhoz workers, and about 2 million stayed heavily taxed independent farmers.[12] Historians differ in their interpretations of the effect of collectivization. Some think of it as a war against the peasantry, others as a way of modernizing Soviet agriculture. Some see peasants using the "weapons of the weak": foot dragging, evasion, minimum compliance, dissembling, feigned ignorance, lying, slander, and sabotage. By 1935 many peasants put their effort into private plot production because they could sell this produce in nearby markets and make more money from this than their wages on a collective farm.[13]

While generational differences were strong, some middle-aged women like Tatiana I. Pankratova and Maria T. Senatskaya also became udarniks (who fulfilled the assigned norms of productivity). Such women's stories were also featured each year in the newspapers on International Women's Day, March 8. In the 1920s, Pankratova had been a poor brick worker, but her exemplary work made the District Party Committee invite her to manage a hog farm in 1934, and she made it flourish. In a discussion with Moscow reporters, she explained her life since the revolution. Before the revolution, she was a poor nobody, but now she was invited to meetings and dinners. She told reporters to relate her story.[14]

Another heartwarming story is that of Liubov Semenets. Prior to the revolution, she earned 35 rubles a year as a nanny and field hand in a kulak household. In 1929 she and her mother joined a collective farm and took adult literacy courses. In 1934 Liubov became a tractor driver and joined the Komsomol. As a tractor driver, she earned 573 labor days per year, a carload of wheat, and 1,500 rubles. She was able to buy an iron bed with a mattress, wool and silk dresses, shoes, and books.[15]

Obviously Semenets was an unusual worker. Later in the decade, Soviet statistician M. A. Vyltsan found that more that a fifth of peasants still participated only symbolically in the collective farms. He found that 4.6 million collective farmers earned no work days in 1937, and 8.5 million earned less than fifty work days a year.[16] (These may have been housewives who spent most of their time in child care and household production, having little time to devote to kolkhoz work.) To spur production, the government obviously needed to call attention to women like Semenets, hoping that others would follow her good example.

Still, English journalist Mrs. Cecil Chesterton, who made two trips to Russia during the 1930s, saw tremendous improvement in peasant women's lives. Initially, she thought life drab and miserable, but by 1934 the diet and the standard of living had improved for many. The communal dining room of the model kolkhoz she visited had heat, electricity, and a radio. For their midday meal, farmers had soup, vegetables, and apples to eat and cider or tea to drink. The women's dorms were airy with whitewashed walls, iron bedsteads, brightly colored quilts, rugs, pictures, and flowers. On productive farms near Moscow, where farmers could market their vegetables, mushrooms, flowers, and fruits at good prices, family income generally increased from 2,000 rubles in 1932 to 6,000 rubles in 1937.[17]

Rural life included a mixture of triumph, struggle, and destruction. For millions, it was a time of dreams come true with new educational, job, and management opportunities. Many obtained a better standard of living, acquiring dishes, sewing machines, beds, overcoats, and shoes. Most gained access to elementary school, some to technical and higher education; some obtained motorcycles or even trips to health resorts. Still, life on the farm remained toilsome, and many women continued their agricultural work with only wooden implements, despite industrialization. Moreover, dekulakization and collectivization also brought pain and devastation to several million others as the section on disenchantment shows. While young women often smiled about their work, as the "Collective Farm Worker" picture shows, older women did so less.[18]

Collective Farm Worker *(Library of Congress)*

B. Songs and Celebration of Rural Women

> Do not call, cuckoo
> I am now a shock worker,
> I am now a wealthy woman.
>
> Y. M. Sokolov, *Russian Folklore*

Pictures in newspapers and women's journals, as well as movies and peasant songs, extolled the virtues of working on collective farms and showed heroines of labor. Some of the following songs show the transference of young girls' loyalty from the household to the collective farm and broader society:

> My husband drove me away, and my father beat me,
> My stepmother was not kind to me.
> But in the collective farm I became,
> Like all the others, a free woman.[19]

> I am very seldom at home now:
> I am sitting in the club over a book
> I am not wasting my time,
> I am following political events.

> In the field there are resting places everywhere.
> If you want to take a breathing spell,
> You can listen to the radio
> And read the newspaper a while.[20]

Some chastushki rhapsodized about the tractor, falling in love with it, becoming a tractor driver, or a tractor driver's wife:

> All around is the field, all around is the field,
> And on the field is the tractor.
> And is it not possible that some day
> I shall be a tractor driver's wife?

A variation in the last two lines reads:

> And is it not possible that some day I shall be
> A tractor driver myself.[21]

Leading kolkhoz workers might lead a brigade, or become an udarnik and earn high rewards:

> Broad is the road that leads into the field.
> Over the field a light wind is blowing.
> Our tractor driver's name is Pasha,
> She wears a bright red kerchief.
> There behind the tractor's wheel
> The girl is sitting like a king.
> Her tongue is very sharp,
> She is a real brigadier.[22]

This song spoke of the shock worker as a wealthy woman because these women often received higher wages than others as well as presents and perquisites including vacations in Sochi and other desirable places. In the mid 1930s, some young dairy maids vowed to exceed milk production at their farms. Stakhanovite Evdokiia Piliukh milked 4,256 liters from her cow in 256 days. The following song could have been written about her:

> We, milkmaids on the collective farm,
> Will swiftly turn out our work:
> We work in the shock-brigade fashion,
> We want to live in the Stalin way.[23]

Other ditties deified Lenin and Stalin:

> I will buy a portrait of Lenin,
> And put it in a little gold frame.
> He brought me out into the light,
> Ignorant peasant woman that I was.[24]

Some of these songs are more believable than others. Some smack of heavy-handed Soviet propaganda. Certainly women predominated among rural shock workers and Stakhanovites. Some were milkmaids, others beet and potato harvesters—like Mariia Demchenko and Klavdiia Epikhina, still others tractor drivers like the famous Pasha Angelina and Daria Garmash. One milkmaid near Leningrad vowed: "We shall fight for 5000 litres of milk from each cow." Certainly the words of Daria Garmash in her memoirs express her love of driving a tractor:

> Here, on the first day of plowing, I keenly felt the depth of my love for my chosen profession. I celebrated my triumph, rejoiced at the fulfillment of my dreams, experienced what that happiness is to be occupied with one's favourite work. "There is no force," I thought, "that could tear me away from the fields."[25]

C. Generational Differences

While some peasant women saw their lives improve during the mid-1930s, others continued to oppose collectivization and remained independent farmers. On her visits to various farms in the 1930s, the British writer Mrs. Chesterton observed this phenomenon. At the Lenin Commune near Moscow, she met a well-educated Komsomolka named Natasha, who went to the countryside to move peasants into the collective farms. While she drew many into the kolkhoz, she was unable to persuade her parents to join and take advantage of the modern conveniences, such as electricity. Her parents remained independent farmers, even though they could barely produce enough to pay the heavy taxes levied on their farm. Children of such parents sometimes migrated to the cities or joined a collective farm. Chesterton thought Stalin had miscalculated the peasantry because 20 percent resisted collectivization and preferred to retain their holdings despite the high taxes. She also observed a generation gap in peasant women's religious behavior. Old peasants tended to keep religious observances while young ones did not. Whether young women were intimidated or simply disinterested in participating in religious rites and rituals is uncertain. Despite sporadic campaigns to eliminate religion, some churches remained open, and religious rites and rituals flourished.[26]

Some of the fiercest resistance to collectivization centered on religion. Many believers thought the Kolkhoz represented the Antichrist. Some heard rumors of not being allowed to baptize their children if they joined a kolkhoz. Gossip abounded. Numerous women heard of "everyone sleeping under one blanket" and rejected collective farm life due to rumors of loose sexual mores. Those who contested collective farms tended to engage in spontaneous, sporadic rebellions. Lacking organization, farm administrators and party members let these women alone, and little violence was used against them. Later, the government was able to circumvent their unorganized demonstrations, and they eventually died out.[27]

Another generational difference was access to education. In the 1930s, elementary education became available to young peasants, as schools were established in villages and collective farms. Literacy became widespread among the youth, while reading corners were set up to teach older illiterate women. But many were unable to pursue these opportunities because they had hard lives demanding all their time and energy—children to raise, gardens to tend, livestock to care for, cooking, cleaning, and mending to do, plus working on the kolkhoz. Many older, married women were too exhausted to take advantage of the literacy courses.

D. Disgust among Peasants

1. Louise Huebert

> How beautiful was the Tchongraw of my childhood! It was a village like no other in the Crimea and my people had made it so before Stalin made it a Kolkhoz.
>
> Louise Huebert

Soviet sources mostly proclaim the stories of peasant women who succeeded in the new system of collectivization. It's harder to find memoirs of disaffected peasants. Unusual sources are available from the American Historical Society of Germans from Russia museum in Lincoln, Nebraska. They include the stories of German farmers living in Ukraine and Crimea who were literate, kept diaries, and wrote their memoirs in exile after migrating to the West at the end of World War II. Two such accounts are found in Louise Huebert's *I Heard My People Cry* and Hilda Mielke's *Border Crossing: A Bridge of Hope, An Oral History*. Their sagas tell the stories of their families' responses to collectivization and their lives during the 1930s. Huebert's book recounts her extended family's unsuccessful attempt to leave the Soviet Union during 1929 to 1930. She indicates that her family was fortunate to sell their land, houses, and implements before going to Moscow to obtain visas to emigrate to Canada. Louise's mother, Elizabeth, kept a diary and recorded that their trip to Moscow in September 1929 took two days by train. She noted: "Peter has gone to Canada, my sister Mariechen Koop to Brazil and Suse is waiting in Moskva to emigrate. Now it is my turn ... why am I so nervous?" The story as told by Louise continues:

> The Hueberts all had (internal) passports for the trip to Moskva. They expected to live in the city maybe a month—maybe longer—with carefully laid plans. *Opapa* Heinrich Huebert had rented an empty summerhouse on the outskirts of Moskva where they planned to stay

together. They were my grandparents Heinrich and Maria Huebert with their children; *Tante* Mariechen Huebert with her husband Nick Enns and their children; my parents Nikolai Huebert and Elizabeth Koop Huebert with six month old Mary; also *Tante* Nettie Huebert and Uncle Gerhard Huebert....

At the Bureau of Emigration the Huebert men stood in long lines and moved from floor to floor to get all the signatures on their many papers. Every day it was the same. At night they returned cold and dirty from the sooty, snow piled streets with their hair and clothes smelling of smoke from the coal burning engines....

"It won't be long now, Elizabeth," my father said the night they returned with all the visas signed. "After tomorrow we sit and wait"....

The next day the heavy freeze had broken. It turned warm enough to snow. The Huebert men were first in line visas in hand, to sign papers for permission to emigrate and for a departure date. They were shown into a waiting room where an official in the uniform of the GPU (Soviet secret police) drew them aside. My father was at first surprised, then became tense and wary.

"Why GPU? Up to now we have dealt with civilians. Stalin's GPU is a law unto itself," he whispered to Gerhard beside him.

"Go home and wait for a notice from our office. We'll let you know when you can depart," said the official with a smile. His quick wave told them they were dismissed.[28]

But that night they heard the wail of sirens, and the police came to take all the men.

"Heinrich Huebert?"

"Yes, that's me—"

"We have papers here for all the men in this house. You will come with us"....

"You will come with us immediately. Get dressed. No baggage. It'll be warm where you're going. You won't need much. Hurry!"[29]

Nikolai intervened to say that they had visas, and there was some mistake. But the GPU just told them to hurry, and the five Huebert men left with them. It turned out that Russia's borders had been closed, and they were unable to leave. The women were taken by the GPU the next night, and they were all returned to Tchongraw in the Crimea. It was a time of great change. Foreigners had to stop traveling, no one was allowed to emigrate, censorship began, Russians could be exiled for speaking to foreigners, and no more foreign newspapers or books were allowed.[30]

The Huebert family had first come to Tchongraw in 1918. They had built a remarkably lovely village with straight, tree-lined streets and fruit trees and flower gardens at every house. The houses of the grandparents were large and had lush pear and apple trees. Lilac, magnolia, mulberry, and cherry trees all bedecked the village. Forests of ash and oak had been planted and grown wonderfully tall by the mid-1930s. Although everything in the village was controlled by the ruling Soviet, the place remained lovely because the German families kept it that way. However, when collectivization came, the sheds and houses were requisitioned by the Soviet to store animals, and when Gerhard Wiens died, the Soviet made offices and a Machine Tractor Station (MTS) of his big house.[31]

As Louise remembered it as a child, everyone got a job under collectivization:

> My uncle Frank Klassan was appointed to look after the horses and Uncle Gerhard Huebert was a good mechanic, so he operated the MTS. He serviced farm machines that had been purchased from America by the village Volostshod. A whole row of combines stood in the MTS yard for many years and none of them worked. Although my uncle was very conscientious the machines took a long time to fix because he couldn't get parts. Only a few of those parts could be tooled by hand. When a part was bad little could be done. Therefore my people had little use of those combines.
>
> Soon after I was born (1930) Stalin decreed the *Internal Passport System* laws and everyone had to have a passport to work. We had to show a passport to travel anywhere in the country—guarded them with our very lives.
>
> How beautiful was the Tchongraw of my childhood! It was a village like no other in the Crimea and my people had made it so before Stalin made it a Kolkhoz. When that happened Opapa Heinrich Huebert received nothing. He lost all his investment, his lands, and my people lost their village. Everything changed. All the fields were turned into one large farm and Tchongraw became my people's prison. That is what happened throughout Russia....
>
> Stalin passed a *Decree on the Punishment of Collective Farmers for Failure to Fulfill the Obligatory Norm of Labor Days* so my father had to work very hard. Even in the rain he rose before the sun and worked very late because there was always work for him to do. On Sundays he was free to be with us and some Saturdays he could stop work at noon....
>
> During seeding and harvest my father Nikolai drove the tractor to earn extra *Trudodnye* (labor day credit points) for the number of

hours he worked. He could never be ill. Revenues from Tchongraw's harvests went to the ruling Soviet to pay the *Kolkhoz*'s expenses—poll tax, a *Vollwirtschaft* tax, village food expenses and village fire insurance. Only after all those expenses were met was my father paid, and then not in rubles—always in produce. According to the number of *Trudodnye* he earned my father was given so much grain, so much corn—so much this and so much that. He was also given *Talon* (paper coupons) that we exchanged at our little village store for sugar and salt. Any family that had only one worker to earn credit points, as we did, found themselves with very little of anything. Nikolai was given a few rubles during the year. They were only enough to pay his personal taxes, so the ruling Soviet got their rubles back.

We suffered greatly because very little was left in Tchongraw for us to eat.... My family's only vegetables came from a tiny plot Mom and we children were allowed to plant in the summer. All Tchongraw's grain harvests, livestock, and produce were sent north to feed Stalin's cities and the wealthy.... We knew Stalin was building a strong war industry. He justified starving us to build up our country which we were told was a hundred years behind those in the west. It was obvious our lives didn't matter. During the world-wide Great Depression of 1932 even the little bit we had was worth absolutely nothing and yet Tchongraw always had a market for all its grain and produce—the ruling Soviet just took it. I remember our Komissar (appointed Russian official, head of the Volostshod) always took photographs of the wagons that left Tchongraw.

Such harsh production and harvest quotas were demanded of every Kolkhoz in Russia. Perhaps we in Tchongraw were even luckier than most because in Ukraine the farmlands had been laid waste by civil wars and in 1932–1933 for the second time, millions of people died in another "man made famine."

It was after my brother Nick was born in 1932 that my mother wanted to go into the fields to work so my family would have more credit points.

"You're not strong enough and the children are too little to leave alone," my Dad said. Then he added, "But I don't know what there is to do ... our grain is almost gone ... the new harvest isn't even underway yet—"

Those were words no child would forget. From then on we children were never given enough to eat and I was always hungry. I watched my parents go without bread so I could eat and mother ate very little so Dad would stay strong enough to work. In 1934 my mother was very thin when she became pregnant with her fourth child. A Russian doctor insisted she have an abortion.[32]

Two years later, in 1936, the NKVD (a later name for the secret police) began locking up the German farmers from the village of Tchongraw. The local Komissar began arresting the men aged sixteen to sixty in June 1936. About the same time, some dispossessed peasants—or "untouchables" as they were called—arrived from Ukraine. Louise describes them as follows:

> By the thousands of thousands they fled across the face of Russia. We called them untouchables. They were forced into bankruptcy by the Ruling Soviet and stripped of their citizenship rights—vital passports destroyed. Driven out of their villages they feared for their lives and for the lives of anyone who might try to help them. Whole families were driven into exile. They fled to Siberia or hid in Russia's northern cities—fled to forests in the far north—to the Ural Mountains or to Wologka. They fled in terror by the thousands to try and live off the land. We were told that if they went to northern cities like Moskva the Ruling Soviet took them by the trainloads to the Ural Mountains and left them there. Many fled to the Crimea—and so to Tchongraw....
>
> ... I was not too young to know about the purges. People were persecuted, exiled, or imprisoned in Gulags to disappear forever— "Red Terror"—the words were etched into my young mind. Stalin had expanded the Tsar's Gulags until all of northern Russia was a vast prison camp and prisoners were used to run mines, cut timber, build canals and factories and repair railroads. Millions of people were enslaved. Entire classes of people were being removed ... Ministers of churches were among the first. In 1935 it was my mother who taught me to pray. It was *Opapa* Heinrich Huebert who continued to read to me out of his Bible with tears rolling down his cheeks.
>
> From the day I saw the first Black Maria, an awesome dread rolled over Tchongraw—fear of torture—being taken away. Fear lay behind my parents' words when they awoke and fear went to bed with them. "Will our family be broken up?—" I heard them ask. Every night my parents spoke together when they thought I couldn't hear.
>
> "They're removing more men from villages all around us," said my mom one night. "They haven't come back to Tchongraw—"
>
> "Our town is more protected," said my dad. "Maybe it's because we're up here in the hills. Also, I know our families are very good to their Russian field workers."
>
> "It's only a matter of time, Nikolai—" was the last thing I heard Mom say every night before I fell asleep.[33]

The roundup began in Tchongraw in July 1936 when a man named Klaus, who wanted to be elected to the Volostshod, was discovered to have failed to declare a relative living in Germany. This was against Soviet policy. When the authorities found out, the Komissar harassed them all. As Louise records the conversation, the Soviet official slammed the tables and swaggered around the hall shaking his fists, shouting:

> "This town's going to feel it! You're going to feel it!" He threatened all the people of Tchongraw.

This was the story Louise remembered:

> My people believed that incident began the purge of Tchongraw. The removal of most of my uncles and male cousins over sixteen. From that night onward the terror unleashed upon my people grew and grew.[34]

In the midst of Tchongraw's terror, some untouchables arrived needing housing and passports. Louise recalls this event and records one young girl's words as follows:

> Margaret began, "My family had to run from our village ... they chased us. We lost our land and house, all our things ... only they let me keep my shoes ... what I had on. Papa couldn't pay taxes so they auctioned, sold everything we had ... everything"....
>
> Then Margaret continued. It was the Komissar who drove us out and we all had to run. No one could talk to us or help us. Even my *Tante* Greta or my *Omama* (granny), they couldn't help us. *Tante* and everyone, they were all crying. The Komissars made people yell at us ... awful, evil words. *Omama* wouldn't and ... oh ... my *Omama*! They hit her ... my *Omama* ... poor *Omama*." Choking sobs shook her body so hard that Mrs. Brugge held her in her arms.
> I had never heard such things. I held my breath. I didn't want to be sent outside. The kind of horror that was in that very room even I, a child, knew what it felt like—could taste it icy cold—could see it on my father's face....
> Then Margaret began again. When we reached the end of our village the Komissar ... he shot my dog. Then he yelled, "If you return here we'll kill you! We'll find you!" ...and we had no food, nowhere to go. We ran out over the grasslands ... we hid. Papa said we couldn't go near people. I know they'll kill people who help us.[35]

Louise's parents realized that they needed to take one of the untouchables, so they did. Although they had scant food, they shared it with the young girl named Margaret. Eventually, room was found for most of the family and they worked on the kolkhoz.³⁶

As Louise remembered it, the Red Terror and purges came to her village in greater force in November 1936. She writes:

> More cars came to Tchongraw all that fall. Like frothing waves the fear ebbed and flowed—swallowed my people one by one—by twos and threes. Men and young boys over sixteen disappeared into prisons and Gulags. My aunts and girl cousins went to work in fields to feed themselves and their children and to meet Stalin's harvest quotas. The Russian Komissar of our Volostshod was a former peasant field hand who had worked for one of our villagers. He lived outside of Tchongraw. That man was a very rough man—rude and arrogant with his new power.
>
> "Who's going to be next?" I heard the words from my parents' bedroom over and over in the night and the words *Red Terror*—always those words—*Red Terror*. Then I learned what *Red Terror* really meant for my people. Walter's father, our friend and cousin Mr. Toews was the elected vice-president of our *Volostshod*—and Mr. Toews was *Verschlept* (forcefully removed, imprisoned, and tortured). Uncle Gerhart Huebert was the first to tell my father. He hurried home late that afternoon to find our barn door open and light from a lantern spilling out onto a corn pile in our *Vollwirtschaft*. Gerhard walked through the open door and pushed it closed behind him. Inside he heard footsteps and sweeping.
> "Nikolai?" he called....
> "Nikolai? Have you heard?" asked Gerhard. "Toews was summoned to the Village Soviet last night. NKVD have taken him to be interrogated."
> "No!" Nikolai sat down heavily on a bench. "He's a good man, Gerhard. What could they possibly say against him?"
> "I don't know? ... he's even part of our Volostshod. It's frightening. Nikolai, I'm frightened."³⁷

The arrests proceeded until the NKVD had imprisoned all eligible men between the ages of sixteen and sixty. When Mr. Toews and Frank Klassan were released from prison and returned to Tchongraw in January, both had been badly tortured but never talked about what had been done to them. Then in January, Louise's father was incarcerated in Simferopol on trumped-up charges. A few days later the NKVD returned to get her mother to sign a form that was later used to incriminate her husband.³⁸ Louise recalls the NKVD ordering her mother to fill in the form:

"Fill in your husband's full name, his birthday, and where he was born," ordered the officer. He was getting impatient.

Elizabeth was afraid to question. She did as she was told. What harm could it do? I watched as she filled in the few questions.

"And here—age and religion." He jabbed at a bottom line. "You are Christians."

Elizabeth froze—pen in the air. "Why have you taken my husband? He's a good man and is needed by his family."

"There—on the bottom—sign it. Sign it!"

"It doesn't say anything . . ." said my mother.

"Sign! It doesn't have to say anything, Mrs. Huebert."

"What is my husband accused of?"

"Sign! You are not supposed to read that—it isn't written here. Your husband is only in for questioning—Sign!" he said fiercely.

Mother sat mute.

All of a sudden that officer leaned over little Nick and threatened her in a loud whisper, "You have children to take care of, Mrs. Huebert—sign! It will be easier for you and your children."

She did.

They didn't just leave. We children climbed up beside Mother on the bed as they walked through our two rooms in their fierce looking jackboots—tall, shiny, black boots. They quickly stripped our rooms—took Grandfather's Bible, all our belongings, everything they could carry. What they didn't take they dumped and stomped on. Over and over they—stomped!—stomped! Those high, flashing jackboots were frightening to look at—cruel heels—kicking, crunching, crushing ... They just went on and on. One NKVD went to the shed and took our pig away—our only meat. Everything they took from us. On the bed my mother held us tightly to her. We children were too frightened to cry.[39]

In March, Elizabeth was allowed to visit her husband, Nikolai. She and other wives were allowed to go to Simferopol to visit their husbands in prison. When they met, they had to sit at opposite tables. He asked her how she could have signed a paper denouncing him of poisoning the town well. She realized that this was an accusation hard to disprove. She told him the paper she had signed was blank. Then he cried. They told each other of their love, and he could see she was far along in her pregnancy. She thought he would be home before the baby was born, but he wanted her to bring the baby to him for him to see in prison. When Elizabeth took their new baby to visit Nikolai in May 1937, the guard at first refused to let Nikolai touch the new baby. Finally another guard took the baby to Nikolai so he could hold its tiny hand and stroke its cheek. Then Nikolai cried and cried. Elizabeth and the other children also cried. It was the last time they saw their father.[40]

On the train from Simferopol, Elizabeth told her daughters: "The Lord is with us. He will protect us. He will carry us in his arms like the lambs of the field." Slowly Elizabeth became calm and resolute. One day she told the children: "I will teach you how to survive. You must survive and you must get out of Russia."[41] After the prisoners left Crimea, Elizabeth received a postcard with her husband's address, and she wrote many letters to him, but after three years she learned that he had died and her last letter was returned to her. It turned out that Nikolai had not died, but he had lost the right to correspond. Louise was seven years old when her father was arrested and deported to the Gulag. It was also seven years since her parents had tried to emigrate from Russia.[42]

While one might think this was the final calamity of the Huebert family, it was not. After taking all their goods except their beds, the local komissar forced them out of their homestead. He bellowed:

> "I don't care where you go, Mrs. Huebert! Just vacate the rooms!" he shouted. "Your husband is gone and those two rooms are too big for one adult. Children don't count." Waving his arms over his head he screamed, "Out! Out! Out! We have a family coming for those rooms." With that he spun around and strutted out of our yard like a preening rooster.[43]

That winter, Louise's grandmother died. Two years later, in 1939, her grandfather died. By the summer of 1939, most of the men of their village had been imprisoned. One of Louise's aunts invited her to come to live with her in a nearby town. It meant one less mouth for her mother to feed. Eventually, her mother had to return to working in the fields, and the children had to help her with the housework and other chores. Slowly, life and their food supply improved. They were able to get some animals, and her mother Elizabeth sold some of the lambs' wool at the market in Simferopol. They also traded their butter for eggs. Life was looking up, and the children were playing games when the German army arrived in the summer of 1941. The story of their exodus during World War II, however, is the subject of another book.

2. Hilda Schulz Mielke

> Our village established an underground information network. Whenever Mama went to town, our German mayor would tell her when the soldiers would conduct another raid. Papa resisted because he thought times would change. He hoped one day to farm freely again.
>
> Hilda Mielke

A tale similar to Louise's is told by Hilda Schulz Mielke, who was born in 1925, the fifth of eight children, to a prosperous, literate, peasant family in the Ukrainian village of Rogowka, forty-five miles west of Kiev. Like Louise's family, Hilda's family did well before collectivization. Their farm consisted of sixty-nine acres, and they raised wheat, rye, oats, and potatoes. They also possessed fruit trees, milk cows, pigs, chickens, and a small flock of geese and ducks. Their livestock provided them meat, the chickens eggs, and the cows milk and butter. Her father also tended bees, which produced honey. They also had four horses used for farming and pulling wagons. They enjoyed a good life. The farm met their needs, and they earned extra money from the local market, where they bought fabric, clothes, and other supplies. During the first six years of Hilda's life, they were well to do. But when collectivization was introduced, high quotas and taxes were levied on private farmers. Her family struggled to meet the requirements, and they illegally concealed food to sustain themselves. They buried potatoes in the field and hid sacks of flour to make sure they would have enough to eat. Finally, they were unable to meet the government quotas. Her father read and kept abreast of the political news. He disseminated this information and was then identified as a member of the resistance. When he wasn't able to fulfill his obligations, a warrant was issued for his arrest and he became a hunted man.[44]

Red Army soldiers were stationed in nearby Zhitomir, and they made frequent visits looking for Hilda's father. She describes their forays as follows:

> When the soldiers appeared on the horizon, my mother would turn white and scream for Papa to hide. Most of the time he hid in a hole concealed behind a kitchen cabinet. If he was outside, he would hide in the barn under the straw or in the growing grains. Because they were unable to catch him, the soldiers increased their visits. When that proved unsuccessful, they came mostly at night. When Mama heard

the horses in the yard or the knock on the door, she loudly whispered, "Papa, they're here again" and the scramble began. The fear of Papa being captured was a heavy emotional weight upon Mama.

Our village established an underground information network. Whenever Mama went to town (it wasn't safe for Papa to go), our German mayor would tell her when the soldiers would conduct another raid. Papa resisted because he thought times would change. He hoped one day to farm freely again.[45]

After collectivization and the famine of 1930–31, her parents secretly decided to move to a German collective in the town of Andrejew, twenty-five kilometers away. It was her mother's hometown, and her father spoke to the mayor of the town and arranged for thirteen sleds to quietly come and take their belongings to their new home at four o'clock one winter morning. No one in their old village saw them leave, so no one could report them to the police. Their new town, Andrejew, was divided into Ukrainian and German sections. Initially they got along because both groups resented communism. Hilda's family moved into a wooden house of four rooms. Two rooms were taken by one family with seven members, and her family occupied the remaining two rooms. The children slept in one room, and the parents in the kitchen. They were able to keep one milk cow, a lamb, some geese and ducks, but the rest of the animals had to be given to the collective farm. In 1932 famine struck their area, and people fought over food. Her father traded his gold ring in Zhitomir for bread and supplies. God was gracious to her family, and they remained healthy despite their dire circumstances.[46]

As Hilda remembered this time in her oral history:

> The Central Committee director gave each family in our village a half hectare of land for their own garden, and Papa took great pride in his plot. It was our primary means of survival. In the springtime when the weeds (like sorrel and nettles) came up, we picked them and added them to our soup. We feared we might be poisoned by eating the wrong weeds, but there was nothing else to eat.
>
> During the summer there was naturally more food to eat, but the food we raised had to last all year long ... We had a couple of apple trees plus cherry, plum, and pear trees in our yard ... Besides eating our harvest fresh, we dried and packed any extra produce in preparation for winter.[47]

Since their garden was so productive, neighbor children often stole fruit and vegetables from it. Recalling their family work situation, Hilda remarked:

> Each day from spring through fall Mama and my older sisters went to work on an assigned farm. They would work from sunrise to sunset. The largest crops were wheat, rye, barley, oats, and potatoes ... Potatoes were a basic staple of food for almost every meal. Potato scraps and peels were used over and over again, boiled in water to extract a broth for soup. When the potatoes turned soft or spoiled, they were turned into vodka; and in the Ukrainian section of town, vodka was plentiful....
> I was too young to work in the fields. I was around ten years old, still a child; so my responsibility was to care for our animals and prepare meals for my family. But I wanted to play, forgetting my responsibilities, which often resulted in a spanking when Mama came home. It was a hard childhood. Papa worked year round in the state-owned horse collective. He cleaned out stalls and provided fresh feed and bedding for the horses, working into the evening and through the night after the horses were brought in from the fields. He slept during the early part of the day and worked in his garden in the afternoon. He also helped around the house, making life a little easier for Mama.
> Papa remained a strong follower of the political scene. I see him so vividly, smoking hand-rolled cigarettes and reading the newspaper. He was a heavy smoker. Often during breaks at work, he spoke out against the Russian bureaucrats. When word of his ranting reached Mama, it raised her fears that one day the sate officials would arrest him....
> I started school when I was eight and stopped when I was twelve. School began after harvest. We met in a home in the middle of the village, a half hour away. I was in a class of twenty to twenty-five children, all about the same age. We learned to read and write; we also studied history and math and were given lots of memory work. Most of my schooling was in German; but as the Communists gained greater control, our schools were taught in Russian; only one hour of German study was allowed each day. During recess we played games similar to volleyball and tether ball, and many of the children played chess. When I turned twelve, my mother took me out of school to work along side her on a farm. It was so sad to work a field for the entire year and not receive any of its bounty. But the human spirit is adaptable, even under these circumstances.
> Our Lutheran church, which had originally been founded by Moravian missionaries, under Communism was closed. All bibles were confiscated. My family hid ours and read it to us in secret. Our church was reopened as a community center and dance hall.

Our social life consisted of folk dances and plays directed and performed by village members. I remember a number of our villagers also played the accordion, violin, guitar, mandolin, and trumpet. One time when I was twelve, I tried to join the adult dance. An older man grabbed me by the neck and threw me out of the hall. He told me, "Children are only supposed to watch."

One Christmas, the tree in our community center was beautifully decorated with candles and draped with cookies, candies, and nuts. Balls of cotton were used to simulate snow. One of the men of the town dressed up like St. Nickolas but got too close to the burning candles and lit his costume on fire. The men threw him on the ground and put out the fire with their coats. Still he was severely injured and almost died. It was very scary.[48]

Like Louise, Hilda became aware of the purges as a youth. She describes the process in the following words:

Over a period of three years, thirty men from our village were arrested by Russian secret police (GPU). Mama knew it was only a matter of time when they would come for my father. In October 1937 around midnight, the GPU pounded on our door. The police from Zhitomir forced our German mayor to direct them to where the Schulzes lived. When they arrived, my younger siblings and I were frightened and began to cry. My two older brothers, Hermann and Willy, remained quiet in the back room because they feared that if they were seen by the police, they also might be imprisoned.

Papa opened the door. "*Bistra, Schulz, Bistra Bistra*" (faster, faster) the soldiers yelled. As Papa slowly dressed, Mama hurriedly packed extra clothing in a bag. The soldiers kept yelling, and Mama began to weep. As Papa was escorted from the house, Mama and my youngest brother Walter put on their clothes and followed at a distance, out of view.

It was dark when Papa and a handful of other men boarded a truck. Before the truck left, Mama overheard my father ask our mayor to deliver a message to her. "Tell Mama not to cry for me. Tell her to pray to God that she is able to stay with the children." He also asked that Mama would make him some warm gloves. Mama quietly cried; and as the truck departed, a horn blew. Mama said the sound was like the truck was moaning sorrow.

The next day Mama found out that the men were taken to Tschernichow, our neighboring village and imprisoned. She learned they would be transported to Zhitomir in a few days. Because cold weather had set in, Mama wasn't working during the day and went every day to the prison. But she was never allowed to speak to or see my father.

She dropped off clothes and gloves a number of times, never sure if he received them. She also delivered food, but she never knew if it even reached him.[49]

Only once after his imprisonment did her brother and mother catch sight of her father. Hilda later learned that her father was killed fifteen days after being arrested. Her sister Margarethe visited Ukraine in the late 1990s and investigated their father's death. She learned that the GPU had pulled over to the side of the road and shot the men when they were being transferred to Zhitomir. Those not killed were transported to Siberia and often died in work camps. Only a few survived.[50]

After her father's arrest, the local communist leader directed their family to move out of their house into a collective closer to Tschernichow. The Central Committee wanted a planned community that looked neat and orderly. As Hilda remembered this period:

> Each home was a half kilometer from their next door neighbor and included a half hectare of land for a garden. We dug a large hole in the ground near the site of our new home and covered it as best we could with boards and straw and slept in it until our home was finished. The dismantling and transfer took a few weeks while it rained and snowed a number of times. I became very ill with something like pneumonia and had to spend eight days in the hospital. When I came home, our home was finished. It was shameful, but it was better than nothing.
>
> We shared four rooms with my brother Hermann, who had married, and his family. They lived in two rooms while our family lived in the other two. We had a little lean-to shed attached to the house with doors that provided protection for our cow, pig, and some chickens.
>
> Every day we carried fresh drawn milk in buckets to the community collective, about a twenty-minute walk. There the cream was mechanically removed and churned into butter which was then transported out of our village. The remaining skim milk was brought back home. Mama blended squash into the milk for a simple soup broth. She added whatever greens were available, and then we dipped dried pieces of bread for a meal. We received an allotment of flour after each harvest from which we had our own bread.
>
> Our quota of eggs had to first be met before we kept any for ourselves. What remained, Mama kept in reserve for visiting guests. When she prepared the eggs, she used flour to stretch them further.
>
> Because this was the first year in our new home, we didn't have our own well. Water had to be carried from a well far away. It was

winter, and we wore woolen socks covered by wooden shoes; yet still our feet were continually wet.

The fuel sources for our stove were cow dung and peat moss. The dung naturally dried in pasture. Peat moss was harvested throughout the summer and placed on stakes for drying in the sunshine.

Once a year we were permitted to harvest wood. It was during winter and only under the direction of the Central Committee. A work foreman appointed ten to twelve people to ride a horse and buggy to a forest thirty-five kilometers from our home. I participated once. We rode two persons per buggy and stayed ten days to cut wood for the government and ourselves. I helped saw small branches and stack wood. The wood was often too wet to burn; it would take a season or longer to prepare it for burning. At the wood-cutting camp, we slept on the floor in a barn. A small stove radiated minimal warmth and was used for meal preparation. Cleanliness was not a priority, and everyone got lice. When the wagons were stacked full of wood, we returned home....

During winter months our evenings were spent with handwork: making clothing and crocheting gloves and socks. Mama would work late into the evening spinning black and white yarn on our home loom; and she was the first one up in the morning, either knitting or preparing meals. During the day, whenever we had heavy snowfall, we were directed by our foreman to shovel roads or clear it away from homes in town.

Sunday was our only day off. We spent the day with village friends playing games like Alter Saue (Old Pig). We also made a ball from cattle molt, and with a stick tried to take the ball away from an opponent. One of my favorite group games was Mein Platz is lear, Mein Platz is lear, Ich moechte Erich Hier (My place is empty, My place is Empty, I'd like Erich over here). The person who was named would have to run over to the team that called him or her.[51]

In many ways, Hilda's oral history mirrors Louise's. Both girls were young children during the 1930s, and both lost their fathers in 1937. Both families had to struggle to survive. Indeed, life seemed to be looking up for them, and they both wrote about enjoying life and playing games before the war. Initially, the German invasion didn't alter their lives too much. In Hilda's village, the church reopened and the German-speaking people felt freer than under the Soviets. However, Jews in Zhitomir were killed, and Ukrainian and Russian youth from their village were deported to Germany to work. The German-speaking population was favored with extra sugar, flour, and clothing. Of course Hilda and other German-speaking farmers were pleased by these kindnesses. As the Ukrainian partisans organized, however, life for the Germans deteriorated. The German mayor had his eyes poked out by resistance fighters. And a nearby German village was burned. Hilda's neighbors organized a night guard to protect themselves. As the war wound down, both Hilda's and Louise's families decided to leave with the German army. In wagon caravans, both families traveled through Ukraine, Poland, and Germany. Their families eventually made it to the British and American sectors in Germany, and later emigrated to the United States and Canada.[52]

Of course, war for Ukrainian and Russian peasants meant a bleak existence. While the Soviet purges had declined after 1939, deportation of youth to work in German factories and serve in the army began in 1941. Food remained scarce as the Germans deported grain to their homeland.

Other Russian farmers during the 1930s were also experiencing disruptions. Well into the decade, Russian peasants used wooden plows, sowed crops by hand, harvested with sickles and scythes, and threshed grain by hand. Only after industrialization began producing plows and threshing machines did some women's lives improve. Most farms lacked the equipment they needed to farm well. Rural overpopulation and the harshness of collectivization, deportation of "kulaks," and grain requisitions pushed millions out of rural areas.[53]

3. Collectivization

> The woman could not have recognized Mother, now a crippled woman without teeth, who looked ninety years old. She had a dirty kerchief on her head and wore baggy, ill-fitting clothing.
>
> Helen Dmitriew

The Communist Party's first Five-Year Plan, 1928–32, included the collectivization of farming. Initially the party defined collective farming as a voluntary process, but peasant resistance to joining kolkhozes proved greater than expected. As a result, the party resorted to coercion, harassment, use of the Red Army, grain requisitioning, and famine to detach peasants from their land, exile recalcitrant ones, and gather obliging ones into communal farms.

Technically, the collective farm, or kolkhoz, was an artel—a sharing of land, animals, and implements—where people lived in private houses with gardens and orchards. Eventually, the kolkhozy became more like cooperatives, and members were allowed to have a few animals and private plots for growing vegetables. Initially, all herds of animals were owned in common, and most peasants opposed this policy when collectivization began. They believed that others would not care for their animals properly, so they slaughtered their cows, sheep, and pigs, thus creating a terrible meat shortage in urban areas. Lack of animal manure also reduced grain yields for several years.

In the 1920s, Soviet planners did not expect collectivization to produce famine instead of abundance. They thought collectivization would modernize Soviet agriculture, making it more productive. They did not foresee peasants slaughtering their horses and cattle to avoid giving them to the hastily organized communal farms. Nor did they anticipate the worldwide depression that reduced the government's ability to acquire foreign-made tractors. In July 1929 only a few hundred thousand peasants lived on state or collective farms. But by March 1930, 14 million households had been reorganized into 111,000 kolkhozy, and by 1933, 210,000 kolkhozy occupied 80 percent of the land. Since each household involved at least four

Reading the Paper to a Brigade of Vegetable Growers, *1937*, Alexandrov, Leningrad Oblast (St. Petersburg Photo Archive)

members, collectivization involved millions of people. Such radical change initially provoked chaos, confusion, and contentious behavior more than cooperation.

4. Dekulakization

The party treated those deemed "kulaks" brutally. Technically, kulaks were those who paid others to help with farming operations, and there were about eight hundred thousand kulak households according to the 1926 census. If each household had four to five members, then the number of households constituted about 4 million people. In the 1930s, "kulak" came to mean those who resisted collectivization. Part of the government campaign was the policy of "dekulakization," or the getting rid of kulaks as a class. Redistributing four or more million people proved a painful process. Some were exiled from their villages, becoming "untouchables"; some were arrested, imprisoned, shot, or sent to forced-labor camps. In some cases, half of a village was wiped out in the liquidation process. Organizers drove the kulaks out of their houses and took their cows. Strangers, who didn't know the area, were put in charge of the kolkhoz as managers, and nothing went well. Some farms suffered a series of directors, many of whom were drunks. Some kolkhozes wouldn't take widows with children. What were they to do?[54]

The term "kulak" meant different things. To Soviet policy makers, it had come to mean those who resisted their policies, as well as the older definition of wealthy farmers, like Hilda Mielke's family. In contrast, the American journalist Maurice Hindus, who periodically returned to Russia, thought that Russian kulaks were not well to do but thrifty, hardworking farmers. He noticed that when these people were deprived of their property, exiled from the village, and then reinstated, they felt no desire to work hard because they might be dispossessed a second time.[55] Hindus gives other examples of miserable, dispossessed kulaks. Some wailed because they didn't want to leave but wanted to die and be buried in their native village.[56] Hindus indicates that exiled kulaks having a son in the Red Army who would intercede for them were often allowed back to their area. However, exile could kill as well as break people's spirits, and many who survived were never strong again.[57]

His tour of Russian villages in 1929–30 sheds light on peasant attitudes toward collectivization. He explains that it was adopted as part of the party's first Five-Year Plan in 1928 but was not implemented until 1929. In January 1930 the party declared a dekulakization policy to liquidate the kulaks as a class. One official told Hindus that peasants had their own five-year plan: Every one had his own five-year plan, at the end of which he wanted to become a kulak.[58] So, the government and many farmers were at loggerheads.

Hindus identified various problems in collectivization. He saw generational differences, such as the youth not being afraid of the kolkhoz even though they weren't sure what it was. No rancor existed among them. They were happy to hear promises of entertainment, including a reading hut, a cultural center, drama circles, plays, and movies at the larger farms. However, older farmers often opposed collectivization. They were suspicious of kolkhozy, where "bedniaks," or poor peasants, predominated. They thought the poor peasants were poor farmers, and they didn't want to work with them. Disorder, dissension, and slovenliness were chronic problems among poor peasants, and middle and wealthy farmers feared being adversely affected by them and their ways.

Hindus's book *Red Bread* is anecdotal rather than statistical and analytical, yet it includes useful material and touching vignettes. He tells about a Jewish landlord and cattle breeder who was squeezed out by the Soviets' high taxes. His eldest son was not allowed to study at the university because of his social origins, and life became more and more threatening for the family. Finally the Jewish rancher decided to give all his land and cattle to the kolkhoz and become a herder. Three families settled in his house, and he and his wife retained only two rooms. He seemed content to be as poor as everyone else. He resented the poor management of the kolkhoz because he had been a good manager. Still, he accepted Soviet rule and the kolkhoz.[59]

5. Memoirs of Peasants' Dekulakization

Soviet sources do not tell us about the pain of dekulakization, but some memoirs published since the fall of the Soviet regime do. Accounts of the followers of Father Sebastian, published in 1999, describe their exile to the steppe in Karaganda. Their reports are fairly similar. They describe how families were dumped on the steppe without food, water, or housing in 1931, and how some of them survived by living in dugouts. A few of their remembrances are cited in the following sections.

a. Tatiana Izyumova

> By spring, practically no people were left in settlement 13; everyone had died off.
>
> T. A. Izyumova

Tatiana Izyumova tells the story of her family's exile in the following words:

> My parents were special-status exiles. They were exiled from the Volgograd Province in 1931. There were my mother, father, and three children. They were brought to the barren steppe, to Settlement 13, which is almost ten miles from Temirtau. There were twenty-five thousand people in that settlement, and every one made dugouts in the steppe. By winter they had erected something like a shed out of brushwood, and ten families lived in the totally unheated shed. There were no windows, the roof barely covered the shed, and everyone lay on plank beds with practically no clothing. Sometimes my father would come home from work, and my mother and all the children would be lying there covered with snow. He would brush off the snow and ask, "Are you alive in there?"
>
> "Yes, we're alive." There was nothing to eat or drink. My older brother once found a block of wood, brought it to my father and said, "Papa, chop up this block and heat some tea up for us." At that moment the commandant walked up, took our father by the collar, and held him under arrest for three months because of that piece of wood.
>
> By spring, practically no people were left in settlement 13; everyone had died off. Our family was spared by a miracle—even the children and my mother. Then they were moved to Tikhonovka, where there were five-apartment dugouts, made from clay and elm wood. That's where I was born, in 1939.[60]

b. Maria Andrievskaya

> That's how our luck was, that's how our life went on in tears, poverty and sorrow.
>
> M. V. Andrievskaya

Maria Andrievskaya's account resembles Tatiana's. She writes:

> In 1931, we were exiled from the Saratov province. They brought us to Ostrovka in cattle cars and then they tossed us to the ground like cattle. I remember it all now as if it had been yesterday—rain was pouring down in buckets, and we collected the rainwater and drank it. I was then five years old, my brother was two years older than I, my little sister was three years old, and there were two infants—five children in all, plus my mother, father, grandmother, and grandfather. In the Saratov Province we were farmers and had always gone to church. They brought us to Osakarovka in a special train, to the barren steppe where we didn't sleep for two whole days. We sat on the ground next to our father and mother and held tightly to their legs. After two days, some Kazaks came in wagons, seated us in them and brought us to Settlement 5. As they were bringing us, we asked our father, "Papa, papa—where will our house be?" He said, "Soon, we'll be there soon, wait a little." They brought us to Settlement 5 and we asked, "But where's the house? Where's our house?" There was nothing there, just a pole with the inscription 'Settlement 5,' and soldiers on guard, so that we wouldn't run off. They brought us to the river Ishem, and again they tossed us to the ground. We children were bawling. Our father went and chopped down some poplar trees, and then we dug out a square hole and arranged the sticks in rows on the ground to make a shelter. We lived on the ground in the dugout until the Feast of the Protection of the Theotokos (October 1). On the Feast of the Protection, one and a half feet of snow fell. In the morning my brother woke up and said, "Mama, Grandpa's freezing and I'm freezing from him." We rushed over, but Grandpa was already finished, dead.
>
> We built barracks. The teenagers and adults carried sod on their backs for three and a half miles. After the Feast of the Protection we were settled in these barracks—there was no glass for the windows, nor were there doors. Our father was still alive then, and he would pour water in a washtub. The water would freeze, and he would take the ice and set it in the windows in place of glass. Two hundred people were sent to these barracks. In the morning you'd get up, and over here there would be ten dead people, and over there would be another five. We would carry off the corpses. I can't forget that. A Mordvinian family of twenty lived with us, and only two of them escaped to Russia. The rest died off. They brought eighteen thousand people to Settlement 5, and by spring five thousand were left. Our father died in 1932, and a month later our mother gave birth, and the six of us children were left, together with our blind grandmother. And how did we live? By begging. Our mother forbade us to steal: "No, daughter, never fill yourself on someone else's food. It's better for you to go out there

with your hand out." And so I went. Someone might give something, while someone else wouldn't, and would kick you out.

Then our newborn brother, younger sister, and grandmother all died. We began to grow to adolescence, and we went to work in a children's' brigade. In 1937 they tried to force our mother to go to a collective farm, but she didn't want to go. They said to her, "You know what you are? You're a kulak." They sentenced her to three years and sent her to the Far East. We children were left alone. My brother was fourteen years old, I was twelve, my sister was ten, and my younger brother was eight. We worked in the children's brigade, begged, worked as nurses for children, and spun yarn. We would bring and feed each other with whatever they would give us. That's how we lived for three years. Then our mother was freed, and soon the war began. They took my brother and he was killed at the Front. That's how our luck was, that's how our life went on in tears, poverty and sorrow.

In 1955 we became acquainted with Elder Sebastian. He blessed our whole family to move to Mikhailovka. Yes ... then we began to live as though in Paradise. A year after his blessing we had built a house. We were always near him and brought all our needs or sorrows to him. "It's all right," the Elder would say. "Put your hope in God: He won't abandon you." He always helped us by his holy prayers, of which we sinners were, of course, unworthy.[61]

c. Maria and Olga Orlova

> In the morning they'd get up and drag off the dead bodies. We didn't mourn over the dead there. It was beyond us.
>
> Maria Orlova, *Elder Sebastian of Optina*

Maria and Olga Orlova's sagas resemble those of Tatiana Izyumova and Maria Andrievskaya. Maria writes:

> My parents were deeply religious people. When our family was accused of being kulaks and was dispossessed in 1931, my father said, "This is what God has sent us. We have to drink this cup." They arrested my father and detained him separately from us, and many years passed before we were reunited. They brought my mother and the four of us children to Kompaneisk, to a bare hillside where there was neither water or bread. We dug a burrow in the ground and Peter, Olga, Alexandra and I lived in it. Our mother was pregnant and gave birth prematurely. Mother suffered greatly. Our hole was covered with blood; there was blood spattered on our clothes, and there

was nowhere to wash them—the steppe was all around. "Daughter," my mother implored, "find a small stone and throw the clothes over it. Wet them with a little water and scrape them with a knife." I was little, and I still didn't know how to wash clothes.

Then they began building dugouts. They would dig clay, pour water on it, knead it with their feet and make bricks. They made barracks that had neither windows nor doors. In the barracks were plank beds, and people would lie on them, covering themselves with whatever they could find. In the morning they'd get up and drag off the dead bodies. We didn't mourn over the dead there. It was beyond us. Our mother would only pray and read Akathists (prayers and chants to the saints), and we would sit beside her: "Mama, we want to eat! Mama, let's eat!"

"Wait—I'm almost done reading the Akathist."

"Mama!"

"Hold on, there's just one page left." She would drag out the time. "I'm finishing up right now, and then god will help us." She would finish reading, take a piece of bread, and cut off pieces from it. And we'd point with our fingers; "Who's that for?"

"That's for Peter."

"And who's that for?"

"That's for Maria, that's for Olga, and that's for Alexandra." That's just how it was. We'd scrape up all the crumbs, and our mother always tried to give us some of her ration. How did we survive—how? It's unbelievable, since it was impossible to survive there! . . .

But how god helped us! We all grew up and received a higher education. Peter graduated from the academy. Olga and Alexandra are doctors, and I'm a teacher. God preserved us through our mother's prayers; it's a miracle that we remained alive.[62]

d. Regehr Family Letters

The German Mennonite Regehr family account of dekulakization and exile differs from the preceding stories in that it consists mainly of letters written to family members in Canada. How these letters were sent and how replies came, especially money and parcels, remains a mystery. The letters were mainly written in Gothic script during the years 1931 to 1937 and decades later were translated and published by family members in Canada. Presumably the stranglehold of the NKVD became tighter in 1937, when their letters ceased. While the family was evicted from their farm in the Mennonite community of Altonou, Ukraine in October 1930, and the father of the family, Jasch

DISGUST AMONG PEASANTS 253

Regehr, was arrested and imprisoned, it was only after his release in May 1931 that the entire family was sent by boxcar to exile in the Ural Mountains. They survived the week-long trip without food or water and were fortunate to be taken to a barracks to live. So, unlike the families in the preceding accounts, they did not have to live in a dugout in the earth.

Their greatest blessing was their extended Mennonite family in Canada, Germany, and Altonou, Ukraine, all of whom sent them money and parcels, which prevented their dying from hunger. The teenage children in the family worked felling trees in waist-high snow during the winter and also worked in the mines—all without boots or warm clothes. For their heavy labor, they received small amounts of food. Family members who didn't work received even smaller amounts of bread, so without the victuals that relatives sent, they would have died of starvation. The desolation was profound, however, and the following letters reveal how difficult life was for families in exile.

In a letter dated February 1932, the father of the family, Jasch, describes the problems of his son Peter's work and surviving:

> Oh, that poor boy is still somewhere in the forest, if he is still alive. People are beginning to swell and some have already died. Yesterday an adult died of Hungertifus (hunger typhus) and 2 children from a neighbouring barracks died of malnutrition. Those who must subsist solely on what they receive here do not survive, it is just not enough....
> ... They have already traded their gold rings for flour. I believe they got 1 pud flour per ring. Many are doing this just to remain alive. My dear little wife will go to see if she can trade hers for flour. But I do not have one. But nothing seems to go very far. One "nyg" of flour is only enough for baking twice. Then it too is gone. Many have traded their clothes, and even their bedding, for bread. For a good pillow you can get 2 pails of potatoes. And so, the people soon run out of goods, and finally are completely out of bread! This happens mostly among Russians.[63]

The Regehr family kept mainly to their own kind, that is, German-speaking Mennonites. When their son Peter became interested in courting a German Lutheran girl in their camp, they disapproved of that. Fortunately for the Regehr family, Mennonites in several countries somehow found ways to send them money to buy food. Describing his daughter and son's work, father Regehr wrote in August, 1931:

Liese wrote us a little bit about her work in the last few days. They were sent to a river and had to cut wood for the winter and float the logs onto the water. The house in which they live is also on the water and floats along with the logs. They have to heat the house every day, since it is so cold on the water. The boys have to work with the logs from early until late (about 17 hours) and are wet the entire day. They are not allowed to go and change clothes. It often happens that they fall into the water, but that makes no difference—there is no halting, no slowing down, always forward! The logs jam where the water is shallow. They must loosen the jam with dynamite, and many times serious accidents occur in the process. Large pieces of log fly high into the air and at times the little house is damaged. My dear little wife just cannot get over it, and intends to walk there and see for herself.... The workers get only 1¼ ... black bread, 1 fish, and 2 cups sugarless tea, per day! And nothing more! They suffer terribly from malnutrition. Children, especially young children 2–4, die here every day.

Well, dear Geschwister (sister), we trust you will help us! What do you think? We have been brought into a region where almost nothing is available. Here a pail of potatoes costs 5–7 rubles, a cucumber costs 35–50 k., a bunch of onions no larger than walnuts cost 10 kop. per bunch. Then you get a small idea how costly life is here—and we are without money. We received packages from Germany. We have had little news from home.... Did you receive our letter? It was the third one sent from here.[64]

Jasch's wife, Maria, also sends a letter and complains about the weather and lack of food, but she indicates that their faith helps them survive, writing:

> It is a hard road, and we cannot understand it, but we believe because: "All things work together for the good to them that love God." (Rom. 8:28) So we are comforted and do not despair![65]

Two of the Regehr children ran away from the camp, but they were tracked down and returned. They were severely punished and imprisoned, but their daughter Liese ran away three times, trying to return to her fiancée in Altonou. The family settles into various places but is moved farther and farther north in the Urals. After two years, father Regehr dies. He was weakened by hard work, lack of food and medial care, and worry about his family. One of the letters Jasch wrote in March 1933 before he died contained the following words:

> I am barely able to write. My feet are so swollen. I can hardly walk on them. The doctor insists it is an infection from bad food and

malnutrition. I really do not wish to get well—but God can determine that! My dear Marie, Liese, and Tina went to Kizel today. They wanted to get flour and barley at the store. Oh, how hard it is! The time is 3 p.m. and they left at 6 a.m! If the Kommandant meets them some place, he would definitely take everything away from them and most likely send them to the Schlansnoge (isolation cell). I am really frantic and can hardly wait until they get back. But maybe the Lord Zebaoth is with them and will guide them unobserved through the enemy camp.

Dear Geschwister, will there be a Gideon for us? Oh, what if we do not receive word from our dear children? Here people are being sought and taken. When the worker comes from work, dead tired, he is still forced to take a spade and dig in the plot—and the Russians then scatter seed into the plot. Friends, you have no idea how cruel the guards are! The Kommandant just came in and wanted to confiscate our ration cards because we cannot go to work. Searches occur every day. I think they want to bury us alive. Dear friends, are there people like that where you live?[66]

By May 1933, Jasch is in failing health, but he hangs on until October. In addition to their pleas for money and food, the Regehr family also begs to be remembered, so the translators of the letters titled their book *Remember Us*. In 1934 food is more plentiful and life becomes easier. The Regehrs get a plot of land where they can grow potatoes. By the second Five-Year Plan, some of the younger children are in school, and the family hears from their relatives in Ukraine. Each Soviet holiday, they hope to be allowed to return home, but they are kept in exile for years. Finally, the son Peter is arrested and shot in 1938, the mother is arrested and imprisoned for a year and a half, and one daughter is detained for ten months. All hopes for leaving the Urals are dashed when Germany invades the Ukraine in the summer of 1941. The Regehr family is kept in exile throughout the war. Only in the 1990s do two daughters, Lena and Mariechen, emigrate to Germany, where they write short accounts of their lives in exile. Mariechen titles hers "So Life Went On," which shows the stoical attitude she adopted to survive the long years in the Urals.[67]

6. Factors in Peasant Resistance

Because 10 million nuclear families had just gained separation from their extended families during the 1920s, many of the wives in those families had just recently escaped their mother-in-law's and father-in-law's control. They were probably reluctant to have a strange, collective farm administrator telling them how to live and work. Nor were they happy to surrender their recently acquired land and livestock to an inefficient collective farm manager. Although families were allowed to keep a small plot of land near their house with a few fruit trees after 1932, this did not always satisfy them. Finally, women's work on the kolkhoz counted less than men's. The time they spent on housework and child care earned them no labor days, as work was calculated and paid. So, they had less incentive to support the kolkhoz. Rumors about families having to share beds, blankets, and spouses were rife, undermining their trust in collective farms.

For all their communal work, a family might receive only half of the harvest. Usually the government took a quarter to a third of the kolkhoz grain, and a quarter was saved for seed, leaving less than half to be distributed to all the kolkhoz families.[68] Traditional ways were also hard to overcome. When incubators were introduced to increase egg production, women often resisted this change. A professional agronomist sometimes had to be brought in to explain how an incubator worked. Usually, young people were more responsive to new technology.[69]

Relations between middle-income peasants and the government had not been good prior to 1927. Since the revolution, peasants found they could buy very little at the market for their grain, so they planted less and ate what they produced, as Hilda Mielke's family story illustrates. Because the government needed grain for the workers in the cities, it began to once again requisition the peasants' grain, paying low prices for it. To get even with the government, many of these farmers decided to plant less. This retaliation didn't work because the government just took their grain, even the grain set aside for seed. So, hostile feelings, which had existed before collectivization, intensified.

Soviet ethnographers found collectivization in the village of Viriatino in Tambov province provoked severe class struggle. Some well-to-do kulaks set fire to kolkhozniks' property, usually to a threshing barn or a shed. Fearing to come out into the open, kulak men conducted their antigovernment agitation through their wives, sisters, and mothers. At the collectivization meetings, all the women of Viriatino at first opposed the organization of collective farms and yelled,

"We don't want to." Eventually, the mood in the village changed, but not before Communists from outside the village came to live and work in the fields of the kolkhoz because of unrest in 1933.[70]

Poor peasants had been easier to organize into the collective farms because they had nothing to lose and something to gain. Agitators promised poor farmers nurseries for the women, machinery for the men, entertainment for the youth, and security for the aged. Kulak women usually were treated more leniently than men since they were allowed to work as nannies at the construction sites, while their husbands had to build the new cities of Magnitogorsk and Cheliabinsk. Large numbers of kulak men were sent to construct the Baltic–White Sea Canal, to build new industrial sites at Magnitogorsk and Cheliabinsk, to harvest trees, and to mine coal in Siberia.

7. Untouchables

> Just having us at her table put her at risk, for if the authorities discovered she was helping two runaways her whole family would suffer.
>
> Helen Dmitriew, *Surviving the Storms*

One Russian girl, whose family was exiled to Siberia, tells of the conditions there. Helen Dmitriew describes how her father, who was the head of a cooperative store in the countryside, was denounced in 1929. Their family barely survived in Prokopevsk, Siberia. Her father was taken to work in the coal mines, where hundreds of men perished from lack of food and exhausting work conditions. Both horses and men perished in the mines. Typhus and dysentery raced through the barracks, and only 8 of 350 children survived. Grandparents and parents died in their camp. After she nursed her father and mother back to health, they decided to escape from the camp in 1932. Her father escaped first, and she didn't see him for many years. It was too dangerous for him to make contact with other family members. She and her mother decided to walk hundreds of miles from Siberia to European Russia, and it took them months to do this. Sometimes friendly villagers gave them food, lodging, and clean clothes. Sometimes a relative took them in for a few days and fed and clothed them. When they encountered distant relatives in Bolotsk, they were not recognizable. As Helen recalled:

The woman had never even seen me. Suddenly my mother stopped, gasped, and exclaimed, "Liuda! Is that really you?"

The woman became even more serious. "Who are you?" she asked.

"It is a miracle of God," continued Mother. "Do you really not know me, Liudochka? I'm Tat'iana, remember me?"

"Tania, my dear! How could I not remember how we always played together and shared secrets."

They hugged while I stood by and watched as they cried and exchanged questions. Mother pointed at me, emphasizing that I was her daughter, a martyr who saved her life.

Liudmilla Smirnov invited us into her home. The house was new. Her husband worked for the railroad. Railroad workers, like miners, were specialists who had privileges. They did not live in luxury but were in a much more comfortable position than other people. Their house was clean and orderly. It felt strange to sit down on chairs in a kitchen. We were dirty and ragged with thousands of lice.[71]

After eating and washing, Helen and her mother told Mrs. Smirnov their story. Then they realized their presence would endanger their hostess. Nevertheless, Liudmilla was exceedingly affectionate and helpful to them. Since her husband was away for a few days, she felt safe taking them in for a while, but she warned them not to go to Novosibirsk to Helen's uncle's. Mrs. Smirnov told them he had a good job and four children, and our arrival on his doorstep could ruin him and destroy his comparatively peaceful life.[72]

This story shows how dangerous it was to help exiles. Even relatives, who might want to help, could not do so out of fear of "the authorities." It turned out that it was even dangerous for them to go to Helen's brother's in Belarus. Some train rides enabled them to get near his village, where he had been a teacher since the 1920s. Several years later, however, her brother was denounced for not declaring his "kulak" social origins.[73]

Having to wear a mask to disguise one's social origins took a toll. When Helen finished secondary school, she decided to become a teacher and study at the Vitebsk Pedagogical Institute. To do so, she declared herself an orphan to disguise her social origins.

In exile, horrible living and working conditions doomed thousands of kulaks. At construction sites, women were often given inside jobs as janitors, food workers, or even maids. While there were goodly numbers of kulaks, the Soviets dubbed anyone who resisted collectivization a kulak, thus swelling their numbers. Between 1930 and 1932, about 9 million peasants, including unknown numbers of kulaks, left the countryside, emigrated to the cities, worked in factories, on construction sites, or even as maids. To soften opposition to collectivization, Stalin blamed local leaders for its excesses. In his speech "Dizzy with Success" on March 2, 1930, he did not reject the policy of collectivization but suggested that party members should lead, not frighten the peasants into the kolkhozy. As the regime relaxed its campaign after Stalin's speech, the kolkhoz population temporarily declined from 14 million to 6 million.[74]

8. Famine

Contrary to economic planners' expectations, kolkhozy proved inefficient. Lack of horses and machinery, starvation wages, and low morale produced poor grain yields. Seeing little correlation between their work and pay, peasants planted less grain than normal in 1931–32, thinking they could change government policy by refusing to produce set quotas. Moreover, some kolkhoz managers were drunks, embezzlers, illiterate, or untrained. Poor management in turn contributed to low productivity. Farmers felt cheated by poorly educated accountants who did not correctly calculate their labor days for their wages. Some farm managers misled local, regional, and provincial party bosses in their reports. Some feared reporting actual crop production, inflating figures to please their superiors. A combination of factors—low yields, misrepresentation of productivity, slovenliness, and ruthless grain requisitions in 1931–32—all contributed to the famine of 1932–33.[75] Grain requisitioning also forced peasants off their farms and into the kolkhozy. Famine and death were especially prevalent in Ukraine, Georgia, and along the Volga in 1933 because of the draconian grain requisitions in 1931 and 1932, which resulted in 3 million to 10 million deaths.[76]

9. Low Productivity of Kolkhoz

Even those who escaped dekulakization and famine found life difficult. Women earned the lowest wages on the kolkhozy, and they worked hard on their family plots to augment family income. Officials mounted a campaign to involve older women in kolkhoz production and to shame young people into working more efficiently. Newspapers praised grandmothers as good workers if they fulfilled their quotas.[77] During the second FYP, however, grain production increased, and families received more grain and wages for their labor. As more tractors were produced in new industrial centers, the mechanization of agricultural work increased productivity.

Lingering patriarchal culture also disenchanted some women as men continued to dominate family life, collective farm management, local soviets, and party organizations. Despite Soviet contentions that kolkhoz work offered women economic independence, wages in-kind were not paid to individuals but households. Dowries in the form of women's labor days remained under male control. Collective farm chairmen simply transferred a woman's dowry of workdays from her father's household to that of her father-in-law or husband.

The division of labor remained with women performing 41 percent of the productive work on the kolkhoz, presumably field work; 76 percent of the "unproductive work," perhaps work on the family household plot; and 95 percent of the household work. They received only 34 percent of wages paid because their work was "less valuable" and they earned fewer labor days than men. Most tractor drivers and machine operators were men, who received more labor days for their work than women who did nonmechanized work. While tending the family vegetable plots was essential for a family's survival, it was not classified as productive work and received no wages. Household work left women less time than men for reading, rest, or sleep. The English observer E. M. Delafield noticed that women on a farm near Rostov engaged in heavy work from 5:15 a.m. to 9:30 p.m. during the summer.[78] Other sources told of peasant men marrying a wife to help with the summer work and then divorcing her after the harvest. Stories abounded of Communist men divorcing their old peasant wives and taking younger, educated wives.[79] Only in the mid 1930s did the government pursue a policy of Stakhanovite work, or intense work, in the countryside. Often it was young women who were attracted to the use of technology—tractors, incubators, and scientific farming— who became hard working, diligent heroines of labor in the rural areas. Mary Buckley tells their story well in her book *Mobilizing Soviet Peasants: Heroines and Heroes of Stalin's Fields*.

Although most migrant peasant girls found employment in the cities and at construction sites, not all were so lucky. Some found not jobs but prostitution. Visiting Moscow prophylactoria in 1930, American doctor Rachelle Yarros noticed that most of the residents were peasant migrants eighteen to twenty-three years old, who lacked education and vocational training.[80] Only as industrialization increased did the number of prostitutes decline.

Farm Machine Workers, Rostov on Don, *1930s (Library of Congress)*

Chapter Seven

Working Women

> At first, everything was just as strange to me. I did not feel at home. But now I understand everything clearly. It is good to know what the machines are for and how they must be handled. One gains confidence and is no longer afraid. I'm going to attend a course for mechanics every evening next month. I should like, later, to be employed in the electricity works. It is so beautiful, peaceful and clean there.[1]
>
> Katia, a worker from the countryside

In the cities and at new construction sites, generational differences remained strong. Young women like Katia became energetic and enthusiastic workers supporting the Five-Year Plan (FYP). For older married working women, factory production proved more difficult. Towns grew quickly and housing remained as crowded as in the previous decade. Many families still lived in one or two shabby rooms, as the picture by Petrov-Vodkin shows.

They lived, ate, and slept in the same few square meters. During the first plan, 1928–32, wages were low and living conditions harsh. Food, clothing, housing, and childcare facilities were inadequate, and family life was difficult to maintain. However, workers did pay low rent and receive subsidized food like bread and milk. No doubt workers appreciated social services, like vacations and sanatoriums for recuperation, which the socialist government provided. Hundreds of thousands of peasant migrants like Katia may not have perceived urban conditions as harsh, since they were accustomed to hard farm labor and primitive dwellings in the countryside. Moreover, by 1937, their ranks had swollen to roughly 8 million women workers and 16 million men mostly living in crowded conditions.[2] Older workers suffered from the speed-up in production, shoddy equipment, poor safety procedures, and lack of investment in industry after 1937, when defense spending increased and consumer goods again became scarce. Yet for many younger workers, life continued to be an adventure.

K. S. Petrov-Vodkin, Alarm, 1934

A. Problems of Older Workers

The generational differences that existed among peasants also plagued workers. As the Petrov-Vodkin picture of a working-class apartment shows, older, married women often were not only exploited by their toil and meager wages but also by dingy, crowded living conditions.

Working-class life could be a rather dingy, shabby affair, requiring the sharing of one or two rooms among four people. Some textile workers engaged in strikes when their families' bread ration was threatened. In the spring of 1932, textile workers outside Moscow went on strike to protest poor food supplies. Generally, textile workers had been receiving sixteen kilograms of bread per month, but in March their bread rations were cut. This provoked rebellion. Some male and female textile workers objected to the speed-up in production, having to do more work for the same pay. Textile plants had old machinery, and this made it difficult to meet the ambitious targets of the FYP. The Ivanovo Industrial Region contended with shock work quotas, poor work conditions due to the use of inferior domestic cotton, reduced pay, food shortages caused by collectivization, and food rationing. Although the workday was reduced from eight to seven hours, this proved no victory for workers because they had to tend more looms and fulfill new higher-output targets.

While many textile workers were married, some were not and lived in simple hostels. Whether single or married, food became scarce for everyone during collectivization, and the better lives that women expected did not materialize. They could not bear their children's hunger. Women engaged in acts of protest that would not provoke their dismissal or arrest. When a call to meet in a general assembly with government and plant officials in Ivanovo was rejected, they decided to strike. Because textile workers had a low rate of party affiliation, fewer high-ranking officials were available to control disgruntled workers. After a week's strike, party leader Kaganovich was dispatched from Moscow to deal with the strikers. He promised improvement, restitution of the sixteen kilos of bread per month, and reduction of the unrealistic work targets that industrialization had imposed.[3]

Other problems emerged when village migrants and wives of first-generation working men found it difficult to adjust to modern, urban life. They brought their traditional, often superstitious culture with them to the city. One worker at Kuznetsk found it almost impossible to persuade his wife to leave her old life and join him at the construction site. Kulaks had told his wife "you will all die of starvation in this new city." He found it impossible to change his wife's mind, so he left her with the young children and took only his eldest son with him. Later this worker's wife wrote:

> My neighbor Avdotja says that there are many Kirghiz in the place and that they steal children. She also thinks there will soon be another war and then there will be starvation and misery in the factories! I do not want to come![4]

A trial in Magnitogorsk revealed that workers as well as their wives needed to be brought into modern life. Many didn't realize that typhus had earlier been a serious problem in the barracks, and they didn't want to have their children treated when they fell ill. One worker's wife, Lubov Anyekova, failed to report her son's illness and tried to hide him from the doctor because she knew nothing of hygiene and was afraid of modern medicine. At her trial, she said that she was afraid the child would be taken from her and put into the hospital. She heard that children often got mixed up in the hospital. However, she realized at the trial how wrong she had been and said she was anxious to be rid of the epithet "pernicious element." She was willing to attend a course for illiterate people. The Social prosecutor made a note of her declarations and obliged citizen Anyekova to also attend a course in hygiene.[5]

B. Idealistic Udarnik and Stakhanovite Workers

> Among women, cases of absenteeism and bad discipline are less frequent than among men. Women participate more in socialist competition and in shock work. They are better workers.
>
> Anna Balashova, udarnik worker

Russian youth responded to the industrial challenges of the FYP and traveled long distances to help build the cities of Magnitogorsk and Kuznetsk. Sometimes frightened by city life, they persevered until they found jobs. One daughter of farmers, Katia, left her village and traveled to Kamah and then to Stalinsk. Most of the people there came from the village she did, walking and talking just like her. They spoke a language she was used to. Initially she worked as a brick maker. Illiterate, she was unable to advance because she could not understand instructions. So, she went to the Likbez, or liquidation of illiteracy course. Good at her lessons, she learned to read, write, and calculate. Eventually she progressed to operating the lift, or freight elevator, in the blast furnace works. While the clean yet spartan workers' barracks

Interior View of Textile Workers' Hostel, 1932, Leningrad
(St. Petersburg Photo Archive)

shown in the photograph is crowded, it may have been welcomed by eager young peasant women migrants, who often came from dirty villages to the cities to work. They may have found such living conditions an improvement over life in a rural hut.

Young people who worked hard, joined the Komsomol, and participated in shock-brigade work—producing more than the prescribed norm—could reap financial, social, and educational benefits. Some were sent from their factories to Moscow to study at the Communist University for two years. One such young woman was so overwhelmed she cried at leaving her fellow workers: "I find it so hard to leave the brigade. One feels lost and abandoned on this train ... going away. One feels so much at home in the brigade!" Certainly, working together with other idealistic young people gave many a sense of purpose in their lives. Some had interpreted NEP policies as a betrayal of revolutionary values and saw the new Five-Year Plans as opportunities to sacrifice for their country. Some regarded their work as a "labor front," much like the military front during the Civil War. They saw their hard work as waging war but with other weapons.[6]

During the second plan, 1933–37, food, clothing, and other consumer goods became more plentiful, wages increased, and housing improved, especially for udarnik and Stakhanovite workers. In both periods, there were particular banes and blessings that made Soviet working-class life unique. During the 1930s, the number of female factory workers increased from 1.2 million in 1926 to 3.4 million by 1939.[7]

Udarnik Anna Balashova could be the woman shown making farm machinery. Her memoir tells about her devotion to her work and to the Communist Party in the late 1920s and early 1930s. She won prizes for her "shock" work in overfulfilling the norms of her textile mill. Her dedication earned her six months of party training. Reading on her own, she was also instructed in party history, from which she became acquainted with various political deviations. She could tell that Trotskyites were "wrong" and were simply "posing as defenders of the working class." Later, she was the leader in a work commune, where one salary was shared equally by all, but the shared wages did not last, as she indicates:

> At first things went well, and we worked with enthusiasm. But here's what happened. Skilled workers were paid no more than unskilled workers, even though those who were skilled worked much more and spent more energy than if they worked by themselves. As a result many workers lost interest in their work, and a month and a half later the commune fell apart.[8]

Balashova went on to study at the Trade Academy and in 1931 was made foreman of the quality control department of Trekhgorka Textile Factory in Moscow. She was elected a member of the party committee and continued as a delegatka, or factory representative. Describing the situation among the workers at her factory, she said:

> We have achieved a great deal thanks to the work of our women's representatives. We prepare all campaigns, shock work, and socialist competition with our activists, and then among the female masses. Recently we had a meeting for the new arrivals, most of whom were fresh from the village. We pay particular attention to the new cadres of women workers. They are the most backward politically. We have been successful at reeducating them. Within a short time many of them apply to join the party....
> Work among women is not easy, but it is an important, necessary, and interesting aspect of party work. I give it everything I've got.[9]

Since Balashova had only one child and was divorced, she was freer than many working-class women to participate in political activity and to take her work seriously.

C. Hard Lives during Industrialization

> In the beginning of the Plan it was impossible to obtain butter, milk, eggs, kerosene, galoshes, tea, sugar, clothing, shoestrings, almost anything, without standing in line for many hours under rain, snow, or scorching sun. Soon, standing in line did not help. The stores were empty.
>
> Markoosha Fischer, Moscow housewife

Urban life could be a dingy, shabby affair when workers shared one or two rooms with several family members. In the spring of 1932, textile workers outside of Moscow went on strike to protest poor food supplies. Housewife Markoosha Fischer, who was married to an American journalist and enjoyed a rather special status, observed that as NEP ended and the first economic plan expanded, food and other commodities became scarcer. She noted:

> Private enterprises catering to everyday necessities of life were abolished, and the government concentrated chiefly on the expansion of heavy industry. Large quantities of victuals—butter, eggs, and meat—were shipped abroad in exchange for foreign machinery.... Ration cards were introduced for almost everything, but little could be bought with the cards. There were different cards for factory workers and office workers, for wage earners and dependents, for children and adults. They gradually grew into large-sized booklets with coupons of the most varied and difficult color schemes. Shopping became a shrewd art. Leaving the house in search of food, we equipped ourselves with newspapers, jars, boxes and cans. No wrapping or receptacles of any kind were furnished in the stores, and one never knew in advance what was to be found on that day.[10]

As the first and second plans advanced and working-class life became more difficult, some party leaders decided to develop a women's movement composed of housewives of well-paid, leading officials to help improve the lives of poor workers. These volunteers called *obshchestvennitsy* began to beautify workers' barracks and reform kindergartens and nurseries. In May 1936 wives of the Commanders of the People's Commissariat of Heavy Industry called upon women in the Soviet Union to join the movement, and there was an immediate response from the wives of the Commanders in the People's Commissariats of Communication, Transportation, and Roads. These well-to-do housewives launched kindergartens, nurseries, Pioneer Camps, cafeterias, buffets, literacy circles, and even a children's wilderness sanatorium. They also introduced branch clinics, amateur theatricals, courses in flower arranging and gardening, the Red Cross, Osoaviakhim (civil defense), libraries, newspapers, schools, gymnasiums, and a children's resort. Galina Shtange's husband was a transport engineer, and her diary tells of her work in a Muscovite nursery in the mid-1930s. Shtange worked for a short time in this community work until her family life intervened and she felt she had to help her children full time. As she explained in her diary:

> I was completely engrossed in my work for two months. I found my element and felt wonderful, in spite of being so tired. I managed to get some things done; and I could have done a lot more, but such was not my fate! Circumstances will not let me be distracted, even for a moment, from what's going on at home.[11]

Her son, Borya, had a baby boy and inadequate space to live in, so she felt she had to help him and his family, who were living in their dacha until a larger apartment became available. She gave up the volunteer work that she loved so much and took up cooking, dishwashing, and diapers to help her family.[12]

There were profound generational differences in women's work. Many Soviet youth felt a sense of mission and purpose building socialism in their country in the 1930s. Life in the cities, even in barracks, was often a step up from rural poverty. The countryside was overpopulated and employment scarce for some Soviet youth. So, millions migrated into the cities during the 1930s. While the work and living conditions seem harsh to us today, they were probably no rougher than agricultural work. Still, the living conditions of married women workers remained brutal, as they faced living in crowded housing and food shortages during collectivization. Indeed, food supplies improved only during the middle of the decade.

Chapter Eight

Education

They told me that if I wanted, I could leave the rabfak and go to Moscow to study—supposedly I had sufficient knowledge to do that. I was determined to go to Moscow. And so I went, planning to enter the Krupskaia Academy of Communist Education.

Sofia Pavlova, student and Komsomolka

Like other aspects of society, Russian education was a mixed affair in the 1930s. While the highest ranks remained male dominated—55,000 male academics and professors to 24,000 females—women teachers outnumbered men 540,000 to 429,000. By 1937, 1.7 million Soviet women were engaged in cultural, educational, and medical work. Elementary education was widely extended to the rural population,

Alexander Rodchenko, Sports Parade, *1935*

and increasing numbers were able to complete five years of school. However, teachers and doctors were still concentrated in urban more than rural areas.

Many girls were never able to make up for their lack of education as children. Poverty-stricken peasants often lacked shoes and clothes to attend school. So, although elementary school was technically free, in fact it wasn't always as available to the poor as it appeared. In an interview, Irina Kniazeva told how she had to take care of younger siblings in the 1920s and never got to go to school. Although the government established liquidation of illiteracy centers in the city and countryside, and Irina attended one briefly in the 1930s, she learned only the "ABCs" and how to sign her name. She never learned to read. The mother of three children, she had to work very hard for her family to survive and had little energy left over for study. However, her own children obtained five years of schooling, and one son became a tractor driver.[1] She and others like her remained rooted in the old ways and traditions.

Still, enterprising peasants, supported by their collective farms, the Komsomol, or the party, boarded at regional high schools and universities. In some families, all the children obtained higher education. An American fellow named John Scott married a Russian woman named Masha in Magnitogorsk in the mid-1930s. At that time, he was working as a welder and she as a teacher. After World War II, they came to the United States, and Pearl Buck interviewed Masha Scott. Masha recounted how the children in her peasant family obtained higher education and became physicians, economists, engineers, or teachers, like herself.

In Kalinin Oblast, members of the Red Banner Collective Farm jointly decided who would receive scholarships for study. Some students joined the Komsomol or the party to gain scholarships, which paid the costs of university or technical education. The Medical Institute at Smolensk University sought financial resources from the Ministry of Health, and 60–70 percent of its students received scholarships in 1932. Ordinary grants paid 27 rubles per month, but party funding paid 60–75 rubles per month—an inducement to join communist organizations. According to Masha Scott, outstanding students got higher stipends, while those who failed their exams lost their allowances. Good students usually helped poorer ones. Although stipends were often small, Masha and her siblings found theirs adequate to cover room and board, books, and entertainment. In addition, students in major cities received free tickets to theater and musical performances. While the Smolensk Archive describes crowded dormitories and meatless cafeterias, Masha found her food rations adequate: tea for breakfast and borscht, meat, potatoes, and fruit compote for lunch and supper.

While Masha and her siblings found the dorms crowded, their conditions were not as bad as those at the Smolensk Medical Institute, where two hundred students lacked places to sleep in 1931. Still, Masha complained about her crowded conditions at a party cleansing, and as a result she and her sister received better accommodations. She was better off than students who lacked clothing, books, and other necessities.

To avoid harsh working conditions upon graduation, some students of peasant origin transferred to Moscow, so they would not have to remain in the countryside as poorly paid medical workers or teachers. Rural doctors sometimes lived two hundred miles from the closest town, lacked medical and pharmaceutical supplies, and lived in substandard housing. Still, Smolensk University offered upward social and economic mobility to poor peasants, and their quotas of 50 percent female students in the medical and pedagogical faculties enabled more women than ever before to obtain higher education. Masha's engineering college was evenly split between male and female students, but the medical faculty where her sister studied had 75 percent female enrollment.[2] Doctors earned such low pay in the 1930s that many had to work two jobs to survive. Since most doctors were required to work only five hours per day, having a second job at another clinic or hospital was not quite the imposition that it was in England or western Europe. In 1933 a visiting British doctor James Purves-Stewart noticed that doctors earned only 250 rubles per month—about the same as an unskilled worker. However, the ones that he spoke to believed that they were sacrificing for a better future for their country, which the Five-Year Plans would produce, and they didn't seem to mind their low wages. Moreover, he thought the health and social services available to Russians in the cities were adequate—subsidized rent; child care; free medical treatment in sanatoriums, convalescent homes, infirmaries, and polyclinics; paid vacations; and pensions. He visited an abortion clinic and found that hygienic abortions, which the Soviet government had introduced in 1918 to prevent death from unhygienic abortions, were free or cost only twenty-five rubles. Doctors used no anesthesia for abortions or childbirth.[3] Under Stalin, however, the Soviet government drew up a more stringent abortion policy in 1936, and this procedure became less available and more costly. Medical care in rural areas lagged behind that in the cities. Abortions there tended to be unhygienic, doctors were paid only two hundred rubles per month, and drugs and equipment could be in short supply.

Many young peasant women took advantage of favorable quotas to pursue higher education. Large numbers became teachers, doctors, dentists, engineers, and agronomists. By 1932 peasants accounted for 11 percent of medical students in Moscow, and in 1933 they represented 20 percent of those in higher education. To achieve these goals, party chiefs sometimes ordered villages to send their youth to regional cities to train as professionals. As a result, the number of peasant women studying agronomy increased from four thousand in 1928 to nineteen thousand in 1933.

In addition to providing free theater and opera tickets, student unions also organized excursions, vacations, and volunteer work in factories and farms. Students often taught literacy classes, formed drama groups, or helped workers make their own newspapers. Indeed, Masha's university class had a newspaper in which they published student poetry. While studying chemical engineering, she also worked in a chemical factory and lab. Her sister, who was a medical student, interned in a hospital. As university students, they all went skiing and skating and participated together in the paramilitary activities of Osoaviakhim, a civil defense organization that especially appealed to young people. According to Masha, students in her circle did not emulate the flapper look and shunned lipstick and makeup. They thought it better to be modest than chic, to dress simply. Many even wore their hair in braids. However, they all loved to dance the fox-trot.[4]

Not all young peasant women proved good students. Tractor driver Pasha Angelina, in one of her writings, confessed that she had difficulties keeping up at the Timiryazev Academy of Agriculture when she was sent there to study in the late 1930s. Only semiliterate from her studies at the secondary school in Staro-Byeshevo, she found her courses at the academy challenging. She succeeded, but not everyone did.[5]

Another generational difference was in the sorts of jobs that young peasant women could get. Some like Pasha Angelina became well-paid tractor drivers. By 1934 several thousand women headed collective farms, managed dairy farms, worked as udarnik milkmaids, and drove tractors. Still, these women had to be tough to withstand the criticism of those who initially rejected their nontraditional behavior. Tractor driver Daria Garmash reportedly rejected her patriarchal fiancé, who objected to her wearing trousers and unfeminine behavior in driving a tractor.[6]

In the 1930s, young peasant women who left for the city did not have to become servants, as had been the custom earlier. They had more choices. When they first went to the city, some started out as domestics, then worked in a factory, then studied in the rabfak, and then became technical workers. In the 1930s, 26–41 percent of factory workers had peasant origins.[7]

Peasant girls who immigrated to the cities and became maids or factory workers usually obtained rudimentary education and absorbed Soviet culture. Some were embarrassed by their mother's old ways and refused to have them raise their children, fearing bad results. In her memoir of life in the 1930s, Markoosha Fischer noticed that her house worker, Frossya, went to evening classes to become literate and citified. When she had a child, she brought it up according to modern rules of feeding and hygiene. Frossya was afraid to let her mother raise her son for fear she would give it the "soska," an old rag filled with chewed-up bread, and that her baby would choke to death. Although Frossya was happy to have her country relatives bring her food to supplement her meager rations, she rejected the old-fashioned childrearing practices of village women.[8]

Still, many Russian women were content to have their mothers care for their children while they worked and studied. For example, Elena Ponomarenko succeeded in becoming a journalist because her mother took care of her children after she divorced her husband. Elena worked in the daytime, but her mentor, Nikanor Petrovich, sent her to evening school for adults, and she studied in the evening until 1:00 a.m. Highly motivated, she finished seven grades in two years.[9]

Soviet education made huge inroads in the countryside in the 1930s. The state provided schools and libraries and chose the books that children read. It told teachers how to interpret their tests. The government tried to inculcate new ideological values among the children, but it is unclear how successful they were. It all depended on the teachers, the kolkhoz chairman, and the families of the children. The ideas of Socialist Realism, of positive heroes and heroines, gender equality, and happy endings in building collective farms and industrialization were proclaimed at school and in the Komsomol.[10] However, these ideas probably had to be reinforced at home in order to mold children's behavior. Poor peasant families like Pasha Angelina's (the tractor driver) and Masha Scott's (whose siblings all pursued higher education) were open to education, upward mobility, and becoming the new Soviet citizens. Since education in the countryside was limited to four years in the 1930s, it seems that the informal education by mothers remained the predominant form. Girls were still taught cooking, cleaning, child care, weaving, knitting, crocheting, embroidery, gardening, and animal care by their mothers, and all this took time. Even when women worked in kolkhoz agriculture, their household duties still took most of their time. Thus, peasant culture generally remained patriarchal and traditional.

A. Harsh University Conditions

> When I arrived at the Pedagogical Institute in Vitebsk in the fall of 1935, I did not have a place to stay because there were not enough places in the student dormitory. I became depressed and sat in a corridor with a group of new female students.
>
> Helen Dmitriew, student

Higher education was open to peasants, workers, and children of the intelligentsia. After 1936 university education became more open to children of priests, kulaks, and former gentry-class officials. Initially, those with dubious "social origins" had a difficult time and were sometimes denounced to the authorities. While higher education had been somewhat tolerant of "bourgeois" professors and children of the intelligentsia in the 1920s, party policies stiffened against these categories in the early 1930s. Moreover, there were purges of students as well as professors in institutions of higher education. Often, conditions of study were harsh—lack of dormitory space and food made study difficult. Helen Dmitriew recounts her experience in trying to find housing at Vitebsk Pedagogical Institute in her memoir *Surviving the Storms*:

> Many of them were in the same situation and had to find at least a corner to call home. One girl, named Roza Goldman, came up and joined in the general conversation. She was pleasant to everyone. When she learned that I didn't have a room to live in, she immediately suggested that I go to her parents' home, hoping that perhaps they would help me. The Goldmans were a loving Jewish family. Although poor, they had their own small house. The father worked in a factory, and the mother was a dressmaker, which explained why Roza was so well dressed. Of the three children ... Roza was the eldest.
>
> I lived with them for an entire year, until I was assigned a place in the dormitory. Many times I didn't have even a kopek, but these kind people shared everything they had with me. I slept in Roza's room on a small bed with a straw mattress. I didn't have any possessions of my own except for a few poor clothes. Food was very sparse. Although I received a monthly stipend for good academic progress, I could never make it through the month.
>
> I spent most of my free time in the library. The institute often had student parties and dances, but I did not participate. Even though I would have liked to enjoy an active social life, I didn't have any clothes or shoes appropriate for going out. Claiming to be an orphan spared me unnecessary explanations and problems, especially having to produce required documents about my social origin. Being an orphan simply made it easier to exist.[11]

In addition to the lack of space and clothing, food was also scarce, as Dmitriew remarked in her memoirs:

> I often contemplated how our people could endure all this fear and deprivation. Students in any country experience some shortages, but the way we lived meant we often went to sleep hungry and were glad for a piece of black bread and hot water tinged with the horrible smell of chlorine. At lectures in the auditorium, it was difficult to concentrate. My head swam and colored spots spun before my eyes, all caused by incessant hunger. No one dared to complain about the shortages, although we all understood each other's plight.[12]

278   CHAPTER EIGHT: EDUCATION

The daughter of a former landowner, Antonia Berezhnaia, indicates that as a teenager higher education was closed to her and she had to work in a factory in Tula. She even became a shock worker, producing more than the prescribed norm. However, in the mid-1930s she married and moved to the Urals. There she was employed as a metallurgist and was elected to the town soviet. A dedicated worker, political activist, and student, she describes her life thus:

> And in the Urals things were also very complicated for me: I had a family, but all the same I entered an institute of higher education, and in '40 I graduated from UPI, the Urals Polytechnic Institute, with a specialization in refractory materials.[13]

B. Problems of Social Origins

> I feared that the people at the institute would expel me if they discovered my (kulak) past: my exile in Siberia, my escape, and my claim to be an orphan, when in fact my mother and perhaps even my father were still alive, weighed heavily upon me.
>
> Helen Dmitriew, student

In the Urals and the hinterlands, it was easier for those with a past to disguise themselves, obtain higher education, and get better jobs. While Antonia Berezhnaia was able to work without hindrance in the Urals, not all children of "former people" were so lucky. Elena Dolgikh was the daughter of rural school teachers. Her father died in 1917, and her mother returned to her father's home in Siberia with her five children. Elena's grandfather was a well-to-do peasant, a kulak, and she was later dogged by her "social origins." Although she had been adopted by an aunt and uncle and had attended school in Biisk, she was later denounced as a kulak while attending the teachers' college there. She describes her situation as follows:

> While I was a student at the college, I was editor of the wall newspaper. At that time, there were such wall newspapers. They were put out by the yard. Yes, I served for three years straight as editor. Then suddenly, a letter came to the college, to the Komsomol organization, demanding to know just why a kulak girl was studying there....
>
> It was the first year that I was getting the scholarship, so I had bought myself a cheap fur coat and something to wear on my feet. I

had very little money, so I also had to economize on food. Well, they called a special meeting of the Komsomol to discuss the matter. The director, who was a communist, came to my defense, saying that I was one of the best, one of the most progressive students, and so on.... They didn't expel me from the college, nothing like that. But there were some who wished me ill. Suddenly a man came from the district Komsomol committee and chewed out the Komsomol members for being apolitical and so on and so forth. "Look," he said, "here's a document that proves that this one is from a family of dispossessed kulaks."[14]

Although the director helped her write a letter to the soviet denouncing her "kulak" past and family, rumors still circulated about her. Eventually, she was expelled from the school. By this time her "adopted" parents were living in Krasnoyarsk, and they took her in. The director of the Biisk School wrote letters of recommendation for her to the teachers' college there so she could complete her studies. She taught language and literature in a school for young workers in a district center in Krasnoyarsk territory. After her mother and two siblings came to live with her, she was denounced again and lost her job. Then she married and moved to Tomsk, where she got another teaching job.[15] However, her life as a teacher was not easy, as she complains:

> And you know what the life of a teacher was like then—meetings, conferences, homework to correct, and the wages were really low, hardly more than a cleaning woman got. At least a cleaning woman could work several jobs at once, but just try to teach at more than one school at a time.... We couldn't afford to dress well or have nice shoes or boots. You'd want one thing, and you'd have to wear something else. In general, I've lived all my life in need, all my life ... it's as if all my life I lived under the sword of Damocles.[16]

C. Education and Upward Mobility

> It was the raikom's (Party's) decision to send us to study. At the rabfak there were few girls, in general.
>
> Sofia Pavlova, Siberian Komsomolka

Still, the 1920s and 1930s were times of tremendous upward mobility for hundreds of thousands of women whose social origins were "correct." Millions of talented peasants and workers became low- or

280 CHAPTER EIGHT: EDUCATION

mid-level white-collar workers in the bureaucracies: teachers, doctors, agronomists, even engineers. Countless stories of these women are recorded in Soviet newspapers and journals. In the 1930s more women than men trained and worked as teachers, doctors, physicians' assistants, pharmacists, dentists, and other medical personnel. Tens of thousands of women also made inroads into engineering, law, and other professions. According to the 1939 census, 700,000 women were occupied as teachers, 75,000 as doctors, 29,000 as pharmacists, 12,000 as dentists, 32,000 as engineers, and 5,500 as judicial personnel.[17] As Markoosha Fischer observed in her memoir:

> But the young and the strong, people with active minds and bodies, gave themselves unquestioningly to the great task of rebuilding Russia. They carried the spark of enthusiasm in the factories, offices, mines, colleges, and homes, and bore uncomplainingly every unbelievable hardship. It was the ardor of these people which covered the old backward Russian land with a huge net of modern dams, roads, power plants, highways, railroad lines, factories, and waterways. The new giant industrial enterprises, Magnitogorsk, the Dnieper Dam, Kuznetsk, and others, could hardly have been built without the utmost devotion, initiative, and sacrifices of their directors, engineers, and workers.[18]

Successful Sofia Pavlova was the daughter of peasants and working-class people who supported the Bolsheviks prior to the revolution. She received an excellent education in a small Siberian town and had just begun gymnasium when the revolution occurred. Then she was drawn into Komsomol work among youth, especially girls in the early 1920s. During the Civil War, Sofia worked for a special military unit of the Cheka (secret police). She had a Mauser firearm and hunted down the remnants of Civil War soldiers belonging to White General Kolchak in Siberia. Joining the party in 1921, she was sent to the Tomsk rabfak to study in 1922. As she remembered:

> Mainly there were returnees from the civil war, young men who were already quite grown up, and for some reason there were Germans. The guys really courted us. They really went after me.... The student body was largely composed of returnees from the civil war. From the Red Army. Because everyone had either a Mauser or a revolver....
>
> There must have been a stipend. I don't remember what we lived on. Money we had. But in addition to being secretary of the Komsomol organization for institutions of higher education in Tomsk, I was also the organizer and leader of meetings for women delegates in the city....

We would go to the factories. There we set up meetings at the municipal level for women delegates. Yes. Or rather we convened meetings at the municipal level for women delegates and also for women delegates at the factory level. I was a member of the district Komsomol delegation and thus responsible for these delegate meetings. This continued until 1924.[19]

In Moscow, Sofia studied to teach in the rabfak schools. She especially loved history and even attended some of Nadezhda Krupskaia's lectures. She graduated as an instructor for factory apprenticeship schools and met her future husband at the school. They married and had a son. With her mother's help caring for her son, she continued her work for the party and worked as a teacher at an oblast party higher school. In 1931 her husband was called to Moscow to write for *Komsomolskaia Pravda*, and she went there to teach world history in the Communist Universities for Workers from the East and from the West. She also taught at the Moscow oblast Komsomol School, and she enrolled at the Institute of Red Professors in the World History Institute. A diligent party worker as well as history teacher, Sofia eventually became a world history professor at prestigious Moscow State University in 1937—the same year that her husband was purged.[20] So, she symbolized the working-class woman who made it—acquiring education, working for the party, married with children, yet afflicted by the purges and losing the love of her life.

While several million women moved up in Soviet society during the 1920s and 1930s, not many discuss the difficulties involved. One writer who does interweave these themes in her fiction and memoirs is Antonina Koptiaeva. In her analysis of Koptiaeva's work, literary critic Anna Krylova argues that a toll was exacted when women moved from peasant or lower middle-class background to writer. She found Koptiaeva experienced anxiety and hope in her adjustment to Soviet intellectual society. At one point she describes Koptiaeva's anguish as follows:

> Koptiaeva represented the moment of cultural crossing through her initial entrance into the Lenin Library, which she figured as her "promised land"—a place where she did not yet belong but which she had come to conquer. The bright electric light exposed "all the darns on her old dress," her feet felt awkward in her worn-out shoes. She fought against the physically-felt otherness in the world of learning with "determination and even anger," with strong belief in herself, and

with rudeness towards those who doubted her. Out of this struggle emerged a new person, solid, changed, empowered, and enriched by books. The official self re-emerged at the end of the sketch, as a result of the long and painful process of acculturation which faced those who were upwardly mobile.[21]

Like many others, she lost not only her husband in the 1930s but also two babies. So while advancing professionally, her personal life proved painful.

Krylova suggests that Koptiaeva's emergence from cultural and gendered otherness became the main theme in her fiction.[22] However it was only in her memoir, published in the 1970s, that Koptiaeva expressed her demoralization after her second husband's death. During the time of Socialist Realism in the 1930s, negative topics like debilitation and anxiety were not openly discussed in Russian literature.

Krylova also analyzes writer Vera Panova's internalization of correct speech and writing in the 1920s and 1930s as she moved from uncultured, lower middle-class young girl to featured journalist. She describes Panova as "self-made, self-educated, self-mannered, and self-corrected." Like many others, Panova lost her job as a journalist when her second husband was arrested in the 1930s. Thus, she not only lost the love of her life but also her livelihood and sense of self. She had three children to support and could not get a job. She wrote a letter begging Stalin for an opportunity to work, to again become part of society. Having worked as a journalist for more than fifteen years, Panova was at a loss how to live. Work made her feel needed somewhere outside of the home.[23]

Throughout the Soviet Union, women pursued higher education. In 1932, 33 percent of university students were women, and by 1937, 38 percent of students were women. This compared very favorably with the situation in England, where 26 percent of university students were women, and in Nazi Germany, where just 13 percent of students were women. In 1932, Soviet women constituted 2.5 percent of professors, 8 percent of the docents, and 33 percent of university assistants. In addition, there were large numbers in the Commissariats of Education and Heavy Industry and many scientific institutes. Certainly the government had a lot to be proud of.

One unintended result of the purges of the intelligentsia was high employment for new graduates. As Raisa Orlova remembers her university life, she notes:

After the destruction of 1937, vacancies appeared in the state, Party, and ideological sectors. Vacancies that required filling.

The graduates of 1939, 1940, and 1941 did not go looking for work—the work came looking for them. I filled out applications in dozens of departments, including the Party Central Committee, the People's Commissariat of Foreign Affairs, and the Council of People's Commissars. Like the majority, I had the opportunity of choosing.[24]

Later she recounts the idyllic life of many university students in the 1930s. She remarks in her memoirs:

> The Institute of Philosophy, Literature, and History stood out among the other institutes of higher learning in Moscow in those days. The best surviving professors in the humanities, who had avoided the prisons or exile, or who had succeeded in returning from there were Nikolai Gudzy, Aleksei Dzhivilegov, and Selishchev.... The era of the Proletarian Cultural and Educational Organization (Prolekult) and Left Front of the Arts (LEF) had come to an end. A different era had arrived, when the "ship of modernity," could be, and had to be re-manned and not depleted.... The interval was a very brief one: by 1936, the crusade against formalism had begun with an article about Shastakovich, "Muddleheadedness Instead of Music," in *Pravda*.[25]

In those days, the sons and daughters of highly placed and important fathers entered this Moscow Institute. Leonid and Raisa read the announcement for applications in the newspaper, applied, and were accepted to study there. A year later, almost all the students from privileged families became "children of the enemies of the people." Yet her world was not disturbed because the institute represented a special group whom she called her second homeland. This was the place where she was born into her profession, where she developed good relationships with other students, and "the place on earth that is closer, dearer, and more beloved to you."[26] (This is similar to the way some Americans felt about graduate school in the 1960s and 1970s.) As she describes it,

> For many of us the institute became the second homeland. Not only a counterweight to our first homeland, but bound by thousands of threads to it. At the same time it was an independent and relatively stable community, with its own mores, even with its own language, and without a doubt with its own personal makeup....
>
> We used to hang around the institute from morning to night whether we were busy or not, and we were always waiting for

someone. It was embarrassing and awkward to go home alone; besides, no one wanted to go.²⁷

Like many of her generation, Raisa felt like she lived among the chosen, those destined for great things. As a classmate put it, they were living in a great country, and they wanted to work, study, run, draw, and play better than everyone else, faster than everyone else, more beautifully than everyone else. Living during the Five-Year Plans in the 1930s, they felt that they were living the good, new life. They believed that they "would be the first generation of happy people." No one would have believed that there was a price being paid for their happiness. They would not have believed anyone who told them of the horrors of collectivization or the terror of the purges.²⁸

Generally, parents kept their fears about the purges and the news of arrested friends secret from their children. Still, shadows fell on their sunshine. One classmate, Yelka Muralova, was expelled from the Komsomol section because she was the daughter of "an enemy of the people." Raisa and her friends protested to the district committee, but it didn't help Yelka, who was soon arrested like her parents. However in 1936, Raisa and her friends felt virtuous for having tried to help a friend. Moreover, few university student Komsomol members defended arrested family members in the mid 1930s.²⁹

Indeed, Raisa, her husband and many others played a game called "Uncover the enemy." She remembered this in the following way:

> He very much liked to play an absorbing game. Wasn't he the one who had devised it? "Uncover the enemy." Plays were being printed in all the magazines of those days about the "enemies of the people." The object of the game was to determine who the enemy was from the list of characters, without reading the play. And one could be successful most of the time. The hack playwrights used to array their negative characters in appropriate names.³⁰

In the late 1930s, Elena Skrjabina decided to enroll in the Leningrad Pedagogical Institute of Foreign Languages because she feared her husband would be purged, and she would need a better job in order to support their two sons. The illustration is her university photo and record book from the People's Commissariat of Enlightenment. This gave her not only status but security as well. She studied French and did outstandingly well in all her subjects, including political

Elena Skrjabina's university record book (Iowa Women's Archives)

economy, or Marxism. Like other students, Elena was required to take exams once or twice a year in all her courses.

D. Women Teachers and Professors

> At the end of my first year I was selected for professorial rank. At that time professors were selected in all institutions of higher learning by their own professorial collectives. I began to be called "Professor Bek." I was not vain but being selected was nice for me, of course.
>
> Anna Bek, professor and physician

Harsh living conditions that plagued university students also beset those living far away from Moscow and Leningrad. Helen Dmitriew records her experiences trying to find a decent apartment when she first began teaching in 1939–40 and some of the other indignities she had to contend with:

> I received an appointment to Yazvinskaya Secondary School, approximately eighty kilometers from the city of Vitebsk. I was glad that this school was near a railroad station, since it would be possible to go to the city more often on my days off. Many of my friends were sent to out-of-the-way places, far from any means of communication, but no one could refuse an appointment.
>
> When I arrived at the school, I immediately went to see the director, Vladimir Pavlovich Kozlov. He was an obtuse, uncultured man, with a Communist Party membership card in his pocket. His wife was the same. She was uneducated and a great gossip.
>
> It was not pleasant to have to associate with such people. There weren't enough apartments, so I was given a small room next to the

director's apartment at the school, without even a lock on the door. Another female teacher, a snoop for the director and his wife, also lived there. None of the teachers liked her, and they tried to avoid her. The remaining teachers lived in the village—some with relatives, and others in rented apartments (more accurately corners) in the huts of collective farmers. Thus began my career as a teacher.

I arrived at the school before the celebration of the October Revolution.... Everyone was required to be present ... I sat in the first row, next to the director himself. This celebration was to be marked with a program....

A history teacher approached the director and said, "Vladimir Pavlovich, I want to sing a song called "The Komsomol Heart Is Broken."

"Absurd!" he retorted: "How can a Komsomol heart be broken? Sing something else!"[31]

In addition to these problems, teachers earned meager salaries. Bearing all this was difficult. However, some of the most heart-rending stories concern rural teachers during collectivization. While most historians focus on the attacks against the peasants in pushing them into collective farms and in exiling "kulak" families, few have discussed the violence that party members and collective farmers perpetrated against defenseless female teachers in the early 1930s. A good account of these outrages is found in Sheila Fitzpatrick's book *Education and Social Mobility in the Soviet Union, 1921–1934*. She quotes various Soviet sources telling of the rape and abuse of women teachers; others speak about the economic crimes committed against them:

> The brutalization of rural life also affected teachers. There was a remarkable increase in reported cases of rape, or undesired sexual intercourse forced on a female teacher by Soviet officials. The assumption of a Soviet *droit de seigneur* was not a new phenomenon: "Officials passing through (the village)—education department inspectors, various representatives of Soviet cooperative organs—prefer 'cultured surrounding' and invariably seek lodging for the night in the school. It has become a tradition." But observers found a qualitative as well as quantitative change in this epoch of class warfare. In one typical instance, local officials 'specially went to Yablonskaya school to see teacher Orlova, the daughter of a kulak sentenced to eight years for anti-Soviet activity, and Kustova, the daughter of a priest. There they organized a drunken party and forced the teachers to sleep with them ... (One of the officials) motivated his infamous suggestion with the statement: "I am (Soviet) power; I can do anything," knowing that

such statements would have particular effect on Orlova and Kustova, since they are of alien class–origin. As a result of his tormenting, Kustova came close to suicide.[32]

According to Fitzpatrick, women teachers also suffered from economic abuses:

> In some cases, the teachers were de-kulakized as prosperous peasants, either because they were married to such peasants or had their own plot of land. But there were also cases of victimization of teachers who were personally unpopular in the village or had come in conflict with local authorities. In one reported instance, the widow of a Communist killed in the Civil War was de-kulakized "essentially because she had more than once driven the local 'activists'—the secretary of the village soviet (a candidate member of the party), the local cultural official (also a party member) and the secretary of the local cooperative organization—out of the school where they intended to hold a drinking party." Since she had no "means of production" to confiscate they took her clothes and cooking utensils and tore up her books. Another woman teacher was de-kulakized on the grounds that she was a priest's daughter: "when she produced documents to show that she was the daughter of a peasant, they declared that her mother visited the priest, and therefore it is possible that she is the priest's daughter."
>
> In the period of reassessment after Stalin's 'Dizzy with success' speech of March 1930, the Smolensk authorities found that 63 teachers had been wrongly subjected to de-kulakization—almost one tenth of all the cases so classified in the region under investigation.
>
> But the majority of teachers had to face ... entry into the kolkhoz. It ... was "a mass phenomenon. In some (areas) it was voluntary, but in some the trade unions published a mandatory resolution on compulsory entry." In one district in the Urals, 98% of teachers became kolkhoz members in 1930/31. Nevertheless, some thousands of teachers fled from Russian schools in the spring and summer of 1930, probably to avoid being forced into the kolkhoz.
>
> The teacher's position as a kolkhoz member was ill-defined, especially if he had not previously held and cultivated a plot of land. One of the major problems was that the teacher received an individual salary from outside the kolkhoz, and was entitled to certain privileges such as vacations and pensions which were not available to other kolkhozniki. The kolkhozy were unwilling to allow him to use these privileges, and frequently insisted on taking a proportion of his salary. In theory the kolkhozy had no right to make financial demands on the teacher beyond exacting 3% of his annual salary in entrance dues. In

practice, the new kolkhozy were desperately short of money and, according to Narkompros, claimed from 25% to 100% of the teacher's salary for the common treasury. In addition, the kolkhozy often expected the teacher to do his share of work in the fields and serve as kolkhoz accountant, sometimes in addition to work in the school and sometimes in place of it.[33]

Just as the personal could be political for students, so it was for teachers and professors in the 1930s. Anna Bek, a psychology professor, tells of a party order to leave Novosibirsk, where she liked teaching and was close to her daughter and grandchildren, to take a position in Tomsk in 1931. As her memoir reveals, despite an auspicious beginning, she ran into problems with the party hacks at the university. The head of diamat—dialectical materialism, or the Marxist-Leninist political philosophy department—forced her to resign in 1934. She describes this situation in her memoirs:

> I worked in Tomsk for four years. The first three years went so well for me that this period could be called the pinnacle of my ascent up the stages of public life. I was beautifully situated materially, especially when the pedagogical institute moved from Semashko to Kiev Street into a large two-story stone building. I was given a big room on a side corridor. In the same corridor I had a room for my pedology and psychology laboratory, and a third door led into my lecture hall. It turned out to be a comfortable private residence for me. The students and administration treated me in a friendly way.... One of my first thoughts was, "How pleased my father would be if he were alive." My psychology course, including information on reflexology, no longer met opposition since Pavlov's teachings had been recognized and his discoveries were (now) acclaimed as works of genius. With the coming of the third, decisive year of the Five-Year Plan I was awarded a certificate of merit from the party professional organizations and the administration of Tomsk University as "an active and conscious fighter for the Bolshevik tempo of work and study, and a shock worker in socialist construction." It seemed that everything was going well, but it did not turn out that way....
>
> At the beginning of 1934 a new head of the diamat department appeared, Comrade Laizan. On the face of it he was a pleasant, good-natured person, not like an introspective philosopher. He considered it his job to organize a circle on dialectical materialism among the scientific researchers. I signed up for the circle immediately and attended all its meetings conscientiously.[34]

Bek was not very "politique," and she told Laizan soon after entering the Marxist circle that she found the meetings boring and unproductive. She suggested that the laws of dialectics be discussed on the basis of materials from various disciplines. She thought this would produce a more lively exchange of opinions. But her suggestion was received in "cold silence." She criticized the diamat discussion on the psyche. She thought Laizan and the other Marxists were familiar with political ideas, but not "the works of the Marxist classics," which she had studied thoroughly. At one point, she joked: "If you convince me that the psyche is not material, then coming into the circle a materialist, I will go out a Hegelian."[35]

Not long after this encounter, Comrade Laizan took advantage of her absence to accuse her of several deviations and to denounce her work on pedology—a holistic approach to child education, including psychology, anatomy, and physiology. When students were called upon to denounce Bek and to point out deviations in her lectures, they refused. One asked "Why is Bek being criticized in her absence?" and the other said he had not noticed anything un-Marxist in her lectures. Learning of the allegations against her, Bek took no offense because she found the accusations base and senseless. Later, she told Laizan: "If you had ever been to my lectures on pedology you would not have imputed such contradictory deviations to me." Still, Bek knew she had to react to these charges against her and on the advice of a colleague she wrote to the Moscow Party Central Committee, to Comrade Stetskoi who specially reviewed conflicts in institutions of higher education.[36]

Unfortunately, Bek acted too late. Laizan had already arranged for a reduction in the number of hours allocated to the teaching of pedology and had removed practical work in pedology from the curriculum. Then Bek remembered the discussions about psychology and pedology at various congresses in the 1920s, and she finally realized that the climate for teaching pedology had changed. While pedologists wanted a holistic approach to child education, those in psychology, anatomy, and physiology wanted specialists to study it.

Bek resolved to leave Tomsk University and return to Novosibirsk in 1934, but she needed a letter of recommendation for her pension, and her superior at Tomsk lauded her teaching but criticized her for not fighting for the "party's general line." Luckily for Bek, party leader

Stetskoi in Moscow had written a better recommendation, and she received her pension. However, when she returned to Novosibirsk to take up her work, she discovered that the Institute for the Protection of the Health of Children and Adolescents had been closed and the Institute of Communist Education had dropped the pedology laboratory where she had formerly worked. Thereafter, her professional life was dogged by disappointments. She wrote about work in sanitary establishments in a 1935 anthology, and the article was published. However, it was not allowed to be distributed because one of the contributors did not follow the party line. After several such setbacks, Bek retired from Novosibirsk University and taught psychology at an evening pedagogical institute. Then fate turned against her again, as she reports:

> The announcement that pedology was a politically harmful science and the persecution of pedologists—almost like that against the enemies of the Soviet order—fell like thunder from a clear sky. Although I was teaching psychology, as a former child development specialist I would be required to disavow pedology in print and point out the harmfulness of the science. I could not do that in good conscience, and for refusing, I was fired from teaching psychology. The path of teaching was closed to me forever.[37]

As a medical doctor, Bek was still allowed to work in a children's polyclinic in the late 1930s, but she considered this a step down from being a university professor. Compared to others caught up in the purges, she was lucky since she was spared arrest and imprisonment. No doubt living in Siberia, away from the internecine struggles in Moscow and Leningrad, protected her somewhat. Writing her memoirs in 1948, she was careful not to criticize the party or Stalin, perhaps fearing retribution for her family. Only those who wrote and published their memoirs in later decades were able to freely discuss their feelings and anxiety during the purges.

E. Technical Intelligentsia

> It is impossible to express in words how I suffered. I had put my whole soul into my work, heard only approval from those around me, and the man who knew me best of all dismissed me from work.
>
> Zinaida Cherkovskaya, proofreader

While many Russian women became part of the intelligentsia, some merged into the technical intelligentsia. One such woman was Zinaida Cherkovskaya, who worked as a proofreader in the 1930s. Zinaida had made an unfortunate marriage to an older man when she was only seventeen years old. She separated from him shortly after the birth of their daughter, when he took up with another woman. Since it was the 1920s, neither of them bothered with a divorce. She learned in 1932 that her husband had been arrested for participating in a workers' organization and was exiled for three years. During the separation from her husband, Zinaida had returned to the countryside to care for her ailing mother and took a position as a proofreader for the rural magazine *Pochinok Kolkhoznik*. She enthusiastically worked for the journal and began to yearn for happiness again. She fell in love with the editor of the journal, P. A. Melnikov, who subsequently became assistant secretary of the raikom (district leader of the Communist Party). Slowly he drifted away from her under the pretext of being too busy to see her. Eventually he had her dismissed. Zinaida describes her disillusionment in the following words:

> Often I was insistently pursued by the thought of suicide. This is cowardice, I know, but I felt that it was easier to die than to live without the man in whom I saw all happiness, all joy for myself. My little daughter forced me to dispel these thoughts.[38]

When Zinaida heard in 1935 that the party had created a case against Melnikov because he was seeing her again, she was crushed. When she learned that they had reprimanded him because of her, she didn't know what to do because she didn't know of what she was accused. Devoted to Melnikov, Zinaida left her work as a proofreader in Smolensk. She felt like a pariah. She didn't want to implicate her sister or father, so she fled her family. Hearing from her husband in January 1936, Zinaida decided to visit him and try to reconcile with him for the sake of their daughter. When they met, she realized that this was a mistake and left him immediately. She realized that she could not live without Melnikov and wrote a letter to the Smolensk Obkom party secretary. (This letter was kept in the Smolensk archive. During World War II, the archive fell first into German hands and then into American, which is how it survived to tell Cherkovskaya's love story.)

I will not be able to fall out of love with him or forget him, and I never want to build my life without him. I met him accidentally in Smolensk, told him how much I had suffered without him, and he told me that I should live only in my work, but that we should not see each other.

But I think I shall go mad. I don't want to be reconciled to it. I cannot get it through my head that in our free country, where the children of kulaks are not responsible for the crimes of their parents, I should be tortured my whole life because my former husband was once sentenced, and I do not have the right to be the wife of the man I love. Though he is a Party member, I am not an alien. I have concealed nothing. I have deceived no one, and I do not want to be a criminal without a crime.

I have recounted my whole life and all my "crimes to you," Ivan Petrovich, more frankly than to my own father. At the cost of my life I would be happy to prove to you the truthfulness of my words.

I trust you implicitly, and whatever your opinion will be on this problem, it will be law for me.[39]

While Zinaida trusted the leading party secretary to save her and her beloved, the purges had turned to provincial leaders by the mid-1930s. So unfortunately for Zinaida, Secretary Rumyantsev himself was discredited and purged. Hence he was unable to help her and her unrequited love.

Chapter Nine
Surviving the Purges

This portrait of a haggard woman by Vladimir Gorb shows a woman who may have suffered the effects of hard work during industrialization or may have lost her husband or relatives during the purges. She certainly looks worn down by life, and both the fast pace of work and the arrests of loved ones hit women hard during the 1930s.

Vladimir Gorb, At the House in Roslavl Town, *1934*

Indeed, as Nelson Demille remarks in his novel *The Charm School*, "It was a time of illusion, delusion, and collusion . . ." Although he wrote his novel during the Cold War, Demille's words could have been written about Soviet people during the 1930s. It was a time of illusion when "true believers"—Komsomol and party members and many others dedicated to industrializing the Soviet Union—were hoping for a better future for their children and themselves. It was also a time of delusion, when people tried to convince themselves that the glitches in industrial production, shoddy consumer goods, and the purges were all a mistake and would soon end. It was also a time of collusion, when many cooperated with the regime because they had no choice and because they thought times were bound to improve. Living through and surviving the purges, they lacked the perspective history affords us today.

While there was a great deal of upward mobility into the intelligentsia in the 1930s, the purges made life precarious for many educated women, especially those educated during the Tsarist period who were considered "former people" and the "old intelligentsia." Certain fields were safer than others. Groups like physicians and elementary and high school teachers were almost immune, but none were completely safe, certainly not academics. Actresses, old peasant women, party members—all could be and were arrested. Engineers and administrators were held more accountable than workers for not achieving the goals of the Five-Year Plans. While workers were seldom prosecuted for slovenliness or mistakes, engineers could be arrested, shot, or imprisoned for delays in construction or production. Trials of foreign engineers and "specialists" in the late 1920s frightened Russian engineers and specialists too, as they threw themselves into completing the Five-Year Plans. Intellectuals, artists, university professors, theater directors, writers, and musicians—even the famous, such as Dmitri Shostakovich—were vulnerable and subject to persecution.

In her book *Escape from the Soviet*, Tatiana Tchernavin estimates that 1 million people had been imprisoned or sentenced to penal camps in 1931. The 1937 Soviet census shows that more than 1.5 million adults and half a million children eighteen and younger were being detained by the NKVD (the name of the secret police during the late 1930s) for political crimes. By 1939 the number listed had increased to 3 million over the age of eighteen and a half million under eighteen. Leningraders suffered more than Muscovites: roughly 90,000 men and 12,600 women from Leningrad Oblast were detained, while 82,000 men and 9,300 women were from Moscow Oblast.[1]

A. Purges and Social Origins

> For who can map the darkness of those times?
>
> Anna Barkova, poet, *A Few Autobiographical Facts*, 1954[2]

In the 1930s, people could be arrested for almost any reason. Sometimes a party member wanted a better apartment and so denounced his or her neighbors. Helen Dmitriew tells the story of her sister, Marina, who was a teacher, and who was sexually harassed by a party member. When she slapped his face, he vowed to get even with her and put her name on a list of "enemies of the people" to be confined. She had to go into hiding for some time to escape his anger. While she was able to evade detention, their brother, Boris, who was also a teacher, was taken away in the early 1930s for hiding his "social origins." Boris had attended the Pedagogical Institute in the mid-1920s and had been a math teacher before his father had been denounced and sent to Siberia as a kulak in 1929. Because math and science teachers were in high demand, and because his courageous sister Marina intervened on his behalf, he was released.

Helen remembered how when she went to school the day of her brother's arrest, other students taunted her, calling her "enemy of the people!" These were the same students who had earlier fawned on her when they discovered that she was the school director's sister. Now she had suddenly become an "enemy of the people." A few years later when Helen decided to study at the Vitebsk Pedagogical Institute, she declared she was an orphan to hide her own "kulak" origins. Her father was living in disguise in Leningrad, and her mother was in hiding at her uncle's in the countryside, and she felt she had to declare herself an orphan in order to study.[3]

Helen Dmitriew recounts how much she hated holidays because she was a burden to her relatives. She writes:

> The worst times of my student life were vacation because I had nowhere to go. Boris [her brother] was always glad to see me, but Zhenia [his wife] disliked me terribly. Marina was married, had two children, and lived far away with our invalid mother, who was hiding from the authorities....
>
> Peter, my sister's husband, was a great fanatic and admirer of the regime, but he loved his wife and his charming children....
>
> I once went to their place for a few days and witnessed an

unpleasant exchange between Peter and Marina concerning our family. "They deserved it and they were banished," Peter uttered with malice.

My sister was at this time serving dinner. She threw a full bowl of borsch on the table. "My family had done nothing to your authorities," she shouted in anger....

He got up, wiped borsch from his clothing, put on his cap, and stalked outside.

Later, Peter returned and apologized to Helen's mother, saying:

> You understand me. I must hold to my line, otherwise we will all be back in Siberia. I don't want my children to take the path that your daughter Lena has experienced.... I am guilty, so please forgive me! We are powerless to change everything that happens around us.

Helen and her mother understood Peter's fears. If the secret police learned that Marina's mother was living with them without a passport and proper documents, they would immediately detain him, expel him from the Party, and deprive him of the right to be a teacher.[4]

While Helen's sister Marina had an indomitable will, Helen's spirits often flagged, as she noted:

> My heart ached, but the sheer force of my sister's will gave me strength and inspired me to hope and plan for a better future. On the other hand, hope was a rare commodity. What was there to hope for? People were intimidated and embittered. Their only thoughts, painted against a backdrop of fear, focused on where to stand in line to obtain a kilogram of bread to feed the family....
>
> When I was in the third year of the institute our family received information from relatives that Father was alive, living in Leningrad and working in an automobile repair plant. A decent person had helped him to get a job and to hide the traces of his past by changing his surname. This news gave me an unbelievable desire to see my father again.[5]

Helen did see her father, but the family was never able to live together. Her mother was ill, incapacitated, and without documents, and her father lived with another woman in a distant city. Survival was a struggle for millions but especially for "former people" and those released from prison.

B. Purges and the Intelligentsia

> A reign of terror such as we had never seen before was drawing near.
> Not only we but all the intellectuals as a class were doomed.
>
> Tatiana Tchernavin, *Escape from the Soviets*

1. Tatiana Tchernavin

In some ways, Tatiana Tchernavin first felt anxious after the birth of her son in 1918 when she found that she and her husband, though both employed, could not provide enough food for their newborn son or for themselves. Fortunately, her husband was able to take a third job at an agricultural institute on the outskirts of St. Petersburg, and the job paid a bottle of milk per day, thus solving their immediate problem as parents. When NEP was introduced in 1921, rationing ended, and family life improved. A remaining indignity for Tatiana in the 1920s was working under rude, dishonest, ignorant, suspicious Communist bosses at the Hermitage. In large enterprises, nonparty workers like herself were under the control and (mis)direction of their Communist bosses.[6]

Tatiana Tchernavin

As the Five-Year Plan was introduced in the late 1920s, rationing was reintroduced, and Tatiana again had a hard time providing food and clothing for her family. Her angst and dread increased during the "show trials" of engineers and specialists in 1927 when she and her husband wondered if they would be taken. After the shooting of "the 48"—food specialists accused of "wrecking" and being "enemies of the Soviets"—in September 1930, their dread increased. As she writes in *Escape from the Soviets*:

> We went about as though we had been poisoned, looking round at every step, starting at every sudden noise, alarmed by everything. The day dragged on wearily. There seemed to be no strength left for work, though sometimes one did it with a kind of desperate energy, to try and forget one's thoughts. Four o'clock brought a certain sense of relief: we would be able to go home once more. And at home one felt more wretched than ever: the rooms and the furniture seemed hostile in their cold sameness and indifference.
>
> My husband and my son came home, and it seemed as though this were our last evening, our last meal together; I could hardly swallow any food, thinking either of the friends who had perished so suddenly, or wondering how much longer my husband would still be with us.
>
> The boy was watching us with frightened eyes. He knew that friends who had such a short time before been well and cheerful, had been to see us, had joked with him, were now killed—but he could not understand why and how. The little girl who sadly sat beside him was a living reminder of their dreadful and incomprehensible fate.[7]

Tatiana tried to quiet her son by telling him that he would understand it some day. She then described their agonized waiting each night for the OGPU to come to arrest her husband:

> When the boy dropped asleep, time dragged on more slowly than ever. My husband and I had nothing to hide from each other: we sat on the sofa and waited. What were we waiting for? There is only one thing that everyone waits for at night, when every minute is filled with the strain of expectation—the OGPU.
>
> Ten o'clock. It was too early for them. We were talking of something else, but more and more slowly and absent-mindedly.
>
> Eleven o'clock. They might come soon now. Loud steps were heard in the yard . . .on the stairs ... My heart throbbed desperately. No, it was not here.
>
> Twelve o'clock. They might come any minute.

"That was how they took F.," my husband recalled. "He had just come home from the office—he had some work to finish and stayed there till midnight. What donkeys we are! How we have worked—and all to earn a bullet through the head!"

"Poor dear F.! How kind he was and naïve as a child! He trusted everyone."

We could scarcely hold back our tears. It seemed unthinkable that that man whom everyone had loved for his sweet disposition, who had never hurt anyone, had been disgraced as a "wrecker" and killed.

Time crept on more and more slowly. Every minute seemed to drag. There were footsteps in the yard: people were returning from evening work, from the theatre ... Some came up our stairs, other walked past, but I listened breathlessly to them all. My mouth was parched; I felt cold and then hot all over. There was a pain at my heart as though it had been bruised.

One o'clock in the morning. The yard was growing quiet; the gates were locked. Half an hour passed quietly. Suddenly there was a sharp ring at the gate. There they were ... sure to be. Thud of footsteps and loud conversation. No, two drunken men.

Two in the morning. The trams stopped. Everything seemed still.... No! There was the hoot of a motor car ... the OGPU car. The revolting, piercing sound came nearer and nearer.... No, it went past.[8]

Their catastrophe came in February 1931, when her husband was arrested, and a month later when she was detained. They took her husband not at night, the usual time, but in the afternoon before their son came home from school. As she describes it:

We had to wait for the OGPU car: with the great number of arrests, there were not enough cars to go round. We sat in silence, looking at each other for the last time. How many men had left home like this and never come back!

An hour passed. The OGPU young man made himself quite at home; he rang up his friends on our telephone, examined books and pictures, walked about the room, carelessly opened and shut the drawers—he was master here. We sat stiffly without moving and looked at each other in silence. One could not speak in front of an OGPU agent. And indeed, what could one say during those last moments? . . .

We started. The boy had not come home yet. Will the father have to go away without saying good-bye? . . .

At last there was a ring.

"It's our son," I said. "May I open the door?"

The OGPU agent nodded.

I let in the boy, and before I had had time to say anything he rushed forward in alarm and stood stock still seeing a stranger by his father's side. He sat down, poor child, and looked at us silently, not understanding what it all meant, what we were waiting for and why we looked at each other so strangely. He was trembling all over, not daring to ask anything.

The OGPU car hooted outside.

"Come along."

We all stood up. This was the end.

For the last time we saw him come up to us to say good-bye, doing his utmost to control his emotion. We could not utter a single word. He held out his hand to me and the boy, looked at us for the last time, and walked out of the room. We let him go his sorrowful way and looked after him in silence.[9]

After her husband's arrest, she realized that everyone would shun them. Some Russians profited from the misery of others. The house committee representative informed Tatiana that she and her son would have to give up one of their two rooms. When she complained that this was improper, he reminded her of her husband's detention. He had guessed that she might be incarcerated as well and wanted to make money by renting her "extra" room, as well as make several thousand rubles by selling the lease on the apartment.[10] She then described how difficult it was during the time of rationing to assemble food stuffs for a parcel to take to her husband and how complicated it was taking it to the prison before going to work:

> Parcels were accepted from nine in the morning, but as I had to go to my work afterwards I had to be in the queue quite early. I left home about seven, when it is still quite dark in winter. The heavy bag kept slipping out of my hands; the tram-car was packed. It was damp and cold; everything one touched was wet and dirty. I was so tired and sleepy that all my inside seemed to be trembling. At the prison gates one had to slip unobserved into the gateway of the house opposite. It is not forbidden to walk past the prison, but if the sentry sees women with sacks he rudely drives them away and threatens them with his rifle—there must be no queue outside a prison, though their sinister closed car rushes about the town collecting victims day and night....
>
> We knew nothing about the fate of our men. Tired and cold, we stood there whispering.
>
> "How long is it since your husband was taken?"
>
> "It will soon be a month."
>
> "Oh, that's nothing! Mine has been here a year"....
>
> "Ah, yes, of course, he is an academician! Yes, yes!"
>
> All were reassured. It was nothing new.[11]

Real joy was when an OGPU officer accepted their parcels and they could leave.

Tatiana's arrest came in March. She had been up late mending her son's clothes, when the OGPU came at one o'clock on a Saturday night. She recounts this event in the following words:

> I had kept hoping it would not happen. It was so dreadful to think that my husband would be left without any help in prison and my little boy alone with strangers.
>
> I had made several attempts to arrange for someone to take care of him in case I were arrested. But *all* my husband's friends were shot, and all my friends were being imprisoned one after another. Three people who had promised to take charge of my son were arrested in succession, and I did not dare to ask for help any more. Besides, I knew that it would not be safe for anyone to give a home to the child, for people were frequently arrested for assisting the families of those who were already in prison. In a case of a certain family that I knew *twenty* persons were imprisoned for helping them.[12]

The hardest part was not seeing all her books, papers, and music thrown on the floor by the OGPU agents but having to say good-bye to her son who was asleep. To waken him with such news was too horrible. She managed to leave her son and bear up during the ride to prison and her initial confinement. Her prison cell was cold, damp, and miserable, but she had a decent cellmate and bore various inquisitions and interrogations disdainfully and well.[13] After seven threatening and bewildering interviews, Tatiana was forgotten about for several months. She was then released and told to return to her old job and her son, who had faithfully sent both his parents the food and clothing parcels they needed.

In jail, Tatiana met various categories of prisoners: wives of prisoners, those who had been abroad, nuns from recently closed convents, pious women who helped churches or priests, wives and daughters of the clergy, criminals, and political prisoners—Mensheviks, Trotskyites, and former Social Revolutionaries, even Old Bolsheviks. Some of the latter had been in Tsarist prisons and demanded better treatment than they were receiving. Usually the politicals were sent to a special prison in Moscow and then to a concentration camp in the northern Urals. The sentences for women in the first categories were usually five to ten years of penal servitude in camps. Since Tatiana only belatedly received her accusation, she was not sentenced, and was eventually released in August 1931.[14]

Tatiana survived the boredom and misery of prison. She easily avoided forbidden things like crying, singing, or talking out loud. She muddled on until she was released. Then she suffered from demoralization. She had lost her taste for life since all of Soviet society seemed to lay in the hands of the OGPU. Her son's voice revived her briefly, but when she went to the Hermitage to claim her old job, as a French art expert, she met her uncouth, unsympathetic boss who told her that he had held her job for two months, but since she had been confined for four months, he had hired someone else. It was traumatic having her old colleagues look at her uneasily. They did not know whether she was still one of them or a "dangerous outsider." She revived somewhat when she got a low-level job working in a library. Slowly, she realized that she was one of the many intellectual "home émigrés" in Russia.[15]

During her incarceration, her greatest anguish was being separated from her husband and son and not knowing whether her husband had been sentenced, and if so, where he had been sent. She found this mental torture the hardest to bear, especially since the OGPU seemed to have forgotten about her and never called her for questioning. She suffered being separated from her son when she saw peasant women, criminals, and some bourgeois women walking with their children during the exercise period in Shpalerka prison. It seemed that educated women like her were denied their children as a special punishment.[16]

The most amazing thing about Tatiana and her family is that they plotted an escape and were able to get to Finland because her husband had been sentenced to work in the northern fisheries. In the early 1930s, families could still make prison visits, and when Tatiana spent time with her husband they planned their departure in detail. She sold all their valuables to obtain warm clothes and food for their journey from her husband's prison camp to Finland. She had to collect travel goods without attracting the attention of the OGPU. Their harrowing escape, documented in the second half of *Escape from the Soviets*, is an exciting read but lies beyond the scope of this book. Her stays with her husband in the Arctic fisheries resemble the situations of the Trotskyites Nadezhda and Maria Joffe in the early 1930s. Both Nadezhda and Maria Joffe were able to have visits with their families, but these lax conditions changed later in the middle of the decade when prison life became harsher.[17]

In the 1930s, countless Russians thought others deserved to be imprisoned. Those who had no family members incarcerated found it difficult to believe that people arrested were innocent. In 1934 the murder of popular Communist Party leader Sergei Kirov in Leningrad struck fear into the hearts of the intelligentsia there, and the purges began there earlier and were more intense than elsewhere. As early as 1935, Leningrad Puppet Theater director Liubov Shaporina began questioning what was happening to Soviet society. Some of the following women's writings show what a bewildering and dreadful time the 1930s were.

2. Olga Sliozberg

In Moscow, Olga Sliozberg heard her maid's story about her family being arrested in 1930 and deported as kulaks, but she was loathe to believe it. Her husband was convinced that the struggle against the kulaks was necessary and that somehow the maid's spouse was not so innocent. Only when Olga and her husband were arrested themselves in 1936 did they begin to understand that something was wrong in Soviet society. Olga's husband had been a lecturer at Moscow State University and she herself an economist, so they had lived rather well. They were both amazed when one of her husband's colleagues denounced him, and he was taken away. She mentions in her writings:

Olga Sliozberg

No, it was impossible; it couldn't happen to me, to him! Of course there had been rumors (just rumors—it was only the beginning of 1936) that something was going on, that there had been arrests.... But surely all this applied to other people, it couldn't happen to us....

But I believed in the justice of our courts. My husband would come back, and this alien smell and topsy-turvy apartment would be no more than a dreadful memory.

After that a strange period began.... Friends and acquaintances spoke to me in a special tone of voice; they were clearly afraid of me. People would cross the road to avoid me. Others became especially attentive, but this was heroic on their part, and both they and I knew it.

One old man, a member of the Party since 1908, came to visit me one day and said, "Put your affairs in order; you may be arrested as well. And remember, answer their questions, but don't say anything you needn't; every unnecessary word will lead to endless further questions."

But my husband's innocent! Why are you telling me all this—you a Bolshevik! So you don't believe in justice either?

He looked at me and said, "Remember what I've told you."

I felt it beneath my dignity to listen to his advice and tried to go on living as if nothing had happened.[18]

Not long afterward, Olga was incarcerated, and her children were left with their grandparents. In the Lubyanka prison Olga noticed:

> The unhappy people in prison were the Communists. They kept assuring everyone that there had been a counterrevolutionary plot, and that if mistakes had occurred in liquidating the conspirators—well, when you chop down trees, the chips are bound to fly. They would say that you had to amputate the gangrenous part from the live body in order to save the organism as a whole.
>
> If you asked them why the interrogators beat people up and forced them to give false testimony, they would simply say, "It has to be done," to which there was no possible rejoinder.
>
> All of them were convinced that Stalin had no idea what was going on in the prisons, and they were constantly writing him letters.
>
> They would accuse themselves of a criminal lack of vigilance. It was very hard for them. Hardest of all was the fact that, while they stubbornly defended the justice and good sense of the authorities' actions, they themselves were gradually losing faith.
>
> Yet they had devoted their entire lives to the Party. They had been its children and foot soldiers.[19]

In the Lubyanka and Butyrki prisons in Moscow and then in

Solovetsky, a former monastery turned into part of the Gulag, Olga tried to make sense of what was happening. Women had different reactions to imprisonment. While Olga wanted to understand what had happened, some just wanted to forget all the pain. Olga wanted to survive and tell about it. This would give her life meaning. One of Olga's cellmates couldn't fathom Olga's tormenting herself trying to understand what was happening. This cellmate, an art historian, believed that they had fallen into the hands of bandits. All they could do was somehow struggle through and survive the terrible years.[20]

After three years of severe confinement, Olga and others were treated to a respite in Suzdal. She describes their stay in the following words:

> But the greatest surprise awaited us on the way to the washhouse, where we were taken as soon as we arrived. It stood in the middle of a flowering cherry orchard! And for three years we hadn't seen trees, the sky, the moon, or rain! We had taken our exercise in walled-in prison yards paved with asphalt, and been made to look at the ground as we walked. We had been constantly submerged in the revolting smells of prison; disinfectant, slop buckets, boots, cheap tobacco, and the flesh of ill and unwashed bodies. And suddenly here we were amid a cherry orchard in full bloom!
>
> The moon was up, and all the leaves were glimmering; bedecked with flowers, the trees whispered in the breeze.
>
> We were seized with excitement. We breathed in the smell of the earth, the flowers, the trees, surreptitiously snapped off a twig to chew. The bittersweet taste of cherry wood pierced our hearts. We longed to fling ourselves on the earth and drink in its aromatic freshness with our entire bodies!
>
> We lined up to wash. Being ill, I was allowed to go last so that I could spend as long as possible in that marvelous garden....
>
> Our prison cell was housed in a wooden building, and before the Revolution had been a monk's cell.... None of the furniture was screwed to the floor, and the cell felt much like an ordinary room ... you could see churches, a bare springtime wood, the silhouettes of crows and jackdaws flitting over the trees, and even an apple tree in blossom![21]

Commenting on her stay at Suzdal, she noted:

> Human beings need both so much and so little!
> So much—because we need beauty, it seems, as well as bread. And yet so little, because it sufficed for us to be to able to see the

sky through our window and to walk once a week through our orchard. I have known many fine things in my life, heard Chaliapin sing and Rachmaninoff play, seen beautiful paintings and read wonderful books—but the sky in Suzdal and the flowering cherry orchard remain with me as the strongest aesthetic experience of my life.[22]

Needless to say, Olga never again found such charming conditions in exile. On their way to the Far East, they stopped at a bathhouse that had a mirror, and Olga did not recognize herself. She remarked:

> There was a wall-length mirror on the landing upstairs. It had been three years since we'd last seen ourselves, and being women, after all, we all rushed to have a look in the mirror. I stood in the crowd and stared, unable to figure out which of the women was me.
>
> Suddenly I recognized my mother's tired, mournful eyes, her graying hair, the familiar melancholy set of her mouth . . .
>
> It was me. I stood there gaping, unable to believe that I was no longer a young woman whom strangers in the street would call "miss," but this sad, middle-aged woman who looked at least fifty years old.[23]

Several years of work outside in the severe cold in Siberia aged her even more. She returned to Moscow to see her family only in 1946. Like many other political prisoners, she was rearrested in 1949 and only rehabilitated in 1956. Like so many, the purges cost her twenty years of her life.[24]

3. Markoosha Fischer

> A severe purge was on. But it affected chiefly the narrow circles of active Soviet and foreign Communists. Within these groups life had turned to tragedy. But the population in general, my Soviet friends, the hundreds of people in our house, went unconcernedly their usual ways.
>
> Markoosha Fischer, housewife

While some of the intelligentsia in Leningrad understood that things had gone wrong since Kirov's murder in 1934, many did not know how to interpret the trial of Kamenev and Zinoviev, which marked the beginning of the intense 1936–38 purges. Markoosha Fischer, the

Russian wife of American journalist Louis Fischer, was surprised that in touring the countryside in 1936 her husband had noticed none of the peasants concerned about the trial and execution of the Old Bolsheviks. Louis told his wife that in the provinces and villages hardly anyone even mentioned it. Russians were totally absorbed in the feverish activities connected with a bumper crop. They were unmoved by the trial. Later, Markoosha heard almost identical words from Maurice Hindus, the émigré Russian-American journalist, who had just returned from a prolonged trip through Russia.[25] Following this event, attacks were made on German Communists exiled in Russia, and Markoosha was told not to speak German in public. Writing about this, she herself observed that little talk was heard about the purges in the fall days in 1936. Life was still filled with activity and hope.[26]

It seemed to Markoosha that the populace was more intrigued by the Spanish Civil War than the purges. However, as the decade wore on, life became more compromised. The Fischers gave no more open houses. No more gay parties. Their wide circle of Soviet friends narrowed to a few. No more American or British tourists came to the Soviet Union seeking them out. The purges hit hard when her neighbor, Grigory Belensky, whose boss was arrested and secretary committed suicide, was awaiting arrest. When he was finally taken by the GPU, his wife Natasha lamented:

> "What shall I live for now? I will never see Grigori alive again. He is not young and he is a very sick man. They know it. They know he can't live if he hasn't got his diet and his medicines. I begged them to permit him to take his pills along. They refused. And I begged them on my knees not to take Lenin's letters and picture away. You know what they said? "A traitor's house is not the place for it!" Well if Grigori can be called a traitor of the Soviet Union, then life is worthless for me!"[27]

Natasha's lament shows that while far fewer women than men were purged, their suffering was intense. According to the NKVD figures of those incarcerated in large cities, women represented 20 percent to 25 percent of the total. For example, in January 1937, 18,000 men and 4,000 women were detained by the NKVD in Leningrad, and 20,500 men and 3,900 women were detained in Moscow.[28]

Markoosha thought the purges of high officials in light industry, transportation, and agriculture were disrupting the production of consumer goods, and the year 1937 brought renewed shortages of food and commodities. "But the masses accepted the government's explanation that the shortage came because the purged men were sabotaging and wrecking Soviet industry and that as soon as the new men repaired the damage the shortage would disappear." When Markoosha asked a woman, "How is it that we had plenty of everything during the years when these men who are supposed to be traitors and saboteurs were working in industry?" The woman almost denounced her to the GPU. Tired of the hypocrisy and insincerity of life, Markoosha felt as if she were suffocating. She was also weary of lying to her children to agree with the misinformation they were given at school. So she and her family decided to leave the Soviet Union at the end of the 1930s. It proved more difficult than she expected, and it took interference from friends of her husband in Washington to arrange her exit visa.[29]

4. Lydia Chukovskaya

> To think that all these women were the mothers, wives and sisters of terrorists and spies! They looked like perfectly ordinary people, just like in a streetcar or shop. Except they all looked tired and baggy-eyed. "I can imagine how terrible it must be for the mother to learn that her son is a saboteur."
>
> Lydia Chukovskaya, *The Deserted House*[30]

Lydia Chukovskaya's novel, translated as *Sofia Petrovna* and as *The Deserted House*, revealed some of the bewildering features of Soviet society during the purges of the 1930s. It could not be published, even abroad, until 1965. Her novel showed the fear, confusion, and despair that gripped Soviet society. It depicted the reaction of ordinary Leningraders to the terror. Her focus is the world of Sofia Petrovna, which served as a microcosm of Leningrad itself. The heroine lived in disbelief—first of the arrest of a doctor, who had been a colleague of her husband, as part of the Doctor's Plot of 1936; then of the arrest of her beloved boss, the director of the publishing house where she worked; and then of the second rejection by the Komsomol of her friend and confidant Natasha. When Sofia complained in a letter to her son Kolya about Natasha's unfair treatment, he replied in standard Soviet phrases:

Lydia Chukovskaya

But Kolya replied that injustice was a class concept, and vigilance was essential. Natasha did after all come from a bourgeois, landowning family. Vile fascist hirelings, of the kind that had murdered comrade Kirov, had still not been eradicated in the entire country. Class struggle was continuing and, therefore, it was essential to exercise the utmost vigilance when admitting people to the Party and the Komsomol. He also wrote that in a few years Natasha would, no doubt, be admitted, and strongly advised her to take notes on the works of Lenin, Stalin, Marx and Engels.[31]

Later, Kolya himself is arrested, and Sofia can't understand how this could have happened. Friends tell her to go to the procurator's office to find out what was happening. Standing in line for days and weeks trying to obtain information about her son's arrest, Sofia began to recognize the other women in her position:

> She was soon able to pick out at a glance which of the people in Chikovskaya Street were not casual passers-by, but holding a place in line, even in the streetcar she could tell by their eyes which of the women were on their way to the iron gates of the prison. She became familiar with all the main and back stairs of the building along the embankment, and had no difficulty finding the woman with the list wherever she would hide. She knew now that, when she left home after a short sleep, wherever she went—on the street, on the staircase, in the corridors, the hall in Chikovskaya Street, the embankment, the

prosecutor's office—she would always find women, women and more women, old and young, in kerchiefs or in hats, alone or with children, or with babies, children crying from lack of sleep and frightened, silent women....[32]

She kept trying to find out what her son had done. A true believer, an ardent Komsomol member, and an avid worker and inventor, Kolya would never have done anything wrong unless enticed by some woman. She kept wondering what Kolya had been arrested for? Who was going to try him? When would the misunderstanding finally be over, and when would he return home? Only after many months does she receive a letter from Kolya telling her that he had been denounced by a former classmate, arrested, imprisoned, beaten, and exiled before anyone could help him.[33]

While Sofia wandered around in a daze not understanding what was happening, her son's best friend, Alik, realized the score early on. At one point he asked Sofia's friend, Natasha:

> "What do you think, Natalya Sergeyevna?" he asked, his bright eyes looking her straight in the face from behind his glasses. "There, in prison, are they all equally as guilty as Kolya? All those others standing in queues somehow look an awful lot like Olga Petrovna."[34]

Indeed, Alik was expelled from the Komsomol for refusing to denounce Kolya. Hearing of Kolya's ten-year sentence to remote camps for terrorist activity, Alik finally decided that the investigators were scum. He told Sofia that saboteurs must have gotten into the NKVD and were running the show. They were the enemies of the people. He somehow knew that Kolya's confession had been forced from him, even though his mother was no longer sure of her son's innocence.[35]

The final tragic scene comes when Sofia goes to her friend, the doctor's wife, who tells her not to appeal her son's sentence. If she does, she will make it harder on her son and will draw attention to herself. Despairing, Sofia burned her son's letter and settled into the strange mental world she had come to live in.[36]

One of the most touching events in the novel is the suicide of Natasha—Sofia's friend and helper. She leaves Sofia a note saying:

> Maybe everything will turn out all right, and Kolya will come home, but I haven't the strength to wait for that. I can't make sense of the present phase of the Soviet regime. But you must go on living, and

my dear one the time will come when it will be possible to send him parcels, and he will need you. Send him canned crab, he used to like it. Thank you for everything and for what you said about me at the meeting. I am sorry for you, about what you have suffered because of me.... When Kolya returns, ... tell him I never believed anything bad about him.[37]

In her letter, Natasha referred to Sofia's defense of her at a publishing house meeting when the new director tried to blacken Natasha's reputation, and Sofia corrected his distortions. Later, Sofia found her job in jeopardy, and resigned before being fired and blacklisted, as Natasha and Alik had been. The feelings evoked by the novel are disillusionment, disbelief, and incredible sadness.

5. Olga Freidenberg

> For us, the first clap of thunder was Gorlovsky's arrest. He had been to Moscow and on his return learned that he had been dismissed. He went back to Moscow to plead his case. That was where he was arrested. Nothing more was heard of him.
>
> Olga Freidenberg, *The Correspondence*

The diary of Olga Freidenberg (1890–1955), her correspondence with her cousin Boris Pasternak—who later won the Nobel Prize for his novel *Dr. Zhivago*—and her memoirs show the stress university professors experienced in the 1930s. She wasn't arrested or purged, but

Olga Freidenberg

her brother and sister-in-law as well as colleagues in her department at Leningrad University were incarcerated. Just trying to get her books and articles published was extremely taxing. She wrote four books, but only one was published; eighty articles but just thirty were published. In the midst of doom, she kept functioning.

Describing the situation of society in the early 1930s, she wrote in her diary:

> The era of Soviet Fascism was coming into being, but we still accepted it as a continuation of the revolution with its thirst for destruction. We still did not know who Stalin really was and believed that there was some program behind him.[38]

In 1932 some prerevolutionary requirements—such as academic courses, examinations, and degrees—were reinstituted. According to literary critic Nina Perlina, Olga agreed to become chair of the department to prevent incompetent bureaucrats from taking over the Classics Department at Leningrad University. For this position, Olga had to complete her PhD, and she did this by presenting her work *The Poetics of Plot and Genre*, written several years previously. She realized that the establishment would exact payment from her, and it did. While her work was published in 1936, it was soon denounced in the government newspaper *Izvestiia*, banned by the state publishing organization, and even confiscated from bookstores. Some colleagues sought revenge for her success.[39]

In the 1930s, a campaign began against "formalism," which could mean anything censors or the secret police intended. It was launched against intellectuals. For Olga Freidenberg it meant that her creative approach to Greek culture and literature as well as her writing style were suspect. An unknown writer attacked her in *Izvestiia*. Charges against her cousin Boris Pasternak led to his having a nervous breakdown in 1935. Olga described the situation among academics as follows:

> Gorlovsky was loved and respected and pitied. Everyone was deeply dejected. Then punitive work began at the institute. A leading article in our university newspaper of January 14, 1935, bore the following headline in big letters: DISCOVER PEOPLE'S SECRET THOUGHTS. The affair of Gorlovsky and his ilk clearly indicates that Party ranks in our Institute are not what they ought to be....
> ... The interregnum and the audacity of the political police caused unrest among the students. This brought on a wave of demagoguery

by student leaders and Party dictators. Ida Snitkovskaya, Party Secretary at our institute, assured me that the Party trusted me and therefore was asking me to lower the marks of children of white-collar workers and raise those of the children of blue-collar workers. I refused point blank.

The atmosphere became unbearably charged. Some of the students began intriguing, informing, creating a feeling of secret discontent, fault-finding, and censure. My nerves were constantly strained to the utmost; I was worried and indignant. The incessant ringing of the telephone kept me in expectation of something crushing and unspeakable. Middle-class students complained to me of the intrigues and insults of working-class students, and everything taken together— the rumors, the ringing of the phone, the whispered stories, the latest news coming from second- and third-hand sources—poisoned my life and shattered my nerves.

Demagogic devastation made deeper and deeper inroads. The department began to crumble, to rot at the root.[40]

Academic life got harder as the decade progressed. Writing in her diary in 1936, Olga remarked:

> At the very beginning of May 1936 my *Poetics of Plot and Genre* appeared. I wrote that book over ten years, day and night, while at work and at rest, on holidays and during vacations.
>
> At last it was published and sales began to mount. Three weeks after it came out, it was taken out of the bookstores.
>
> On September 28, in the "bibliography" section of the newspaper *Izvestiia*, a review by Ts. Leiteizen entitled "Harmful Gibberish" was published with the following editorial note: "The article we have published about Olga Freidenberg's book demonstrates the sort of scholars the Leningrad Institute of Philosophy, Literature, Linguistics, and History is training and the sort of 'scholarly' works it is producing"....
>
> Can you conceive what it meant ... to suddenly receive such a crushing blow? Oh, the news we were forever expecting in fear and trembling! News that reached one by phone, that overtook one on the street, that came crashing into one's home, that ripped off the door of every refuge![41]

Olga later relates how family and friends encouraged her to make a public acknowledgment of minor errors to save the book as a whole. Recanting was repugnant to her. Instead, she wrote directly to Stalin. Like others, she believed in local scoundrels, and asked for his intervention. She didn't initially realize that Stalin was directing the terror from above. She felt calmer after appealing to Stalin, but people at the university began avoiding her. Friends ceased calling on the phone. Only her faith in the tradition of scholarship sustained her. She felt overwhelmed by whispers and rumors. Her life felt poisoned. Still, she went on giving lectures and attending meetings at which students despised her, and where colleagues isolated her in a ring of empty chairs. In those days, she learned what cowardice was.[42]

Luckily for Olga, Commissar of Education Volin intervened on her behalf. He was a high-ranking censor and had been a tutor to Stalin's children. Having studied her book, he found nothing in it contrary to Marx's teachings. In an interview in Moscow, he assured her that there was no reason for her book to be confiscated and withdrawn from sale. He thought she wouldn't be bothered again and that her good name had not been sullied. If she had any further troubles, she should contact him.[43]

After this interview, the atmosphere at the university completely changed. "Everyone was affectionate. Everyone smiled." People expressed sympathy and congratulated her.[44] However, another blow fell the next day when an ominous notice appeared in *Izvestiia* yet again, declaring that the patience of the academic community had ended and the university should understand the significance of pandering to her.

She asked her cousin Boris to have Communist Party leader Nikolai Bukharin intervene for her. But it was too late. Bukharin himself had fallen under suspicion and house arrest. Eventually Volin phoned the editors of *Izvestiia* and told them that Olga Freidenberg was not to be restricted. Still, this turmoil took its toll on Olga, Boris, and others dear to them.[45]

Writing in her diary later that year, Olga expressed her distress about the difficulties publishing her work. She agreed with Boris who remarked, "Analysis is looked upon as condemnation. Everything must be praised." Still, she resolved that the important thing is to preserve one's identity and go on working.... When questioned about her style, she asked the censor if he thought her cousin Boris Pasternak could write differently? She argued that academics, like writers, express themselves in certain ways. After these encounters with the authorities, she wrote:

> "It's absurd to deprive oneself of the air one breathes at home. Were it not for all these meetings and confrontations I could be happy."[46]

Tragedy awaited Olga as the decade wore on. In her memoirs, she reported events in Soviet society as follows:

> I do not know how historians will describe 1937. This was a whole year ... of political plague, pestilence, and flood—horrible, irresistible, and unfathomable. Its meaning was clear only to Stalin, who moved through the country like death. He undertook the merciless massacre of the population and cut off the people's head. From then on only the truncated torso remained alive. Such a version of myth was not known to mankind ...[47]

While Stalin was purging party leaders like Bukharin, Olga lamented in her memoirs that a "pestilence also struck the university, slew many of her colleagues, and ruined the morality of the survivors." Moreover, her brother Sasha and sister-in-law Musya were arrested and exiled. While Musya was allowed to receive parcels, her brother was not. Still, she stockpiled food for him in the event he would one day be able to receive parcels. Later, during the blockade of Leningrad in World War II, these food parcels helped her and her mother survive.[48]

6. *Lydia Ginzburg*

> Tonight I couldn't fall asleep for hours; I was overwhelmed by terrifying thoughts. During the day you are continually distracted by the minutiae of ordinary tasks, but at night when there's nothing else to keep you busy, thinking about daily life can be truly agonizing.
>
> Lydia Ginzburg

Like Olga Freidenberg, Lydia Ginzburg also felt the changes in academe. The university was tarnished when literary and cultural institutes like the Leningrad Institute of the History of the Arts were closed

Lydia Ginzburg

in 1930 on charges of "formalism." Fear and suspicion led to the disintegration of collegial relationships, making academic life at the highest levels difficult. Ginzburg chronicled some of these changes in her life as a litterateur. She wrote about the "ever present fear" of the time which was countered by acts of heroism, enthusiasm, creativity, and amusement. She also discussed her fall from literary historian to children's writer. Her journal entries on "melancholy" and "depression and writing" reveal the psychic stress of the period on one academic and yet her resiliency as well.

On melancholy, she writes:

> People tend to be melancholy (sic) in the morning and in the evening; day light dispels and engulfs it. I never fear evening melancholy because it is natural, the result of physical and mental fatigue, or vexation over an unsuccessful day, or even boredom, which appears when you're no longer in a state to work but don't know how or want to relax.
>
> But morning melancholy I fear like a disease or a moral fall.... It is not a weight, but a void, a nauseating feeling, recalling the nausea brought on by an empty stomach, by hunger.
>
> ... I get a morning attack only during the worst, most meaningless periods in my life. It basically reflects my fear of a meaningless, difficult, and joyless life. It usually occurs in bed before I rouse myself to wash and have breakfast. It can extend to cold, physical numbness, and to the horror of being unable to move in order to start the processes of getting up, dressing and eating, with which I must begin the bad day that lies ahead.[49]

On depression, Ginzburg presents a picture of what was happening to her profession during Stalinism:

> I suddenly understood that what we had avoided thinking about in earnest had already happened, that for almost two years now many of us, myself included, had lost our profession. When other people were going to pieces over the idea of losing their positions and their property, we were losing our profession and the people closest to us.
>
> It turned out to be not just something temporary, but an irreparable deterioration of our fate. Lacking the reciprocity and continuity of our occupations and interests we were losing touch. Stated more bluntly: we had ceased to relate to literary history and to scholarly activity in general.... Such a discovery was not easy to think through clearly; and then another year had to pass before it could be put into words. People have degenerated, grown cold, and forgotten under

the convenient cloak of putting it off. Not very long ago, in fact so recently it makes me laugh, I finally uttered for the first time the words that my dissertation—my book about the poetry of the 1830s—would never be written....

I feel no connection to scholarship, nor to literature. I am seemingly a free literary professional with whom contracts are easily concluded for children's books.... There are many such people nowadays, somewhere between literary specialists and hustlers.

... So my instinct for interpretation and for realizing my thoughts in writing saved me from utter despair. This is how we can utilize humiliation, grief and even emptiness, transforming them into literary material.[50]

By the late 1930s, terror in Stalinist Russia had intensified. Children of purge victims were being arrested. In 1932, Dr. Alexandra Kanel along with two other doctors refused to sign a false death certificate stating that Stalin's wife, Nadezhda Alliluyeva, had died of acute appendicitis. Dr. Kanel lost her job in 1935 and died the next year. In 1938, Dr. Kanel's two daughters, Yulia and Nadezhda Kanel, were arrested and imprisoned. Nadezhda was pregnant when imprisoned, and the authorities forced her to have an abortion. After several months of intense interrogation, a ray of light came to Nadezhda's prison cell in the form of Ariadne Efron, the daughter of poet Marina Tsvetaeva. Ariadne parodied the guards' visits, making the women laugh. Nadezhda remembered their good times together remarking:

> Despite the frequent interrogations and the sheer tedium of our life in prison, Alya and I didn't take things seriously at all. Knowing that we were completely innocent, we were sure that the most they could give us was three years' exile. We agreed to meet up after our release and even decided where—in the town of Voronezh, for some reason.[51]

Forty years later, Ariadne remembered how she and Nadezhda had ushered in the 1940 New Year together:

> It's almost the New Year again. At this time I always think back to the extraordinary New Year's Eve that we celebrated together: the remarkable circumstances (even I find them hard to credit now) and the remarkable closeness we felt for one another; the Kremlin chimes (I can hear them still), and hearts filled, in spite of everything, above all else, with faith, hope, and love . . .[52]

7. Lydia Seifullina

> Here and there, people ask these questions and they reproach me, saying that I don't want to see our success, don't want to participate in our country's socialist reconstruction. No, comrades, I do, but my experience as a writer, as well as my sense of responsibility, don't allow me to produce low-quality work.
>
> Lydia Seifullina

The plight of Russian intellectuals is also seen in the lives of writers like Anna Akhmatova and Lydia Seifullina. They had trouble getting rations and having their work published. Seifullina, who was popular in the 1920s, found it impossible to write in the 1930s. Like many of her counterparts, she was uncomfortable praising industrialization and collectivization. In 1934 she explained:

> I could write about Magnitogorsk, where I spent a few days. I could do this ... but I don't feel comfortable with this material, I don't feel the way I felt when I was writing about life in the countryside or "The Lawbreakers." I need to know this new life better. Don't forget that I came here from another world.... The greater part of my work and my life were spent in the country, and it is not easy for me to turn to the new topic of industrial urban life.[53]

Seiffulina's husband was purged in the 1930s, but she continued to work as an educator and journalist. Out of touch with the Soviet countryside, she chose not to write about it at all.

8. Anna Akhmatova

> In those years only the dead smiled.
> Glad to be at rest:
>
> Anna Akhmatova, "Requiem"

While Anna Akhmatova was not allowed to publish her poetry in the 1930s, she continued writing. Akhmatova suffered agonies when both her son and her lover, Punin, were arrested. Fears that they might be beaten and killed ruined any happiness she might have had. While her son survived two imprisonments, Punin perished in the Gulag. These poems and picture show the toll the decade took on her. The beautiful, carefree young woman of the prerevolutionary period has disappeared, and these works reveal the pain she experienced in the

1930s. One poem captures the terror of the time:

> I hid my heart away from you,
> As if I threw it into the Neva ...
> Tamed and wingless
> I live in your house.
> Only ... at night I hear squeaks.
>
> What's there—in the strangers' twilight?
> The lindens of Prince Sheremetyev ...
> House spirits calling back and forth ...
> The little black whisper of disaster
> Cautiously draws near,
> Like the murmur of water,
> And hotly presses to my ear—
> And mutters, as if it means
> To mess around here all night:
> "You wanted comfort then,
> Do you know where it is—your comfort?"[54]

(1936)

Her poem "Autumn" laments:

> They took you away just at sunrise,
> After you, like a mourner, I came,
> In the dark parlor children were weeping,
> The icon case candle guttered.
> On your lips the chill of an icon,
> Deathly sweat on your brow ... Can't forget!
> Like the wives of the Streltsy, I will
> Howl under the towers of the Kremlin.[55]

(1935)

A year earlier she had written another bitter poem called "The Last Toast." It reads as follows:

> I drink to our ruined house,
> to the dolor of my life,
> to our loneliness together;
> and to you I raise my glass.
>
> to lying lips that have betrayed us,
> to dead-cold, pitiless eyes,
> and to the hard realities:
> that the world is brutal and coarse
> that God in fact has not saved us.[56]

(1934)

CHAPTER NINE: SURVIVING THE PURGES

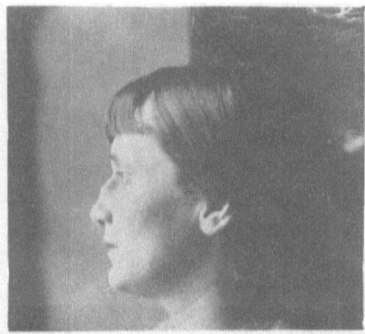

Anna Akhmatova, 1930s (Anna Akhmatova Museum, St. Petersburg)

This picture reflects some of her personal sadness, as does her famous poem from this period, "Requiem," which was written during the period 1935–40 and published abroad in 1963. It documents many women's suffering.

> Prologue to "Requiem"
>
> In those years only the dead smiled.
> Glad to be at rest:
> And Leningrad city swayed like
> A needless appendix to its prisons.
> It was then that the railway-yards
> Were asylums of the mad;
> Short were the locomotives'
> Farewell songs.
> Stars of death stood
> Above us, and innocent Russia
> Writhed under bloodstained boots, and
> Under the tires of Black Marias.[57]
>
> 4.
>
> Someone should have shown you—little jester,
> Little teaser, blue-veined charmer,
> Laughing-eyed, lionized, sylvan-princessly
> Sinner—to what point you would come:
> How, the three hundredth in a queue,
> You'd stand at the prison gate
> And with your hot tears
> Burn through the New-Year ice.

How many lives are ending there! Yet it's
Mute, even the prison-poplar's
Tongue's in its cheek as it's swaying.[58]

5.

For seventeen months I've called you
To come home, I've pleaded
—O my son, my terror!—groveled
At the hangman's feet.
All is confused eternally—
So much, I can't say who's
Man, who's beast any more, nor even
How long till execution.
Simply the flowers of dust,
Censers ringing, tracks from a far
Settlement to nowhere's ice.
And everywhere the glad
Eye of a huge star's
Still tightening vice.[59]

8.

You will come in any case, so why not now?
Life is very hard: I'm waiting for you.
I have turned off the lights and thrown the door wide open
For you, so simple and so marvelous.
Take on any form you like.
Why not burst in like a poisoned shell,
Or steal in like a bandit with his knuckleduster,
Or like a typhus-germ?
Or like a fairy-tale of your own invention—
Stolen from you and loathsomely repeated,
Where I can see, behind you in the doorway,
The police-cap and the white-faced concierge?
I don't care how. The Yenisei is swirling,
The Pole Star glittering. And eyes
I love are closing on the final horror.[60]

9.

. . .

I fall upon my knees, I pray
For mercy. It makes no concession.
Clearly I must take away
With me not one of my possessions—

Not the stone face, hollow blanks
Of eyes, my son's, through pain's exquisite
Chisel; not the dead's closed ranks
In the hour of prison visits;[61]

. . .

Epilogue

I

There I learned how faces fall apart,
How fear looks out from under the eyelids,
How deep are the hieroglyphics
Cut by suffering on people's cheeks.
There I learned how silver can inherit
The black, the ash-blond, overnight,
The smiles that faded from the poor in spirit,
Terror's dry coughing sound.
And I pray not only for myself,
But also for all those who stood there
In bitter cold, or in the July heat.
Under the red blind prison-wall.

II

. . .

I have woven for them a great shroud
Out of the poor words I overhead them speak.[62]

9. Anna Barkova

The poet Anna Barkova was not as careful nor as well known as Akhmatova. Her critical views of the Five-Year Plans got her arrested in the early 1930s. In the third stanza of a poem written in 1932, Barkova questioned the "faith of the fatherland" in the following words:

> And with a slave's quiescence
> We shall pay our blood-stained toll,
> In order to build a useless
> Heaven of concrete and steel.[63]

In another poem written during imprisonment in Karaganda in 1935, Barkova questioned:

PURGES AND THE INTELLIGENTSIA   323

So I am a woman, a Poet:
Now, tell me: what purpose has that?
Angry and sad as a she-wolf
I gaze at the years that are past.[64]

10. Natalia Sats and Larisa Lappo-Danilevkaia

> The most awful thing (was that) I was wild with fear. Fear that if something happened to me, then everything would be lost. I was afraid for my son, for my mother, for my father. Wild fear—always!
>
> Larisa Lappo-Danilevkaia, "A Mother in Exile"

While the memoirs of most educated purged women in the 1930s revealed only gloom and doom, some wives of "enemies of the people" were able to survive, almost thrive, in exile. Two such women were Natalia Sats, a director of the Moscow Children's Theater during the 1920s and 1930s, and Larisa Lappo-Danilevskaia, who also had theater connections in Leningrad before she was exiled. Both these women showed incredible spunk, robustness, and outspokenness. In prison, Sats demanded library books, pens, and paper so she could study during her imprisonment and emerge a better person. Lappo-Danilevskaia demanded special treatment from NKVD personnel and often got it. She asked for extra days to prepare for her exile to Kirgizia, and she was given eleven days instead of the usual twenty-four hours. Moreover, she was able to take her mother and child into exile with her, while Sats was able to have visits from her mother and child. These strong family bonds, which they were able to maintain in prison and exile, seemed to strengthen them. Few others were able to keep their children near them.

In exile, Sats directed plays and used her creative talents. No doubt this helped her survive. That and the visits of her mother and child emboldened her.

Lappo-Danilevskaia was able to visit her husband in exile in Kazakhstan shortly before he was due to be released in the late 1930s. However, someone denounced him, and she was unable to move to his place of exile or to work near him, as they had planned. After one short visit to his camp in Karaganda, she never saw him nor heard from him after he was sent away from his protected place of exile. As she remembered it:

That was another cheery affair. So I go out there. I arrive. He meets me. He was the head of transportation. In excellent standing. Well, so, we two met. I had an acquaintance in Karaganda, whose husband was in prison, and I'd known her in Rostov. The two of us corresponded, and I had already arranged to visit her, and then on to my husband. And we met there, my husband and I, and something very interesting came to light. This car was coming along from the camp. We were spending the night with my acquaintance. The car comes. The son of the camp director was sitting in that car.... He (my husband) introduces me, everything's fine. We drive, drive, and drive, drive and drive, somewhere out into the steppe. I look, and there are people on horses. They stop the car. A mounted patrol. They stop the car: "Who's this, who's this, and who is—this?" "This is the head of transportation's wife," said the director's son. That was it, they didn't touch me. Once it's put like that, I mean, the head of transportation.... And what did we discover? That on the day I arrived, visits (from family members to prisoners) had been stopped. And when I was traveling, I was already traveling illegally!!![65]

During her five-days visit, Lappo-Danilevskaia had met with the camp director, and she, her husband, and the director had agreed that she would come to work at the camp as a volunteer worker since her husband was supposed to be released within the year, when his three years of exile would be over. Instead, he was denounced and disappeared shortly afterward. She was proclaimed the wife of an "enemy of the people" and was exiled to Frunze, the capital of Kirgizia. However, she was allowed to take her mother and son with her. This all happened around 1938–39. A friend was not afraid to help her and gave her money to survive in Frunze for a while. She admits that she was afraid to go alone, so her mother and son went with her. Her father was ill and unable to travel.

Her mother also had a good attitude. As they were traveling to Frunze, she and her mother declare:

> "Mother ... I always wanted to ride, travel—it's wonderful! See—it's wonderful." And imagine, Mother said, "(If we hadn't been exiled) we'd never have got as far as Central Asia! Wonderful!" Nothing dreadful, we'll get along. When I had talked to that Pashin, he laughed loudly and said, "Oh, good Lord, won't be even half a year! What would it last a long time for?" Can you imagine?[66]

In Frunze, Lappo-Danilevskaia behaved in a spirited way with the NKVD officials. When told to go to a kolkhoz to live and work,

PURGES AND THE INTELLIGENTSIA   325

she refused. She realized that she couldn't support her family there. So she insisted on staying in the capital city, Frunze. With the money her friend had given her, she was able to rent a room in a hut. She applied for various jobs and seemed to have landed one with a theater, but after initially welcoming her, they checked her documents and after discovering her exiled status, they didn't hire her. As her rubles dwindled, she began making garments to earn money. She had designed her own clothes in Leningrad and even made some for friends, but she had never sewn for cash before. So, she made use of her many talents in exile. While waiting for a job, she had to report to the NKVD commandant's office every week.[67]

Eventually, a job opened at a library. Because educated personnel were in short supply in Central Asia, Lappo-Danilevskaia landed the job despite her status. She worked as director in what became the State Scientific Medical Library of the Kirgiz SSR. Through luck and pluck, she was able to stay in her position for almost a decade before she was denounced. Unlike her husband, however, she had a friend in the Communist Party, who helped her appeal to the Central Committee to be reinstated in her position. In her memoirs, she says:

> In short, I organized a library in the medical institute, then, you see, I found that (order from the Ministry of Health) and I showed it to the (officials at the institute) and said that I was organizing the republic's library for the Ministry of Health. And I got my way: at the ministry, I wrote a letter to Moscow, and I gave it to them to sign. With the minister's signature, in the name of the minister. And I became the director of the republic Scientific Medical Library. So that's how I slipped through . . .[68]

After Lappo-Danilevskaia was denounced, she again resorted to sewing to survive. Her appeal to the Central Committee in Moscow was successful, and in the 1950s she was reinstated in her job and was given back pay. Rehabilitated in 1957, she returned to Leningrad with her son. While others often had difficulty obtaining rehabilitation documents, Lappo-Danilevskaia did not. Compared to most exiles, she lived a charmed life. Still, she admitted how fearful she often was and how difficult it was to live with all her thoughts fettered until Gorbachev. Describing her fear, she wrote:

> You know, it's hard for me to say (how I coped with this fear).... Here's what it was: I have a child, I have to, I have to (be strong)—I

don't have the right to fall apart! I have a child, I am responsible for him. And in general, I have my mother and father, too, though they died later.[69]

C. Purges of Social Revolutionaries

"Still, we're really very lucky! There aren't many people in the USSR who can get together and say all they think, without fear of being denounced to the GPU!" This was the everyday mood of the exiles. They did not expect that they would be allowed to say or do anything much in the near future, but they did not abandon hope altogether.[70]

Galina Zatmilova, SR

While the Socialist Revolutionaries (SRs, or agrarian socialists) had been accorded fairly lenient treatment in prison in the 1920s, and while some SRs were working in exile in the Ural area to help build socialism in the 1930s, many were arrested in February 1937. This time, the regime was severe, and after their arrest they were shot, imprisoned, or sent to labor camps. A convert to the SRs, Galina Zatmilova tells how she became disenchanted with her job as a literacy teacher at the Aromil cloth mill, which was situated in the countryside. There, she witnessed collectivization and dekulakization first hand. In her memoir, "A Part of History," she describes her disillusionment with the following words:

> Then I saw de-kulakization and collectivization with my own eyes. It left a terrible impression, although I later learned that the Aromil rural soviet was much less brutal in its actions than was the case elsewhere. Those crowds of people driven out of their homes, the wild howling of the women, and the wailing of the children, were so awful that I did not recover for long after. I applied to leave the Komsomol. Neither the reproaches of my comrades nor the knowledge that I was condemning myself to oblivion could alter my decision. They expelled me. I had loved belonging to that large organization, now I was on my own. Next came my divorce, which had been brewing up for some time. I could not stay in Sverdlovsk anymore. In July 1930 I left for Shadrinsk, a town some three hundred kilometers away.[71]

In Shadrinsk, Galina met some SRs and married one—Pavel Yegorov. Pavel was devoted to the SRs and told Galina that although he loved her, he had no intention of altering his status as an exile. He had resolved to remain in prison and in exile until the authorities had ceased persecuting dissenters. In 1931 he believed that wives of political prisoners were not sent to prison, but they had to deliver parcels there for their husbands. This was before the mass purges of the late thirties. While the SRs were scattered in the northern areas, Galina and Pavel had no desire to go there and decided to live in Ufa, where some of the Left SR leadership such as Maria Spiridonova, Ilya Mayorov, and Irina Kakhovskaya lived. There, many SRs banded together in communal apartments and helped each other financially. In Ufa, Pavel complained about the dekulakization of the Kuban area. He didn't know how he and his friends could stand it.[72] Some thought Russia was no better than before the Revolution of 1917. Still, Galina described Pavel's thoughts regarding their situation as upbeat even in 1936.

Things changed drastically during the trial of the Old Bolsheviks Zinoviev and Kamenev in the summer of 1936. Some of the SRs could not understand how Zinoviev had confessed to planning to assassinate Stalin, but Ilya Mayorov remarked that Zinoviev had never been a decent person, so there was no reason to expect him to behave properly now. In February 1937, the NKVD came to arrest Galina's husband. When she went to check with friends to find out who else had been taken, she was seized. The NKVD allowed Galina to return home, wash, and pack suitcases for her and her husband. They were not so considerate in many other places, and women were often taken away in a summer dress with no winter clothing.[73]

While Galina did not report being beaten by the NKVD, she was questioned nonstop for five days at a time. Sleep deprivation was called "the conveyer." The authorities wanted Galina to admit to certain political conversations and to being a member of the SRs. She refused to do either one. She thought the NKVD had listened to all their conversations for years, so why did they need her to confess? Apparently it was necessary for court purposes. Moreover, she was never enrolled as a member of the SRs, so she couldn't confess to that charge. Since she was not cooperating, they began to question her nonstop for fifteen to sixteen nights at a time. Prisoners were forbidden to sleep during the day, so she was incredibly sleep deprived. Eventually, her interrogators stopped questioning her and asked her to sign the documents they had assembled. Since she didn't think she was incriminating anyone else, Galina signed the documents. Later a friend told her that they no longer needed her testimony and that was why they stopped questioning her. She was then sent to Kolyma, where she served a ten-year sentence. In Kolyma she married a peasant who had been exiled as a kulak, and they lived in Kolyma and then southern Siberia. Not until 1960 did she return to Moscow and Leningrad.[74]

D. Purges of Communist Party Members

> At the newspaper my head was in a spin. People kept whispering that yesterday so-and-so was arrested, and someone else had been picked up today. You hardly knew whom to write about, or what to say.
> Yelena Sidorkina, editor

1. Yelena Sidorkina

While Olga Sliozberg found Communist Party members the unhappiest people in prison, peasant party member Yelena Sidorkina's account makes one think that she was more bewildered than unhappy. Yelena belonged to the Mari people and had percolated up during the Communist period. Born in 1903, she had trained as a teacher and then joined the Komsomol and the Communist Party. She worked for Zhenotdel, the women's section of the party, in the Mari capital of Yoshkar-Ola. Yelena was even chosen to study at the Communist University for the Toilers of the East in Moscow. Her studies were interrupted when she was elected a member of the regional party committee and summoned back to Yoshkar-Ola. She was serving as editor of the local newspaper, the *Mari Commune*, when she was taken in 1937. Arrests had begun in 1936, and no one knew whose turn would be next. In her memoir, "Years Under Guard," Yelena recorded her confusion:

> During the election campaign for the USSR Supreme Soviet, for instance, the chairman of the regional executive committee, Pyotr Andreev, was nominated as a worthy son of the Mari nation. The Party campaigned actively on his behalf, and his portrait and biographical information were published in the press. That was mid-November 1937. By the end of the month, he had been arrested as "one of the most vicious enemies of the people."

Nobody knew what tomorrow would bring. People were afraid to talk to one another or meet, especially families in which the father or mother had already been "isolated." The rare individuals foolhardy enough to stand up for those arrested would themselves be automatically nominated for "isolation."

My own ordeal began on 27 November 1937. The knock at the door came at about one o'clock in the afternoon, as I was preparing the midday meal. Outside stood NKVD investigator Ukhov, People's Commissar for Internal Affairs. Karakharov wished to see me, he said.

I asked him to wait while I changed my clothes. Then I went into the living room and told my husband that the NKVD had come for me.... I tried to calm him. I was not guilty, I said, so it was obviously a misunderstanding, and everything would soon be sorted out....

I went into the bedroom and got my revolver. It had been issued to me after I was attacked one evening by a man we had criticized in the newspaper. I knew how to use it. We'd been taught to shoot back in the Civil War "special detachment." For a moment I held the gun in my hand and hesitated: a bullet in the head, and that would be the end of my worries. There was no evidence against me, however; I had done nothing wrong. The thought of my husband and daughter restrained me. Why should I cause them additional grief. People were bound to taunt them that I must have felt guilty if I shot myself. I put the gun down and hid the bullets so that my husband would not find them. Then I put on my coat, took my Party card, my passport, and some money, and went out to join Ukhov. My daughter had still not come back from school so I could not say goodbye to her, but I told Marusya, the maid: "I'll be back soon."[75]

Instead, she was gone eighteen years. Strangely, she never thought of turning her gun on the NKVD, only on herself. (Similarly, several high-ranking party members—like Mikhail Tomsky, Grigory Ordzhonikidze, and Stalin's own wife, Nadezhda Alleliueva, shot themselves—but not Stalin.) Yelena underestimated the NKVD. She had revered it as the right hand of the Party and the faithful guardian of the revolution.[76] She felt as though she had fallen into the hands of the fascists. She described her experience in the following words:

> It hurt me that such people could exist and call themselves Soviet investigators when everything they did discredited the Soviet system and undermined its authority. Even real enemies of the state should not have been treated like this. They were treating their comrades, people they had worked with, even worse than the fascists did. The fascists, after all, were tormenting their opponents. These people, who

called themselves Communists, tortured those who had dedicated their lives to the Party.

Later on I thought a lot about this. I realized that something was going very wrong in our country. The prisons and transit camps were filled with Old Bolsheviks and Party workers. And almost all the leading officials in the Mari republic, from top to bottom, passed through our prison: beginning with regional and district Party committee secretaries, Soviet officials, the staff from the courts and procurator's office, down to collective farm chairmen and their staff. Almost half the members of our regional Party organization, some two thousand Communists, were in jail. So every other person was an "enemy of the people?" It was quite unbelievable!

I tried pointing this out to my interrogators, and gave specific examples. There had been thirteen chief editors of the Mari Commune since it came into existence, and all of us were now in prison. We were long-standing Party members; some had fought in the Revolution and the Civil War, others had held leading Party posts. Why would such people attack the system they had struggled to create? The interrogators wouldn't consider any logical arguments.[77]

When Yelena tried to protest NKVD behavior and refused to hand over her party card to them, they simply called a member of the Party City Committee who came to the prison and took her membership card from her. Like others, Yelena was questioned for seventy-two hours at a time. When she was too exhausted to know what she was doing, she signed papers incriminating herself. Later she was sentenced to ten years in corrective labor camps and five years' loss of civil rights by the very judges she had earlier appointed.[78]

2. *Olga Berggolts*

> Thinking people ... were unable, quite unable to speak out against the politics eating away at the theory, and stayed silent, and tormented themselves desperately ...
>
> Olga Berggolts, diarist, 1930s

Another banished writer was the poet and party member Olga Berggolts. Her first husband, from whom she was divorced, was slandered, arrested, and shot in 1938. About the same time he was arrested, she too came under suspicion and lost her party card and membership in the Writers' Union. After several months, she was reinstated in the party, but then a few months later, she was detained on trumped-up charges, beaten unmercifully, and finally released after nine months in prison. Her imprisonment caused a miscarriage, leaving her disillusioned not only with the party but also with the petty, vindictive nature of the people who attacked her. In prison, Berggolts realized that the other women she met were equally innocent and there only on trumped-up charges. She wrote many poems about her experiences during 1938 and 1939, but none of them could be published until after Stalin's death. Some were printed during the "thaw" in literature under Nikita Khrushchev in 1965.

In her poem "The Ordeal," written in 1938, Bergholts bitterly comments:

> . . . And you'll have the strength again
> To see and realize
> how all that you have loved
> will start tormenting you.
> And like a werewolf, suddenly
> It will appear before you,
> and a friend will slander you
> and another will reject you.
> And they'll start seducing you,
> they'll order you: "Give up!"
> and your soul will writhe
> in fear and anguish.
> And you'll have the strength again
> to repeat just this one thing:
> "I shall never give up
> all that I have lived by!"
> And you'll have the strength again
> remembering these days,
> to call to all you've loved:
> "Come back! Come back . . ."[79]

Equally poignant was her poem "My Country," written in 1939. It reads:

> All that you send: the unexpected disaster,
> the savage ordeal, the fierce joy—
> I shall endure and pass through.
> But do not deprive me of trust and sharing.
>
> Then it will be as if the window has been sealed again

with an iron plate, grim, rusty . . .
Suddenly death will come in this unjust
estrangement—suddenly it will make no difference.[80]

In her secret diary about the Soviet period, she recounted the lies and trauma of everyday life. She had her husband bury her diaries during World War II because she wanted to keep a record of what had happened. In one excerpt she writes:

> If I survive they will be useful for writing the whole truth. About our limitless faith in a theory, about our sacrifices in the name of making that theory a reality—it seemed possible the theory could be realized. About the way politics then ate away the theory, concealing itself beneath the theory's banners, about how years passed of unthinkable, suffocating lies ... years of terrible lies, years of the most agonizing duality in all thinking people who were faithful to the theory and saw that in practice, in politics, everything was the other way round, and were unable, quite unable to speak out against the politics eating away at the theory, and stayed silent, and tormented themselves desperately, and voted for people to be excluded, even though they were convinced of their innocence, and lied, lied involuntarily, dreadfully, and were afraid of one another, and did not spare themselves, and wildly, desperately tried to believe.[81]

Apparently the need to lie and deceive oneself led to terrible alcoholism, and Berggolts was hospitalized and treated for this disease several times long after her imprisonment.

E. The Purges—Knowing and Not Knowing

Books and diaries of survivors help us understand the lives of Russian women during the time of terror. Writings from the 1930s provide glimpses into the issue of "knowing" and "not knowing" about Stalin's orchestrating of the purges. It seems that people in different social strata and in different parts of the country became aware of the presence of spies and arrests of innocent people at various times. In Leningrad, the assassination of party leader Kirov in December 1934 sparked a witch hunt that frightened much of the "old" intelligentsia. Some—like Markoosha Fischer, Elena Skrjabina, and Vasilevna Shaporina—surmised and "knew" that Stalin was behind the purges and torture. Of course, many ordinary citizens as well as some party members and intellectuals continued to believe that those accused of wrongdoing were actually guilty.

1. Elena Skrjabina

> Everybody was in a downcast mood, and all types of repressions were expected.... We were not deceived in our forebodings of misfortune.
>
> Elena Skrjabina, white-collar worker

Coming from the despised gentry class, Elena Skrjabina was careful about what she said after the revolution. She noticed that most others also began to watch their words and not complain about the shortages of food and supplies during the time of collectivization. She observed:

> There was sufficient bread in Leningrad; however, one item after another would disappear from the stores; first it would be butter, then sugar, then cloth. One would have to stand in line for hours. Russians had become used to lines; and no one protested, knowing that protest was dangerous. Spies were everywhere. Any misplaced word could mean jail or Siberia. People were afraid to make the least criticism; and if anyone did say something it was preferable not to answer for one could be involved in "counter-revolutionary propaganda." During the many years since the Revolution, people had become used to keeping quiet.[82]

Fear increased in Leningrad after the assassination of party leader Kirov. Describing the situation, she wrote:

> A few days after the murder, the Party Committee announced a purge at our institute. This purge took place in the following manner. At a general gathering of all the employees and workers, one or another colleague who was undergoing scrutiny that day would have to get up and relate his complete pedigree and history not only about himself but also about his parents, his grandfathers, and grandmothers. Of course, everyone tried to represent himself as a genuine proletarian never having had any property, having studied on pennies from his working father or his charwoman mother. Sometimes everything went fine.[83]

Sometimes people contradicted the stories told at the "chistka," or party cleansing. Then Party members were reprimanded or removed from their positions. Sometimes they were arrested, imprisoned, or even shot. Soon after Kirov's murder, tribunals of university professors took place, and mass arrests began. Several detentions among the Skrjabins' acquaintances occurred, and one of her neighbors was taken by the NKVD. Her husband began to feel guilty that he had not been arrested. They lived in dread in 1935.

Yet, in the summer, life seemed calmer, and they shared a dacha outside of Leningrad with some friends. Elena became pregnant with their second child, and life seemed not so bad until they received news that her brother, George, who had served in the Red Army, had been arrested. Like others, his trial was held by a troika behind closed doors, and no one knew why he had been arrested. Several months later they learned that he had been shot.[84]

More and more of their acquaintances were arrested, and soon the Skrjabins began to worry that he would be next. So Elena decided to study at the university so that in the event of her husband's arrest, she would be able to support their family. Having studied French and German as a child, she entered the institute of foreign languages. She was an outstanding student and received a stipend, so she could give up her day job and become a fulltime student.[85]

While she was advancing at the university, life was becoming grimmer in the Soviet Union. Her husband lost his job because of his nonproletarian origins, but a highly placed benefactor saved him and Elena. The purges intensified under Nikolai Ezhov, during 1936 to 1938, and even more under his successor, Lavrenty Beria. Eventually, even her Communist neighbor became disenchanted when her own husband was arrested—just like any other "enemy of the people." While Lyubov Kuryakina had always insisted that the Soviet regime made no mistakes, she realized how easily this happened when it was her own husband who was taken away by the secret police. Elena concluded:

> Unfortunately, until a person experiences something himself, sympathy and compassion are usually only superficial. With Mrs. Kuryakin, however, even superficial compassion had been lacking since, until now, she had believed the Soviet government to be invincible. For her, the only people arrested were subversives and enemies of the people who were undermining the foundations of the state. When it turned out that an enemy of the people was her own husband who, like her,

had been a true supporter of the Soviet state, she would not even try to conceal her new anti-Soviet attitude.[86]

Life's struggles continued in 1939. Elena was hoping to finish the university and did so just as the war with Finland broke out. But that and World War II are another story, beyond the confines of this book, but told in her volume *Siege and Survival*.

2. Markoosha Fischer

> We tried to keep up our normal routine and normal spirit as if nothing were happening, as if it would be possible to return soon to the bright hopeful atmosphere of only a few months ago.
>
> Markoosha Fischer, *My Lives*

Markoosha Fischer recorded how the purges slowly spread from the highest levels of party members to the rank-and-file party membership and then to the Red Army, and from non-communist officials down into the ranks of teachers, office workers, factory directors, engineers, physicians, actors, students, scientists, and writers. She remembered:

> People tried to escape by listening to old operas and reading classics and history and visiting museums. But as hard as we tried, it soon became impossible to think about anything else but executions, arrests, and exiles. Our boys would bring home stories about the purged parents of their schoolmates.[87]

Her servant, Niura, believed Stalin's explanations of the purges. She thought that all the Old Bolsheviks were traitors and wanted to kill Stalin and bring back the landowners. As Maroosha understood it:

> Niura truly represented the mentality of the woman and man in the street. She was, like most Russians, warmhearted and responsive to human troubles. She felt sorry for purge victims and helped them in secret if she could. But she was not bothered by political doubts and accepted every official utterance as gospel.[88]

Markoosha knew she had to be careful what she said around Niura since she believed Soviet propaganda and might make her employer pay dearly for frankness.[89]

3. Anna Larina

> Ordinary people could not understand how military heroes could have become enemies and wreckers. Some, however, thought they deserved the bullets they got.
>
> Anna Larina, Bolshevik

It was easy to hear people's comments about Soviet propaganda and whether or not people believed the official party line. On a transport to prison, Anna Larina overheard the following conversation among other travelers about the shooting of several military commanders:

> They themselves confessed; they did! You can't hide from the evidence.
> Excitedly, the people tried in vain to figure it all out.
> But look who tried them, commanders like Blyukher, Budyonny, and Dybenko! What are they doing trying people when they themselves should be tried! . . .
> But then a passenger in an embroidered Ukrainian shirt declared with sudden boldness, "I don't believe what they say about Yakir!" Sitting not far from me, he was flushed with agitation. "You can write a hundred pages in that paper, and still I won't believe it! I knew Iona and fought under him in the civil war, so I know what kind of man he is. A fascist hireling? That's absurd, a filthy lie! He's Jewish, you know, so like hell he needs fascists! . . .
> "Then tell me why it's necessary to kill off such military commanders, if they're innocent? That would only strengthen the enemy's hand!"[90]

4. Galina Shtange

> Today there's been a Demonstration going on since morning, with a Parade. Everyone is cheerful, there's music and singing everywhere, the streets are full of people . . .
>
> Galina Shtange, housewife and diarist

In her diary for 1936, Galina Shtange expresses her love for Stalin but gives no analysis of the trials. She simply puts the newspaper clippings in her diary. At one point, she says, "Last night Stalin's new Constitution was adopted. I won't say anything about it; I feel the same way as the rest of the country, i.e. absolute, infinite delight." Later she notes that when she was invited to a program in the

Kremlin, she did not feel as much awe as she expected. However, she was nearsighted and did not see everything clearly. She adds:

> My main reaction was a feeling of intense pride in being in the Kremlin, in this historic hall.
>
> I listened very carefully and wrote down everything I could. The most memorable impressions for me were when the delegation of children of the commanders of the Moscow Garrison came up and Stalin reached out to them, pulled them up to the rostrum where he was standing, and enfolded two of them in his arms in a warm, fatherly embrace. It was so touching to watch that tears welled up in my eyes. The procession of children's delegates, all dressed in white sailor suits, was a beautiful sight to see.[91]

Since Shtange's husband had been arrested and imprisoned in 1928, she may have been very careful about what she wrote in her diary. She may have felt free to describe her family's life and struggles but careful to include only positive remarks about Stalin and Kaganovich—at least for the years 1936 and 1937. She seemed to know she should avoid criticizing party leaders.

Many like Shtange had to conceal their feelings from their friends and relations. After World War II, one mother explained this to her daughter, confessing:

> ... she said she was crying because in Russia, the country she loved, one could no longer have a real conversation even with one's closest relative or friend. Fear filled every heart; you became a hypocrite. One expressed false feelings and concealed one's true feelings.[92]

5. Liubov Shaporina

> I am one of those happy ones, but that state, the gloom of the abyss, is exhausting, terminally exhausting. Like walking through a cemetery pitted with freshly dug graves. Who will fall in next, will it be you? And it's already so commonplace, you're not even scared anymore.
>
> Liubov Shaporina, diarist

Others, like Liubov Shaporina, founder of the Leningrad Puppet Theater, began questioning the purges and almost went mad. After the arrest of several friends and acquaintances in June 1935, she noted in her diary:

Life goes on, it tangles around you like a ball of yarn and you have no time to think or share in the grief of others, all you can do is try to ease your own private sorrows.[93]

Two years later, in January 1937, after the trial of several leading party figures, she commented:

I was getting my hair done yesterday at the hairdresser's. The radio started broadcasting Vyshinsky's speech for the prosecution. My Figaro spread his hands in the air, leaned over toward me and whispered, "I can't make any sense of it—the entire leadership!"[94]

After hearing Old Bolsheviks like Radek and Zinoviev "confess" to treachery, she asked herself, "And what about the things that are not being said at the trial? Think how much more terrible they must be." When foreigners questioned the confessions of former party leaders, Liubov merely wondered what hypnosis was for anyway![95]

Several months later, she complained:

The nausea rises to my throat when I hear how calmly people can say it: He was shot, someone else was shot, shot, shot. The word is always in the air, it resonates through the air. People pronounce the words completely calmly as though they were saying "He went to the theater." I think that the real meaning of the word doesn't reach our consciousness—all we hear is the sound. We don't have a mental image of those people actually dying under the bullets....
The puppets are my refuge. A fairy tale. A living fairy tale.
God forgive the living and give rest to the dead.[96]

After hearing of people being shot in the middle of the night at the Peter and Paul Fortress in Leningrad, Liubov verged on hysteria and madness:

To spend all night hearing living people, undoubtedly innocent people being shot to death and not lose your mind. And afterwards, just to fall asleep, to go on sleeping as though nothing had happened. How terrible.

A month later, she asked herself:

How can you find the strength to live, if you let yourself think about what's going on all around you?[97]

6. Lydia Chukovskaya

> And Sofia Petrovna makes an attempt to believe simultaneously both the prosecutor and her son, and as a result, she loses her mind.
>
> Lydia Chukovskaya, writer

While Lydia Chukovskaya flirts with madness in the thirties, one of the heroines in her novel *Sofia Petrovna* becomes unhinged. The book, set in 1937 and written in 1939, was not published until the cultural "thaw" of the 1960s. The novel's main character, Sofia Petrovna, is a clerk in an office, and she tries to make sense of the purges when her beloved son is arrested and declared an "enemy of the people." Chukovskaya writes:

> Sofia Petrovna for her own part knows full well that Kolia (her son) did not commit and could not commit any crimes, and that he is dedicated heart and soul to the Party, his dear factory, and Comrade Stalin personally. But if she would allow herself to believe herself and not the prosecutor and the newspapers, then ... then ... her universe would shatter, the earth would cave in under her feet, and the spiritual comfort in which she had so pleasantly dwelled and worked and which she had affirmed, would crumble into dust.[98]

Chukovskaya remarks further:

> Sofia Petrovna is not capable of generalizing from the visible and experienced, and reproaching her for this is wrong, because in the mind of an ordinary person such events seemed like systematically arranged absurdity; how can one comprehend organized chaos? And how do this all alone? A wall of terror solidly separated each person from those who were suffering likewise. The majority of people, that is, millions were like Sofia Petrovna, but when the consciousness of a nation is deprived of all documents and all literature, when the real history of entire decades is substituted for by a fabrication, then each mind is left to its own devices and experience, and reduced to a lower level.
> ... For many years my novel existed in a single copy — in a thick school notebook, in purple ink. I could not keep the notebook at home: I already had three searches behind me and a complete confiscation of property. My notebook was kept by a friend. If it had been found, he would have been executed.[99]

Chukovskaya then revealed the difficulties she had publishing her book during the early 1960s. Expelled by the Writers' Union in the

1970s, she and her works were rehabilitated only under Gorbachev during Glasnost in the 1980s.

7. Valentina Kamyshina

> On March 1, 1938, my husband was arrested ... and was convicted to ten years imprisonment under strict isolation and without correspondence privileges. Under what article of the statutes he was accused, I was never able to learn, despite many appeals to magistrates and governmental officials.
>
> Valentina Kamyshina, wife, mother, worker

Another poignant story of a shattered life was told by Russian defectors after World War II to Harvard professors for a translation project. Valentina Kamyshina's account is titled "A Woman's Heart." In her memoir of the 1930s, she tells of her husband's arrest and her efforts to find him and send him packages. She describes her life as follows:

> When I received the announcement that my husband had been sentenced and was being sent to the far north, I began to watch the prison trains going out.
>
> The nights were cold; it was raining. Maybe it didn't always rain, but when I think of those nights the rain is always there. The trolley had stopped running. One had to walk far out of town to the stations. Every night prisoners were shipped out from freight stations at different ends of the city.
>
> Since it was impossible for one individual to cover all stations, several wives in the same position as I joined together. Every evening we would meet and decide who would go to what station and there call out the names of all the husbands. Officially this was forbidden. We were cursed in the vilest language by the guards. Police dogs were sent at us ... I was afraid with every fiber of my body to see him among these sad, bent figures with hands behind their backs. I loved him, I was proud of him, that is why I didn't want to see him in this degradation. It seemed to me that if I should see him something horrible would happen; what, I could never imagine. Every night I went through this fright. Every night I went to see the prisoners leave. And it never happened—I never saw my husband. Thus he went out of my life, forever. Others met theirs, fainted, went into hysterics. The soldiers cursed violently, chasing the prisoners ever faster with their bayonets.
>
> Morning brought another torture. On my job I hid the fact that

my husband had been arrested. I was listed as a divorced woman. It seems that I was never so gay and witty as at that time. I never had so many admirers as then....

Finally I decided to call upon the prosecutor of the Republic himself. In my naiveté it seemed to me that he would be able to give me the information sought.[100]

After one twelve-hour wait, Valentina was finally told that "maybe her husband did nothing. The action might have been 'prophylactic.'" This shattered her. Ten years under strict isolation for a prophylactic measure! All her entreaties at the NKVD offices yielded no information about her husband. Finally, some of the officials told her to get married again and then she could live where she wanted, even return to the city to care for her aged mother. After divorcing her husband and marrying a new one, she and her husband applied to the NKVD to return to her native city only to be refused. The person who had advised her to marry told her it was all a joke. Describing her state of mind, she says:

> I was dazed when I came out of the NKVD building. I walked a block, maybe two, then I sat down on a doorstep. I remained there for a long time, several hours.... My last hopes were smashed and I saw all the tortures I had gone through.
> It was all just a joke . . .[101]

After the war, Valentina left Russia when German troops withdrew, and she met her third husband, who had been a prisoner of war, in Germany. She concluded:

> It was not easy—leaving your friends, your native town, your homeland—to go to the unknown. But there was no other way.[102]

8. Nina Kosterina

Something frightful and incomprehensible has happened: they arrested Uncle Misha.... They say that Uncle Misha was involved with some counterrevolutionary organization. What is going on? Uncle Misha, a member of the Party from the very first days of the Revolution—and suddenly an enemy of the people![103]

Nina Kosterina, teenage diarist, 1937

Most of the women's writings about the purges present the experiences of adult women in the Soviet Union during the 1930s. However, *The Diary of Nina Kosterina*, also published during the "thaw," shows that even teenagers were filled with anxiety about the arrest of relatives. Nina Kosterina's *Diary* reflects the turmoil and uncertainty she felt trying to understand what was happening in her society. A staunch Komsomol member and activist, she was disturbed by the arrests and trials of Old Bolsheviks, and she began to question what was happening. In an entry for February 7, 1937, she writes:

> The terrible trial is over. Of course, they will be shot. How could it have happened that old revolutionaries who had fought for decades for a people's government became enemies of the people?[104]

A few weeks later, she writes on February 21,

> "Loss after loss: Kirov, Kuybyshev, Gorky, Ordzhonikidze—our old guard is dying off."[105]

By April 1937 Nina's tone had changed from one of mild confusion to near panic. She's writing about the confinement of the father of her school chum Stella. "He was a department chief at the People's Commissariat of Heavy Industry. They say he was a wrecker."[106]

Later at the summer cottage that her family rented, the owner was picked up for Trotskyism. Nina was there when the NKVD came and also wanted to search her family's things. When they arrested the landlord, he could not refrain from sobbing as his little daughter clung to him and cried.[107] Reflecting on these events, Nina notes:

> I thought about it for a long time. I remembered the arrests of Irma's and Stella's fathers. Something strange is happening. I thought and thought, and came to the conclusion: if my father also turns out to be a Trotskyite and an enemy of his country, I shall not be sorry for him!
> I wrote this, but (I confess) there is a gnawing worm of doubt...[108]

Still, her doubts lingered. After school started in September 1937, she met with the Komsomol organizer, and he asked her about her school friend Laura, whose parents had been arrested. She again wondered what was happening:

> Grandmother is crying. I cry. Where has Ilya disappeared to? And what if they should arrest my father too? No, no, I have faith in my

father! He is a Party member, an old Civil War partisan, he never was and never will be an enemy of the people.[109]

Just a few months later, the blow fell. She received a letter from her father saying he had been expelled from the party and dismissed from his job. He told her:

> I shall not go into details: at your age much will still be unclear to you. But you must remember one thing: you will need a great deal of calm and endurance now. I do not know as yet how events will turn for me. But even in the worst case, you must be sure that your father was never a scoundrel or double-dealer, and has never blemished his name by anything dirty or base.... Be steadfast! ... We shall live through and overcome all ordeals.[110]

By May 1938, it was apparent how dangerous life had become. Her Uncle Misha was back, but he had been arrested when trying to intercede for his brother. Although Misha had only been detained and then released, his time with the NKVD had been harrowing.[111]

In September 1938, Nina learned of her father's arrest in the Far East. It was a terrible blow. The nightmare plaguing her was whether her father was also an enemy. Like many others, she thought it all a terrible mistake. Her mother remained calm, going places to appeal her husband's arrest and writing to the authorities. Her mother also thought it was a misunderstanding that would soon be cleared up. At school, Nina remained active in the Komsomol, in charge of the young Pioneers. She tried to cheer herself up by thinking of the pleasant summer, but she felt lonely without her father's guidance. In early September 1938, she wrote:

> And now I feel as though a rope were tightening around my throat. Such despair comes over me that I have no strength to shake myself, to unbend my back and look people boldly in the eye....
> Desolation and gloomy silence at home. Nobody is doing anything. Grandmother cries all the time—our father was her favorite son-in-law.... To top it all, there is no news of Uncle Ilyusha. He should have been here from Transbaikal by now, but he has disappeared. We have decided the he was probably arrested too.
> Mama is looking for work. With father here, we never knew want. Now everything is falling to pieces....
> And I am sunk in a deep, gnawing depression. Everything is either repulsive or meaningless.

And now all the young Kosterins—my father and Uncle Misha—
are supposedly enemies of the people. How can I, their daughter in
flesh and blood, believe this?[112]

For some strange reason, she was not dismissed from the Komsomol, even though she tried to disqualify herself because of her father's arrest. In fact, she was even elected to the Komsomol committee for mass cultural work. However, her father's arrest did disqualify her from attending an institute of higher education in Moscow, and she was forced to study in Baku instead. Her relatives couldn't understand why she hadn't lied during her interview and told the director that she didn't know about her relatives' situation. But, Nina knew her Komsomol honor demanded honesty, not "getting on" in the system.[113]

By August, 1939, her life had become a nightmare, as her diary indicates:

I feel so strange—suspended in a vast, monstrous vacuum. What can I do? Where can I turn? I keep feeling that it is all a dream—a nasty, ugly dream. In a moment I'll wake up and everything will be as before, fine, straight, and clear. Can my "practical" aunts be right, and I must really "accommodate myself," and hence lie and become a kind of tentacled creature, "an octopus"?[114]

Although Nina went to Baku to study, her mother intervened and she returned to Moscow for autumn classes. The 1940 New Year was funereal. "Father was absent, and Uncle Ilya, after a few drinks, began to talk about his long months in prison. Some of the details were dreadful. I am terrified at the thought that my father may have had to endure such things too."[115]

On November 18, 1940, Nina confided in her diary that her Komsomol leader, Nina Andreyevna, had been morally and physically crushed by her husband's arrest. She resigned her position at school and intended to leave Moscow to live in the provinces among new people. With her departure, Nina felt she had lost the last friend of her youth.[116]

On November 30, Nina wrote of her father's sentence as a "socially dangerous element" and his five-year sentence of imprisonment in Siberia. To survive, Nina devoted herself to her studies, social activities, and love. Little wonder that Nina threw herself into the war effort a few months later in June 1941. Joining a partisan detachment, she was killed in action in December 1941. Years after his release from prison, Nina's father published his daughter's diary during the "thaw." It was later translated into English.[117]

9. Valeria Gerlin

> Everything turned out badly for me, but not the worst. The best of the worst or almost the best.
>
> Valeria Gerlin

While Nina Kosterina's diary shows how one teenager came to grips with the purges, an interview with Valeria Gerlin shows how young children from well-to-do Communist families internalized the Stalinist terror, learning not to talk about her parents who had been arrested. Because relatives were not told that their kin had been shot, she hoped for her father's return from the age of seven until fourteen. Then, she realized that all her fantasies of her father appearing to her on the street, when she was walking home from school, were just dreams. She suddenly knew that he was never returning. Her mother had been allowed to correspond with her because her mother was only a wife of "an enemy of the people," and in exile she had the right to correspond with family members. Still, Valeria learned not to talk about the purges.

Luckily, Valeria was not sent off to a state orphanage, as most children of "enemies of the people" were; her mother had been able to place her with close friends. Moreover, Valeria's nanny was also taken in by them. So she had some continuity in life. Still, her inner world had been shattered when her father, who was a high-ranking member of the GPU and a Communist, was arrested. At school, she heard children talking about others who were the children of "enemies of the people" and she felt bad. She had only one or two friends. She remembered:

> We did not talk about this. You know, somehow, in some strange way, they didn't even tell me what I shouldn't talk about, but I knew what I shouldn't talk about. That's what we were like already. You know, moreover, I didn't ask about anything at home. I loved the people who were raising me very much, especially Nadezhda Vasilievna. I never asked about anything.[118]

A precocious child, Valeria had collected money for Spanish children during the Civil War before she was six years old. It broke her heart when the Soviets made a pact with Hitler in August 1939. She remembered:

> There were times when I really suffered, that was in 1939 or 1940. The Molotov-Ribbentrop Pack. On the way to school, I walked past the German embassy, where a red flag with the swastika hung. And every day, that was traumatic for me, literally every day. As for the people raising me, I don't know what they thought, at least what he thought; she was very simple, the woman. So she said that, well, this is the way it is, they are doing what they have to do, so it is necessary, and so forth. I never asked any questions. But after all, these were the Fascists, how could they do this? It was terrible.[119]

After the war, Valeria was reunited with her mother, who came to live outside of Moscow. Yet, in 1949, Valeria was banished as a child of an "enemy of the people." Her mother stayed with her in her place of exile until 1954. Then Valeria became a teacher, wife, and mother. After Gorbachev came to power, she remarked: "I have had the impression my whole life, well, with the exception of the last 12 years, let's say, that everything turned out badly for me, but not the worst. The best of the worst or almost the best."[120]

10. Anna Larina and Nikolai Bukharin

> They'll sort it out, you know. It'll get cleared up.
>
> Anna Larina to Nikolai Bukharin, 1936

While many Soviet citizens realized something was wrong in their society, some like Old Bolshevik Nikolai Bukharin developed elaborate rationales to explain the arrest of other famous party members. Huge numbers of purge victims, Party members, intellectuals, and other frustrated citizens wrote to Stalin asking for explanations of the purges or intervention in the cases of relatives and friends. In intellectual circles, Bukharin was known as the "Intercessor" because he initially interceded with Stalin for clemency for writers like Osip Mandelstam, Boris Pasternak, and others in the early 1930s.

A touching account of "knowing" and "not knowing" is Anna Larina's book *This I Cannot Forget: The Memoirs of Nikolai Bukharin's*

Widow, which was published abroad in 1994. It's a fascinating account of the time because it tells about her fifty-year effort to exonerate her husband. Although she was only twenty when she and Bukharin married and only twenty-three when they were arrested as "enemies of the people," she seemed more politically savvy than her husband, who was an Old Bolshevik. Larina recounts continued attempts by Bukharin to telephone and write to Stalin, asking for intervention in his arrest and trial. Bukharin refused to believe that Stalin was behind his detention. He thought Yagoda and the NKVD were in charge and played on Stalin's morbid suspiciousness. In Larina's opinion, just the opposite had happened: Stalin had perverted the NKVD.[121]

Larina suggests that it was a form of self-protection that kept Bukharin from admitting Stalin's involvement in the purges. Other Old Bolsheviks like Mikhail Tomsky and Grigory Ordzhonikidze committed suicide when they realized what was happening. Bukharin somehow thought he could continue to influence Stalin, as he had successfully intervened for many purge victims in the late twenties and early thirties. Only as his arrest drew near in 1937 did Bukharin tell his wife, "If I could have foreseen such a thing, I would have run a mile away from you!" He would not have wanted to compromise her by marrying her. She tried to comfort him, but only at the bitter end did Bukharin wonder if Stalin had lost his mind.[122]

NKVD interrogations by former acquaintances and admirers like Laverty Beria and childhood friend Andrei Svedlov shocked Larina. She was unprepared for the terror when it happened to her. Likewise, Vera Shulz was unnerved when she saw that her arrest warrant had been signed by Andrei Vyshinsky. He had been the rector of Moscow University when she attended classes there. She found it odd that he had become Stalin's chief prosecutor.[123] While Bukharin and other party members thought Zinoviev and Kamenev might have been guilty of betraying the state, they knew they were innocent. They tormented themselves trying to reconcile these "misunderstandings."

Interpreting this period includes figuring out why some wives of high-ranking functionaries were tortured and shot but others—like Natalia Sats, Anna Larina, and Mariia Joffe—were not killed and instead arrested, imprisoned, interrogated, and exiled to labor camps for years or decades. Larina insists that she was not physically tortured during interrogations. Yet Anna Akhmatova's son told of terrible beatings of purge victims when he was arrested in the 1930s. Nadezhda Joffe and Evgenia Ginzburg also tell of other women prisoners who were physically tortured, while they were not. One explanation about Russian women's survival focuses on women's lack of power and prominence in the government and party. For some reason, Stalin seemed content to humiliate and intimidate Old Bolsheviks like Lenin's wife, Nadezhda Krupskaia, and his sister, Maria Ulyanova.[124] Others, like the SR Vera Figner and Old Bolsheviks Elena Stasova and Alexandra Kollontai, were merely shunted aside, wielding no power in the Party or government after the mid 1920s, and hence posing no threat to Stalin.

In 1937 Beria warned Larina not to try to vindicate her husband. Just mentioning him could lead to her death. She took his advice seriously and spoke of him only to trusted friends. Initially, she had spoken of Bukharin and his unfair trial to a woman "planted" in her cell. So, she learned to be silent. It was one way to survive.

F. Righteous Russians during the Purges

Just as there were "righteous gentiles" in Germany and Eastern Europe saving some Jews during World War II, so too were there "righteous Russians" trying to help falsely accused purge victims and their families. As the decade of the 1930s progressed, however, people became more and more frightened of helping purge victims. According to Markoosha Fischer, she initially helped others but did so less and less as the decade progressed and terror spread.

Chapter Ten

Religion in the 1930s

> Hope was a rare commodity. What was there to hope for? People were intimidated and embittered. Their only thought, painted against a backdrop of fear, focused on where to stand in line to obtain a kilogram of bread to feed the family.[1]
>
> Helen Dmitriew, student, 1930s

Three social institutions helped women survive during the harsh 1930s: religion, marriage, and family life. Despite the antireligious campaigns of the League of the Militant Godless, closing of churches, and persecution of priests in the late 1920s and early 1930s, religion did not die out in Russia. While some hoped and believed in the religion of socialism, millions of peasant women remained true Orthodox believers, and many women in the cities, on collective farms, or even in concentration camps found traditional religious values sustaining. The 1937 Soviet census recorded 26 million female Orthodox believers and several hundred thousand Catholics and Protestants.

A visiting British doctor, Sir James Purves-Stewart, attended Znamenskaya Church in Leningrad in 1933. He noticed the richly decorated building and icons with no sign of pillaging. He saw several priests in richly embroidered vestments and heard a mixed choir of men and women singing in glorious voices. Mainly middle-aged and old people made up the devout worshipers in the congregation. His guides also showed him a mosque that was used for antireligious propaganda six nights a week but open for Islamic services on Fridays. In both Leningrad and Moscow, he observed that some churches and cathedrals were being used for antireligious instruction, some were being destroyed, and some had been turned into museums, schools, or workers' clubs. He reported that in Leningrad religious funerals were tolerated and that they were distinguished by black coffins; Communist and worker coffins, by contrast, were white, red, or yellow, and musical bands played socialist songs at these funerals and grave sites.[2]

350　　　CHAPTER TEN: RELIGION IN THE 1930S

In Smolensk Gubernia, an area not far from Moscow, a Communist archive revealed that party members were too busy and understaffed to conduct effective antireligious propaganda campaigns in rural areas. Believers, such as the German Lutherans and Mennonites, organized their own kolkhozes. Some Smolensk party members still baptized their children, had icons in their homes, and attended church. As late as 1936, there were 852 houses of worship and 836 priests and ministers in the Smolensk region. Smolensk city had four Orthodox churches, one synagogue, a Roman Catholic church, and an Evangelical church.[3] Figures are available for Smolensk because during World War II the Communist Party archive there fell into Nazi hands and later into American. Much of the information from that area is available in Merle Fainsod's book *Smolensk under Soviet Rule*.

A. In the Countryside

> "I don't want people coming to visit and find no icons in our house."
>
> Russian villager

During collectivization, several thousand churches were closed, yet religious practices did not die out partly because they were woven into the fabric of village culture. Private devotions to one's own icons in one's own hut could not be stamped out. Adherence to religious beliefs was one reason some women resisted collectivization, and as previously noted, some peasants thought they couldn't have their children baptized if they joined a kolkhoz and so refused to join the collective farms. Older village women tended to keep the traditional rituals regarding birth, marriage, and death. According to Soviet ethnographers, villagers in Tambov and Smolensk Gubernias still kept icons in their homes so that everyone who came to visit would see them. People in rural areas were reluctant to defy village conventions. One explained: "Nobody in our house prays. I've forgotten how myself. But all the same we keep the icons. An empty corner without icons doesn't look right."[4]

Although the religious significance of holidays was not emphasized so much, people kept the old traditions. Before a church holiday, they cleaned the house, hung fresh curtains, put a fresh coverlet on the bed, decorated the entranceway, and took a steam bath. The holidays of Christmas, Easter, Michaelmas, and the village patron saint's day were times for rest and feasting. Women did no spinning, weaving, or work during these holiday periods.[5]

According to Soviet ethnographers, even after collectivization many farmers continued baptizing their babies, and all families had christening celebrations even if they did not baptize their child. Godparents were chosen for the new baby, and a special dinner took place with relatives bringing food. Gifts of money and clothes were given, and singing and dancing took place. Rural dwellers retained funeral rites and rituals. If no priest was available to conduct a service, relatives read scriptures over the dead and women sang funeral laments. Singers of these chants were often in a trance-like state. The rhythm and words helped them communicate with both the living and the dead. Families also served a supper following the burial of their beloved and held the traditional Orthodox remembrances on the ninth and fortieth days following a beloved's death.[6]

In the 1930s, Helen Dmitriew found it safe to engage in religious rites with friends and relations in the provinces and small towns. For example, when she married her sweetheart, Anton, in Belorus, she didn't have time to ask her parents for a blessing, so her landlady blessed her instead. She recorded the incident in the following words:

> A devout woman, she loved me as her own daughter. She was very pleased when I told her that I was to marry Anton and confessed that she had told Alexander not to waste his time with me since I was obviously becoming serious with Anton.
>
> How I wished that my relatives could be present at this celebration, but this was impossible. When Anton and I were ready to go, my landlady made the sign of the cross over both of us and kissed us. "Let this be a substitute for family blessing," she said tearfully.[7]

In his book *Red Bread*, Maurice Hindus discussed religion and described how some Russian Orthodox priests lost their homes and gardens. Some were able to rebuild and could accept change as God's will. One priest's wife said:

> "Nu (well) let us not grumble too much. It is God's will. He gives and He takes. He blesses, and He punishes, so let it be."

Some wooden country churches fell into disrepair and collapse as

Destruction of Church, Leningrad Oblast, 1936 (St. Petersburg Photo Archive)

priests aged and died off. Children sometimes renounced their priestly parents so that they could "get ahead" in life. Market towns, however, often kept a church as a safe meeting place as well as for worship. It could serve as a "slap at the Soviets."[8] Still, Komsomol and party members sometimes turned churches into club houses or schools or tore them down, as the picture from Leningrad oblast shows.

According to Hindus, one priest whose home was confiscated was given land, and he built a new house. His wife was a good gardener and provided them with vegetables. She also cared for a cow and hens. But some priests missed colleagues and other priests with whom to talk. Some priests borrowed books from the village library and even disputed with the local party members on philosophical problems, including the existence of God. Most priests still baptized children and conducted funerals in 1930. During the New Economic Policy (NEP), some wealthy businessmen paid to renovate local churches. However, after 1930 NEPmen disappeared and penalties against the clergy increased. During collectivization, many churches were closed and some dismantled.

In *Red Bread*, Maurice Hindus noted that many of the small wooden buildings in the cemeteries, which held banners and icons for public processions and funerals, were abandoned and falling apart. Still, the 1937 census reported the existence of twenty-nine thousand priests (mostly in Moscow and Leningrad oblasts) and twenty-five hundred nuns.[9] Many in these groups had to disguise themselves, so the true number was probably much higher. Nuns had to work or be arrested in the 1930s, so some worked in hospitals or even on collective farms during the day and then participated in home worship when they were free. At least this was the story of several who lived and worked near Karaganda in the 1930s. Their unusual story is told by Tatiana V. Torstensen in *Elder Sebastian of Optina* and includes the following information:

> Mothers Barbara and Febronia, who had been arrested with the Elder, were not given a sentence. Mother Agrippina was sent to the Far East, where she was freed a year later. She wrote to Fr. Sebastian about her intention to go to their home village, but he blessed her to come immediately to Karaganda. She came in 1936 and was able to meet with the Elder. He proposed that she buy a small house in the settlement of Greater Mikhailovka, close to Karaganda, and settle in it; she was to come to see him every Sunday, "if only there is some vehicle going in that direction." Two years later Mothers Febronia and Barbara came to Karaganda. A house was bought on Lower Street—a small, old storehouse with a caved-in ceiling. In it they fixed up two rooms, plus a kitchen and a vestibule. There was also a garden with a well. Mothers Agrippina and Barbara found work in the hospital in the New City while Febronia, because poorly educated, worked on a collective farm. Other nuns as well came to Karaganda—Kira, Martha and Maria. They settled in nearby Tikhonovka. The nuns became acquainted with believers and began secretly to gather for common prayer. When they learned that Fr. Sebastian was in Dolinka, the believers began to help him. On Sundays the nuns would come to see the Elder. In addition to groceries and clean linens they brought him the Holy Gifts (Communion), cuffs and an epitrachelion. They would go out to a small grove, where the Elder would receive Communion and the sisters would confess and commune also. The prisoners and the camp authorities came to love the Elder. The love and faith in his heart had conquered malice and enmity. He led many in the camp to faith in God—and not only to faith, but to *real* faith. When Fr. Sebastian was released, he had spiritual children in the zone who, after their terms, went to him in Mikhailovka. Many years later, when the

church was opened in Mikhailovka, the residents of the Dolinka Central Industrial Gardens went there and recognized in the noble-looking Elder-priest their former water-bearer.[10]

The story of religious life in the 1930s is continued in the memoir of Vera Tkachenko, Elder Sebastian's cell attendant. She recorded the miracle of abundant of food:

> I became acquainted with Fr. Sebastian in 1939. I was eight years old, and he had just been released from prison. I was then living at my aunt's house on Lower Street. My aunt was a believer and we often went together with the Elder from house to house and prayed. When my mother died I became extremely close to him, since he felt sorry for orphans. He would say, "If I had not been an orphan myself, I would not have had such compassion for others." Then Fr. Sebastian said, "I'd like to take you in." I was then eleven years old. He settled me with a nun, where I lived under the Elder's supervision. When I turned sixteen, he took me on as his cell-attendant, and I constantly lived by him and took care of him.
>
> When we lived on Lower Street, we used to all eat from one dish. Five or six people would sit at the table and Fr. Sebastian would sit with us. It would happen that we would all be very hungry, but they could only set one dish for all of us. "No," I'd think, "I won't get my fill." And a miracle would happen! There would be food left over in the dish, and everyone would be full. How was he able to do that? I don't know.
>
> Our church was still unregistered at that time, so for ten years we went from house to house to pray. For example, it would be necessary to go to Fyodorovka to pray, and the Elder would say, "Let's get up at half past four and go to Fyodorovka." And we'd all get up and go on foot to Fyodorovka. I'd carry the books at my shoulder, Fr. Sebastian would take a stick and bundle, and Mothers Varya and Grusha would be there—they were the Elder's choir. There we would pray, and at half past seven he would bless me to go to work. (It was forbidden to not work—all who did not work were investigated.) When I would come back from work—again I had to go and pray. We used to go from one end of Karaganda to the other, because it was impossible to serve continuously in one place.[11]

1. Lifting of Some Restrictions, 1936

Once the kolkhozes became productive in the mid-1930s, the

Communist Party seemed less worried about the church's impact in the countryside, and the 1936 Soviet Constitution legally lifted civil restrictions against priests and their family members. A few bold priests tried to run for election in 1937, citing this article in the Constitution, but the government found ways to invalidate their request and eliminate them from the ballot. However after 1936, priests' children could attend university without restrictions. Given the purges in the late 1930s, priestly families probably still did not breathe easily.

The blurred lines between mystical religious practice and magical incantations remained, and women kept their quasi-religious rites and rituals. They continued using special healing incantations for sick children and guarded against the evil eye falling on a new born child or its mother. Old rituals hung on, and young mothers were not allowed to touch a dead body. Only old women sang laments for the dead. Mothers-in-law knew the scripts for healing illness. Older women assisted in childbirth and knew the rituals for protecting young mothers.[12]

Certain village women possessed magical incantations to punish thieves or return women's husbands to them. In Pokrovskoe, Vologda oblast, a woman recounted her skill in using magical words to inflict sadness upon an absent husband. In an interview, she remarked:

> A woman came to me: "Heal me ... My husband has left me, he lives in Moscow." I wrote down the words for her: "Morning-light—summer lightning, lovely maiden, take from God's handmaiden ... this sadness, inflict it on (Igor), so that he doesn't pass an hour, doesn't pass a minute, eats no eating, drinks no drinking, smokes no smoking, (only) grieves and yearns for God's handmaiden (Tamara)." I came home, and she comes to me: "Grandmother, my husband—he came back to me from Moscow!"[13]

B. In the Cities

1. Helen Dmitriew

> No matter how the godless authorities of the Soviet Union tried, it would not be possible to expel faith in God from the hearts of the Russian people.
>
> Helen Dmitriew, *Surviving the Storms*

From memoirs of the period, it appears women in urban areas had to be more discreet in performing religious rites and rituals. In a visit to the factory where her father, who had escaped from Siberia, worked, Helen Dmitriew noticed that illiterate peasant women workers who lived in the Leningrad factory barracks in the late 1930s crossed themselves while lying in bed, so no one would notice in the darkness. Writing her memoirs years later in the United States, she then pondered:

> Seeing this, I thought to myself that it is not possible to kill the deep religious belief that has become rooted in our people throughout the centuries. No matter how the godless authorities of the Soviet Union tried, it would not be possible to expel faith in God from the hearts of the Russian people. The peasants were and continue to be the foundation of Orthodox tradition. Without unnecessary questions, analyses, or criticisms, they preserve that deep faith, which they guard like a small spark in their hearts.[14]

Later, when these same women workers asked her if she would like to go to celebrate Christmas Eve, Helen hesitated:

> At these words my heart started to pound. Yes, I very much wanted to go with them. I was glad to be assured that not all religion had died in the hearts of these simple but wonderful people. I knew that faith in God had given me strength and patience to endure all difficulties, to struggle with fear, and to emerge as the victor over death. How many times had death visited my door? How many times in my struggle for life had I slammed my door shut when death knocked?
> Yet now, when they suggested that I go with them to pray in a small chapel in a cemetery where an old priest spared from execution and exile and not fearing anyone, celebrated the ritual of our Orthodoxy in secret, I was frightened. "No, I cannot go," I told Anna Yakovlevna.
> Everyone in the group stared at me. There was neither contempt nor hatred in their eyes, but understanding of what a visit to a church could mean: expulsion from the institute. Fear stopped me. My faith was strong, but when the question was of life or death, weakness and self-doubt set in.[15]

2. Elena Skrjabina

> Now we had to be very careful and not say anything that might be misconstrued. This was not easy since there was only one common kitchen for all four families living in the apartment.
>
> Elena Skrjabina, memoir

In her remembrances, Elena describes the baptism of her second child in the late 1930s and her mother's keeping icons in their apartment and the communal kitchen. When a Communist family moved in, her mother had to remove the icons from the kitchen, and they all had to become more careful. When it was time to baptize their baby, the priest recommended christening him at home, not in the church. One of Skrjabina's neighbors helped in the christening. She was a believer but did not tell her son-in-law, who was a Communist. Elena recalled the events as follows:

> Stepanida Svanovna crossed herself fervently during the time of the service and helped the inexperienced godmother hold the child. Mother had observed all of this; because my husband and I, according to the rules of the Orthodox Church, did not have the right to be present at the christening ceremony.[16]

3. Alexandra Berg

> What a mercy god has shown to me, a sinner. I was on the brink of death. This was a miracle.
>
> Alexandra Berg

Alexandra Berg had belonged to a clandestine religious study group in Moscow in the 1920s, and she stayed in it until her arrest in the 1930s. (Her memoir, which she wrote after she was eighty years old, does not include many exact dates.) In camp she experienced a miracle when some criminal elements in her barracks saved her from exhaustion and near death. This was an unlikely event because educated women and the criminals seldom associated in the camps. They usually detested each other, so this was remarkable. Later, she tells of meeting one of her "angels" in Moscow in 1939. She writes:

Many years went by. The year was 1939 and I was working in Moscow. I had finished the University of Moscow and was working in the Institute of Sciences making experiments on white mice and rats and testing different drugs, viruses, and microbes on them. I married Viacheslav. One day while I was shopping in a store I heard, "Good morning, Alexandra Fedorovna."

I turned around and saw before me a woman with a charming and pleasant face who was well dressed. I looked again and realized that she was the criminal, Katia. We hugged and kissed, and I wanted to ask her how she was, but she only said, "Give me your address."

I did, and she disappeared into the crowd without saying goodbye. I was surprised and stayed in the store for a while longer. Ten o'clock that evening my apartment bell rang and I opened the door. Katia walked in, took off her coat silently, and said "I am sorry I did not say goodbye, but I couldn't" and before she even entered the room she asked: "Would you let me stay with you for two months?"

I don't know what my face was saying, but I answered, "Of course, Katia, do stay." But I thought, "She will rob us."

... Katia stayed with us for over two months. My children and my husband loved her, and she was never a burden to anyone. In the evenings when we used to pray together, we did so in front of her. Father Piotr came down from Yaroslavl and served the liturgy, and we were not afraid of Katia. When we prayed she always stood but only seldom made the sign of the cross. After Father Piotr served, she walked over to him and asked him to give her a little time for a talk, but it took a long time. Later, about a year later, Father Piotr told us, "An amazing woman, your Katia. She has a surprising soul, it is truly Christian, but her life is so complex and difficult."

Katia would come home at different times of the day or evening sometimes even around eleven at night, so I just gave her a key to our apartment. One morning Katia came to Viacheslav and me and asked us to give her a blessing. She hugged the children, venerated the icon of the Mother of God of Kazan and, as always, just left....

What Katia was doing and where she went I never asked.... On the day that Katia had asked us to bless her, I went as usual to take the children to their grandmother, after which Viacheslav and I went off to our respective places of work. When I came home that evening, I saw a clean cup in the middle of the table and under it a note:

My dear ones, thank you for your trust, and for everything.
I love you, remember Ekaterina.
Katia.
P.S. the bundle is for you, it is clean.[17]

Katia has underlined the word clean, and Alexandra's friend Father Herman explained that clean meant the money was honestly gained.

He advised Alexandra to give one third of the money to the poor and to keep the rest. Alexandra believed that everything in life has a purpose, and the money was a godsend to her family, truly a miracle. She mused that it was a miracle that a thief who had done several stints in prison for stealing suddenly behaved so well in their household.[18]

In fact, Alexandra was graced with several miracles in her life: once saved by "criminals" in camp, and then by Katia's gift. Another time she was saved from robbery and possibly rape and death by thieves in Moscow, and she records this event as follows:

> I was walking at eleven thirty at night on Malaya Nikitskaya Street. It was windy and cold and there was no one else in the street. The houses were old ones, with deep gateways. I prayed and thought, I have to get to the tram stop as soon as I can, but I was going to have to walk for five or six minutes more to get there. I was scared. I passed a tall house, and suddenly two men came out and pushed me into the gateway. I was trying to say something when a third man grabbed me by the throat, pulled out a knife, and said "Shut up or I will cut you up! Let's take her to the basement quickly!"
>
> They pulled me into the basement and took the shopping bag with my purchases and my purse with my money.... They started searching me to see if I had any other valuables on me. I had a large gold cross on a chain hanging around my neck. They took off my jumper, and I was left in a dress with a torn collar. The cross on its chain was still on me.... It was useless to scream, to ask, to beg—they were merciless. I felt like a compressed knot and put all my spiritual ego into a prayer to God, to His Holy Mother, and to my spiritual father, Father Arseny. I was not afraid of them, but of dirty violence done to my body. Two of the men were standing next to me while the third, obviously the chief, was pulling money, documents, and pieces of paper out of my purse. Under the light of a hanging lamp he carefully was reading everything, but he put the money in his pocket. I could only pray to God in a disorganized way, asking for the assistance of His Holy Mother and of Father Arseny. The third one attentively was reading a little piece of paper he had pulled out of my purse. He suddenly asked, "What labor camp were you in?"
>
> I was so shocked that I did not understand his question. "How long did you stay in a labor camp? And which one were you in?"
>
> I answered. He looked at me attentively and said, "Hey guys! Give her back her clothes."
>
> He pulled the money out of his pocket and put it back in my purse saying, "Go home and know that you'd better not say anything about us."

I realized that the Lord and the Birthgiver of God, as well as the prayers of Father Arseny, had saved me. I walked over to the third one (the chief), bowed low to him, made the sign of the cross, gave him my hand, and said, "I thank you."[19]

Alexandra heard the chief thief say that he too had been in the camps and for that reason returned her things to her and released her unharmed. For Alexandra it was a "miraculous liberation, an indescribable miracle!" She walked to the tram, glorifying God, His Holy Mother, and St. Nicholas the Wonderworker. She arrived home, cried, went to the icons, prayed, and then peace returned to her. She was able to tell her husband about the incident in full detail. She thought "what a mercy god has shown to me, a sinner. I was on the brink of death. This was a miracle."[20]

Later in her memoir, Alexandra tells of her spiritual director Father Arseny's thirty years in the labor camps, and the trials of Bishop Afanassy who spent twenty-seven years in camps of various kinds. The biographies of churchmen like Father Arseny and Father Paul Florinsky indicate that the relatively laissez-faire religious policy of the 1920s had been replaced with a harsher one in the 1930s. Most of the monasteries were closed by 1927 and the monks dispersed. While Farther Arseny's spiritual group of lay men and women continued to meet secretly in Moscow during the 1930s, he was arrested for the second time in 1931 and banished to Vologda for five years, and then arrested and imprisoned from 1939 until 1958. Although Father Paul Florinsky was a gifted scientist and useful to the regime, he rejected the newly appointed Soviet metropolitan of the Russian Orthodox Church, Sergius Starogorodsky. As a result of his opposition, he was arrested and sentenced to ten years of servitude in 1933 but was shot in 1937. Berg's memoir also included the story of Bishop Afanassy Sakharov, who indicated that of his 33 years of being a bishop, he spent 33 months serving his diocese, 32 months free but out of commission, 76 months in prison, and 254 months in exile and forced labor.[21]

Indeed, church closings and desecration became more draconian in the 1930s. Empty ecclesiastical buildings deteriorated, and some were used for unholy practices. Village churches were often converted to club houses, some cathedrals became museums, and some monasteries were drawn into the Gulag system. The Solovetsky monastery was used to house prisoners and prison officials, while the

Nikolo-Pesnoshky monastery became a prison for the criminally insane. After 1933 the Boris and Gleb monastery in Dmitrov, outside of Moscow, was utilized by the NKVD prison camp guards and officials of the Moscow-Volga Canal, which was built by two hundred thousand exiled kulaks, criminals, and other prisoners.[22]

C. In the Camps

> To be where all this misery will have an end.
>
> Maria Regehr

As I argue in an article titled "Surviving Imprisonment in the 1930s: Social and Religious Experiences of Soviet Female Prisoners," in a Festschrift to my professor Jaroslaw Pelenski, memoirs of many camp survivors are often texts of terror and hope, showing women triumphing over dehumanizing imprisonment for years, even decades. Though they tell of torture and inhumane treatment, they also attest to some of the marvels of the human spirit. Their writings show prisoners bonding together into surrogate families, sharing mutual support and affection. They also reveal the kindness of cellmates. Some educated women temporarily escaped the horrors of camp life through intellectual activity, such as composing imaginary letters or mentally translating Russian poetry into French. But it was their religious experiences that fortified and sustained many. It was the Holy Spirit, the Supreme Good, St. Seraphim, and God who sustained several of them during their times of torture, terror, and distress. While luck, age, occupational skill, and a "talent for life," helped women survive, it seems that social bonding and a deep religious life also consoled them.[23]

1. Maria Joffe

In one Siberian camp, Maria Joffe was repeatedly put in punishment cells because she refused to recant her Trotskyite views. Still, it was in the punishment cell that she found spiritual comfort. A crack in the door let a "ray of light into her kingdom of darkness." This miracle helped her breathe more easily again. Slowly, she began to feel differently and accepted her ordeal. She believed that the darkness and punishment were necessary for her to see the light and to understand the miracle. During this experience, she mentally asked her son to give her his suffering, to let it fall on her. Slowly, she felt a small spark of happiness and peace. She no longer felt abandoned and believed the miracle would strengthen her. She knew the Holy Spirit would be with her the rest of her life. After this mystical experience, she felt she could withstand interrogation and no longer feared losing her communist honor during intimidation and torture.[24]

2. Evgenia Ginzburg

> Something intervened something at first sight accidental, but which was really a manifestation of that Supreme Good which, in spite of everything, rules the world.
>
> Evgenia Ginzburg

Another political prisoner, Evgenia Ginzburg, describes her social and religious experiences slightly differently. She found that while ordinary friendships took years to develop, in the prison processing rooms, women got to know each other well within a few hours. Ginzburg found that life, light, and human kindness kept breaking through the gloom that surrounded her.[25] In her memoirs, she describes a manifestation of this "Goodness" in her life:

> Each time my indestructibly healthy body found some miraculous way of preserving the flicker of life from extinction ... something intervened something at first sight accidental, but which was really a manifestation of that Supreme Good which, in spite of everything, rules the world.[26]

She came to grips with prison life, realizing "you comfort yourself with the thought that suffering lays bare the real nature of things, and that it is the price to be paid for a deeper, more truthful insight into life." These insights strengthened her, enabling her to survive decades of imprisonment and exile.[27]

3. Marie Avinov

> "St. Seraphim help me."
>
> Marie Avinov, *Pilgrimage Through Hell*

Gentry-class Marie Avinov was a Russian Orthodox believer, and her religious experiences in prison differed substantially from those described by Joffe and Ginzburg. Imprisoned following her husband's arrest, Avinov prayed to her patron saint St. Seraphim, and she experienced miracles in gaol and during her exile. She met Russian Orthodox nuns, theosophists, Communists, kulaks, even criminals. During her first detention, Abbess Mother Tamara befriended her, telling her to look for the hint of the Creator in everyone, and she would find it.

Her second incarceration, however, produced a profound moral and spiritual crisis. She could no long pray. Only gradually did "faith in the wisdom that shaped her life and gratitude for the breath of life" sprout in her again. Slowly, she found the ability to look at ugliness and find beauty in it. Eventually, Avinov was deported to a prison in Kazakhstan. Finally, she was sentenced to exile and dumped in a Kazakh village, where she had to report weekly to the NKVD. Put off a train in a small village and left to starve, she felt calm and prayed, "St. Seraphim help me." Aid came in the form of an exiled Ukrainian woman named Seraphima who sheltered her. It was a miracle being rescued in Central Asia. As Seraphima told Avinov, "think no more of Prison ... we're all in God's hands, and He will watch over us." They became friends, sharing food and fending for each other.[28]

4. A Dispossessed Peasant

Heartfelt prayers of German-speaking Mennonites exiled from their home in Ukraine to the northern Urals during dekulakization are found in letters written by the Regehr family to siblings in Canada in the 1930s. These letters were saved and translated into a book titled *Remember Us*. They are a testament to the faith of people in distressing conditions. Mr. Regehr writes to his sister in Canada that they have had little food in exile, and the parcels and money the relatives and friends have sent have kept them alive. He is certain God is watching over them, as he says in his letter of June 1932:

> Yes, dear Geschwister, if we did not have God as our comfort we would have perished long ago. But our trust is in the Shepherd of Israel, who does not sleep nor slumber, but keeps a watchful eye over everything. In spite of all our trials and tribulations we have often experienced God's help. It is especially evident in that He makes you so

willing to help. We are often touched to tears by what all of you together do for us—that you still regard us of so much worth. May God bless all the givers as well as the gift, and give us here ever thankful hearts. Everything must come from Him who can do everything and who has everything. We wish you the best of health and ask, please write more—and both write. We are happy to read.²⁹

Maria Regehr, the mother of the family, writes in a mournful letter to the family in Canada in October 1932:

> But just as God wills. Even though we must end our life like this, we still know that this momentary affliction is not worth the glory that will be revealed to us. A better lot is awaiting us there. Papa, parents, and many loved ones are awaiting us there. It will be glorious there. That is where I want to go with my loved ones—to be where all this misery will have an end. I wish you the very best of health, and good well-being. Would love to see you face to face. May God grant that it will happen soon.³⁰

Other dispossessed peasants were also able to keep their religious faith and continued praying in the most austere conditions in Kazakhstan. One memoirist notes: "The special status exiles who were believers used to gather in groups to pray. When the nuns Martha and Maria were released from Dolinka and sent to Tikhnovka, they told us that the Optina Elder Father Sebastian, would soon be released from Dolinka as well. We began waiting for him." He was released shorted before World War II. Until the war, priests often conducted services secretly in peoples' homes or in the forest. However, as part of the war effort, Stalin encouraged the Russian Orthodox Church to pray for Russian victory, and he allowed some churches to reopen and some priests to practice more freely.

Chapter 11

Marriage

> No wedding bells until you graduated from university. And by the time we did that, the war had started. That's how it was.
>
> Vera Malakhova, physician

While the 1930s were generally a time of economic, political, psychological, and social stress, a good marriage helped sustain many women. Russians in all ranks continued to fall in love, marry, and have children. Family life could be a bulwark against the uncertainties of life. Unfortunately, marriage was often broken by desertion, high divorce rates, and the purges, which separated husbands, wives, and children. Male deficits in the population caused by World War I, the Civil War, and epidemics after the revolution meant that not all women could marry. The highest marriage rates were among women aged fifteen to twenty-nine and thirty-five to thirty-nine. Older women were more likely than men to be widowed.[1]

The intelligentsia was particularly hard hit by the purges in the 1930s, so there were many widows as well as abandoned and divorced women in that segment of the population. Thousands of women were detained, sentenced, and exiled after their husbands were arrested, shot, or imprisoned. While sometimes their children were raised by relatives, often this was not possible, and in such cases their offspring were sent to orphanages, where they were ridiculed as the children of "enemies of the people." Once collectivization was accomplished and the famines of the early 1930s ended, life was not as precarious for peasants. Not so many peasant women were purged or exiled in the middle or late 1930s. Working-class families were not so prone to investigation or purges. While factory managers were often arrested for incompetence when the Five-Year Plan was not fulfilled, workers were merely reprimanded for sloth. However, low wages paid to both men and women made women's work necessary for families to survive. Full-time work created additional stress in family life. Marital and parental relationships suffered because of women's lack of time and energy and people's miserable living conditions.

The censuses of 1937 and 1939 show a deficit of 6 million Russian men, so not all women could marry in that decade. One woman medical student remarked:

> We had been brought up to think—and this was reinforced by life itself, 1937 and 1938 had taken their toll—that until you got on your feet, received your diploma, and were able to earn something, you shouldn't get married, because heads of families were all sitting in prison; there were no grown men around. It was a different matter for young fellows, but for a girl—until you had your diploma, a profession, and regular wages coming in, there was no use even thinking about getting married. It was completely out of the question![2]

While this was the voice of reason speaking, young girls continued to fall in love and to dream about their ideal mate. In a diary entry, Nina Kosterina tells of the fellows she fell in love with in Moscow, and then describes her ideal man in the following words:

> This does not mean that he must be a model of high intellect. But he must answer my inner needs. I must feel that he is a man who understands my thoughts and emotions. He need not like what I like or share my opinions in everything. No, but we must be on the same level. This is what I dream about.[3]

A. Peasants

> Love is even more trouble
> What with caring and forgetting.
>
> Maurice Hindus, *Red Bread*

Peasant women enjoyed very high marriage rates. Maurice Hindus gives some fascinating accounts of peasant courtship and marriage during the first Five-Year Plan. He notes that in the villages he visited, peasants still dressed up in their best clothes on Sunday and had fun dancing and singing in the afternoon. Young people no longer wore lapti (foot coverings) but shoes, not homespun dresses but clothes bought in the city. They even had underwear. In the evenings, groups went to the outskirts of the village to court. At dusk, couples broke away to court in ways that he remembered from earlier times. One difference was that in addition to discussing dowries, they also talked about free love and women's independence.[4]

Although weddings were a little precarious during collectivization, many traditions continued. Secular weddings were called Red Weddings, and those in church White Weddings. Hindus noted that during one church wedding service, the groom was unable to recite a prayer to one of the saints, and this was a source of great embarrassment. It also showed a decline in religious knowledge among some youth. Yet, according to Soviet ethnographers, most rites and rituals lingered on. Weddings never took place during the penitential seasons of Advent or Lent. Brides still prepared their dowries, including a feather bed, three covers for it, sheets, blankets, quilts, down pillows, pillowcases, curtains for the kitchen shelf, curtains for the windows, a lace tablecloth for the table under the icons, two plain tablecloths, dresses for the bride, shirts for the groom, and four towels to drape over icons. (Towels were used to cover the icons when couples made love.)

Brides still sang wedding laments. Some of the words in the songs changed, but not all. Singing occurred before the ceremony, on the way to the church in the wagon, and afterward at the house of the bride and groom, where everyone ate and sang more songs. Wedding guests brought food—cheese, sausage, and bread—and drink—vodka and home brew—all of which produced much merriment.[5] Chastushki, or songs about love and marriage, remained the most popular. Ethnographers no longer collected or published religious verse, although it probably continued to be memorized.[6]

Researchers like Laura Olson argue that collectivization diminished men's public power in the village, transferring it to the kolkhoz chairman, Komsomol members, and local party chairmen, but it left women's more covert power as keepers of tradition intact. This meant that the traditional ways of doing things remained. Girls got engaged, parents had considerable say in their choice of partners, village needs often took precedence over those of an individual bride, and women's domestic chores remained similar to those of their mothers.[7]

An example of village needs taking precedence over the brides' is recorded in the words of Aglaia Paramonova D., born in 1918 in a village in Arkhangelsk Oblast. In response to an interviewer's question of whether she had wanted to marry her husband, Aglaia said that she "got used" to him. He was a former kulak, exiled to the north, and after working in her village, her father hired him to do carpentry work.

The kolkhoz chairman sent Aglaia and her future husband, Aleksei, to a logging camp, where they worked together. When they returned, he asked her parents for her hand, and they married. Her father had only daughters, so by marrying Aleksei, Aglaia brought a man into the household, which is what her parents wanted. She accepted her parents' direction and married the person they chose. She was obedient and resigned—virtues in village girls well into the 1930s.[8]

Aglaia also remarked that sometimes men did not get to marry the girl they loved but had to marry the one chosen by their parents. She said: "That's how it was! The father, the father and mother commanded. That's how it was." She also remembered songs that married women sang, especially one about a young girl forced to marry an old man. The song told of a young wife running away from her husband and the consequences:

> He beats my body as much as he wants
> Oh, I submitted to the old man.
> Bowed to his right foot,
> I won't do that anymore,
> I'll kiss you, my dear (her new love.)

Aglaia indicated in the interview that her husband didn't scare her, beat her, and there were no bruises.[9] Still, her interview shows the strength of patriarchy in the family the 1930s.

Peasant women's autobiographies are scarce, but one appearing in the 1990s tells of a woman's two unhappy marriages in the 1930s. Irina Ivanovna Kniazeva's first husband supposedly loved her yet abandoned her and took up with her girlfriend when she was pregnant with their second child. Her father was so mean he threw her out of the house in the dead of winter, and she had to live with relatives in a village in Siberia. Irina married again, as she relates in an interview:

> And then a second husband turned up after six years. He seemed to be okay. He kept asking and asking. But I was afraid to get married. I said: "I have two children. How can I marry? Their own father threw us out. Is this one going to feed us?" And so it turned out. Well, all the same, I ended up marrying him. He wouldn't leave me alone. So I got married, but he was not a good man. Oh, he was not a good man! God forbid there should be such people. He beat me and cursed me out and swore all the time, and he drank and drank and drank. That's how it turned out. So I got married for a second time. He was the father of my

fourth child. One died; three were left. And Iurka had just been born—he was only twelve days old—when he, too, took off, left me. Again I was abandoned. And all I had was an awful little hut.[10]

Like many husbands and fathers in the 1930s and subsequent decades, he paid no alimony to her for raising their son.

Another Siberian woman, Elena Ponomarenko, tells how some patriarchal traditions did not change, and how she was deceived into marrying a suitor she didn't want. At the age of twenty, she was working and taking care of her elder sister's children. Both her sister and brother-in-law had died in a typhus epidemic, leaving three orphans for Elena to care for. Elena left her good job in Novosibirsk to tend her nieces in the village of Iurga. There the physician Arkady Koriaev and the head agronomist Vladimir Suasar fell in love with her. She was pretty and a hard worker, an attractive combination. The two men bet which one would marry her. Both began courting her. She had no time for a man in her life since she was working twenty-hour days, caring for the children and the farm. The men charmed her mother, bringing food for the family. As Elena remembered it:

> Well, I'd come home and Mama would say: "You know, Lena, Vladimir Ivanovich came by and chatted with me; he's such a fine man. He talked with me, he played with the girls, he even got down on all fours and let them ride on his back." Yes. He was such a strong man. Arkadii Ivanovich also came, but he would come and ask for a hunk of bread and a cucumber. Incidentally, they all collected dry rations for us, whatever they received. After all, they weren't married—there were a lot of guys—and they would give everything to Mama. And I begged Mama: "Good heavens, Mama, don't take anything from them." "Lena look, the children want to eat. Why are you making such a fuss?" And she hid the rations from me, but she kept taking them. Well, they kept coming, and this Arkadii Ivanovich made me a formal marriage proposal. Now, when they began to court me, they came to Mama and began to try to win her over, so she in turn would win me over. And Mama would talk to me, and I would say: "I'm not going to marry anyone! I don't have the time right now to get married"....
> Well things went on like that for six months. They both kept courting me. Vladimir Ivanovich took to dropping by ... he said: "I really like you, and I have serious intentions." I replied, "I don't have any serious intentions except to raise these children." And parted with him very coldly.... And just what do you think they thought up? One night I was washing clothes. I'd begun, see, in the evening, there was such a

heap of clothing. Three little girls, oh, how dirty they got everything. I only had time to do it at night. I was washing, and suddenly a messenger from the village soviet came running and said, "You're wanted by the village soviet." Well, I had a cow, they must want me to pay some kind of tax, they must be collecting taxes there. So immediately, without even taking off my apron or anything, I dried off my hands a little and rushed off to the little wooden house of the village soviet. I got there and said "Where? What's this all about?" There wasn't a soul around. On the table lay a book. The messenger said to me: "Sign here." I signed, and, see, just as soon as I signed, he said: "That's all! We've got it!" A door opened, and in came the director of the sovkhoz and various comrades. Arkadii Ivanovich wasn't there, he was absolutely opposed. Well, and everybody came into the room, and Vladimir Ivanovich immediately ran up to me, as if he was going to embrace me. I literally pushed him away, began to wail, and said, "Just what is this?' Well, and how did I figure out what was up? I figured it out as soon as he closed the book, this kid (the messenger) closed the book, and on it was written "Marriage Registry." I thought I was signing for the tax, and here it was the marriage registry. Vladimir Ivanovich immediately signed as well, and everything was done, and I was already married.... I ran home wailing, fell down onto the bench wailing. Mama said: "What is this? What's the matter with you?"[11]

Elena held him off for three nights, but finally her husband cried and carried on so, she yielded. After the birth of their first child, Elena discovered that Vladimir hadn't been a bachelor but had been married before and had a child by his first wife. Soon he started stepping out with different women. Eventually, he deserted her and their child too. So Elena left to go live with one of her sisters for a while. Eventually she obtained higher education and became a journalist.

Nor was marriage easy for achieving, hard-working Stakhanovite peasant women like Pasha Angelina and Daria Garmash. Angelina's husband disliked her zeal for tractor driving and wanted her to stay home and spend more time with their child. So, she divorced him. Daria Garmash's fiancé Nikolai complained about her devotion to her "unfeminine" work, so although he was a handsome fellow, she chose her work over marriage with him.[12] Having a job gave these two women the money and opportunity to be self-defining. Had they been only housewives, they probably couldn't have provided financially for their children. So, while marriage might have helped women survive, it wasn't always a happy arrangement. Perhaps children yielded greater joy.

B. Educated Women

> The only thing is, we have no time to be together; our work is always coming between us, and we see and talk to each other only sporadically, both of us are tired.
>
> Galina Shtange, housewife

Marriage sometimes fell casualty to overwork in the 1930s. While Galina Shtange's marriage survived, her lament was probably a common one. Still, educated people fell in love and married, despite the political and economic difficulties. In urban areas, bosses or superiors sometimes arranged marriages or interfered in them. Teacher Elena Dolgikh tells how her future husband's boss played the role of matchmaker in their marriage. Unfortunately, she was still in love with another man, and eventually her husband fell in love with another woman and divorced Elena, despite their three children and many years of married life together. She also tells how the superiors of her beloved Pavlik forbade him to marry her because of her "social origins." They even intercepted his letters to her.[13]

One tender love story was that of John and Masha Scott. John was an idealistic American who went to Russia to help build socialism in the 1930s. He worked as a welder in Magnitogorsk, and met a teacher named Masha in night school. She was his math teacher, and they fell in love despite their cultural differences. Their life together is chronicled in his book *Behind the Urals* and in a 1945 interview in the United States with Pearl Buck called *Talk about Russia with Masha Scott*.[14]

Another touching love story is told by Soviet journalist and writer Raisa Orlova in her *Memoirs*. She tells of her naive, happy childhood and early, happy marriage to her university classmate Leonid in 1937. Living in an era of self-deceit, she remarks:

> I was a very happy person in my youth. I graduated from the university of happiness without passing through the school of unhappiness. My first genuine love was a happy one, our marriage was a happy one. Over and over again the feeling was reinforced in me that this was the way it was supposed to be, that this was the normal way, that man was born for happiness. Whereas unhappiness and grief were deviations, anomalies.... My very own heroine was Tolstoy's Natasha Rostova, overflowing with the joy of life. And everything bad, everything horrible that subsequently occurred in my life seemed to be a deviation,

a haphazard incident. Over and over again I expected happiness and was unwaveringly certain that everything still lay ahead.[15]

1. Galina Shtange

Galina Shtange's diary, written in the mid-1930s, shows her own happy but hectic life as well as the unhappy marriages of her children. Galina was married to engineer Dmitry A. Shtange in 1903, and they still loved each other thirty years later. Although he was arrested in 1928 at the time of the "Engineers' plots," he was released after a short time in jail. They savored their time together, but he was beset by work as a professor at the Moscow Institute of Railroad Engineers. He had a special commission to finish two books about transport during the Five-Year Plans, and his work undermined his health but not their relationship. In one entry, she remarks, "My one happiness is my Mityachka. With him everything is reliable, stable, permanent. He won't betray me, he won't stop loving me. I am the only one in the world for him, just as he is for me."[16]

2. Anna Larina

A poignant love story was that of the very young Anna Larina (1914–1992) and the older renowned party member Nikolai Bukharin (1888–1938). Bukharin was a friend of Anna's family and closer to her father's age than hers. Anna had grown up knowing Bukharin since they both lived in the Metropol hotel in Moscow, and their families often took their holidays together in the Crimea. In 1930 when she was 16, they fell in love. Initially, Bukharin resisted his love for Anna, but he succumbed in 1934. Their romance lasted as long as he lived. Along with many other Old Bolsheviks, he was arrested, tried, and shot in 1938. In the late twenties, Bukharin had realized that Stalin was not a good party leader, but he was unable to stop his takeover of the party or prevent his policies from harming the population. So, although he was Stalin's friend, he was critical of his policies and ideas. Hence, he tried to resist his attraction to Anna because in some way he sensed his impending doom.

After her father died in 1932, Anna became even more attracted to Bukharin. She wanted to marry him, and they did so in 1934, when she was twenty years old. They had a child just as the noose was tightening around Bukharin in the mid-1930s. She was arrested and exiled in 1937, but she managed to survive twenty years in various camps in the Gulag.[17] However, she was not allowed to take her year-old son with her into exile and prison, and she never saw him again as a child. Because Anna's mother was also arrested, her son was raised by uncles, aunts, and orphanages. Only when he was a young adult in 1956 did he come to visit her in Siberia.

3. *Maria Astafeva*

> I asked Dunia to make sheepskin jackets for Lenochka and me out of Vasia's sheepskin coat and send them to us.
>
> Maria Astafeva, letter to relative, 1933

Some young prisoners in the early 1930s met and married in the camps or upon their release. Some couples were allowed to go into exile together in the early 1930s when conditions in Stalinist Russia were milder than later in the decade. In the early 1930s, couples who were arrested were sometimes allowed to go into exile and live together with their children. This happened to women like Nadezhda Joffe and to Maria V. Astafeva (1910–1937). Joffe was even allowed to take a nanny to care for her children when she was first sentenced in the early 1930s. However, she and her husband were eventually separated, and he died in Siberia. She lived to tell of the atrocities families experienced in her book *Back in Time*.

Astafeva was not so lucky. Born and educated in Harbin, China, she married a Russian businessman and lived in Moscow with him. They were arrested and spent years in camps for "aiding the International Bourgeoisie." In 1933 they initially lived on Anzer Island, Solovetsky camp, where their two children were born. Like Joffe, she employed a nanny for her first baby. But her luck did not last, and she was shot in 1937, her husband in 1938, and their children sent to a special orphanage.[18]

Astafeva's letters to her relatives in the mid-1930s are cheerful, yet she requests food and clothing that they needed to survive in the north:

374   CHAPTER ELEVEN: MARRIAGE

> We need badly three winter hats with earflaps (for me, my husband, and Lenochka) and mittens.... We also need warm stockings, books for Lenochka, a rattle toy for little Nikolushka. If you are going to send a food parcel, please send the most necessary—fats, sugar, milk, onion, garlic, and some dried fruit or compote (for scurvy). It would be great to have scissors, thread for sewing and embroidering, and waistband elastic, and buttons for underwear.[19]

Wives of so-called "traitors" usually received sentences of five to eight years or more. Many believed their own arrest was an honest mistake. They knew they had done nothing wrong but often thought that others were guilty. Few understood the widespread, systematic repression that was occurring. One woman, Iadviga Verzhenskaia, was even warned by a KGB agent to flee Moscow, but she fell ill and couldn't leave. Moreover, she had done nothing wrong and didn't believe that innocent people like her were arrested. She even went willingly to the Lubianka without taking a suitcase with her. She just didn't believe that anything bad would happen to her. Like Iadviga, many wives couldn't understand why they were arrested and why they were separated from their beloved children. None of these women had trials or were confronted with evidence of any wrongdoing. In despair, some went insane or tried to commit suicide. One woman, Liudmila K. Shaposhnikova, was put in a punishment cell for trying to improve the situation of other wives in the camp and for writing petitions. Some women never learned the fate of their children, and some learned only by accident that their children were living with relatives or had been taken to special orphanages, where they were tormented as the children of "traitors."[20]

4. Helen Dmitriew

Helen Dmitriew's romantic life resembled that of many other young Russian girls in the middle and late 1930s. Although she was from a poor exiled peasant family, she had decided to become a teacher. As the daughter of disgraced kulaks, she disguised herself as an orphan to attend a teacher training institute. While she dated many men during her student period, she chose not to marry until she graduated. She was tempted to marry a military man, Lt. Alexander Lomonosov, with whom she had fallen deliriously in love in her third year of studies; it was hard to resist his proposals. Moreover, military families enjoyed better food, housing, and lifestyles than poorly paid teachers. Still, she would have had to move around if she married the lieutenant, and that was easier for women who didn't have a career, which she wanted to have. Despite the low salaries and harsh conditions that teachers faced, Helen decided to remain true to her own dream and plan of becoming a teacher in 1939.[21]

After graduating in 1940, Helen was swept off her feet by a married man named Anatoly, whom she met when she took her gymnastic students to Minsk for a competition. She didn't know he was married and was quite confounded by his wife's and his light-minded attitudes toward marriage. In her memoir, she writes:

> Liudmilla and Anatoly both behaved very calmly throughout the conversation. I was the only one apparently feeling any embarrassment in this situation. I later learned that Liudmilla had lovers and was unfaithful to her husband at every opportunity.... Although from the beginning I had been quite indifferent to Anatoly his attention to my girls and me had impressed me. I nevertheless decided that their lifestyle was their business and that I would not allow myself to become enmeshed in such a situation.
>
> Although I felt as if life had failed me, I endured this breakup, too. The memory of each broken romance did not disappear entirely. I went proudly forward, anyway, in search of my dream. These experiences only underlined once again that life itself is like the ocean waves, which lash and try to swallow you with their strength and carry you away into the depths. If a person's strength of will is weak, then it goes without saying that she will disappear into the waves.[22]

Finally, Helen met the man of her dreams, who was also a teacher in a Russian school. He fell in love with her and asked her about her plans. She told him:

> "I'm not in a hurry. I want to find a man who will be close to me, with whom I can spend my life to the end. I don't recognize divorces. In my opinion that is too heavy a blow in life, and I've already endured enough blows. I want peace, love, and respect."[23]

(The blows Helen refers to are her family's exile to Siberia, starvation and illness there, and her thousand-mile trek on foot back to her homeland with her mother.)

Like other young women her age, Helen desired to express her feelings to her new love Anton, but she feared doing so. At one point she writes:

> Walking next to Anton, I wanted to embrace the whole world. Anton held my hand firmly as I alternated between sad and happy emotions. I wanted so much to hug him and let him know how wonderful he was and how happy I was to know him. Excessive modesty and fear restrained this impulse, for I didn't now what he would think if I expressed my feelings too quickly.[24]

Anton must have read Helen's thoughts because he then kissed her and made a date for the next night. They went to films together and listened to records. The words of one song made a big impression on Helen:

> Our little corner is never crowded for us;
> When you are in it, spring blossoms there.
> Don't leave, so many songs are still unsung,
> Each string of the guitar still rings.[25]

Like many others, they told their stories to each other, and it turned out that Anton's life also contained bitterness. His father had been denounced to the NKVD, and he was beaten to death during an interrogation. This only created a greater bond between them, since Helen's family had been unfairly exiled to Siberia. They married soon after they began dating. They wed not in church but in the local ZAGS office—the civil registrar's office for recording marriage, divorces, and births. It was a simple ceremony, where they recorded their names, place of birth, nationality, and decided whether Helen would keep her maiden name or take her husband's. It cost only three rubles to marry at ZAGS—much less than if they had a church wedding or a party and invited their friends.[26] While their new life together went smoothly, World War II ruined their lives, and Anton was killed a year later by a German sniper. So their true love lasted only one year.

5. Margaret Wettlin

Another touching love story of the mid-1930s is told by the American English teacher, translator, and writer Margaret Wettlin. She went to Russia in the early 1930s to teach English but married a Russian actor named Andrei Efremov and stayed for fifty years. Margaret and Andrei met at a Moscow theater, and she described their attraction in the following words:

> I found interminable the intervals between Andrei's seeing me home one night and calling for me the next. I was falling more and more under his spell. No other man of my acquaintance had ever pleased me so. I had dreamed of marrying a musician, having set my heart on a life associated with art, and music was the form of art to which I was most attuned. But all the arts are one at the source; the main thing was that Andrei was an artist, albeit of the theater. And an impassioned artist. An impassioned thinker, too, with strong likes and dislikes which for the most part were congenial to my own. And he was a dreamer who believed in the future, as could only be expected of one with his buoyant disposition and infrangible optimism.
> All this was true, but—he could not even speak my language, and our backgrounds could hardly have been more different. Why then, was I so sure that he was the man who most answered my needs?
> I could not ignore the physical attraction we felt for each other. But this alone could not have held us together for thirty-six years of extraordinary vicissitudes.[27]

Since they were attracted to each other and wanted children, they decided to live together and legally marry when they went to register their son's birth in 1935.[28] Margaret also tells of heroic Russian wives she met. She admired Eve, the wife of a Russian engineer who worked long hours at Autozavod, where Margaret taught English. This was the time during collectivization when there were shortages of butter, meat, and milk. Housing was in short supply, and most families lived in one room. Eve told Margaret:

> Of course, Margarita ... it is not easy to live this life. A person has to be strong. Very strong ... But always we must build and see the future. We must build a new life or we cannot be happy.[29]

Eve couldn't understand Margaret's friend, another American wife, who had a nice apartment and good food from the stores for foreigners yet left her husband because life was too hard. Eve assumed she didn't love her husband. Eve had no idea that the lifestyle of a well-to-do Soviet worker was quite low compared to others' in the Western world.

Margaret thought the wives of the engineers were special people who dedicated themselves to helping their husbands serve the needs of the new Soviet state. She wrote:

> The point is that the men at the head of the plant in Autozavod had made their choice. And their wives had made theirs, for no one compelled them to be there. They chose to stand by their men, sacrificing themselves to keep the fires going so that their husbands could have hot baths and hot food and guarded rest when they needed it most sorely. Love prompted the wives' sacrifice and elevated them to the pedestal of heroism on which their men stood.[30]

6. Sofia Pavlova

> I was adamant. In such matters, that's the way it usually is; when faced with such situations, people are adamant. Love prevails.
>
> Sofia Pavlova

While stories of men divorcing their wives are common, the reverse also happened. History professor and party member Sofia Pavlova met the love of her life at a sanatorium in the early 1930s. She remarked in an interview:

> Then I left my first husband. This was when I was starting my second year at the Institute of Red Professors. I went to a sanatorium in Solitsyno. And I was done for. I fell in love, and he fell in love with me. I came home and said that I would no longer live with my husband. But there was no particular need for us to get a divorce, since our marriage had never been registered anyway. And so I married for a second time.[31]

Pavlova realized she had been infatuated with her first husband but had not really loved him. Unfortunately, her second husband was a public prosecutor of the Iakut Republic, and he was purged in 1937, just two years after their marriage. So this marriage ended up short-lived.

7. Nadezhda Mandelstam

> Like two blind puppies we were, nuzzling each other and feeling so good together. And how fevered your poor head was, and how madly

we frittered away the days of our life. What joy it was, and how we always knew what joy it was.

Nadezhda Mandelstam, farewell letter to her husband

One of the most tender and romantic love letters of a married woman of the 1930s was written by Nadezhda Mandelstam in 1938 to her husband, Osip, after his arrest and disappearance. She saved this letter and printed it in her memoirs written in the 1970s. Apparently, many women whose husbands had been arrested and imprisoned wrote these last love letters. It reads:

Osia, my beloved, faraway sweetheart!
I have no words, my darling, to write this letter that you may never read, perhaps. I am writing it into empty space. Perhaps you will come back and not find me here. Then this will be all you have left to remember me by.

Osia, what a joy it was living together like children—all our squabbles and arguments, the games we played, and our love. Now I do not even look at the sky. If I see a cloud, who can I show it to?

Remember the way we brought back provisions to make our poor feasts in all the places where we pitched our tent like nomads? Remember the good taste of bread when we got it by a miracle and ate it together? And our last winter in Voronezh. Our happy poverty, and the poetry you wrote. I remember the time we were coming back once from the baths, when we bought some eggs or sausage, and a cart went by loaded with hay. It was still cold and I was freezing in my short jacket (but nothing like what we must suffer now: I know how cold you are). That day comes back to me now. I understand so clearly, the ache from the pain of it, that those winter days with all their troubles were the greatest and last happiness to be granted us in life.

My every thought is about you. My every tear and every smile is for you. I bless every day and every hour of our bitter life together, my sweetheart, my companion, my blind guide in life.

Life can last so long. How hard and long for each of us to die alone. Can this fate be for us who are inseparable? Puppies and children, did we deserve this? Did you deserve this, my angel? Everything goes on as before. I know nothing. Yet I know everything—each day and hour of your life are plain and clear to me as in a delirium.

You came to me every night in my sleep, and I kept asking what had happened, but you did not reply.

In my last dream I was buying food for you in a filthy hotel restaurant. The people with me were total strangers. When I had bought it, I realized I did not know where to take it, because I do not know where you are.

When I woke up, I said to Shura: "Osia is dead." I do not know whether you are still alive, but from the time of that dream, I have lost track of you. I do not know where you are. Will you hear me? Do you know how much I love you? I could never tell you how much I love you. I cannot tell you even now. I speak only to you, only to you. You are with me always, and I who was such a wild and angry one and never learned to weep simple tears—now I weep and weep and weep.

It's me: Nadia. Where are you?

Farewell.

Nadia.[32]

Nadia's premonition about Osip's death was correct. He died in October, and she was condemned to wander around the Soviet Union for several decades before she was allowed to return to Moscow and rehabilitate him.

C. Marriage and Family Difficulties

> The A. N. Tolstoy household has collapsed like a house of cards. My god, how easily people destroy what is dearest to them, just for the sake of pure physiology.
>
> Liubov Shaporina, diary

Family life could be incredibly difficult, even among educated middle-class Russians in the 1930s. Diarists like Galina Shtange and Liubov Shaporina as well as memoirists and poets like Anna Akhamatova and Markoosha Fischer discuss the difficulties of marriage in that period. In her diary, Liubov Shaporina laments the dissolution of writer Alexei Tolstoy's marriage in the late 1930s. This affected her because she was herself divorced from the composer Yuri Shaporin and had enjoyed the company of the Tolstoys as a kind of surrogate family, "an oasis amid the general sadness everywhere." Seeing this marriage fall apart was depressing. She laments Alexei's actions in her diary:

> Twenty years as Natalia Vasilevna's soul mate, talented, grown children, a home, a whole way of life, everything down to drain, gone to wrack and ruin, and for what? Love, passion? Nothing of the sort. Is this genuine feeling? At 53, the old man felt a need for passion. He told Starchakov "I want to love, to love someone, anyone." He became infatuated with Timochoka, Max Peshkov's widow. She wouldn't yield. Natalia Vasilevna found some verses Aleksei Nikolaevich had written to Timoshka and that's where the whole thing started.[33]

When Natalia went to Moscow to beg Timoshka to accept Tolstoy, she asked Liudmila Tarsheva to stay as Tolstoy's secretary and hostess in Leningrad, offering her a salary of three hundred rubles a month plus room and board. Liudmila had asked Liubov's opinion about taking the post and whether she should resign her good position at the library of the Writers' Union. Soon, Tolstoy divorced his wife of twenty years and married his secretary, Liudmila. Tolstoy's friend, A. O. Starchakov, questioned why Tolstoy, who had everything—a country house, a full cup, a beautiful wife—why did he throw it all over for a new wife who slept around? He thought it politically a bad move. People wouldn't take kindly to it and he'd soon feel the effect. Gorky wouldn't be inviting him to bring Liudmila over.[34]

1. Galina Shtange's Demanding Children

> They moved in with Boris's parents in a room that was so small that you could only sit or stand in it, there was no question of taking a step in any direction.
>
> Galina Shtange, diary

In her diary, Shtange records the marital difficulties of her four grown children. They all married, but none happily. One son married three times in fifteen years. Most suffered from money and apartment worries. Some of her children lived in one small room. One son and a daughter had no room for a maid, so her daughter and daughter-in-law had to do all the shopping, cooking, and cleaning. This made it difficult for her daughter to progress in her painting career. It also made it difficult for her sons to be happy because their wives nagged about their poor living conditions. In contrast, Galina and her husband seemed to have a very strong and happy marriage, begun in 1903.[35]

Galina describes her son Boris's life in a 1936 entry:

> Boris, a marvelous person, smart, gifted, and an extremely conscientious worker, but things just haven't worked out for him in life.
> He married for the first time when he was only 20, to Irina's friend Olga Baeva. They had a daughter, Ninochka, a charming girl. Olga is a very decent person—a wonderful mother, a beautiful woman, a hard worker, and outgoing, but she's got an evil streak, just like her mother. The two of them together tormented Boris for seven years until finally

they got divorced. After a year and a half in the doldrums he married again, even less happily. His second wife was a young woman who was interesting and not unintelligent, but neither of them had a speck of love for the other. Plus she turned out to be quite sickly and didn't have the slightest inclination to start a family. So it was that they came together without love, and so too, without discord, they went their separate ways.

Again he pined away in solitude for some time, until he met Dina and married her.

They're into their second year of marriage, and apparently they love each other, but their life is not happy. To begin with Borya has worked in out-of-the-way places, in unhealthy conditions; it really ruined his health, and he even started to lose his hearing. He keeps going for treatment, but it doesn't do much good. Because of his bad hearing, in spite of his many wonderful qualities and all his knowledge, he hasn't been able to advance in his career.

Right now he's an acting sector chief in the Stations Department with a salary of 700 rubles, and for now that looks like about as far as he's going to go. He's held back at work, and it causes him no end of suffering. Naturally they're always short of money; he has to set aside 200 rubles for his daughter Ninochka. He's constantly on the lookout for piecework, which is very hard to come by these days. In general money is a constant struggle for them. He has a hard life, the poor thing, and I can't do anything to help; it's hard on me too.[36]

Galina's son Boris divorced in the late 1920s and early 1930s, when divorce was free and easy. After 1936 Soviet law made divorce more expensive and abortion less available. Each divorce cost more than the preceding one, and each divorce was entered into one's passport and workbook.

Galina describes her daughter's unhappy marriage in the following words:

> Irinochka has a hard life too. She's an artist. She married Boris Shatilov, a classmate from art school. They got married when Mitya (her father) was in prison (1928) and we were in desperate straits, materially speaking, so I couldn't set her up properly with the things she needed, and I had no money to give her either.
>
> They lived in that tiny little room for two years. I'm amazed that they managed to keep their sanity.... After two years they got a fairly good room. But it's just one room for the two of them along with their easels and all the things they use for their painting. In short, they really get in each other's way. Plus they have to do everything themselves; there's no room for a maid, though they could afford one.

My poor little girl has to cook, clean, mend, and fix things, wash dishes, and do all the other little things that have to be done around the house, earn enough to live on, and most importantly, to develop as an artist, which is everything to her. She's exhausted and her nerves are worn ragged. Plus Boris has a difficult personality—he's coarse, selfish and inclined to jealousy.

Irinochka is already a recognized artist who gets good reviews in the press. Her work is included in all the exhibits, and she has a 500 ruble a month contract with the state. She got a state commission— a large painting to commemorate the 20th anniversary of the October Revolution—and she's already done the scenery for several stage productions.[37]

Galina was happy when her son Vanyusha returned to Moscow from Khabarovsk, but she was often torn between trying to help her children and grandchildren and doing her own volunteer work. She says:

> Today is Vanyusha's birthday, and I was out all day long. The whole family is terribly hurt because I'm away for days at a time. They laugh at me ... Vova is especially hurt. "We'll just have to pack our suitcases," he says, "and go on back to Khabarovsk." I simply don't know what to do—I can't give up my work, and I can't give up my family either. Tomorrow I was supposed to apply to the Local Committee to get Sashenka accepted into the nursery. Valya (Galina's daughter-in-law) really wants him to go there, it's hard for her to take care of him, but I can't understand how you can entrust your own child to strangers, unless you absolutely have to, just so you can have some more free time.[38]

Galina complains in her diary that her daughters-in-law gave her and their husbands nothing but heartache:

> I didn't find anything to cheer me up at home either. My sons Borya and Zhenya are all worn out, they look terrible; we haven't gotten any letters from Vova, and meanwhile Olya sends bad news—Tolya nearly died of furuncular angina, and they're utterly destitute. And I don't know what I can do to help. Money is awfully tight.... Their wives are throwing fits. Valya says, "I've decided to take Sasha to Khabarovsk, let Vladimir stay here to finish his studies and get his degree. This way of living isn't enough for me. I want to work. I can do it in Khabarovsk, since my Mama's there and she can take care of Sasha."
>
> In my day mothers didn't think that way, and they weren't in such a big hurry to put their babies in nurseries and dump them into the hands of strangers; they brought them up themselves. When you tell

her, "But a child could very easily catch some infection in the nursery and die," she says, "Well that's natural selection. If he makes it, that's fine, if he doesn't, there's nothing to be done about it." That's how today's young mothers think and just imagine what it's like for me to listen to it, when I was always ready at any moment, and still am, to this very day, to give up my life for that of any one of my children.

And Tatyana is simply insufferable. She has an offensive, rude, insolent way of talking. And acting, too. I find out that Zhenya has been working every day until four or five in the morning. It turns out that she's pushing him to finish his studies at the Institute as soon as possible. I got terribly upset. What can you do with dear ones who behave like that?[39]

Galina's only happiness is with her beloved husband Mitya, and they are both too exhausted to enjoy each other's company. Galina and her children seemed to ignore the advice of Soviet sociologist Anton S. Makarenko. He advised parents to have more than one child and to avoid spoiling them. But as Galina's diary makes clear, her children have neither the space nor money for more than one child. Also, Makarenko cautioned mothers not to be martyrs, but Galina's diary again shows how difficult it was for mothers to follow their own desires and ignore the needs of their children and grandchildren.[40]

2. Markoosha Fischer

> Family quarrels always took place in the presence of children. There was only one room so where could the children go?
> Markoosha Fischer, 1930s

Echoing some of Galina's observations about how crowded housing increased the stress in marriage, Markoosha Fischer commented:

> On our floor we actually saw examples of the misery brought to families which had to live in one room. There were violent hatreds, divorces, and unhappy children. Newlyweds had to move into the small room of the young husband's parents. They quickly ruined a happy marriage. Another couple got divorced but had to stay in their room together and after a while she brought her new husband into the room.... Many people, otherwise kind and intelligent, were nervous from lack of privacy and sleep in the noisy apartment, and from too little food and too much work. They found an outlet in trivial scandals and bickering.

Our neighbors were often petty in their squabbles. They could fight over a pencil or a piece of string. But their spirit was far from petty when important issues were at stake, and there was much friendliness and warmth in them. It would have been almost impossible at times to bear those years had it not been for the help of friends and neighbors. Russians are always responsive to other people's troubles and they had ample occasion then to help one another.... They shared their food with those who had less. Serving tea to visitors, they would bring to the table every bit of sweets they could find in the house.... There was much sickness due to over crowdedness and malnutrition. We all helped nurse one another. Neighbors took children out for a walk when adults were sick, or sat with sick children when their parents went to work. They lent one another wearing apparel, food, chairs, kitchen utensils, and money.[41]

3. Wives of Prisoners

While life was difficult for women in all classes, it may have been hardest for women whose husbands were arrested as "enemies of the people" and charged with "wrecking." Wives of arrested factory managers, party or government officials, or leading personnel of any type were generally imprisoned soon after their husbands. True grit seemed to sustain these women who lost not only their spouses but their children as well. In prison, they often formed surrogate families to survive emotionally and physically. Apparently women in many kinds of jails and prisons formed such groups for emotional sustenance. Prison memoirs of Russian women imprisoned in the late 1930s indicate that Russian women also bonded together to protect themselves from the NKGB (People's Commissariat for State Security) administration and from imprisoned criminals, who often preyed upon them. Generally, they provided food and emotional support for each other.

a. Surrogate Families in Prison

Maria Joffe, Evgenia Ginzburg, Anna Larina, Marie Avinov, and Natalia Sats all mention surrogate families in prison in their memoirs, which were written years, even decades, after their incarceration. Joffe belonged to an intellectual and artistic group whose members took care of each other. When Joffe was released from seven days of solitary confinement, her cellmates gave her food and shielded her from the prying eyes of the guards so she could sleep. One of their group even prostituted herself to get additional food, which she shared with the circle of friends. Joffe was often asked to regale the prison interrogator with stories of Scheherazade so he wouldn't have time to torture some of the women.[42] Ginzburg's friends saved her from working outside when a commandant took a dislike to her. Her "family" bribed camp officials to assign Ginzburg easier inside work, so she could survive. Friends obtained eggs and precious food to sustain her when she was working outside in Kolyma, Siberia, where the weather and work could have killed her.[43]

While Soviet youth were brought up to love Stalin and believe that life was joyful in the 1930s, children of purge victims were not so blessed. In her memoir, Anna Larina notes that she was deprived of her year-old son when she was arrested and sent to Tomsk prison in 1937. There she met sixty other mothers, some of whom had their babies with them. There the prisoners made clothes for the infants. Inadequate food and prison living conditions made children's survival precarious. Likewise, children brought up in state-run orphanages faced many challenges as well. Believing their parents were "enemies of the people," they developed conflicts. Ruffians and hooligans in the orphanages could also make children's lives miserable. The 1937 census indicated half a million young people eighteen and younger were under NKVD control. So the lives of mothers of purge victims, like Joffe and Larina, were not easy.[44]

Marie Avinov's surrogate family included several groups of nuns, who shared food with her and helped her adjust to prison life and survive two imprisonments.[45] Natalia Sats seemed to have the widest circle of helpers in prison. As a theater director, she found even the criminals—the bandits, pickpockets, and thieves—could teach her about the playwright Maxim Gorky's underworld. She tried to rehabilitate them by using them in her theatrical productions, which the administration allowed. Nor did she shun the help of political prisoners whose husbands had been high-ranking party leaders before being slandered for "wrecking," as her husband was. Her surrogate families were quite disparate, and even some of the criminals provided tea and a good bunk when she needed them.

Sats was lucky that her mother was able to intercede for her, visit, and bring information about her children. Most of the women prisoners never saw or heard from their children or relatives once they were arrested. Sats's mother intervened with the authorities for her daughter, and Sats was allowed visits from family members. After a request to the Minister of Internal Affairs (NKVD), she was allowed to do theater research in prison. She obtained a cell, notebooks, and books to write theatrical history. She told the NKVD that she could be more helpful to society when she was released if she used her time in detention for self-education. She wrote Marxist analyses of Shakespeare's and Moliere's plays, focusing on the roles of women and children, but what she wrote had to remain in the prison archives. The last few years of her sentence, she spent in a minimum-security camp on the Volga, and her mother and children visited her there. In the camp, she organized musical productions, using even displaced Polish musicians who had fled the Nazis.[46]

b. Plight of Nonimprisoned Wives

Wives of arrested men usually faced incredible struggles. Valentina Kamyshina tells of her plight, especially her difficulties when her employer discovered her husband's status and fired her.

> I had to keep silent. I would have been fired immediately had the news of my husband's internment reached the office. And I had a sick mother and my sister's little daughter on my hands. Being the wife of a prisoner, it was practically impossible to find another job....
> My office found out that my husband was an "enemy of the people." I was fired, and soon thereafter sent out of the city. In the beginning, with great effort and the help of friends, I was able to obtain various unskilled jobs—as a scrub woman in theaters, or as a laundress. Later I took up embroidery. I earned little at this work, but it kept me occupied.[47]

D. Unequal Marriages

Unequal marriages continued to exist in the 1930s. Sometimes it was the wife who was better educated than her husband, and sometimes it was the husband who was the better educated. Some were happy, others not.

1. Happy Unequal Marriages

> We women must take a daily interest in how our husbands' work is going, in how they lead the Stakhanovite movement and in how to help Stakhanovites to increase productivity and the quality of their work.
>
> Stakhanovite housewife

Some happy unequal marriages involved male Stakhanovite workers and their wives. In the late 1930s, the Soviet government lauded women who turned all their attention to making their husbands more productive. This situation usually happened among well-educated men but sometimes among lower ranking but well-paid men as well. Women whose husbands earned high wages could afford to stay home making life cozy for their spouses. However, they were also encouraged to make life at their husbands' enterprises more comfortable for the workers there. Called *obshchestvennitsy*, or public-spirited activists, they were expected to engage in socially useful work—improving the barracks where ordinary workers lived, helping in daycare programs and camps for children of workers at their husbands' enterprises, and generally making the lives of workers cleaner and more cultured. Rewards that Stakhanovite workers and their families enjoyed included more consumer goods, such as bicycles, record players, wristwatches, better housing, holidays in the Crimea, invitations to party conferences and congresses, and fame through newspaper publicity. Films glorified industrial and rural shock workers and Stakhanovites. Needless to say, these "unemployed" housewives were more common in urban than rural areas.[48]

Some helped their husbands study to pass examinations. At a wives' congress, many expressed how proud they were of their Stakhanovite husbands and of how well they lived. One commented:

> I helped my husband to become a first class engineer. (Applause). Now he earns 800 rubles. (Retort: "Appropriate!") Now we have everything and we are beginning to live well. Workers abroad only dream of such a life, but here the dream is real. I bought our son a camera and I'm going to buy our daughter a piano.[49]

2. Unhappy Unequal Marriages

> I am loath to part with him—he is such a good hearted and splendid fellow, he loves me sincerely and, conscious of the impending disaster, he begs me: "Don't leave me, I am still young, I will study." I, too, love him. It seems to me I could make a valuable man of him.
>
> Zoya Petrova, *Komsomolskaya Pravda*

Kollontai's short story "Thirty Two Pages" about "unequal" unregistered marriage in the 1920s found echoes a decade later. While a common story in the 1920s was about a man who became upwardly mobile, joined the party, and then tried to enlighten a reluctant wife, an educated woman falling in love with an uncultured man remained a social problem. It was discussed at length in *Komsomolskaya Pravda* (Young Communist Truth) and the *Moscow News* in the 1930s.

One example was the missive of Zoya Petrova, who wrote to *Komsomolskaya Pravda* seeking advice about marriage. She asked, "What am I to do?" As a university-educated agronomist from an intellectual family, she found herself regretting her marriage to a twenty-five-year-old, hard-working combine operator whom she had met on a state farm. After falling in love with the young man and becoming pregnant, she realized he didn't fit in with her family. Her parents resented her marrying a "semi-educated man who was shy, silent, and boring company." Yet Zoya was loathe to part with him.[50] However, when she asked herself "Is it worth the struggle?" her answer was "No." The struggle was too hard.

Her letter provoked 250 responses from people in varying professions and jobs. One student at Dniepropetrovsk pharmacy school reminded Zoya of the example of Maria Demchenko, who started life as a simple peasant girl but had become a student and would soon be an agronomist. Thirty-eight tractor drivers from the Shatsk Machine Tractor Station wrote reminding Zoya that she had received her education free, and her duty was not to boast of her education but to impart it to others. Some other respondents confessed to the same problem but had resolved it by helping their wives or husbands become educated. One writer suggested that Zoya didn't know what true culture was and that she suffered from "swell headedness."

A synopsis of the letters indicated the following:

A Stakhanovite operator who grows and widens his general knowledge is a new intellectual. The friendship and love of such a man should be the source of joy. Marriage of a girl agronomist to such a man cannot be termed "unequal."[51]

E. Marriage and Maids

> My first maid was Frossya, a little village girl from the Klin region. She did not know much about keeping house but she was a friendly, warm-hearted soul, and we got along splendidly for four years.
>
> Markoosha Fischer, housewife

While we don't yet have the words of the half million Russian servants or house workers describing their own lives, we do have some information about this group of women. A fascinating account of the need for maids is found in Markoosha Fischer's memoir *My Lives in Russia*. She explained:

> Apartments devoid of any labor-saving devices, plus lengthy shopping hours, made householding a complicated affair, and Soviet women had to have someone to help them keep house if they wanted to do anything besides household work.[52]

The American welder John Scott was surprised that his Russian wife Masha wanted to hire a servant at Magnitogorsk. He told her that most American women did their own housework, and he was amazed that she, a former peasant, expected a servant to care for their child, clean the house, and cook. However, Masha insisted they have a maid, and they hired an exiled young kulak girl as their maid and nanny.[53]

Like other educated women, the teacher Margaret Wettlin had a variety of servants and a host of different relations with them. One servant named Marusia seemed to have a cavalier attitude toward work that Margaret found typical among peasant migrants. Still, they had a congenial household with Marusia, as the following account reveals:

> Marusia was a characteristic village type, cheerful and imperturbable on all occasions. She attached no importance to forgetting to give us a message left by a caller or to being an hour late with dinner because her girlfriend had dropped in to see her. "Nichevo!" (It's nothing!), she would say with a disarming smile.[54]

In Mongolia, Margaret was more pleased with their servant Fenia. The latter was taciturn, modest, and respectful. She was a good worker—washing the clothes, scrubbing the floors, chopping wood, making fires, cooking—but not talkative, even though she spoke Russian.[55]

Margaret observed that most professional families had servants. Sometimes they needed overseeing and reminding of their tasks. Some maids were unpleasant, but the supply was abundant during collectivization when there wasn't enough food for farm families and many young girls fled to the cities to eat with a family and work as a maid.[56] When she lived with her in-laws in Moscow, Margaret described the situation as follows:

> Sasha, the maid, ... volunteered to work for us when she quarreled with her mistress across the hall. Sasha would sleep in the kitchen as most maids did in Moscow. An apartment in this house enjoyed the rare advantage of having gas—a gas stove in the kitchen and a gas water heater in the bathroom. Most Muscovites depended on public baths to keep them clean, and oil stoves to cook their food.[57]

In her memoirs, teacher Tatjana Tchernavin described her need for a maid:

> In order to obtain food one has to keep a servant—unless the family is lucky enough to have an old aunt, a grandmother or some other relative who is not fit to go out to work and can look after housekeeping. Otherwise one risks being left without anything to eat.
>
> This is how a Soviet house-wife's day is mapped out. At seven o'clock in the morning she must run out to fetch the bread and take her turn in two or three queues outside the co-ops which open at nine. The co-ops might be selling something that can be bought on the ration cards: salt, cereals, soap—and it is essential to be there before the goods are sold out. Then she must scour the neighbourhood to see if anything is being sold without ration cards: half-rotten potatoes, cabbage, tinned fish, etc. If it happens to be a day on which sugar or butter can be had on children's ration cards, or margarine on the first category ration cards, she must leave everything and stand in a queue for hours. In case of complete failure she must run to the free market and in the general crush and hustle snatch something as cheaply as she can—a piece of stale meat or fish or a doubtful sausage. And in any case she must stand in a queue for paraffin, for all cooking is done on primus stoves and there never is enough oil. Soon after three

o'clock she must run home, light the primus stove and do her best to cook something more or less eatable with the bad and scanty provisions. About five, all office workers, factory hands, students, and schoolchildren come home to the overcrowded flats where many families live together.[58]

It is not difficult to find a servant: all the peasant girls who in the summer manage to eke out a livelihood on collective farms, kitchen gardens or derelict individual small holdings, in the autumn try to get into towns where they hope to go into a factory. Their reasoning is simple enough: the State robs the peasants, both on the collective and on the individual farms, but feeds factory workers. Obviously it is more alluring to receive two and a half pounds or even one pound of bread a day on a ration card than to produce the bread and be left in winter on starvation rations or without any rations at all with nothing but cabbage, mangle-tops, dried fungi and chaff-soup. Besides, in the country a girl has no chance of buying any clothes or shoes.[59]

Fifty rubles per month seemed to be the standard wage for servants. While factory workers earned 100 to 120 rubles per month, they had to pay for board and room, which servants did not. Wages did not buy much: shoes cost one hundred rubles and an overcoat two hundred. Tchernavin had a succession of servants. During the 1930 outbreak of Soviet terror, her son became ill, and her husband had been forced to go to Murmansk to work. She was swamped with work at the Hermitage Museum and found herself in need of a servant. Usually her servants stayed a year or two, and she had had peasant girls, widows, and divorcees without alimony, since under the new Soviet law alimony was paid only for children, not to former spouses. Since her family was small and her husband's and her wages were good, they could afford a servant. When her son was in the hospital, a friend suggested a servant girl named Masha. At first Masha worked diligently but then did less and less.[60]

Eventually, Tchernavin's servant Masha became an informer for the GPU and spied on her employer. Tatjana discovered this when she was arrested and realized that the evidence against her had come from her maid Masha. At one point Tchernavin had burned some letters and photos that she thought might be incriminating. Since it took longer to dispose of these papers that she anticipated, she had asked Masha to help her. Later, Masha revealed this to the GPU. Tchernavin was then arrested and detained for five months in Shpalerka prison. Her husband had already been arrested and incarcerated at Kresty

Prison in Leningrad and then exiled farther north near Murmansk. Thus, their son was left home alone, without either parent.[61] As the decade progressed, the government, through its trade unions, encouraged all maids to report on their employers, so women became more cautious of even their most trusted servants.

Chapter Twelve

Osoaviakhim

Osoaviakhim, a popular civil defense organization, attracted all ages. Young pioneers participated in defense drills, at times equipped with gas masks. Boys and girls as well as men and women wanted to learn to fly and do parachuting. Pictures abounded of women learning to fly and parachuting out of planes. Even housewives participated in Osoaviakhim, doing their civic duty in the apartment houses where they lived.[1]

A. Housewives and Osoaviakhim

> Factories, schools, clubs, and apartment houses introduced courses in first aid, protection against air raids and poison gas, as well as in elementary military drill, topography, and sharpshooting ... in the summer of 1936, the number of these courses greatly increased.
>
> Markoosha Fischer, housewife

While Osoaviakhim, or Russian Civil Defense, had been founded in the 1920s, it became more widespread in the mid-1930s. It became more timely after Adolf Hitler took power in Germany and during the Spanish Civil War. Markoosha Fischer thought the Soviet government was gradually preparing people for war. In her memoirs, she observed:

> The lessons of Madrid and Barcelona were studied not only by the German military but also by Soviet housewives. The Spaniards cared for their wounded and children, the way they met their food shortage and other civilian problems were discussed in Moscow Red Cross groups.
>
> Our house had one of the best-organized groups in the neighborhood.... The educational grades of those attending the classes ranged from college graduates to illiterates. The latter were taken care of by the more educated ones. I helped the house plumber's wife, Marisha....
>
> We also made regular inspections of apartments. The main purpose was to prepare them for air raids, incendiary bombs, and instantaneous evacuation....

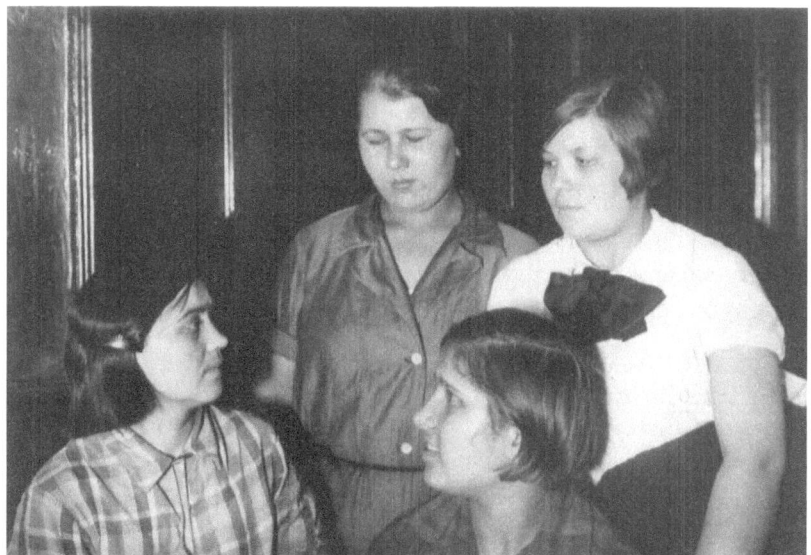

Efimovsky, Osoaviakhim Instructor and Club Spiridonov Members, *1936, Leningrad Oblast (St. Petersburg Photo Archive)*

Besides inspecting the apartments, I was given the job of leading first-aid courses for children. Like their adults, they were being mentally prepared for war as early as 1936, and they had their assigned place in the civilian defense setup.... A large section of the park had been turned over to civilian defense. Booths filled with tear gas, open-air first aid courses, instruction in the handling of machine guns, small tanks and airplanes attracted as big a crowd as the entertainment and sport sections of the park. Prizes were given to the best contestants in shooting, skiing in gas masks, parachuting, fire fighting, and passing quizzes on civilian defense problems. Women participated as enthusiastically as men.

In the middle of the winter of 1936–1937 one or another of the women in our groups disappeared following the arrest of a husband, father, sweetheart, or brother. She could no longer put her mind on dressing wounds or running around in a gas mask.... In 1937, during the great Red Army purge, when the leading generals were executed, many of the officers living there were shot or exiled, and their wives disappeared too. Others took their place, some of them soon disappeared too. Nobody ever said a word about this, but red eyes and a choked voice often betrayed anxiety for friends. General Eideman, the man who had built up Osoaviakhim (Defense against Chemical Warfare), into the most powerful factor in Soviet civilian defense, was shot after a secret trial in June, 1937. Hundreds of leading members of the rank and file of Osoaviakhim and the Red Cross were liquidated in the purge. New people took over. For a while the civilian defense activities suffered. But, on the surface at least, the breach was soon healed and the preparations to defend the country continued.[2]

Similar comments about Osoaviakhim can be found in the diary of Muscovite housewife Galina Shtange. She participated in activities in her apartment building, and her diary for 1936 sounds quite patriotic. In one entry, she wrote:

> Of these, I went through the civil medical defense and chemical weapons defense training, and at present I have two badges certifying my completion of that training. I wanted to join the permanent medical defense squad of our building, but unfortunately my age (51) and the state of my health (a bad heart) won't allow me to sustain such physically demanding work. Still, I consider myself obliged to be ready for any encounter with enemies, which we have plenty of and therefore I plan to enroll in a nursing course in the fall.[3]

B. Youth and Osoaviakhim

> I've decided to go to the stadium every free day. Yesterday I spent four hours there—running, jumping, rowing, riding a bicycle, and throwing grenades. I passed in rowing and high jumps. I had an excellent time.
>
> Nina Kosterina, diary, 1938

While many young people belonged to organizations like Komsomol and Osoaviakhim, not many wrote their memoirs or had them published. An exception was Nina Kosterina, who was featured earlier in the chapter on the purges. Initially, she was part of a pampered party elite. Seeing Petrov-Vodkin's picture of his daughter with a globe, one could imagine this to be Nina Kosterina in 1936.

A true believer in the Komsomol and her own Komsomol honor, Nina was confused when her father was arrested and imprisoned as an "enemy of the people" in the late 1930s. She was discombobulated and had a hard time studying for her university exams. In a diary entry for July 1940, Nina writes about her interest and participation in sports. She doesn't describe her sports experience as part of

K. S. Petrov-Vodkin, Portrait of Daughter with a Globe, *1936*

Osoaviakhim, but it might have been. She says:

> I often go to the stadium. I am excited about football, running competitions, and so on. On the 10th there was a grandiose event at the stadium: a repetition of the physical culture parade. What majesty and beauty! And then I have become a swimming enthusiast....
> All this takes up enormous amounts of time. This is how time is spent by this ordinary girl "on the brink" of college.[4]

In 1938 Nina had been involved in throwing grenades, which suggests that she was involved in some form of military training. Nina's sports and Osoaviakhim experience stood her in good stead when she decided to volunteer for a partisan detachment after World War

II began. Just two days after the Nazi invasion of June 21, 1941, she wrote in her diary, "Well, then, I am ready.... I want action, I want to go to the front."[5] In a November entry, she wrote that she was joining a partisan detachment and described the weeding-out process in Moscow. She didn't mention having been trained in shooting and parachuting, but she may have been. She wrote:

> At the Central Committee they had a long discussion with us. Several people were winnowed out. Others left themselves, realizing the full seriousness and danger of the task. Only three of us remained. And we held out till the end. "This is grim, demanding, dangerous work," the Central Committee official warned us. And I was terrified of one thing only—that in the process of training and checking they might discover that I am nearsighted. They'll kick me out. They say we shall have to parachute down. That's the easiest thing of all. We shall act singly, at best in pairs. This is the worst of it.... In the woods, in snow, in the dark of the night, behind enemy lines.... Oh, well, obviously I am not climbing up onto a safe warm feather bed atop the kitchen stove![6]

Nina performed her first partisan action safely and returned to Moscow, but she never came back from the second one in December. Much later, after her father's release from prison and his rehabilitation, he published Nina's diary in the journal *Novy Mir*. Later still, it was translated into English and published in the United States.

While it is hard to uncover figures for the number of young girls in OSO, Raisa Orlova's memoirs suggest that like Nina Kosterina she too belonged to a military organization, probably OSO. A university student in the 1930s, Orlova remembers her experiences, as follows:

> In the summer of 1936, after the end of our first year at the institute, we were in military camps near Moscow. There, one evening, after our military exercises, we learned that Gorky had died. We gathered in a single tent. One student received Gorky's *Italian Tales*. I don't recall that Gorky loomed large in our thoughts before, but at that moment we felt like orphans. The authorities would not give us permission to attend the funeral. So we organized our own impromptu procession without their permission, made our way on foot, and formed part of the over-all procession.[7]

Like Nina with her dedication to partisan work, Orlova writes about the relief that her husband and friends felt when the war began. She writes:

Like many of our contemporaries, he (Lyonya) gave a sigh of relief when the war began. The line between friends and enemies became the line at the front.[8]

Before the war, Komsomol members and university students had a host of duties to perform. They taught in literacy classes, helped with collectivization, and participated in the League of the Militant Godless organization and in Osoaviakhim military training. Paramilitary organizations were attached to educational institutions, factories, and even collective farms. Many thought war inevitable, and college students practiced battles in the snow. Osoaviakhim trained women in sharpshooting, flying, parachuting, and other military skills. These activities were time consuming, but they also provided camaraderie.

One Soviet university student of the 1930s described sharpshooting and camping as great fun. At that time, some women studied engineering, interpreting, and even piloting at military educational institutions. A company of women usually marched in the military parades on Red Square in the 1930s. They wore uniform coats, calf-length skirts, and high boots. While female interpreters often served in the armed forces in Central Asia, others served in army intelligence or the medical corps.[9]

World War II sniper Roza Shanina with her rifle, 1944.
Photo by A. N. Fridlyanski (Wikimedia)

N. Yanov, Osoaviakhim Aero Club Members, Leningrad Factory, *1936*
(St. Petersburg Photo Archive)

In the 1930s, aviation became a craze in the Soviet Union, and many young girls fell in love with daring pilots. Girls as well as boys were attracted to the pilot training that Osoaviakhim offered. Aviators made daring exploits and scientific advances. In 1934 aviators rescued men from the ship *Cheluskin,* which was stranded on icebergs in the Arctic. The heroism and adventures of Russian pilots were celebrated in song, particularly in chastushki:

> Ah, we have such aviation,
> Aviators who are brave young fellows!
> They have added glory to the whole land,
> They have brought back the Cheluskin's crew![10]

> My heart has been smitten
> By the aviator Kamanin.
> Oh, that I might be among the icebergs,
> And that he alone might fly out![11]

> Today I dreamed a dream,
> What a delightful dream it was!
> Molokov fell in love with me
> And invited me to come to Dickson![12]

Our aviators are heroes!
There's not a day but this is what we hear:
Kokkinaki has gone up high,
Alekseyev has gone up higher still.[13]

Girls may also have been drawn to Osoaviakhim's parachuting practice because the air force was more open to women's participation than the army or navy—the more established branches of the military. Just as a few young gentry-class women became pilots in World War I, so some Russian women responded to challenge and adventure in the 1930s, studying to be aviators, glider pilots, and paratroopers. The 1926 census shows 378 women in the military. Those who were determined, like Nadezhda Sumarokova, even became instructors in the Military Aviation Academy in 1926. Heroines like the World War II pilot Marina Raskova reinforced young girls' dreams about becoming pilots.[14] Raskova was a pilot and navigator, and became the first woman navigator in the Soviet Air Forces in 1933. During World War II, she convinced Stalin to allow her to organize three regiments of women pilots. For her, for Nina, and many others, World War II came as a relief and an outlet for youthful idealism and self-sacrifice.

Conclusion

Reading about the harshness of industrialization, the tragedies of collectivization, and the pain of the purges makes one wonder how Soviet society continued to function in the bleak 1930s. Several factors seemed to help unify the country. One was millions of women gaining access to higher education and professional employment. Another was party propaganda about "building socialism in one country." This especially appealed to idealistic youth, some of whom helped build the Moscow Metro and many of the new cities like Magnitogorsk and Kuznetsk. Yet another was the enthusiasm of idealistic young workers in the cities and countryside in udarnik and Stakhanovite work. They received higher wages than others, scarce goods, better housing, vacations in desirable places like Sochi and the Crimea, medals showing their diligence and heroism, and fame in having their pictures prominently displayed in national newspapers and women's journals.

Another unifying feature in Soviet society was the adulation of marriage and motherhood. Wives of engineers and well-paid officials were acclaimed as *obshchestvennitsy*, or social volunteers. They too were pictured in the newspapers and appeared at conferences with Stalin and high-ranking party officials. Likewise, mothers of large families were awarded medals and bonuses. Their faces were also featured in newspapers and women's journals that proclaimed their heroic work in raising the birthrate.

A third factor was patriotism, which undergird many Soviet citizens in their work in the harsh 1920s and 1930s. Many were motivated by love of country rather than the Communist Party. A surge in Soviet nationalism was fueled by propaganda in the 1930s. Certainly fear of war with Japan when it invaded Manchuria and threatened Siberia in 1933, and Hitler's election in Germany and his saber rattling strengthened Soviet nationalism.

A final factor was hope. Hope for a better future sustained many Russians. Elena Skrjabina writes in her book *Siege and Survival* of wanting the future to be better for her children and future generations. This belief bolstered her spirits during the difficult 1920s and frightening 1930s.[1]

Afterword

A final thought is what would have happened to Russian society if the Nazis had not attacked and destroyed so much of what the people had produced? Would Five-Year Plans in the 1940s have enabled the government to continue building workers' apartments, club houses, gymnasiums, theaters, and other socially useful infrastructure? We don't know. While industry may have flourished, it seems that rural life may have stagnated. The British physician James Purves-Stewart, who made a two-day trip across Ukraine by train in 1933, failed to see any tractors, combines, or machines in the fields. He saw only farmers using hand scythes to mow the grain and horses drawing harrows. The visiting American photographer Margaret Bourke White saw Russian women working with wooden rakes as late as 1941.

It seems sad that contemporary Russian society has not come to grips with the terror and suffering of the 1930s. This omission does not help the victims and their families, many of whom have survived. While the group Memorial has and does discuss the crimes of the purges, the Russian government has begun harassing this civic organization and makes no effort to deal with those horrific times. As a result, pain is pushed down, this topic is avoided, and Russia remains a deeply wounded society.

As the nineteenth-century literary critic Nikolai Dobroliubov asked, "When Will the Day Come?" We too wonder when will the day came when the terrors of the Soviet era are reported as such. People wonder when the government will apologize for the purges, harsh industrialization, and destructive collectivization and dekulakization? We don't know.

We only know that when Russian society chooses to revisit this period, it will find resilient Russian women's remarkable poetry and prose telling of the horrors and providing much evidence to reflect upon. As one writer observed: "When the consciousness of the nation is deprived of all documents and all literature, when the real history of entire decades is substituted for by a fabrication," then society cannot stand the chaos.[1]

Notes

Notes to Chapter One

1. Vera Broido, *Daughter of Revolution: A Russian Girlhood Remembered* (London: Constable, 1998), 75–76.
2. Countess Alexandra Tolstoy, *I Worked for the Soviet*, trans. by the author in collaboration with Roberta Yerkes (New Haven: Yale University Press, 1935), 2.
3. Marietta Shaginian, quoted by Laura Goering, *Russian Women Writers*, vol. 2, ed. Christine D. Tomei (New York: Garland Pub., 1999), 1195–96.
4. Shaginian, *Russian Women Writers*, 1196.
5. Irina Ivanova Kniazeva, "A Life in a Peasant Village," in *A Revolution of Their Own: Voices of Women in Soviet History*, ed. Barbara Alpern Engel and Anastasia Posadskaya Vanderbeck, trans. Sona Hoisington (Boulder: Westview Press, 1998), 124.
6. Elena G. Ponomarenko, "From Peasant to Journalist," in *A Revolution of Their Own*, 136–37.
7. Chris J. Chulos, *Converging Worlds: Religion and Community in Peasant Russia, 1863–1917* (DeKalb: Northern Illinois University Press, 2003), 171n44.
8. Sofia N. Pavlova, "Taking Advantage of New Opportunities," in *A Revolution of Their Own*, 54–55.
9. Pavlova, "Taking Advantage," 57.
10. Pavlova, "Taking Advantage," 58–59.
11. Pavlova, "Taking Advantage," 59–60.
12. For information about SR Kakhovskaya, see Galina Zatmilova, "A Part of History," in *Till My Tale Is Told: Women's Memoirs of the Gulag*, ed. Simeon Vilensky, trans. John Crowfoot et al. (Bloomington: Indiana University Press, 1999), 174n.
13. Sula Benet, trans. and ed., *The Village of Viriatino: An Ethnographic Study of a Russian Village from Before the Revolution to the Present* (New York: Anchor Books, 1970), 278–79.
14. Rhoda Power, *Under the Bolshevik Reign of Terror* (New York: McBride, Nast & Co., 1919), 41–44. Power had worked as a journalist in the United States before going to Russia to serve as a governess for a wealthy merchant family in Rostov-on-Don. Rhoda Power was the sister of famous English historian Eileen Power.
15. Power, *Under the Bolshevik Reign*, 62–45.
16. Power, *Under the Bolshevik Reign*, 55–57.
17. Power, *Under the Bolshevik Reign*, 58.
18. For this quote, see Elizabeth A. Wood, *The Baba and the Comrade: Gender*

and *Politics in Revolutionary Russia* (Bloomington: Indiana University Press, 1997), 141.

19. Jane McDermid and Anna Hillyar, *Midwives of the Revolution* (London: University College London, 1999), 190–91.

20. For a good discussion of the problems of Zhenotdel, see Marcelline Hutton, *Russian and West European Women, 1860–1939: Dreams, Struggles, and Nightmares* (New York: Rowman & Littlefield, 2001), chap. 5, and Wood, *Baba and the Comrade*, 139ff. (Hereafter Hutton's 2001 citation is referred to as *Russian Women*).

21. L. Katasheva, *Natasha, a Bolshevik Woman Organiser: A Short Biography* (New York: Workers Library, 1934), 48–49. (Natasha was Konkordia Samoilova's name used in the party. Most of the Old Bolsheviks had such names; i.e., Lenin, Stalin, etc.) For statistics about women's participation in the Civil War, see Wood, *Baba and the Comrade*, 56.

22. Katasheva, *Natasha*, 51.

23. Samoilova as quoted by Katasheva in *Natasha*, 60–61.

24. Samoilova as quoted by Katasheva in *Natasha*, 61.

25. See Katasheva, *Natasha*, 62.

26. As quoted and analyzed by Wood in *Baba and the Comrade*, 94.

27. As quoted by Wood, *Baba and the Comrade*, 94.

28. As quoted by Wood, *Baba and the Comrade*, 95.

29. V. I. Lenin, *Women and Society* (New York: International Publishers, 1938), 11–12, 17–19.

30. Hutton, *Russian Women*, 236–39, and Nadezhda Krupskaya, introduction to Lenin, *Women and Society*, 6.

31. Igal Halfin, *Terror in my Soul* (Cambridge, MA: Harvard University Press, 2003), 222–24, 230–31.

32. Anne E. Gorsuch, *Youth in Revolutionary Russia: Enthusiasts, Bohemians, Delinquents* (Bloomington: Indiana University Press, 2000), 100–103.

33. Isabel Tirado, "The Komsomol and the Krest'ianka: The Political Mobilization of Young Women in the Russian Village, 1921–1927," *Russian History* 23, nos. 1–4, 345–66, and "The Revolution, Young Peasants, and the Komsomol's Anti-Religious Campaigns, 1920–28," *Canadian American Slavic Studies* 26, nos. 1–4 (1992), 97–117. See also Heather DeHaan, "Engendering a People: Soviet Women and Socialist Rebirth in Russia," *Canadian Slavonic Papers* 41, nos. 3–4 (September–December 1999), and Glennys Young, *Power and the Sacred in Revolutionary Russia: Religious Activists in the Village* (University Park: Pennsylvania State University Press, 1997). All these writings comment on the crude, sexist attitudes of male Komsomol members toward young women.

34. Tolstoy, *I Worked for the Soviet*, 196.

35. Tolstoy, *I Worked for the Soviet*, 197.
36. Tolstoy, *I Worked for the Soviet*, 198–99.
37. Heather DeHaan, "Engendering a People," 442–44.
38. Alexandra Kollontai, "Vasilisa Malygina" and "Sisters," as translated by Cathy Porter in *Love of Worker Bees* (Chicago: Academy Press, 1978), 152, 180–81; Marcelline Hutton, "Voices of Struggle: Soviet Women in the 1920s: A Study in Gender, Class, and Literature," *Feminist Studies*, Fall 1991, 65–80; Hutton, *Russian Women*.
39. Kollontai, "Vasilisa Malygina," 152, 180–81; Hutton, "Voices of Struggle"; Hutton, *Russian Women*, 431.
40. Kollontai, "Sisters," 212–22.
41. Kollontai, "Love of Three Generations," in Porter, *Love of Worker Bees*, 206–9.
42. Tolstoy, *I Worked for the Soviet*, 145.
43. Anna Pankratova in Reginald E. Zelnik, "Perils of Pankratova" (Seattle: Herbert J. Ellison Center for Russian, East European, and Central Asian Studies, University of Washington, 2005), 14–17, and Maria Joffe, *One Long Night: A Tale of Truth*, trans. Vera Dixon (London: New Park Publications, 1978).
44. Anna Barkova, "Selected Poems," in *Till My Tale Is Told*, 213–15.
45. Berberova's novella *Cape of Storms* (Paris, 1948–50) shows the precarious lives of ordinary people after the Bolshevik takeover as well as the lives of émigré Russians in Paris. Life was not easy there either. Since history usually belongs to the victors, such sympathetic portraits of bourgeois women did not appear in Soviet publications, yet their tale was told to émigré audiences.
46. *The Diary of Nelly Ptashkina*, trans. Pauline de Chary (London: Jonathan Cape, 1923), 54–61, diary entry Moscow, February 1918.
47. *Diary of Nelly Ptashkina*, 149, diary entry Kiev, November 1918.
48. *Diary of Nelly Ptashkina*, 108–9, diary entry Kiev, May 1918.
49. *Diary of Nelly Ptashkina*, 109, diary entry Kiev, May 1918.
50. Kyra Karadja, *Kyra's Story: Reminiscences of a Girlhood in Revolutionary Russia* (New York, William Morrow, 1975), 30–31, 34, 43.
51. Karadja, *Kyra's Story*, 90, 95–97.
52. Maria Shkapskaya, "No Dream," in *An Anthology of Russian Women's Writing, 1777–1992*, ed. Catriona Kelly (Oxford: Oxford University Press, 1994), 237–38.
53. Marina Tsvetaeva, *Selected Poems*, trans. Elaine Feinstein (Oxford: Oxford University Press, 1993), 34–35.
54. See Iuliia N. Danzas, "From the Protocol of Interrogation," and Veronica Shapovalov, introduction to *Remembering the Darkness: Women in Soviet Prisons* (Boulder, CO: Rowman and Littlefield, 2001), 97–106.
55. See Vera Fedorovna Shtein, "Letters," and Shapovalov introduction to

Remembering the Darkness, 263–67.
56. Tolstoy, *I Worked for the Soviets*, 17–63.
57. Tolstoy, *I Worked for the Soviets*, 136–37.
58. Tolstoy, *I Worked for the Soviets*, 70–72, 106–14, 145–47.
59. Olga V. Sinakevich, "Epiphany in the Taiga," in *Remembering the Darkness*, 257.
60. Sinakevich, Epiphany in the Taiga," in *Remembering the Darkness*, 259.
61. Hutton, *Russian Women*, 235; Marguerite E. Harrison, *Marooned in Moscow: The Story of an American Woman Imprisoned in Russia* (New York: George H. Doran, 1921), 140–44, 230–99.
62. Berta Babina-Nevskaya, "My First Prison, February 1922," in *Till My Tale Is Told*, 104.
63. Babina-Nevskaya, "My First Prison," 105.
64. See Marguerite E. Harrison, *Unfinished Tales from a Russian Prison* (New York: George H. Doran, 1923), 13–14.
65. Harrison, *Unfinished Tales*, 194–95.
66. Olga Romanova, "A Voice from the Wilderness" (1923), in *Letters from Russian Prisons*, published by the International Committee for Political Prisoners (New York: Albert & Charles Boni, 1925), 20–25.
67. *Letters from Russian Prisons*, 61.
68. *Letters from Russian Prisons*, 62.
69. *Letters from Russian Prisons*, 118.
70. *Letters from Russian Prisons*, 192, 198–200.
71. *Letters from Russian Prisons*, 223–27.
72. *Letters from Russian Prisons*, 26.
73. *Letters from Russian Prisons*, 26–27.
74. *Letters from Russian Prisons*, 27.
75. *Letters from Russian Prisons*, 27–28.
76. G. M. Yudenitch, "The Road to Exile," *Letters from Russian Prisons*, 30–31.
77. Maria Spiridonova, *Letters from Russian Prisons*, 74–75.
78. Galina Shtange, "Diary," in *Intimacy and Terror: Soviet Diaries of the 1930's*, ed. Veronique Garros, Natalia Korenevskaya, and Thomas Lahusen, trans. Carol A. Flath (New York: New Press, 1995), 170.
79. Angelica Balabanoff, *Impressions of Lenin* (Ann Arbor: University of Michigan Press, 1964) and *My Life As a Rebel* (New York: Harper, 1938); Rosa Luxemburg, *The Russian Revolution*, ed. B. Wolfe (Ann Arbor: University of Michigan Press, 1961).
80. Aida Basevich, "How I Became an Anarchist," in Shapovalov, *Remembering the Darkness*, 129.

81. Anna P. Skripnikova, "Why Weren't You Crying?" in *Remembering the Darkness*, 79.
82. Basevish, "How I Became an Anarchist," in *Remembering the Darkness*, 134–37.
83. Shapovalov, *Remembering the Darkness*, 147.
84. Evgeniia I. Iaroslavskaia-Markon, "My Autobiography," in *Remembering the Darkness*, 42–43.
85. Markon, "My Autobiography," and files about her case in Shapovalov, *Remembering the Darkness*, 59, 63.
86. Nadezhda Mandelstam, *Hope Abandoned*, trans. Max Hayward (New York: Athenaeum, 1981), 202.

Notes to Chapter Two

1. Sofiya Parnok, "Through a Window-Light," in *Anthology of Russian Women's Writing*, 259.
2. For information about the Russian Orthodox Church and women on the eve of the Revolution, see William G. Wagner, "Orthodox Domesticity": Creating a Social Role for Women in *Sacred Stories Religion and Spirituality in Modern Russia*, ed. Mark D. Steinberg and Heather J. Coleman (Bloomington: Indiana University Press, 2007), 119, 136.
3. Young, *Power and the Sacred*, 229–30; also, *Vsesoiuznaia Perepis' Naseleniia 1926 goda, Kratkie svodki* (Moscow Statistika, 1928) (1926 Soviet Census), vol. 34, hereafter cited as *Perepis' 1926*.
4. David Ransel, "Sites of Veneration, Sites of Memory: The City of Dmitrov and Its Spiritual Symbols," in *Everyday Life in Russian History: Quotidian Studies in Honor of Daniel Kaiser*, ed. Gary Marker, Joan Neuberger, et. al. (Bloomington, IN: Slavica, 2010), 145–46.
5. Archpriest Sergei Lebedev, *Consoler of Suffering Hearts: The Life, Counsels, and Miracles of Eldress Rachel, Visionary of Russia*, trans. Xenia Skete (Wildwood, CA: Xenia Skete, 2001), 93.
6. Lebedev, *Consoler of Suffering Hearts*, 94.
7. Lebedev, *Consoler of Suffering Hearts*, 95.
8. Lebedev, *Consoler of Suffering Hearts*, 96.
9. Lebedev, *Consoler of Suffering Hearts*, 106.
10. Lebedev, *Consoler of Suffering Hearts*, 106–7, 169.
11. Vera K. Fleisher, "Daughter of a Village Priest," in *A Revolution of Their Own*, 89.
12. Fleisher, "Daughter of a Village Priest," 90.
13. *Woman Under Fire: Six Months in the Red Army: A Woman's Diary and Experiences of Revolutionary Russia*, trans. Reginald J. Dingle (London: Hutchinson, n.d.), 115–16. Mme X is the name that was taken by the diary writer. Born

a princess in 1898, she was the well-educated daughter of a British mother and Russian father. Her real name is not used because she feared retaliation from the Soviet secret police in London. In 1917 Mme X had joined a women's battalion under the leadership of Princess O, ostensibly to fight in the war but really to protect the Tsar and royal family. She received military training, but her mother ordered her home since she was a minor, and she did not see active military service under the Provisional Government. The Bolsheviks knew of her military training, and that was one reason they drafted her into the Red Army in the summer of 1918. Mme X was unlike the women she commanded in that she was not working class and had not joined the army to receive food and shelter.

14. *Woman Under Fire*, 126–27.
15. Maria Shkapskaya, "No Dream," in *Anthology of Russian Women's Writing*, 241–42.
16. As translated by Barbara Heldt in "Motherhood in a Cold Climate, the Poetry and Career of Maria Shkapskaya," in *Sexuality and the Body in Russian Culture*, ed. Jane T. Costlow, Stephanie Sandler, Judith Vowles (Stanford: Stanford University Press, 1993), 251.
17. Harrison, *Marooned in Moscow*, 130–33.
18. Harrison, *Marooned in Moscow*, 133.
19. Harrison, *Marooned in Moscow*, 133–34.
20. Harrison, *Marooned in Moscow*, 134.
21. Harrison, *Marooned in Moscow*, 135.
22. Harrison, *Marooned in Moscow*, 136–38.
23. Harrison, *Marooned in Moscow*, 138–39.
24. Harrison, *Marooned in Moscow*, 139.
25. Tolstoy, *I Worked for the Soviet*, 234–35.
26. Tolstoy, *I Worked for the Soviet*, 217–18.
27. Raisa Orlova, *Memoirs: The Testament of Conscience of a Russian Writer: A Searching Portrayal of the Troubled Inner Life of a Great Culture*, trans. Samuel Cioran (New York: Random House, 1983), 51–52.
28. Raisa Orlova, *Memoirs*, 52–53.
29. Raisa Orlova, *Memoirs*, 54.
30. Page Herrlinger, *Working Souls: Russian Orthodoxy and Factory Labor in St. Petersburg, 1881–1917* (Bloomington, IN: Slavica, 2007), 132–33.
31. Benet, *Village of Viriatino*, 118–19.
32. Laura J. Olson and Svetlana Adonyeva, *The Worlds of Russian Village Women: Tradition, Transgression, Compromise* (Madison: University of Wisconsin Press, 2013), 90.
33. Vera Panova, "Evdokia," as translated by Helena Goscilo in *Russian and*

Polish Women's Fiction (Knoxville: University of Tennessee Press, 1985), 137.
34. Peasant woman quoted by Ernest Poole in *"The Dark People": Russia's Crisis* (New York, Macmillan, 1918), 225.
35. Glennys Young, "Trading Icons: Clergy, Laity, and Rural Cooperatives, 1921-1928," *Canadian American Slavic Studies* 14 (1992), 315–33.
36. Hutton, *Russian Women*, 203; Young, *Power and the Sacred*, 132, 236–44, 250–52; Elena Skrjabina, *Coming of Age in the Russian Revolution*, trans. and ed. Norman Luxenburg (New Brunswick, NJ: Transaction Books, 1985), 66, 79.
37. Memoir of A. F. Berg in *Father Arseny: A Cloud of Witnesses*, trans. Vera Bouteneff (Crestwood, NY: St. Vladmimir's Seminary Press, 2001), 185–87.
38. Memoir of Berg in *Father Arseny*, 189.
39. Memoir of Berg in *Father Arseny*, 190.
40. St. Paul Florensky, *Salt of the Earth: An Encounter with a Holy Russian Elder: Isidore of Gethsemane Hermitage*, trans. Richard Betts (Platina, CA: St. Herman of Alaska Brotherhood, 1999), introduction, 28–30, 96 (regarding the intelligentsia). For secret groups of students in the 1920s, see, *Father Arseny*, 41–42, 75, 123, 199, 200, 203, 223, 234. This work is a collection of memoirs of members of Father Arseny's circle in Moscow in the 1920s and then as they regrouped around him in the 1960s and 1970s in Rostov. Their memoirs were a response to Father Arseny's question, How did you become a Christian?
41. Tatiana Tchernavin, *We Soviet Women*, trans. N. Alexander (New York: E. P. Dutton, 1936), 11–13.
42. Tchernavin, *We Soviet Women*, 18–27.
43. Tchernavin, *We Soviet Women*, 36–45.
44. Y. M. Sokolov, *Russian Folklore*, trans. Catherine R. Smith (New York: Macmillan, 1950), 640.
45. Sokolov, *Russian Folklore*, 638.
46. Isabel Tirado, "The Village Voice: Women's Views of Themselves and Their World in Russian Chastushki of the 1920s," *Carl Beck Papers in Russian and East European Studies*, no. 1008 (December 1993): 44.
47. Tirado, "Village Voice," 23.
48. Young, *Power and the Sacred*, 165ff.

Notes to Chapter Three

1. Maurice Hindus, *Broken Earth* (New York: International Publishers, 1926), 111–13, 126, 166, 198–200.
2. Hindus, *Broken Earth*, 165; Chris J. Chulos, *Converging Worlds: Religion and Community in Peasant Russia, 1861–1917* (Dekalb: Northern Illinois University Press, 2003), 89.
3. Olson and Adonyeva, *Worlds of Russian Village Women*, 101.

NOTES TO CHAPTER THREE   411

4. Olson and Adonyeva, *Worlds of Russian Village Women*, 61.
5. Tirado, "Village Voice," 24.
6. Tirado, "Village Voice," 8.
7. Vladimir Brovkin in *Russia after Lenin: Politics, Culture, and Society, 1921–1929* (New York: Taylor and Francis, 1998), 138.
8. Vladimir Brovkin in *Russia after Lenin*, 138.
9. Lidiia Seifullina, *Virineia*, trans. Tatiana Osipovich, in Tomei, *Russian Women Writers*, vol. 2, 770.
10. Seifullina, *Virineia*, 770–71.
11. Tirado, "Village Voice," 20.
12. Tirado, "Village Voice," 26.
13. Tirado, "Village Voice," 27.
14. Tirado, "Village Voice," 14; sociologist Anton S. Marchenko, *The Collective Family: A Handbook for Russian Parents*, trans. Robert Daglish (Garden City, NY: Anchor Books, 1967), 27 (originally published in 1937).
15. Tirado, "Village Voice," 21.
16. Tirado, "Village Voice," 29.
17. Tirado, "Village Voice," 32.
18. Tirado, "Komsomol and the Krest'ianka," 364.
19. Hindus, *Broken Earth*, 244–47.
20. Hindus, *Broken Earth*, 244–47.
21. Quote of a peasant woman to Poole, *"Dark People"*, 210.
22. Quoted by Anna Louise Strong, "New Women of Russia Test Lenin's Theories," *New York Times*, 20 March 1927, 14.
23. Marchenko, *Collective Family*, 117, 130ff.
24. Beatrice Farnsworth, "Rural Women and the Law: Divorce and Property Rights in the 1920s," in *Russian Peasant Women*, ed. Beatrice Farnsworth and Lynne Viola (Oxford: Oxford University Press, 1992), 167–82; Hutton, *Russian Women*, 146–49.
25. Tirado, "Village Voice," 33.
26. Yelena Shershenyova, "The New Jerusalem Tolstoy Commune," in *Memoirs of Peasant Tolstoyans in Soviet Russia*, trans. and ed. William Edgerton (Bloomington: Indiana University Press, 1993), 6.
27. Shershenyova, "New Jerusalem Tolstoy Commune," 13.
28. Shershenyova, "New Jerusalem Tolstoy Commune," 13.
29. Shershenyova, "New Jerusalem Tolstoy Commune," 7–24.
30. Quoted in Hutton, *Russian Women*, 139–76.
31. Hutton, *Russian Women*, 148; Nadezhda Mandelstam, *Hope Abandoned*, trans. Max Hayward (New York: Atheneum, 1981), 78, 159, 173, 212, 215, 456.

32. Panova, "Evdokia," 120.
33. Anna Balashova, "A Worker's Life," in *In the Shadow of Revolution: Life Stories of Russian Women from 1917 to the Second World War*, ed. Sheila Fitzpatrick and Yuri Slezkine, trans. Yuri Slezkine (Princeton: Princeton University Press, 2000), 249–50.
34. Anatoly Glebov, "Inga," trans. Charles Malamuth, in *Six Soviet Plays*, ed. Eugene Lyons (New York: Houghton Mifflin, 1934), 335.
35. Hutton, *Russian Women*, 153, 157; Anne E. Gorsuch, "Flappers and Foxtrotters: Soviet Youth in the 'Roaring Twenties,'" *Carl Beck Papers in Russian and East European Studies*, no. 1102 (March 1994).
36. Harrison, *Marooned in Moscow*, 86.
37. Harrison, *Marooned in Moscow*, 88–89.
38. Harrison, *Marooned in Moscow*, 90–91.
39. Margaret Wettlin, *Fifty Russian Winters: An American Woman's Life in the Soviet Union* (New York: Pharos Books, 1992), 102.
40. Skrjabina, *Coming of Age*, 66–67.
41. *The Diary of Nelly Ptashkina*, trans. Pauline de Chary (London: Jonathan Cape, 1923), 124–25, entries for September to October, 1918.
42. *Diary of Nelly Ptashkina*, 131, 126, October 1918.
43. *Diary of Nelly Ptashkina*, 238–39, April–May 1919.
44. *Diary of Nelly Ptashkina*, 244–45, May–June 1919.
45. *Diary of Nelly Ptashkina*, 192–93, January 1919.
46. Mariya Shkapskaya, *The Mother and the Stern Master: Selected Poems*, trans. and intro. Sandra Shaw Bennett (Nottingham: Astra, 1998), 101–5.
47. Shkapskaya, *Mother and the Stern Master*, 105–9.
48. Shkapskaya, *Mother and the Stern Master*, 109–11.
49. Shkapskaya, *Mother and the Stern Master*, 135–39.
50. Mariia Shkapskaia, "Lonely Like a Crane," translated in "Mariia Shkapskaia" by Natalie Roklina, in Tomei, *Russian Women Writers*, vol. 2, 804–5.
51. Anna Akhmatova as translated by Sibelan Forrester in Tomei, *Russian Women Writers*, vol. 2, 928.
52. Mandelstam, *Hope Abandoned*, 215.
53. Mandelstam, *Hope Abandoned*, 225.
54. A. Kollontai, "Thirty-Two Pages," as translated by Rimma Volynska in Tomei, *Russian Women Writers*, vol. 2, 724–25.
55. Mandelstam, *Hope Abandoned*, 118.
56. Mandelstam, *Hope Abandoned*, 208–28, quote from p. 216.
57. Mandelstam, *Hope Abandoned*, 140–41.
58. Skrjabina, *Coming of Age*, 73.

59. Shkapskaya, *Mother and the Stern Master*, 153–55.
60. Ol'ga Forsh, "The Suitcase," trans. Martha Hickey, in "Ol'ga Forsh," in Tomei, *Russian Women Writers*, vol. 2, 665.
61. Forsh, "The Suitcase," 668.
62. Forsh, "The Suitcase," 668.
63. Forsh, "The Suitcase," 670.
64. Forsh, "The Suitcase," 669–71.
65. Anna Ostroumova Lebedeva's quote found in M. N. Yablonskaya, *Women Artists of Russia's New Age, 1900–1935,* ed. and trans. Anthony Parton (New York: Rizzoli, 1990), 49.
66. Tatjana Tchernavin, *Escape from the Soviets*, trans. N. Alexander (New York: E. P. Dutton, 1934), 11–13.
67. Tchernavin, *Escape from the Soviets*, 14.
68. Tchernavin, *Escape from the Soviets*, 14–15.
69. Tchernavin, *Escape from the Soviets*, 22–27.
70. Tchernavin, *Escape from the Soviets*, 29–37.
71. Gorsuch, *Youth in Revolutionary Russia*, chapter "Flappers and Foxtrotters," 116–38, quotation of chastushki p. 134.
72. Gorsuch, *Youth in Revolutionary Russia*, 156–58.
73. Barbara Hedlt, "Motherhood in a Cold Climate: The Poetry and Career of Maria Shkapskaya," in *Sexuality and the Body*, ed. Costlow et. al. (Stanford: Stanford University Press, 1993), 238–54.

Notes to Chapter Four

1. Ella Winter, *Red Virtue* (New York: Harcourt Brace, 1933), 84–85, 109.
2. For information about the contested nature of Bolshevik education and culture in the 1920s, see Gorsuch, *Youth in Revolutionary Russia*, especially pages 17, 29, 31.
3. Irina Sergeevna Tidmarsh, *Memories of Revolution: Russian Women Remember*, ed. Anna Horsbrugh-Porter, interviews by Elena Snow and Frances Welch (London: Routledge, 1993), 62.
4. Tidmarsh, *Memories*, 62–63.
5. Broido, *Daughter of Revolution*, 107–8.
6. Broido, *Daughter of Revolution*, 109, 124–25.
7. *Diary of Nelly Ptashkina*, 40, 120, entries January 1918 and September 1918.
8. *Diary of Nelly Ptashkina*, 34–35.
9. Skrjabina, *Coming of Age*, 39.
10. Skrjabina, *Coming of Age*, 40–41.
11. Skrjabina, *Coming of Age*, 45.

12. Skrjabina, *Coming of Age*, 45.
13. Skrjabina, *Coming of Age*, 45–64.
14. Larisa Reisner, "The Front" (1924), reprinted in part in *Storming the Heavens: Voices of October*, ed. Mark Jones (London: Zwan Publications, 1987), 142–43.
15. Tolstoy, *I Worked for the Soviet*, 176–179.
16. Tolstoy, *I Worked for the Soviet*, 159, 163.
17. Tolstoy, *I Worked for the Soviet*, 163.
18. Tolstoy, *I Worked for the Soviet*, 200.
19. Tolstoy, *I Worked for the Soviet*, 203.
20. Igal Halfin, *Terror in my Soul* (Cambridge: Harvard University Press, 2003), 122–23, 233–35.
21. Troshchenko as quoted by Halfin in *Terror in my Soul*, 123.
22. Igal Halfin, "From Darkness To Light: Student Communist Autobiography during NEP," *Jahrbuchr fur Geschichte Osteuropas* 45, no. 2 (1997): 231–32.
23. Ella Winter, *Red Virtue Human Relationships in the New Russia* (New York: Harcourt, Brace, 1933), 84–85.

Notes to Chapter Five

1. Gorsuch, *Youth in Revolutionary Russia*, 29, 37.
2. Hutton, *Russian Women*, 17, 203.
3. Tolstoy, *I Worked for the Soviet*, 164.
4. Tolstoy, *I Worked for the Soviet*, 165.
5. Tolstoy, *I Worked for the Soviet*, 168–69.
6. Ponomarenko, "From Peasant to Journalist," 137.
7. Ponomarenko, "From Peasant to Journalist," 137, 151.
8. Writing by a delegatka as quoted by Vladimir Brovkin in *Russia after Lenin*, 137.
9. "A People's Deputy, Praskovya Pichugina," *Soviet Literature* 4–5 (1939): 235.
10. Benet, *Village of Viriatino*, 287–90.
11. Maurice Hindus, *Red Bread: Collectivization in a Russian Village* (Bloomington: Indiana University Press, 1988), 52, 58 (originally published in 1931).
12. Hutton, *Russian Women*, 202–4ff. For information about the role of the Bolshukha, domestic chores, and bread making, see Olson and Adonyeva, *Worlds of Russian Village Women*, 66–68.
13. Markoosha Fischer, *My Lives in Russia* (New York: Harper & Brothers, 1944), 27–28.
14. Fischer, *My Lives in Russia*, 28.
15. Marietta Shaginian, "Diaries," as quoted in Tchernavin, *We Soviet Women*, 187–89.

NOTES TO CHAPTER FIVE   415

16. For information about housing conditions in Moscow in the 1920s, see Tricia Starks, "Workers' Bodies in the Workers' State: Prophylaxis and the Construction of Soviet Citizenship," in *The Making of Russian History: Society, Culture, and the Politics of Modern Russia, Essays in Honor of Allan K. Wildman,* ed. John W. Steinberg and Rex A. Wade (Bloomington, IN: Slavica), 112.
17. See Harrison, *Marooned in Moscow,* 151.
18. Hutton, *Russian Women,* 209–12.
19. Ekaterina Strogova, "The Baroness and Her Maid," in *Womenfolk: Factory Sketches, 1927,* trans. Marian Schwartz, in *Anthology of Russian Women's Writing,* 276–78.
20. Ekaterina Strogova, "A Day in the Trimmings," *Anthology of Russian Women's Writing,* 278–82.
21. Ekaterina Strogova, "The Foreman and the Forewoman," in *Anthology of Russian Women's Writing,* 282–85.
22. Ekaterina Strogova, "The Women Run Everything," "Leaders," and "Foreman and the Forewoman," in *Anthology of Russian Women's Writing,* 282–85, 287–94.
23. Balashova, "A Worker's Life," 248–50.
24. Gorsuch, *Youth in Revolutionary Russia,* 9, 38, 63–65.
25. Hutton, *Russian Women,* 218–24; *Perepis' 1926,* vol. 34: 56–75.
26. *Diary of Nelly Ptashkina,* 172–73, Kiev, December 1918.
27. Elena Skrjabina in her memoir indicates that one of their servants hated the new Soviet regime and complained so bitterly and noisily about it at the market that they feared being denounced as anti-Soviet. See Skrjabina, *Coming of Age,* 50.
28. Skrjabina,*Coming of Age,* 54. In the early 1920s, Elena and part of her family were living in Simbirsk, on the banks of the Volga, when the ARA food was distributed.
29. Tolstoy, *I Worked for the Soviet,* 170, 176.
30. Marietta Shaginian's diaries recorded peoples' wages, working conditions, and diet, as reported in Tchernavin, *We Soviet Women,* 187.
31. Richard Stites, *The Women's Liberation Movement in Russia: Feminism, Nihilism, and Bolshevism, 1860–1930* (Princeton: Princeton University Press, 1978), 372–73.
32. Hutton, *Russian Women,* 143.
33. Fischer, *My Lives in Russia,* 32.
34. See Shaginian, "Diaries," as quoted by Tchernavin, *We Soviet Women,* 187; Hutton, *Russian Women,* 145–57; Gorsuch, "Flappers and Foxtrotters," 3–18.
35. Skrjabina, *Coming of Age,* 54.
36. For copies of her Simbirsk Institute Report of 1923, see her file at the Iowa

Women's Archives, University of Iowa.
37. Skrjabina, *Coming of Age*, 56, 68.
38. Skrjabina, *Coming of Age*, 68.
39. Skrjabina, *Coming of Age*, 75–76.
40. Skrjabina, *Coming of Age*, 76–77.
41. Helen Dmitriew, *Surviving the Storms: Memory of Stalin's Tyranny*, trans. Cathleen A. McClintic and George Mendez (Fresno: The Press at California State University, 1992), 2.
42. As quoted by Vladimir Brovkin in *Russia after Lenin*, 152.
43. Olga Freidenberg, diary entry from *The Correspondence of Boris Pasternak and Olga Freidenberg, 1910–1954*, ed. and trans. Elliott Mossman (NY: Harcourt Brace Jovanovich, 1982), 56.
44. Hutton, *Russian Women*, 222–27; citations from 1926 Soviet Census, *Perepis' 1926*, vol. 34: 56–75, 118–19, 142–61; for Leningrad, see *Perepis' 1926, Kratkie Svodki*, vol. 18: 33, 492.
45. Udaltsova, "How the Critics and Public Relate to Contemporary Russian Art," 1915, quoted by Yablonskaya, *Women Artists of Russia's New Age*, 160.
46. Yablonskaya, *Women Artists of Russia's New Age*, 169.
47. Yablonskaya, *Women Artists of Russia's New Age*, 170–71.
48. Aida I. Basevich, "How I Became an Anarchist," in Shapovalov, *Remembering the Darkness*, 132. Basevich was a student in the Institute of the History of the Arts in the early 1920s.
49. Karadja, *Kyra's Story*, 172–79.
50. Osip Brik, as quoted in John E. Bowlt, *Russian Art of the Avant-Garde: Theory and Criticism, 1902–1934* (New York: Thames and Hudson, 1988), 248.
51. See, E. V. Efremova, *Zinaida Serebriakova* (Moskva: Izdatel'stvo ART RODNIK, 2006), 38–55, 72–73; *Sovetskoe iskysstvo 1920–1930-x godov* (Leningrad, Avrora, 1991).
52. Tchernavin, *We Soviet Women*, 99–100.
53. Tchernavin, *We Soviet Women*, 100–101.
54. Tchernavin, *We Soviet Women*, 102–5.
55. Tchernavin, *We Soviet Women*, 105.
56. Pavlova, "Taking Advantage," 60–61.
57. Lidiia Seifullina in Tomei, *Russian Women Writers*, vol. 2, 764.
58. Seifullina, in Tomei, *Russian Women Writers*, vol. 2, 764.
59. Seifullina, in Tomei, *Russian Women Writers*, vol. 2, 769.
60. Seifullina, in Tomei, *Russian Women Writers*, vol. 2, 772.
61. Tolstoy, *I Worked for the Soviet*, 175.
62. Reginald E. Zelnik, "Perils of Pankratova," 14–17.

63. For a fascinating account of Olga Freidenberg's life and excerpts from her autobiography in the 1920s and 1930s, see Nina Perlina, *Ol'ga Freidenberg's Works and Days* (Bloomington, IN: Slavica, 2002), especially chapters 2 and 3, as well as her book *Correspondence*.
64. Freidenberg, *Correspondence*, 57–58; Perlina, *Freidenberg's Works and Days*, 47–55.
65. Freidenberg, *Correspondence*, 85.
66. Freidenberg, *Correspondence*, 87, 89, 122–23.
67. Freidenberg, *Correspondence*, 125.
68. Freidenberg, *Correspondence*, 145–53.
69. Anna Bek, *The Life of a Russian Woman Doctor: A Siberian Memoir, 1869–1954*, trans. and ed. Anne D. Rassweiler (Bloomington: Indiana University Press, 2004), 106.
70. Bek, *Life of a Russian Woman Doctor*, 109.
71. Bek, *Life of a Russian Woman Doctor*, 110–11.
72. Bek, *Life of a Russian Woman Doctor*, 113–14.
73. Bek, *Life of a Russian Woman Doctor*, 114.
74. See Barbara Heldt, "Motherhood in a Cold Climate: The Poetry and Career of Maria Shkapskaya," *Sexuality and the Body in Russian Culture*, ed. Jane T. Costlow, Stephanie Sandler, Judith Vowles (Stanford: Stanford University Press, 1993), 241–44.
75. Leon Trotsky, *Literature and Revolution* (New York: Russell & Russell, 1957), 41.
76. Trotsky, *Literature and Revolution*, 170–71.
77. For a good account of Barkova's short literary life, see "Anna Barkova: A Few Autobiographical Facts" in *Anthology of Russian Women's Writing*, 311–12; see also "Sofiya Parnok," in *Anthology of Russian Women's Writing*, 256.
78. Tchernavin, *We Soviet Women*, 169–72.
79. Tchernavin, *We Soviet Women*, 181.
80. Tchernavin, *We Soviet Women*, 185.
81. Tchernavin, *We Soviet Women*, 186–89.
82. "Anna Akhmatova (1889–1966)" in Catriona Kelly, *A History of Russian Women's Writing, 1820–1992* (Oxford: Clarendon Press, 1994), 209.
83. Anna Akhmatova, "A Brief Word About Myself," *Soviet Literature*, no. 6 (1989): 6–7.
84. Kelly, *History of Russian Women's Writing*, 214–18.
85. Anna Akhmatova, "The Song of the Last Meeting," in *Anno Domini MCMXXI*, 1922, and "The Muse," 1924, as translated in Evelyn Bristol, *A History of Russian Poetry* (New York: Oxford University Press, 1991), 211–13.
86. Translated by Judith Hemschemeyer in Roberta Reeder, ed., *Complete Poems*

of *Anna Akhmatova* (Somerville, MA: Zephyr Press, 1990), from *Anno Domini MCMXXI*, 1922.
87. Anna Akhmatova, "Now All is Sold," trans. Jack Lindsay, in *Russian Poetry, 1917–1955* (London: Bodley Head, 1957), 30.
88. Mandelstam, *Hope Abandoned*, 115.
89. Tchernavin, *We Soviet Women*, 170, 180–82.
90. Vera Inber, "Five Days and Nights," translated by Jack Lindsay in *Russian Poetry*, 72–73.
91. Nina Berberova, *The Italics Are Mine*, trans. Philippe Radley (New York: Vintage Books, 1993), 114.
92. Berberova, *Italics*, 121.
93. Berberova, *Italics*, 121.
94. Tsvetaeva, *Selected Poems*, 53.
95. Tsvetaeva, "The Return of the Chief," as translated in Bristol, *History of Russian Poetry*, 242.
96. Marina Tsvetaeva, for Blok, as translated in Vladimir Markov and Merrill Sparks, eds., *Modern Russian Poetry: An Anthology with Verse Translations* (Indianapolis: Bobbs-Merrill, 1967), 433.
97. Berberova, *Italics*, 126, 143.
98. Mandelstam, *Hope Abandoned*, 119.
99. Anatoly Lunacharsky, "Revolution and Art, 1920–22" and "Theses of the Art Section of the Central Committee of the Union of Art Workers of Narkompros," as quoted in Bowlt, *Russian Art of the Avant-Garde*, 184–94.
100. Bowlt, *Russian Art of the Avant-Garde*, introduction, xxxv–xxxvii; Mandelstam, *Hope Abandoned*, 14.
101. Mandelstam, *Hope Abandoned*; Tamara Glenny, "Unpredictable Past: How the Revolution Betrayed Liubov Popova and the Russian Avant-Garde," *Art and Antiques*, (February 1991), 59–61.
102. Bowlt, *Russian Art of the Avant-Garde*, xxxv–xxxvii.
103. Glenny, "Unpredictable Past," 61.
104. Varvara Stepanova, "Concerning My Graphics at the Exhibitions," Moscow, 1919, as quoted in *Women Artists of Russia's New Age*, 142.
105. Yablonskaya, *Women Artists of Russia's New Age*, 142.
106. Yablonskaya, Women Artists of Russia's New Age, 144–48.
107. Varvara Stepanova, "From Costume to Designs and Fabric," Evening Moscow, 1929, as quoted by Yablonskaya, Women Artists of Russia's New Age, 156.
108. Exter, "Simplicity and Practicality in Clothes," 1923, as quoted by Yablonskaya, Women Artists of Russia's New Age, 140.

Notes to Chapter Six

1. As quoted by John Van Zant in "Now We Amount to Something," *Moscow Daily News*, March 8, 1933, 3.
2. Mary Buckley, *Mobilizing Soviet Peasants: Heroines and Heroes of Stalin's Fields* (New York: Rowman and Littlefield, 2006), 308.
3. Pasha Angelina, "The Most Important Thing," in *In the Shadow of Revolution: Life Stories of Russian Women from 1917 to the Second World War*, ed. Sheila Fitzpatrick and Yuri Slezkine, trans. Yuri Slezkine (Princeton: Princeton University Press, 2000), 308.
4. Angelina, "The Most Important Thing," 308.
5. Angelina, "The Most Important Thing," 311.
6. Angelina, "The Most Important Thing," 311.
7. Angelina, "The Most Important Thing," 313–19; Buckley, *Mobilizing Soviet Peasants*, 27, 67–78. Buckley suggests that meetings with Stalin and promising him to perform heroic feats in agriculture were important features in the lives of these women Stakhanovites.
8. Angelina, "The Most Important Thing," 321.
9. Buckley, *Mobilizing Soviet Peasants*, 272.
10. "Galaxy of Women: Portrait II: Ustina of the Collective Farm," *Moscow Daily News*, March 11, 1933, 2.
11. "Galaxy," 2.
12. Hutton, *Russian Women*, 329; *Vsesoiuznaia Perepis' naseleniia 1937 goda: obshchie itogi, Sbornik dokumentov i materialov*, ed. Iu. A. Poliakov, V. B. Zhiromskaia, E. A. Tiurina, Ia. E. Vodarskii (Moskva: ROSSPEN, 2007), 124 (hereafter cited as *Perepis' 1937*).
13. See Buckley, *Mobilizing Soviet Peasants*, 5–7, for good discussions of different historians' assessments of collectivization.
14. Pankratova, "A Farm Woman Speaks," *Moscow Daily News*, 18 February 1934, 2; Hutton, *Russian Women*, 330.
15. See "We Live Well—The Story of a Woman Tractorist" by Liubov Semenets, *Moscow Daily News*, February–March 1935; Hutton, *Russian Women*, 330.
16. Volytsan's findings in Buckley, *Mobilizing Soviet Peasants*, 22–23.
17. Mrs. Cecil [Ada Elizabeth] Chesterton, *Sickle or Swastika?* (London: S. Paul & Co., 1934), 135, 246–49; Mrs. E. M. Delafield also visited Soviet Russia in the 1930s and saw impressive kolkhozy, which she describes in *I Visit the Soviets: The Provincial Lady in Russia* (Chicago: Academy Chicago Publishers, 1985 (originally published in 1937), 1–79; R. A. Clarke, *Soviet Facts, 1917–1970* (New York: John Wiley, 1972), 74–75; Hutton, *Russian Women*, 329–30.
18. Hutton, *Russian Women*, 331.
19. Sokolov, *Russian Folklore*, 646. For photos of women working with wooden

implements in the fields, see Leah Bendavid-Val and Walton H. Rawls, *Propaganda and Dreams: Photographing the 1930s in the USSR and the US* (New York: Stemmle, 1999), 98–99.
20. Sokolov, *Russian Folklore*, 648–49.
21. Sokolov, *Russian Folklore*, 650.
22. Sokolov, *Russian Folklore*, 650.
23. Sokolov, *Russian Folklore*, 652. For information about Soviet Stakhanovite milkmaids, see Buckley, *Mobilizing Soviet Peasants*, 71.
24. Sokolov, *Russian Folklore*, 653.
25. Buckley, *Mobilizing Soviet Peasants*, 69, 75.
26. Chesterton, *Sickle or Swastika?*, 247–49, 257–59, 263–64; Hutton, *Russian Women*, 327, 357.
27. Lynne Viola, "Babi Bunty and Peasant Women's Protest during Collectivization," in *Russian Peasant Women*, ed. Beatrice Farnsworth and Lynne Viola (New York: Oxford University Press, 1992), 189–205; Hindus, *Red Bread*.
28. Elizabeth Koop and Louise Huebert as quoted by Elizabeth Lenci-Downs in *I Heard My People Cry: One Family's Escape from Russia* (Victoria, BC: Trafford, 2003), 44–46.
29. Huebert quoted in *I Heard My People Cry*, 49.
30. Huebert quoted in *I Heard My People Cry*, 50–57.
31. Huebert quoted in *I Heard My People Cry*, 60–62.
32. Huebert quoted in *I Heard My People Cry*, 62–64.
33. Huebert quoted in *I Heard My People Cry*, 73–74.
34. Huebert quoted in *I Heard My People Cry*, 75.
35. Huebert quoted in *I Heard My People Cry*, 76–77.
36. Huebert quoted in *I Heard My People Cry*, 77–79.
37. Huebert quoted in *I Heard My People Cry*, 79–80.
38. Huebert quoted in *I Heard My People Cry*, 87.
39. Huebert quoted in *I Heard My People Cry*, 87–88.
40. Huebert quoted in *I Heard My People Cry*, 92–93.
41. Huebert quoted in *I Heard My People Cry*, 94–95.
42. Huebert quoted in *I Heard My People Cry*, 95–96.
43. Huebert quoted in *I Heard My People Cry*, 97.
44. Hilda Mielke, *Border Crossing: A Bridge of Hope: An Oral History*, comp. and trans. Lorenz Mielke, ed. Velma Jesser (Lincoln, NE: American Historical Society of Germans from Russia, 2009), 1–3.
45. Mielke, *Border Crossing*, 3–4.
46. Mielke, *Border Crossing*, 4–5.
47. Mielke, *Border Crossing*, 5.

NOTES TO CHAPTER SIX   421

48. Mielke, *Border Crossing*, 5–6.
49. Mielke, *Border Crossing*, 6–7.
50. Mielke, *Border Crossing*, 7–8.
51. Mielke, *Border Crossing*, 8–9.
52. Mielke, *Border Crossing*, 11–21.
53. Hutton, *Russian Women*, 325.
54. Tchernavin, *We Soviet Women*, 109–20, 155; Hutton, *Russian Women*, 327.
55. Hindus, *Red Bread*, 60, 152.
56. Hindus, *Red Bread*, 259.
57. Hindus, *Red Bread*, 247.
58. Hindus, *Red Bread*, 69.
59. Hindus, *Red Bread*, 284–97.
60. Tatiana A. Izyumova, essayist in Tatiana V. Torstensen, *Elder Sebastian of Optina*, trans. David Koubek (Platina, CA: St. Herman of Alaska Brotherhood, 1999), 208–9.
61. Maria V. Andrievskaya, essayist in Torstensen, *Elder Sebastian of Optina*, 215–17.
62. Maria F. Orlova, essayist in Torstensen, *Elder Sebastian of Optina*, 252–53.
63. Letter from Regehr family as translated by Ruth Derksen Siemens in *Remember Us: Letters from Stalin's Gulag (1930–1937), Volume One: The Regehr Family* (Kitchener, ON: Pandora Press: 2007), 101–2.
64. Siemens, *Remember Us*, 73–74.
65. Siemens, *Remember Us*, 75.
66. Siemens, *Remember Us*, 199.
67. Siemens, *Remember Us*, 251–386.
68. Hindus, *Red Bread*, 47, 57–58.
69. Hindus, *Red Bread*, 235–45, 278.
70. Benet, *Village of Viriatino*, 179–80, 282.
71. Helen Dmitriew, *Surviving the Storms*, 7–18.
72. Dmitriew, *Surviving the Storms*, 18–19.
73. Dmitriew, *Surviving the Storms*, 24.
74. Hutton, *Russian Women*, 327.
75. Hutton, *Russian Women*, 328.
76. Hutton, *Russian Women*, 328; *Perepis' 1937*, 6.
77. Hutton, *Russian Women*, 329.
78. Delafield, *I Visit the Soviets*, 53, 79; Benet, *Village of Viriatino*, 254–56; *SSSR Strana Sotsializma*, 74, 88, 117; *Izvestiia*, 22 December 1936, 1; Jiri Zuzanak, *Work and Leisure in the Soviet Union: A Time Budget Analysis* (New York: Praeger, 1980), 183–86, 219–20; Hutton, *Russian Women*, 331, 358.

79. Tchernavin, *We Soviet Women*, 166–67.

80. See Dr. Rachelle Yarros, "Observations in Soviet Russia," *Journal of Social Hygiene* 16 (1930): 455; Yarros, "Moscow Revisited," *Journal of Social Hygiene* 25 (1937): 201; Alice Field, "Prostitution in the Soviet Union," *The Nation*, 142 (25 March 1936), 373–74; Hutton, *Russian Women*, 330–31, 358.

Notes to Chapter Seven

1. F. C. Weiskopf, *Iron, Coal, and Komsomol* (Moscow-Leningrad: Co-operative Publishing Society of Foreign workers in the USSR, 1933), 56.

2. Hutton, *Russian Women*, 324; *Perepis' 1937*, 124.

3. For an excellent account of these events, see Jeffrey J. Rossman, *Worker Resistance under Stalin: Class and Revolution on the Shop Floor* (Cambridge, MA: Harvard University Press, 2005), 1–26, 208–36.

4. Weiskopf, *Iron, Coal and Komsomol*, 57.

5. Weiskopf, *Iron, Coal, and Komsomol*, 42–43.

6. Weiskopf, *Iron, Coal and Komsomol*, 81–82.

7. Weiskopf, *Iron, Coal and Komsomol*, 325.

8. Anna Balashova, "A Worker's Life,", 251.

9. Anna Balashova, "A Worker's Life," 251.

10. Fischer, *My Lives in Russia*, 33.

11. Shtange, "Diary," in *Intimacy and Terror*,170–73.

12. Shtange, "Diary," in *Intimacy and Terror*, 172–90.

Notes to Chapter Eight

1. Irina Ivanovna Kniazeva, "A Life in a Peasant Village," in *A Revolution of Their Own*, 123, 128; *Perepis' 1937*, 126–27, 138.

2. See Pearl S. Buck, *Talk about Russia with Masha Scott* (New York: John Day, 1945), 44, 71–80; Merle Fainsod, *Smolensk under Soviet Rule* (Cambridge, MA: Harvard University Press, 1958), 355–63; *The USSR in Figures for 1935* (Moscow: Statistika Publishers, 1935), 260–63; *SSSR Strana Sotsializma: Statisticheskii Sbornik* [USSR country of socialism: Statistical collection] (Moscow, 1936), 98; Hutton, *Russian Women*, 311–13.

3. James Purves-Stewart, *A Physician's Tour in Soviet Russia* (New York: Frederick A. Stokes, 1933), 144, 161, 169.

4. Hutton, *Russian Women*, 313, 320–21.

5. Pasha Angelina, *My Answer to an American Questionnaire* (Moscow: Foreign Language Publishing House, 1949), 60–62; Hutton, *Russian Women*, 313.

6. Buckley, *Mobilizing Soviet Peasants*, 80.

7. Hutton, *Russian Women*, 330.

8. Fischer, *My Lives in Russia*, 48.
9. Ponomarenko, "From Peasant to Journalist," 146–47.
10. Olson and Adonyeva, *Worlds of Russian Village Women*, 127–28.
11. Dmitriew, *Surviving the Storms*, 35–36.
12. Dmitriew, *Surviving the Storms*, 38.
13. Antonia Aleksandrovna Berezhnaia, "Overcoming an 'Incorrect' Birth," in *A Revolution of Their Own*, 106.
14. Elena Trofimovna Dolgikh, "Under a Sword of Damocles," in *A Revolution of Their Own*, 165ff.
15. Dolgikh, "Under a Sword," 165–69.
16. Dolgikh, "Under a Sword," 170.
17. *Perepis' 1937*, 136–38; 1939 census, *Perepis' naseleniia 1939 g., Osnovnye itogi* (Moscow: Gosplan, 1941), 18–19 (table 37).
18. Fischer, *My Lives in Russia*, 37.
19. Pavlova, "Taking Advantage," 60–64.
20. Pavlova, "Taking Advantage," 65–73.
21. Anna Krylova, "In their own words, Soviet women writers and the search for self," in *A History of Women's Writing in Russia*, ed. Adele Marie Barker and Jehanne M. Gheith (Cambridge: Cambridge University Press, 2002), 253.
22. Krylova, "In their own words," 255.
23. Krylova, "In their own words," 256, 259–60.
24. Raisa Orlova, *Memoirs*, 76.
25. Raisa Orlova, *Memoirs*, 76–77.
26. Raisa Orlova, *Memoirs*, 77.
27. Raisa Orlova, *Memoirs*, 77–78.
28. Raisa Orlova, *Memoirs*, 81–83.
29. Raisa Orlova, *Memoirs*, 87–88.
30. Raisa Orlova, *Memoirs*, 43.
31. Dmitriew, *Surviving the Storms*, 58–59.
32. Sheila Fitzpatrick, *Education and Social Mobility in the Soviet Union, 1921–1934* (Cambridge: Cambridge University Press, 1979), 161.
33. Fitzpatrick, *Education and Social Mobility*, 164–65.
34. Bek, *Life of a Russian Woman Doctor*, 116–17.
35. Bek, *Life of a Russian Woman Doctor*, 117.
36. Bek, *Life of a Russian Woman Doctor*, 118.
37. Bek, Life of a Russian Woman Doctor, 121.
38. Letter of Zinaida Cherkovskaya to Party Secretary of Smolensk Communist Party, as quoted in Fainsod, Smolensk under Soviet Rule, 225–28.

39. Letter of Z. Cherkovskaya in Fainsod, *Smolensk under Soviet Rule*, 229.

Notes to Chapter Nine

1. Tchernavin, *Escape from the Soviets*, 125; *Perepis' 1937*, 6, 245ff.; *Vsesoiuznaia perepis' naseleniia 1939 goda* (Moscow: Nauka, 1992), table I, 229ff.
2. "Anna Barkova: A Few Autobiographical Facts," in *Anthology of Russian Women's Writing*, 311–12.
3. Dmitriew, *Surviving the Storms*, 26–27.
4. Dmitriew, *Surviving the Storms*, 36–37.
5. Dmitriew, *Surviving the Storms*, 38.
6. Tchernavin, *Escape from the Soviets*, 11–12, 22–23, 31–32, 35.
7. Tchernavin, *Escape from the Soviets*, 52–53, 43–50.
8. Tchernavin, *Escape from the Soviets*, 54–55.
9. Tchernavin, *Escape from the Soviets*, 59–60.
10. Tchernavin, *Escape from the Soviets*, 64–73.
11. Tchernavin, *Escape from the Soviets*, 78–80.
12. Tchernavin, *Escape from the Soviets*, 92–93.
13. Tchernavin, *Escape from the Soviets*, 94–118.
14. Tchernavin, *Escape from the Soviets*, 119–23.
15. Tchernavin, *Escape from the Soviets*, 154–64.
16. Tchernavin, *Escape from the Soviets*, 29–61, 130, 139.
17. Tchernavin, *Escape from the Soviets*, 167–315; Hutton, *Russian Women*, 382–83; Maria Joffe, *One Long Night*; Nadezhda Joffe, *Back in Time: My Life, My Fate, My Epoch: The Memoirs of Nadezhda A. Joffe*, trans. Frederick Choate (Oak Park, MI: Labor Publications, 1995).
18. Olga Adamova-Sliozberg, "My Journey," in *Till My Tale Is Told*, 3–6.
19. Adamova-Sliozberg, "My Journey," 22.
20. Adamova-Sliozberg, "My Journey," 38, 45.
21. Adamova-Sliozberg, "My Journey," 43.
22. Adamova-Sliozberg, "My Journey," 44.
23. Adamova-Sliozberg, "My Journey," 47.
24. Adamova-Sliozberg, "My Journey," 49–85.
25. Fischer, *My Lives in Russia*, 143.
26. Fischer, *My Lives in Russia*, 145.
27. Fischer, *My Lives in Russia*, 153–55.
28. *Perepis' 1937*, 252–57.
29. Fischer, *My Lives in Russia*, 165, 194, 210, 233.
30. Lydia Chukovskaya, *The Deserted House* (Belmont, MA: Nordland, 1967),

74–75.
31. Chukovskaya, *Deserted House*, 41.
32. Chukovskaya, *Deserted House*, 81.
33. Chukovskaya, *Deserted House*, 83–84, 141.
34. Chukovskaya, *Deserted House*, 85.
35. Chukovskaya, *Deserted House*, 108–9.
36. Chukovskaya, *Deserted House*, 142ff.
37. Chukovskaya, *Deserted House*, 125.
38. Olga Freidenberg as quoted by Nina Perlina in *Ol'ga Freidenberg's Works and Days*, 126.
39. Perlina, *Ol'ga Freidenberg's Works and Days*, 155–56.
40. Olga Freidenberg, diary entry from *Correspondence*, 153–54.
41. Freidenberg, diary entry in *Correspondence*, 157–58.
42. Freidenberg, diary entry in *Correspondence*, 162–64.
43. Freidenberg, *Correspondence*, 164–65.
44. Freidenberg, *Correspondence*, 166.
45. Freidenberg, *Correspondence*, 164–69.
46. Freidenberg, *Correspondence*, 171–72.
47. Freidenberg as quoted in Perlina, *Ol'ga Freidenberg's Works and Days*, 163.
48. Freidenberg, *Correspondence*, 175–81; Perlina, *Ol'ga Freidenberg's Works and Days*, 164.
49. Lydia Ginzburg, *The Journals*, trans. Jane Gary Harris, in Tomei, *Russian Women Writers*, vol. 2, 1172.
50. Lydia Ginzburg, *The Journals*, 1173–74.
51. Nadezhda Kanel, "A Meeting at the Lubyanka," in *Till My Tale Is Told*, 282.
52. Kanel, "Meeting at the Lubyanka," 282.
53. As quoted in "Lydiia Seifullina," in Tomei, *Russian Women Writers*, vol. 2, 772.
54. Anna Akhmatova as translated by Sibelan Forrester in Tomei, *Russian Women Writers*, vol. 2, 930.
55. Anna Akhmatova as translated by Sibelan Forrester in Tomei, *Russian Women Writers*, vol. 2, 934.
56. Anna Akhmatova, "The Last Toast," in Bendavid-Val and Rawls, *Propaganda and Dreams*, 28.
57. Anna Akhmatova, "Requiem," in *Selected Poems*, trans. D. M. Thomas (London: Penguin Books, 1985), 89.
58. Akhmatova, "Requiem," 90.
59. Akhmatova, "Requiem," 91.
60. Akhmatova, "Requiem," 92.

61. Akhmatova, "Requiem," 93.
62. Akhmatova, "Requiem," 95.
63. Anna Barkova, "Selected Poems," in *Till My Tale Is Told*, 215.
64. Barkova, "Selected Poems," 216.
65. Larisa Lappo-Danilevskaia, "A Mother in Exile," interview in Jehanne M. Gheith and Katherine R. Jolluck, *Gulag Voices: Oral Histories of Soviet Incarceration and Exile* (New York: Palgrave Macmillan, 2011), 78.
66. Lappo-Danilevskaia, "A Mother in Exile," 79.
67. Lappo-Danilevskaia, "A Mother in Exile," 80–81.
68. Lappo-Danilevskaia, "A Mother in Exile," 82.
69. Lappo-Danilevskaia, "A Mother in Exile," 85.
70. Zatmilova, "A Part of History," in *Till My Tale Is Told*, 175.
71. Zatmilova, "A Part of History," 173.
72. Zatmilova, "A Part of History," 174–75.
73. Zatmilova, "A Part of History," 175–76.
74. Zatmilova, "A Part of History," 171–78.
75. Yelena Sidorkina, "Years under Guard," in *Till My Tale Is Told*, 194.
76. Sidorkina, "Years under Guard," 196.
77. Sidorkina, "Years under Guard," 196.
78. Sidorkina, "Years under Guard," 195, 197.
79. Olga Berggolts, "The Ordeal," trans. Daniel Weissbort, in *Twentieth Century Russian Poetry: Silver and Steel: An Anthology*, ed. Albert C. Todd and Max Hayward with Daniel Weissbort (Doubleday: New York, 1993), 571–72.
80. Olga Berggolts, "My Country," in Todd and Hayward, *Twentieth Century Russian Poetry*, 572.
81. Olga Berggolts in Katherine Hodgson, *Voicing the Soviet Experience: The Poetry of Ol'ga Berggol'ts* (Oxford: British Academy/Oxford University Press, 2003), 22.
82. Skrjabina, *Coming of Age*, 80.
83. Skrjabina, *Coming of Age*, 81.
84. Skrjabina, *Coming of Age*, 84–87.
85. Skrjabina, *Coming of Age*, 90–93.
86. Skrjabina, *Coming of Age*, 93–96.
87. Fischer, *My Lives in Russia*, 150–51.
88. Fischer, *My Lives in Russia*, 151.
89. Fischer, *My Lives in Russia*, 152.
90. Anna Larina, *This I Cannot Forget: The Memoirs of Nikolai Bukharin's Widow*, trans. Gary Kern (New York: Norton, 1994), 61–62.
91. Shtange, "Diary," in *Intimacy and Terror*, 181–83.

92. Tatyana Senkevich, "A Soviet Girl's Diary," in *Thirteen Who Fled*, ed. Louis Fischer, trans. Gloria and Victor Fischer (New York: Harper, 1949), 130.
93. Lyubov Vasilievna Shaporina, "Diary," in *Intimacy and Terror*, 339.
94. Shaporina, "Diary," in *Intimacy and Terror*, 350.
95. Shaporina, "Diary," in *Intimacy and Terror*, 351.
96. Shaporina, "Diary," in *Intimacy and Terror*, 352–53.
97. Shaporina, "Diary," in *Intimacy and Terror*, 353.
98. Lydia Chukovskaia, "Process of Expulsion," in Tomei, *Russian Women Writers*, vol. 2, 1134.
99. Chukovskaia, "Process of Expulsion," 1134–35.
100. Valentina Kamyshina, "A Woman's Heart," in Fischer, *Thirteen Who Fled*, 104–6.
101. Kamyshina, "A Woman's Heart," 109–10.
102. Kamyshina, "A Woman's Heart," 110.
103. Nina Kosterina, *The Diary of Nina Kosterina*, trans. Mirra Ginsburg (New York: Crown Publishers, 1968), 35.
104. Kosterina, *Diary of Nina Kosterina*, 31–33.
105. Kosterina, *Diary of Nina Kosterina*, 32.
106. Kosterina, *Diary of Nina Kosterina*, 36.
107. Kosterina, *Diary of Nina Kosterina*, 43.
108. Kosterina, *Diary of Nina Kosterina*, 44.
109. Kosterina, *Diary of Nina Kosterina*, 45.
110. Kosterina, *Diary of Nina Kosterina*, 53.
111. Kosterina, *Diary of Nina Kosterina*, 79.
112. Kosterina, *Diary of Nina Kosterina*, 86–89, 98–99, 127–28.
113. Kosterina, *Diary of Nina Kosterina*, 128.
114. Kosterina, *Diary of Nina Kosterina*, 128.
115. Kosterina, *Diary of Nina Kosterina*, 146.
116. Kosterina, *Diary of Nina Kosterina*, 163.
117. Kosterina, *Diary of Nina Kosterina*, 163–89, introduction.
118. "From Privilege to Exile: Interview with Valeriia Mikhailovna Gerlin," May 2005, trans. Cathy Fierson, in Gheith and Jolluck, *Gulag Voices*, 157.
119. "From Privilege to Exile," in Gheith and Jolluck, *Gulag Voices*, 157.
120. "From Privilege to Exile," in Gheith and Jolluck, *Gulag Voices*, 153.
121. Larina, *This I Cannot Forget*, 284, 293.
122. Larina, *This I Cannot Forget*, 284, 304.
123. Vera Shulz, "Tanganka," in *Till My Tale Is Told*, 153.
124. For stories about the intimidation and humiliation of Lenin's sister and

wife and their dispirited behavior, see Larina, *This I Cannot Forget*, 286, 332–33, 341.

Notes to Chapter Ten

1. Dmitriew, *Surviving the Storms*, 38.
2. Purves-Stewart, *A Physician's Tour*, 45, 51, 59, 156.
3. See *Vsesoiuznaia Perepis' Naseleniia 1939 goda*, Tsentral'noe Statistichechkoe Upravlenia Gosplana SSSR, 112–13; Fainsod, *Smolensk under Soviet Rule*, 430–37.
4. Benet, *Village of Viriatino*, 272.
5. Benet, *Village of Viriatino*, 272–73.
6. Benet, *Village of Viriatino*, 274–75; Olson and Adonyeva, *Worlds of Russian Village Women*, 291.
7. Dmitriew, *Surviving the Storms*, 79.
8. Hindus, *Red Bread*, 272, 275, 283.
9. Hindus, *Red Bread*, 66, 141, 276–78; *Perepis' 1937*, 124.
10. Torstensen, *Elder Sebastian of Optina*, 46–47.
11. Vera A. Tkachenko in Torstensen, *Elder Sebastian of Optina*, 196–98.
12. Olson and Adonyeva, *Worlds of Russian Village Women*, 64, 66, 195–96.
13. Olson and Adonyeva, *Worlds of Russian Village Women*, 253.
14. Dmitriew, *Surviving the Storms*, 47.
15. Dmitriew, *Surviving the Storms*, 48.
16. Skrjabina, *Coming of Age*, 84–88.
17. *Father Arseny*, 195.
18. *Father Arseny*, 195.
19. *Father Arseny*, 196–97.
20. *Father Arseny*, 197.
21. *Father Arseny*, 9–10, 190; Paul Florinsky, *Salt of the Earth: An Encounter with a Holy Russian Elder: Isadore of Gethsemane Heritage*, trans. Richard Betts (Platina, CA: St. Herman of Alaska Brotherhood, 1999), introduction, 30–32.
22. Ransel, "Sites of Veneration," 146, 165–66.
23. Marcelline Hutton, "Surviving Imprisonment in the 1930s: Social and Religious Experiences of Soviet Female Prisoners," in Jaroslaw Pelenski, *States, Societies, Cultures: East and West: Essays in Honor of Jaroslaw Pelenski* (New York: Ross Publishing, 2004), 382–83.
24. Hutton, "Surviving Imprisonment," 376; Maria Joffe, *Odna Noch': Povest' o pravde* (New York: Khronika, 1978), 56–58; Maria Joffe, *One Long Night*, 105–9.
25. Hutton, "Surviving Imprisonment," 376–77; Evgenia Ginzburg, *Journey into the Whirlwind*, trans. Paul Stevenson and Max Hayward (New York:

Harcourt, Brace & World, 1967), 145, 156, 264–65.
26. Hutton, "Surviving Imprisonment," 377; Evgenia Ginzburg, *Journey into the Whirlwind*, 411.
27. Hutton, "Surviving Imprisonment," 377–78.
28. Hutton, "Surviving Imprisonment," 381–82; Marie Avinov with Paul Chavchadze, *Marie Avinov: Pilgrimage Through Hell* (Englewood Cliffs, NJ: Prentice Hall, 1968), 121–32, 143–81.
29. Siemens, *Remember Us*, 157.
30. Siemens, *Remember Us*, 179.

Notes to Chapter Eleven

1. *Perepis' 1937*, 192–98.
2. Vera Ivanovna Malakhova, "Four Years as a Frontline Physician," in *A Revolution of Their Own*, 186.
3. Kosterina, *Diary of Nina Kosterina*, 170.
4. Hindus, *Red Bread*, 38, 52, 54.
5. Hindus, *Red Bread*, 190–209; Benet, *Village of Viriatino*, 117, 239–40, 269–70.
6. Sokolov, *Russian Folklore*, 649–50, 657–58.
7. Olson and Adonyeva, *Worlds of Russian Village Women*, 58, 112–13.
8. Olson and Adonyeva, *Worlds of Russian Village Women*, 113–15.
9. Olson and Adonyeva, *Worlds of Russian Village Women*, 115.
10. Irina Ivanovna Kniazeva, "A Life in a Peasant Village," in *A Revolution of Their Own*, 121–23.
11. Ponomarenko, "From Peasant to Journalist," 141–43.
12. For stories of their work and marriage, see Buckley, *Mobilizing Soviet Peasants*.
13. Dolgikh, "Under a Sword," in *A Revolution of Their Own*, 169.
14. John Scott, *Behind the Urals* (Bloomington: Indiana University Press, 1962); Buck, *Talk about Russia*.
15. Raisa Orlova, *Memoirs*, 14.
16. Shtange, "Diary," in *Intimacy and Terror*, 167, 181.
17. Anna Larina, *This I Cannot Forget*.
18. Mariia V. Kovach-Astafeva, "Letters," in Shapovalov, *Remembering the Darkness*, 269–73; Nadezhda Joffe, *Back in Time*.
19. Kovach-Astafeva, "Letters," in Shapovalov, *Remembering the Darkness*, 272.
20. Shapovalov, *Remembering the Darkness*, 89, 209–14, 237–8, 250.
21. Dmitriew, *Surviving the Storms*, 54–57, 68.
22. Dmitriew, *Surviving the Storms*, 63.

23. Dmitriew, *Surviving the Storms*, 76.
24. Dmitriew, *Surviving the Storms*, 76.
25. Dmitriew, *Surviving the Storms*, 77.
26. Dmitriew, *Surviving the Storms*, 78–79.
27. Wettlin, *Fifty Russian Winters*, 42–48.
28. Wettlin, *Fifty Russian Winters*, 109.
29. Wettlin, *Fifty Russian Winters*, 71.
30. Wettlin, *Fifty Russian Winters*, 72.
31. Pavlova, "Taking Advantage," 70–71.
32. Nadezhda Mandelstam, *Hope Abandoned*, (New York: Atheneum, 1981) 620–21.
33. Shaporina, "Diary," in *Intimacy and Terror*, 342–43.
34. Shaporina, "Diary," in *Intimacy and Terror*, 343–44.
35. Shtange, "Diary," in *Intimacy and Terror*, 173ff.
36. Shtange, "Diary," in *Intimacy and Terror*, 173–74.
37. Shtange, "Diary," in *Intimacy and Terror*, 174–75.
38. Shtange, "Diary," in *Intimacy and Terror*, 178.
39. Shtange, "Diary," in *Intimacy and Terror*, 180.
40. Shtange, "Diary," in *Intimacy and Terror*, 178ff.; A. S. Makarenko, *The Collective Family: A Handbook for Russian Parents* (1937), trans. Robert Daglish (Garden City, NY: Anchor Books, Doubleday, 1967), 98, 111–12, 320–21.
41. Fischer, *My Lives in Russia*, 63–64.
42. Hutton, *Russian Women*, 374–76; Maria Joffe, *One Long Night*.
43. Hutton, *Russian Women*, 377; Evgenia Ginzburg, *Journey into the Whirlwind*.
44. *Perepis' 1937*, 245ff. and table 74.
45. Hutton, *Russian Women*, 381–82; Avinov, *Pilgrimage Through Hell*.
46. Hutton, *Russian Women*, 380; Sats, *Zhizn-Iavlenia polosatoe*, (Moscow, Novosti, 1991), 315–326; *Sketches from my Life*, (Moscow: Raduga, 1985), 263–69.
47. Kamyshina, "A Woman's Heart," 110.
48. Buckley, *Mobilizing Soviet Peasants*, 25, 270–79.
49. Buckley, *Mobilizing Soviet Peasants*, 271.
50. "Unequal Marriages Debated," *Moscow News*, March 10, 1937.
51. "Unequal Marriages Debated."
52. Fischer, *My Lives in Russia*, 47.
53. Scott, *Behind the Urals*, 133.
54. Wettlin, *Fifty Russian Winters*, 65.
55. Wettlin, *Fifty Russian Winters*, 82–83.

56. Wettlin, *Fifty Russian Winters*, 70–82, 132–33.
57. Wettlin, *Fifty Russian Winters*, 103.
58. Tchernavin, *We Soviet Women*, 214–15.
59. Tchernavin, *We Soviet Women*, 215.
60. Tchernavin, *We Soviet Women*, 217–19.
61. Tchernavin, *We Soviet Women*, 223–27.

Notes to Chapter Twelve

1. For pictures of pioneers in gas masks participating in defense drill, see photo in Bendavid-Val and Rawls, *Propaganda and Dreams*, 79; women parachuting in *Propaganda and Dreams*, 116; and paintings of women shooting with a rifle and with gas masks by Aleksandr Samokhvalov, "Osoaviakhimovka," 1932, National Russian Museum, as printed in *Istoriia Russkoi Zhivopisi Pervaia polovina XX beka* (Moskva: Belyigorod, 2007), 33.
2. Fischer, *My Lives in Russia*, 146–49.
3. Shtange, "Diary," in *Intimacy and Terror*, 171.
4. Kosterina, *Diary of Nina Kosterina*, 121.
5. Kosterina, *Diary of Nina Kosterina*, 172.
6. Kosterina, *Diary of Nina Kosterina*, 189.
7. Raisa Orlova, *Memoirs*, 45.
8. Raisa Orlova, *Memoirs*, 43.
9. Nikolaus Basseches, *The Unknown Army: The Nature and History of the Russian Military Forces*, trans. Marion Saerchinger (New York: Viking, 1943), 168; Ellen Jones, *Red Army and Society* (Boston: Allen & Unwin, 1985), 99; Oral Interview in El Paso, Texas, April 6, 1996 (source wished to remain anonymous); Hutton, *Russian Women*, 311–12, 320.
10. As quoted from "Creative Art of the Peoples of the USSR" by Y. M. Sokolov in *Russian Folklore*, 656.
11. Sokolov, "Creative Art," 656.
12. Sokolov, "Creative Art," 656.
13. Sokolov, "Creative Art," 656.
14. "The First Woman Air Commander," *Moscow Daily News*, 9 February 1933, 4; *Perepis' 1926*, vol. 34: 12–13, 172–73; in Hutton, *Russian Women*, 219, 230.

Note to Conclusion

1. Elena Skrjabina, *Siege and Survival: The Odyssey of a Leningrader*, trans. Norman Luxenburg (Carbondale: University of Southern Illinois, 1971).

Note to Afterword
1. Lydia Chukovskaia, "Process of Expulsion," in Tomei, *Russian Women Writers*, vol. 2, 1134.

The University of Nebraska–Lincoln does not discriminate
based on gender, age, disability, race, color,
religion, marital status, veteran's status,
national or ethnic origin,
or sexual orientation.

www.ingramcontent.com/pod-product-compliance
Lightning Source LLC
Chambersburg PA
CBHW022045160426
43198CB00008B/137